Mass Communication
and Human Interaction

Mass Communication and Human Interaction

Robert D. Murphy/University of Kentucky

Houghton Mifflin Company   Boston

Atlanta   Dallas   Geneva, Ill.   Hopewell, N.J.   Palo Alto   London

Part and chapter opening illustrations by Edith Allard

Printed in the U.S.A.

Library of Congress Catalog Card Number: 76-19906
ISBN: 0-395-24433-1

Contents

Two   Special Privileges at a Special Price

Three   Private Ownership and the Profit System

Four   Content and How It Is Selected

Five The Audiences

Six New Technology and New Opportunities

To the Student

Communication is the *essence* of humanity. Through communication individuals bridge their islands of loneliness and through communication societies are formed. The ability to communicate is essential both to individual success and to group activity.

Humans communicate in many ways: with themselves in thought processes; with each other in face-to-face meetings; and through information-processing systems, including the media. This book considers communication at each of these levels and emphasizes the concepts that unify the process in interpersonal and media communication.

People communicate because they like to and because they must. Two strangers thrown by chance into the same room find it almost impossible to avoid sending and receiving messages, by glance and posture if not by words.

Citizens of advanced countries are the slaves as well as the masters of the media. Films, television, radio, newspapers, magazines, and books provide much of the information and entertainment that fill these people's minds and guide their actions.

Enchanted or bored, many persons chain themselves to the media. They spend hours gazing at the television screen. They read newspapers. Most go to the movies. Many read magazines, often to muted radio music. And many boast that they enjoy reading good books.

But nearly everyone complains about the media too. Newspapers and newscasters persecute heroes, conceal the turpitude of villains, or cheapen popular taste with titillating tidbits. Television tries to entertain by serving up endless stock comedies and then treats the public to a long season of reruns.

Why do people put up with it?

Because they must. Those who ignore the media are likely to have little to talk about when they see their friends. The media tell what goods are available at what prices and where to find a restaurant or theater. People must attend to the media in order to satisfy their social and economic needs. And the media reflect what their audiences are seeking, or at least what large numbers of people will accept. The sheer size of audiences demonstrates that.

But the media could do better. Always sensitive to their audiences, they will change if enough people ask them to. They already provide some magnificent material: fine music and drama, firsthand views of significant events, and sometimes wise comment on the latter. As audiences respond to the best in the media they will get better media.

Understanding the media is important because along with interpersonal channels, they have much influence on the shape of society. Information from the media and from other persons affects individual attitudes and public decisions. In a circular process the media affect what people think and talk about and are in turn influenced by what people are saying in their homes and in public meetings.

New technology is gradually providing the tools that will permit more people to participate as senders as well as receivers of information. Eventually it may be possible to provide multidirectional channels so that anyone who will spend the energy can participate fully in the information process that undergirds democracy.

But first comes understanding of the way interpersonal and media communication work. This book is designed to help in that process. It is mostly about the present, but it provides perspective by occasionally looking at the past and projecting into the future.

Part One deals with individual communication processes, the media, and how the two are related. Part Two describes the freedom allowed the media and the responsibilities that are exacted in return. Part Three deals with the owners of the media and other factors that influence mass communication. Part Four considers content and the manner in which it is presented. Part Five discusses audiences and how they respond. Part Six wraps up the theme of the book by considering new technology and new social insights that are creating novel media combinations and opening the opportunity for wider participation in the information process.

The study of communication is particularly rewarding because examples surround nearly everyone at every waking moment. Talking, reading, listening, and nonverbal communication are constant experiences. Understanding the underlying principles enriches these experiences and enhances the effectiveness of the participants. Thus the television viewer, radio listener, student, reader, writer, radical, or socialite can all enhance their daily effectiveness by examining the mass media, not in isolation, but as part of the total communication process. The aim of this book is to do just that—not to train professionals in the technical fields of communication, but to make more effective consumers of the users of mass communication.

To the Instructor

Mass Communication and Human Interaction presents interpersonal and media communication in relation to individual and social action. It uses the basic concepts of the field of interpersonal communication to describe both interpersonal communication and media institutions. If students can learn to view communication as an aspect of behavior, they will understand its relevance to their own lives and to the processes by which social decisions are made.

Since everyone participates in interpersonal communication, students need to be introduced to the concepts of that field; and since nearly everyone in the United States uses the media, students need to understand mass communication. The first course in mass communication appeals to at least three kinds of students:

1. Those who will become professional communicators in the media or related fields
2. Those who will become specialists in the subject matter of communication—future teachers, researchers, and scholars
3. Generalists who will go on to other fields, but who need to understand individual and mass communication in order to be more successful in their business and personal lives and to become effective and discriminating consumers of the media

In the beginning course it is not practical to separate students with different goals, because at this level many students have not formed career plans. This book endeavors to provide the understanding that is needed by students in all three groups. It shows the development of the field of mass communication and the theory that supports it and applies the theory to the world. The book is not over-scholarly, reserving a detailed discussion of theory for later courses. It has likewise avoided a preoccupation with the details of the media, which will be supplied in later courses to students with professional communication goals. Theory is explained without recounting all the details of advanced scholarly studies, and the media are described without including minutiae.

In a semester, students can be taught theory that will help them to understand what is occurring when they engage in a conversation or write a letter. They can learn enough about the media to use the media more effectively and to make realistic demands that the media serve them better.

They can learn the importance of communication in determining social action. On the basis of such understanding they can lead more effective lives.

This book is designed as one of the tools by which an instructor can achieve these goals.

The six major sections of the book can be used as the major course divisions. Part One, The Origins and Development of Communication, deals with basic communication theory and sketches the growth of communication technology and of the media. The material is not intended as a definitive discussion of theory nor a thorough development of the history of communication, but as a starting point to provide an essential frame of reference for later discussions.

Perhaps the early part of the course can be used most productively in encouraging students to think about the essential nature of the communication process; and to consider how it changes in various periods and situations, yet remains essentially the same. It is important for students to recognize that communication affects individuals and society subtly through its manner and its technology, as well as more obviously through its content.

Part Two, Special Privileges at a Special Price, treats the expectations of society for the media and the way the media are controlled by legal sanctions. First Amendment rights are matched with the responsibilities they imply, and the differences between the oughts of the media (ethics) and the musts (legal sanctions) are pointed out.

As this section is being taught, students can gain significant insights into the relationship between the media and government. By pointing out the differences between press-governmental relations in Western democracies and in totalitarian states, the instructor can demonstrate how the media have become an integral part of the social system.

Part Three, Private Ownership and the Profit System, shows how the private ownership system and the necessity for making a profit have affected the media in the United States. Regulatory policies on ownership and advertising are discussed, along with the underlying philosophy that supports them. Students can be expected to develop an appreciation of the manner in which the media are related to economic systems, and the philosophy that is used to justify occasional intervention by the government.

Part Four, Content and How It Is Selected, is devoted to media content, how the media shape content, and the external forces that influence content. Also considered are the various formats in which information is supplied. The information on communication theory presented earlier will help students to understand this material.

Through Part Four students should come to appreciate that communication and the media are essential to society and that communication processes shape society and are shaped by it. Students should be better able to appreciate the fine line that separates information from entertainment and how both affect public decisions. Future consumers of the media can learn to distinguish the media formats and to understand how they affect audience response. Perhaps most important, future consumers and practitioners should understand that in the long run, "Archie Bunker" may be as influential as the evening news.

Part Five, The Audiences, relates what researchers have discovered about the nature of audiences and the effects of the media on individual conduct. Students can be helped to understand how individuals respond to the media, how use of one medium affects the use of another, and how researchers have gone about the task of ascertaining these relationships. With such a background students can better evaluate the controversies over violence and other content generally regarded as undesirable in the media.

Part Six, New Technology and New Opportunities, relates the attempts by the media through new formats and new technology to provide more interaction with their audiences. Interactive communication and the media, essential to a democratic society, are considered in relation to social and technological innovation.

In studying this part students can be encouraged to take an imaginative approach. They can speculate on the future formats of the media and how they will affect lifestyles and society. Having studied traditional controls on the media and the reasons for them, students can be encouraged to reconsider the reasons, discuss whether the controls are needed, and ask themselves how a conscious effort can be made to improve the media by altering the rules.

Part Six provides, too, the opportunity for a discussion of technology. This might include means by which new technology can be anticipated and controlled, so that its effects are channeled in desirable directions. This section emphasizes the manner in which the media can help more citizens to participate in the formation of policy. Technology shows some promise, but social innovation is more crucial still. Some concepts of communication policy are introduced at an elementary level to provide a bridge by which students, whatever their professional goals, can apply their study of communication to their personal and social worlds.

As the manuscript for this book developed, a fine set of critics provided fresh insights and valuable suggestions. Particularly deserving of thanks are Genelle Austin-Lett, Illinois Central College; Eldean Bennett, Arizona State University; James K. Buckalew, California State University, San Diego; Everette Dennis, University of Minnesota; Edward G. Luck, Georgia State University; and John Wiemann, Rutgers University. My wife, Reta Vanderburgh Murphy, provided sound criticism at all stages and conceived the original artwork for the numbered figures.

Robert D. Murphy

ONE

The Origins and Development of Communication

1

Communication: Oil, Glue, and Dynamite

In Copenhagen, where prostitution is not a crime, but public solicitation is, a constable watches the way a woman walks down the street. Is she, by the way she walks, advertising her trade? If she is, the officer's duty is to arrest her. If not, he must not lay a hand on her.

Pity the Copenhagen cop.

He is asked to make a decision based on ambiguous information. The way a woman (or a man) walks may be an invitation—or it may not.

The constable is not alone in his dilemma. Everyone has to make decisions based on incomplete and inadequate information. Everyone takes in information, just as everyone takes in food.

People eat because they like to—and to sustain their bodies. People talk because they like to—and to get along with others.

As food nutrients nourish bodies and strengthen muscles, information fuels minds and guides social contacts.

Simple? Neither the biological nor the mental process is that simple, but the parallel is real. Communication is as important to social life as digestion is to physical life.

As prisoners within their own skins, people must find a way to relate to the objects and events surrounding them. Seeing, hearing, feeling, tasting, and smelling are the ways humans take in information. Information comes from firsthand observation and communication.

Since we use the same receptors whether we gain information by observing or by communicating, we may not make a conscious distinction between the two. The difference is that in observing we are receiving information directly from the environment, while in communicating, the information is channeled through the mind of at least one other person.

Ideally we would obtain all our information by firsthand observation. This would eliminate the middlemen of the information business. We would see for ourselves, hear for ourselves, taste, smell, and feel for ourselves. We would experience for ourselves. A child can explore the nature of a rock by feeling its texture, kicking it, hefting it, tasting it, or throwing it. That is a better way to discover the nature of a rock than looking it up in a dictionary and finding, perhaps, that a rock is "a large mass of stone." Just the same, we can often benefit from someone else's experience. A farmer could spend a lifetime peering at rocks and still learn a great deal from a geologist skilled in scientific analysis.

Ideal as it often is, observation can supply us with only a fraction of the information we need. The world is too large and our bodily resources too limited. We must rely on other people, either directly or through the media.

Friends and associates are handy and effective sources of information about objects and events that we cannot observe for ourselves, but most of us need even greater information resources. For these we turn to the communications media. The media are systems that combine human talents and mechanical devices and that have as one of their central purposes the supplying of information.

The media surround citizens of advanced countries; there is no difficulty in identifying their end products. They are books, newspapers, magazines, catalogues, radio and television programs, motion pictures, computer printouts, records, and tapes.

The media are influential because they supply information on which personal and public decisions are based. To understand our society we must understand communication and the media.

This book is about individual, group, and mass communication and their importance for people and society. We will investigate how communication works both between individuals and in groups. We will inquire into the nature of conversation, and at the other end of the spectrum we will consider the media systems that supply information to vast numbers of people.

The usual terms for these processes are *interpersonal*, *group*, and *mass communication*. Since most people engage in all three every day, we will consider them together, noting the differences and similarities.

The definitions of communication are many. The difficulty of reaching a good definition emphasizes the mystery of the process. We will concern ourselves with more detail later, but for now we will define *communication* as an exchange of meaning by which one mind affects another. Meaning is information that registers somewhere in the mental structure of the receiver.

There, in "the mental structure of the receiver," we will begin our exploration. After all, the purpose of all communications, is to affect the mental structure of the receiver.

Pictures in Our Heads and Reality

Every human being carries around in his or her head a picture of the world, and for every individual that picture is the closest he or she will ever come to reality. Fuzzy or sharp, the picture guides our actions. When the picture is sharp we act effectively; when it is fuzzy our actions will have little to do with the world of actuality. As Walter Lippmann pointed out many years ago, we are forever condemned to act in the real world, but to base our actions on the imperfect representation that we carry in our minds.

The pictures inside our heads change as we take in new information. Each new impression changes our mental outlook in some small way, so that each of us is a little different when we go to bed at night from what we were when we awoke in the morning. But our minds resist change, too. We instinctively protect our individuality by refusing to allow too much or too rapid change. We alter information so that it better fits our preconceptions. That is why the same experience may mean different things to different people and why two persons who have witnessed the same event may tell quite different stories about it.

The picture of the world that each of us carries is uniquely our own because each of us has a unique make-up and undergoes a unique set of experiences. The accuracy of the pictures—the extent to which actuality corresponds to what we carry in our heads—is a matter of fascinating speculation. Since we know that each of us carries a picture at least a little different from that of everyone else, we must assume that all are, to some extent, out of touch with reality. When some persons' perceptions of the world are radically different from those of most other persons, those individuals are regarded as abnormal. Sometimes "abnormal persons" may have pictures that are closer to reality than those carried by others. Future generations say they were "ahead of their time." Galileo was regarded as a heretic by his own generation, as a genius by later ones.

Another genius, fictional detective Sherlock Holmes, showed a London secretary that people are governed by their perceptions of reality, not by reality itself. Jill Nicholson works at the office of Abbey National Building Society of 218–230 Baker Street. Because of her office address, mail addressed to Holmes at 221–B Baker Street is delivered to her company, and she is assigned to answer it. In the 1970's she was receiving six letters a day addressed to Sir Arthur Conan Doyle's fictional sleuth, who, had he ever lived, would have died long ago. Acting on their pictures of reality, frightened people from all over the world still write to seek the aid of the mythical detective.

All of us respond to faulty views of the reality beyond us. Senator Sam Ervin of South Carolina suffered a mild embarrassment of this kind during the Watergate hearings. As chairman of the Senate investigating committee Senator Ervin was trying to get from President Nixon tapes of his White House conversations. The senator was summoned from the hearing room for an important telephone call, and when he returned he glowingly announced that he had just been talking with Secretary of the Treasury George Shultz, who told him that the president was going to make the tapes available. Senator Ervin and the committee vice chairman had hardly finished congratulating each other when it became apparent that Senator Ervin had been the victim of a hoax call. Secretary Shultz had not been on the telephone, and there was no indication that the tapes would be available. Senator Ervin had acted on false information that distorted his picture of reality. The error was quickly corrected, but the episode was particularly embarrassing for the senator because the glow with which he took the poisoned bait and his later discomfiture were broadcast on national television.

Often the results of faulty information are more earthshaking than a senator's momentary embarrassment on national television. Andrew Jackson's victory at New Orleans in January 1815 enhanced the general's political career, but it was utter tragedy for the 700 British and 7 Americans who died; and it was unnecessary tragedy, for the War of 1812 had been concluded two weeks earlier. Word of the peace settlement had not reached New Orleans, so the British and Americans were unaware that they were no longer enemies and had no obligation to kill each other.

Faulty information is one way in which pictures inside our heads are distorted, but not the only way. Two people may receive different impressions from exactly the same information. Our experiences build for each of us a set of preconceptions about the world by which we judge each new bit of information, so the same message may mean quite different things to different people. Much of our public policy is determined only after

Communication: Oil, Glue, and Dynamite

various people have taken time to reconcile the meanings of the same information.

Information, whatever it is, links us with the world outside. It is not a physical thing, although it is carried along channels. It is easy to think of information as being transferred between two individuals. When this occurs it does not mean that something is poured from one mind to another. We know little about what actually does occur, but we can say that one mind has somehow been affected by another.

How We Learn to Communicate

As infants most of our communication is tactile. Being held, patted, stroked, and fed and touching the mother's body provide the original messages that reach an infant. Gradually, as vision develops, the child associates these sensations with smiles from the mother and with sounds as she talks. At this stage the mother's words have no significance; her tone contains the message. From this early world of touch, tone, and facial expression the child gradually learns the use of symbols: a smile may substitute for a caress, a pair of outstretched arms may substitute for a hug. Specialists who work with children have established that the treatment a child receives in these early years is critical to the ability to use symbols.

By the time we become adults we have changed our communication patterns so that we receive most of our information through our eyes and ears. This is partly due to the way our media condition us. None of the mass media tries to provide us information on any regular basis except through our eyes and ears. Occasionally, someone in the media makes such an effort. Sometimes a newspaper will, at the behest of an advertiser, add a scent to its ink so that an advertisement appeals to readers' noses; or a sample of cloth may be attached to a magazine page so that prospective buyers can feel its texture. But these are exceptions.

Even though the media condition us to sight and sound communication, the olfactory, gustatory, and tactile sensations of childhood cling. Media messages are bland compared to experiences that stimulate all our senses. Visiting a Latin American market is immeasurably more exciting than seeing even the most artful film about it. Being pushed by the crowd and brushing against strangers is considerably different from the enforced spectator role assigned to us when we watch a film. Media messages provide secondhand experience.

Our culture also influences the way we learn to interpret messages. Anthropologist Edward T. Hall described the difficulties that arise when a

North American and a South American try to converse. The Latin American prefers to talk at such close quarters that the North American feels uneasy. As the Latin edges close so as to be at a comfortable distance for conversation, the North American slowly retreats. Neither may be aware of what is happening, but both feel thwarted because their respective cultures have established different distances for proper face-to-face conversation. Many other differences in the use of time and space make for difficulties in communication, particularly if the parties to the process do not understand the reasons for their discomfort.

The men and women who study communication have developed a vocabulary they use to describe the process. The words themselves are familiar, but they are used in a special, limited way. To understand the theories of communication we must pay attention to the special way some of these words are used. Six of these words concern us now. They are *symbols, language, channels, media, feedback,* and *static* (or *noise*).

The Uses of Symbols

When children learn to substitute a smile for a caress they are on the road to learning the use of symbols. A symbol is something that stands for something else. (See Figures 1.1 and 1.2.) The behaviorist interprets this as meaning that the symbol provokes something like the same reaction as would the original object (the referent). If children gurgle and coo when their mothers cuddle them and do the same when their

Figure 1.1 Symbols Overcome Language Barriers
General Motors is developing symbols like these for international use on auto instrument panels.

Hazard Flasher Headlamp Cleaner Windshield Wiper Windshield Washer Rear Hood

Fuel Engine Coolant Temperature Seat Belt Charging Condition Front Hood

From the General Motors quarterly *Changing Challenge*, Summer 1974, p. 32. Reprinted with permission.

Communication: Oil, Glue, and Dynamite

Mauldin and his tricks of the trade: A few strokes suffice if you're stumped

WILLIE AND JOE AT YALE

When students and faculty members at Yale decided to start a course in political cartooning this semester, they went straight to the top for a teacher—to Bill Mauldin of The Chicago Sun-Times, whose mordant drawings have earned him two Pulitzer Prizes and syndication in 250 newspapers across the country. So for the past ten weeks, Mauldin has spent Monday evenings with nineteen Yale students selected from an original 300 applicants. The class concentrates on such questions as what separates banal ideas from bright ones, and the fine line between freedom of expression and "unnecessary savagery."

Mauldin also helps the students with their drawing. In one class, for example, he showed them the tricks of the trade for cartoonists momentarily unable to come up with original caricatures: a mustache and forelock for Hitler, a cigarette holder for FDR, a beetling brow for Richard Nixon.

The students love it and consider the course a challenging one. "It's harder to come up with a succinct caption than it is to write a five-page research paper," says sophomore M.G. Lord, who aspires to be the nation's first major woman political cartoonist. Mauldin applauds their efforts. "They're surprising themselves and me too," he says. "It takes real will power not to cop their ideas myself."

Figure 1.2 Cartoonist Bill Mauldin Shows How He Uses Symbols

9

mothers smile, it may mean that since they respond about the same way to the smile as the cuddle, the smile has become a symbol for a cuddle.

If they are to help in exchanging information, symbols must have a common meaning for the sender and receiver. A word, a common form of symbol, may signify a generally agreed upon meaning, or it may require interpretation by the receiver. *Democracy,* for example, despite its frequent use, is a rather vague term that means different things to different people. The word *tree*, on the other hand, indicates a specific class of objects. Its meaning becomes even clearer (that is, leaves less room for interpretation by the receiver) if we refer to a specific tree that is known to the sender and receiver of a message. The first time a word is heard, the receiver tries to perceive its meaning from the context of the message.

Words are only one kind of symbol. Objects become symbols when they signify other objects or ideas. Gestures and facial expressions often convey meaning, so they are symbolic acts. But words are the symbols we use most consciously to transmit messages.

How human beings began to use words is a matter of fascinating speculation. Presumably word sounds evolved from grunts. Gradually, a certain grunt came to have a certain significance. As word sounds became more refined and more commonly shared, human beings had the beginnings of a communication system. Words for physical things such as rocks and animals must have come first. Words for abstractions must have developed slowly over generations.

What Language Is

Words and other symbols are the building blocks of a communication system, but they can convey only rudimentary information unless they are used together. Language is the system in which symbols are related to each other to transmit messages. The language system provides rules by which word symbols are used in concert. Grammar tells us what forms of words to use and how to arrange them into sentences. The English language pattern usually calls for a subject-predicate-object structure. This is varied to add emphasis and interest, but too much straying from the pattern slows down comprehension.

The relationships between words in sentences are indicated by the way they are arranged and by their endings. Nouns in Latin have case endings. If they are the subject of a verb the nominative case endings are used; if they are the object, objective case endings are used. In English, case endings have disappeared, since we depend much more on word order to indicate relationships. This difference is one cause for difficulty as English-speaking students start the study of Latin. Latin sentences can vary word patterns without damaging the meaning, and many Roman orators did exactly that to create an impressive style.

Not all languages use spoken or written words. The system by which drivers signal their intentions to other drivers is a rudimentary language. Members of African tribes send messages by drumbeats. American Indians used smoke signals. Nonverbal symbols were important in early America when only one person in five could read. "Wooden Indians" indicated tobacco shops. Some barber shops still display the red and white striped poles that originated when the operations of the barber also included the dressing of wounds, bloodletting, and other surgery. The riband wrapped around the pole represented the bandage twisted round the arm prior to bloodletting. The three-ball sign is still used by pawnshops. This was adapted from the coat of arms of the Medici family, which started out in medicine (hence the three pills), but later switched to money lending.

In *The Story of Language*[1] linguist Mario Pei says that gestural language may have preceded spoken language, and that under the right circumstances, it might have become humankind's all-purpose message carrier instead of the spoken word. He describes the sign language by which North American Indians of different tribes could carry on elaborate conversations even though they did not understand each other's spoken languages. He cites some of the imagery:

> To indicate that one is sad, for instance, one points to oneself, makes the sign for "heart," then draws the hand down and away in the direction of the ground. A question is indicated by rotating the raised hand in a circle by wrist action; a lie by two spread fingers showing "double talk," or a man with a forked tongue; "friend" by the two forefingers raised together, symbolizing brothers growing up in each other's company.[2]

Pei quotes Charles Darwin's suggestion that spoken language won out over gestural language because it leaves the hands free for other activities.

Symbols and Language as Tools for Thought

It is easy to understand that the exchange of ideas requires symbols and language, but it is difficult to assess the role that symbols and

---

[1]Mario Pei, *The Story of Language*, rev. ed. (Philadelphia: J. B. Lippincott, 1965), p. 17.
[2]*Ibid.*

language play in individual thought. Certainly symbols are necessary for thinking. They range from concrete ones—such as those that represent objects in our daily existence—to abstractions that may remain vague. The human mind contains configurations that cannot be presented verbally. Emotions, although they frequently govern actions, are often said to be "felt" and incapable of description. At the same time, symbols that enter the mind ready-made through communications channels form an important part of the raw material for thinking.

We do not know the extent to which thinking is limited by the symbols fed in by communications. Neither do we know the extent to which its processes are controlled by the system of thought imposed by language. But verbal communication is "precoded" inasmuch as concepts are already embodied in words when they enter the mental context of the receiver. These symbols facilitate thinking, but also limit it.

It has been suggested, for example, that users of English and other languages that have precise words for time adjust more easily to time-bound duties such as keeping appointments on time, reading an airline timetable, or eating regularly. Some tribes of American Indians, on the other hand, which have only vague expressions for time ignore minutes and hours and do things whenever they feel like it. The question remains whether the language patterns determine the customs or the customs determine the language patterns.

Each language system, too, affects the way the mind processes information. English, for example, frequently uses a logical subject-predicate-object structure. English speakers are likely to carry this pattern into their thinking and rely more on syllogistic logic than the users of other languages that follow other patterns. The question can again be raised as to whether the language determines the customs or the customs set the pattern for the language.

At any rate, it is safe to assume that the thinking of persons immersed in a culture and its language is controlled to some extent by the language. If our language does not provide words for certain concepts we are likely to think less about them; and if our language imposes certain patterns for the use of words and the ideas they represent it is more difficult to think in novel ways. Thus we are to some extent prisoners of our language.

Channels

A communication channel is the means by which a message is carried from sender to receiver. Sound waves are frequently used as channels, since they provide the road by which spoken words travel from the sender's larynx to the receiver's ear. Light waves carry messages to the eye of the receiver. Radio waves carry electronic messages on broadcast bands. Telephone lines are the channels that link sending and receiving instruments.

In general, interpersonal communication uses broad channels; media communication, narrower ones. Communications technology has devoted itself to improving and broadening media channels.

The channels in face-to-face conversation are broad and we handle them with little conscious effort. We can listen to the words and simultaneously monitor several other channels. By tonal cues speakers can even tell listeners that they mean just the opposite of what the words are saying. This reverse whammy, called *sarcasm*, heightens the impact of the message.

Eyes use other channels to provide additional information in a conversation. Facial expressions, too, tell a great deal. Julius Fast helped to popularize the subject in his book *Body Language*.[3] Anthropologist Ray Birdwhistell has devoted much of his life to the study of body movements (called *kinesics*) and his work provides much insight into nonverbal communication.

Birdwhistell and others have coded and analyzed characteristic positions and movements. One function of body movement is to act as a cueing agent. When we want to answer a point in a discussion we are likely to uncross our arms and legs and lean forward. When we are finished and ready to listen again we will lean back and may cross our legs again.

Eye contact provides another channel. If we wish to avoid speaking to another person we avoid catching that individual's eye. As children we are taught not to stare, and a violation of this rule is usually interpreted as a hostile act or an attempt to dominate another person. In some societies the opposite is true. Prolonged eye contact is a sign that one is paying proper attention.

Nonverbal channels can carry a variety of messages. Hip-hugger pants, a bare midriff, and a scanty halter send one kind of message. T-shirts and jeans send another. Expensive paintings on the living room wall say one thing about the residents. Two-dollar posters stuck up with tape say something else. Come-hither perfume at twenty dollars an ounce helps to make a certain type of impression. The smell of sweat and garlic-laced breath tell something else.

Channels Narrow in the Mass Media

Media use fewer channels than face-to-face communication and usually limit their appeal to the eye and ear of the receiver. Words are

[3]Julius Fast, *Body Language* (New York: M. Evans, 1970).

the principal message carriers in print. Readers get additional information through the size, style, and arrangement of type and through illustrations. Radio widens the channels over print because it can exploit the rich variety of tonal cues in the voice and can manipulate emotional impact with background music and other sounds. Television and film widen the channels still further by adding sight.

Technology is constantly widening media channels, but media will never match firsthand experience because they must interpose themselves between the event and the individual receiving information about the event. Media always alter the receiver's perception of an event. Sometimes this slanting is deliberate, as when an artist or an entertainer manipulates material to heighten its emotional impact. In good news reporting, slanting is kept to a minimum.

Often receivers benefit from the interposition of the media, as when viewers watch close-up football action on the television screen and have the benefit of instant replay, in which they see an interesting play from a new angle and in slow motion. Such an added dimension changes the perception of reality. The viewers have a different perception of the game from the one they would have gotten if they were seated in the stands. Even the location of fans' seats in the stands will affect their perception. Whether such perception is closer to reality or farther from it is unanswerable since everyone's perception of "reality" will be different.

The Media Carry the Message

In a broad sense, a communications medium is the means of conducting the message through the channel from sender to receiver. In face-to-face communication no mechanical medium is needed. The human body has devices to produce and modulate the sounds that provide words and the body sends messages through actions, poses, and expressions. Messages transmitted in other than firsthand situations need some medium to carry them.

When one writes a letter the paper is the medium that carries the message. A book or magazine makes more elaborate use of the same medium. If one makes a telephone call the wires, switchboards, and other equipment of the telephone company are the media used. Philosophers of communications have regarded buildings as media. The buildings of a city give a message. If there are many churches we have one opinion of the city. If there is a preponderance of bars we have another.

In mass communication the systems that provide information to many people are referred to as the media. Thus radio stations, newspapers, publishing houses, television stations, motion picture producers, and magazine publishing units are media. Characteristically, media transmit information from one sender to many receivers; they require mechanical or electric intervention (printing presses, electronic equipment, and photographic equipment); and overt audience response is relatively light and slow in coming.

Thus the term *media* can refer to the actual substance on which a messages are carried or to the systems that engage in sending messages to audiences. We shall use it, as is customary, in both senses. The context normally makes the distinction clear. The mass media are distinguished partly by the scale on which they operate. Because of their size and the large number of people they reach they have tremendous impact on society.

Point-to-point media may involve elaborate physical equipment, but they serve as extensions of individuals rather than information-generating and transfer systems in their own right. The telephone and telegraph systems, for example, allow individuals to overcome the distance separating them for instantaneous communication, but the telephone and telegraph companies exert little control over the content of the messages carried on their facilities.

Media systems process information in various ways, but eventually it must be converted into a form that humans can understand such as written or spoken language or pictures and slides. A computer stores information on tapes and disks, but it is of no use to humans until it is printed out on paper in words, figures, pictures, charts, or graphs or reproduced as sound.

Feedback

Feedback is information that the sender of a message receives from the receiver. In an ordinary conversation the person who is talking at the moment receives a considerable amount of information from the listener. An interested listener will keep his or her eyes on the talker most of the time, giving occasional nods of the head, sitting in an attentive position, and remaining undistracted through noises and other potential interruptions. The talker, flattered by such attention, is likely to continue the discussion. But if the talker sees that the listener is losing interest, he or she may alter the message to regain attention. If the talker sees signs of puzzlement on the face of the listener, he or she can repeat, rephrase, or use illustrations to clarify the point. If the listener picks up the conversation and becomes the talker, that person in turn monitors feedback from the other. Skillful communication, which includes receiving and reacting as well as sending, provides the key to rewarding conversations.

Feedback is abundant, too, in group situations. Competent speakers "sense" almost at once whether the group before them is interested in what they have to say. Actually, their "sensing" comes from receiving and interpreting messages from audiences so automatically that the process itself is usually carried on below the conscious level. Signs of attention or restlessness come to speakers' eyes and to their ears. Silence or applause are the best music to speakers' ears. Attentive postures and eyes centered in their direction are the visual indicators that their message is going over. Scraping chairs, glances snatched at watches, wistful looks at exit doors, indicate that speakers are in trouble. This kind of feedback tips off speakers that they need to brighten their manner of delivery, insert an illustration or ancedote, or perhaps remedy the situation by talking louder so that their audience can hear them.

In town meetings or gatherings of fraternities, faculties, or commissions, the members who monitor the feedback channels most successfully are the ones most likely to have their suggestions adopted. When is the best time to put a controversial motion before such a group? When is the best moment to bring the discussion to a halt with a call for a vote? The answer lies in the mood of the group, and the best estimate of the mood comes from observing the other members. Are they attentive? Bored? Ready to purge an acrimonious discussion with a laugh? Are the dissenters perhaps ready to tolerate a favorable vote for your motion in order to forestall further debate? Many individuals who are especially successful in bringing groups to their way of thinking seem to read feedback signals instinctively. Timing is an essential factor in influencing group decisions, and even the most effective group leaders can profit from systematic appraisal of the feedback information that is always available in a meeting.

One of the superiorities of individual and group communication over media communication is its fast and reliable feedback. Plenty of stories tell about early editors receiving feedback in the form of threats of violence and even dark hints of lynching parties. These are the exceptions to the general rule that mass media workers usually get little feedback and that it comes too late to alter any message. Reporters may write articles day after day with little or no overt response from their intended readers. The people who program the media need feedback just as much as a conversationalist needs it, but they must spend large sums of money and endure a waiting period to get it. When they do it is meager and considerably less reliable than the rich information lode provided in face-to-face communication. We will consider audience research later, but here we must note that much of it is done to find out what all communicators need to know: Who is listening? How does the message affect them?

Newspapers and radio and television stations as well as the other media get letters from readers and listeners, but the number of people who take

Communication: Oil, Glue, and Dynamite

the time to write is so small that it may not be representative of the views of the audience as a whole. Because feedback is so important, the media spend a great deal of money to find out the same things that people accept and use almost instinctively in face-to-face and group communication.

The opening night of a Broadway play illustrates a two-level feedback system. The players are provided with the instantaneous reaction of the first-night audience, and so they have some idea as to how the production is going over. Still, they wait eagerly until they can read the reaction of the critics in the next day's newspapers.

Static Blocks the Way

The film *Catch-22* opens with scenes on a Second World War bombing base. Alan Arkin, the star, shouts to be heard above the screech of heavy bombers as the noise level becomes intolerable. Striving to hear the words against the background chaos, the audience rapidly gets into the mood of the film by sharing the stressful unease of life at the base.

The producers of *Catch-22* built up the noise to achieve an effect, but the problem is an everyday one. Whenever one person tries to communicate with another he or she is almost sure to have to contend with obstructions to the passage of the message. These obstructions take many forms. Some factories have such a high noise level that conversation is almost impossible. Sometimes a message fails to get through simply because the intended receiver is not paying attention. Daydreaming in class frequently makes it impossible for the teacher to get a message through to every student.

In media systems the obstruction may be mechanical. There is always a certain amount of noise in even the best recording system. In their efforts to keep it at the lowest possible level, sound engineers measure signal-to-noise ratio. The higher the signal (the message) and the lower the noise, the better the system. Radio static and interference with television pictures are well-known irritants.

Anything that interferes with the delivery of the message has been labeled as static or noise by students of communication. It includes interference in the system itself or in the environment. As the example of daydreaming indicates, it can even include the mental state of the receiver. This concept, like the others we are considering, is important in studying communication as a process. For example, speakers trying to get an important point over to an audience may well consider the obstacles they face: lack of interest, lack of ability to understand, traffic sounds from outside the auditorium, perhaps a heckler in the rear of the room.

Sometimes one person's message may become another's static, as when a minister found that the sound of a local rock station was coming over the church public address system when he was trying to preach a sermon. The transmitter was so close to the church that the church public address system picked up the wrong signal.

The Media Versus Interpersonal Communication

As receivers of information we evaluate interpersonal experience differently from the way we evaluate media information. When we listen to the firsthand account of a friend we apply certain standards of judgment. We remind ourselves that this particular friend is inclined to be overemotional, to play up the dramatic, and to sometimes be careless with the facts. We may have the opposite assessment of another friend. The point is, experience has given us some standards of judgment to apply. When we are attending to a mass medium we have fewer standards of judgment. We may know nothing about the reporter who is standing in front of the camera giving the message. We may know nothing about the network's abilities to test the accuracy and judgment of its reporters, and we are likely to know nothing about the mental context of those who give us the news. It is entirely possible—likely, in fact—that the people employed by news agencies will give us a fairer and more honest account of an event than our friends. The trouble is, we have to take that on faith, and since we do, we have credibility problems.

Do we tend to believe Walter Cronkite more than we believe some other newscaster? If so, why? How do we judge the credibility of the anonymous author of a newspaper article? Even if the writer has a by-line, few of us can take the time to investigate the caliber of his or her work. These problems are not insurmountable, but the interposition of the media does require readers or listeners to evaluate the medium itself before they can feel justified in having opinions about the subject matter under discussion.

What is it that conveys credibility? Previous experience with a given source of information is the best guide. When a friend, a newspaper, or a radio or television station consistently provides information that turns out to be correct, it is natural to put increasing faith in that source of information.

Often the media provide information that their audiences have no means of checking—readers and listeners never do find out whether the information they are given is correct. To an informed reader or listener, certain signs provide clues. A report that cites its sources and is specific with details is more likely to be accurate. Reporters often cite their sources and provide information about them to help listeners evaluate them. Knowing a speaker's background helps the audience evaluate what that person has to say.

An authoritative manner often induces people to believe. Simplifying issues and repeating them often induce belief. Neither method makes much sense logically, but they appear to work. Adolf Hitler understood the practice. He described it in *Mein Kampf:*

> The receptivity of the great masses is extremely limited, their intelligence is small, their forgetfulness enormous. Therefore all effective propaganda must be limited to a few points and they should be used like slogans until the very last man in the audience is capable of understanding what is meant. . . .

Hitler combined this technique with violence to make believers of many of the German people. Simplification and repetition are still two of the ways that work for people and organizations who use information for propaganda.

We give up our right to make our own judgment in still another way when we rely upon the media. We have to let someone else decide what events are worth our attention. Before the days of regular commercial news services, investors in Europe would hire correspondents in other cities to write letters describing business activities in the correspondent's area. Presumably it was possible for the investors to instruct their correspondents on what they considered worth knowing and so to control the contents of the letters. Readers of present-day newspapers are not in such a happy position. Reporters who write for them also write for thousands or millions of others. The reporter and editor have to estimate what will be of interest to the most readers, so the interests of any single reader can be only approximated.

The uncertainties exist even when people have perfect confidence in the motives of those in charge of the media. When the audience thinks it may have reason to distrust the motives of the media the situation becomes cloudier still. Anyone working as a reporter or editor becomes the target for attempts by many groups who wish to reach the public ear. Many skillful public relations specialists help such groups tell their messages through the media. To maintain their own credibility, media workers must filter out the worthwhile information from the flood of special-interest offerings.

Another disadvantage is that media naturally distort events. Words themselves are inadequate to describe an event so that we can feel it in the same way we would if we were present. The tremendous compression required by time and space limitations make distortion inevitable. If a speaker talks for forty minutes his or her remarks may be summarized in five hundred words in the newspaper or in two minutes on the evening newscast. With the best intentions and the greatest skill it is still inevitable that the report will be distorted. Most of what the speaker said will be omitted, and what is reported will be overemphasized just because it was selected for transmission.

The process of selection works to distort the picture of events in another way. Because of the limited time and space, news reporters can report only a few of the events that come to their attention. They are successful in their selections to the extent that they report the stories in which their audiences are most interested. With mass audiences this comes down to a decision as to what segment of the audience they wish to please.

The technical problems of the media influence the selection of information and the emphasis it is given. In New York City television cameramen shot seven minutes of film covering a dramatic story of two firemen who were electrocuted. Since the event happened in the evening, the film was rushed to the station and was in the developer by 10:30 P.M. Technicians, striving to have it ready to air at 11:15 as part of the 11 o'clock news broadcast, pushed too hard and ruined the film. The audience got, instead of dramatic film highlighting the tragedy, two lines on the incident, spoken by the anchorman. The station's assignment editor, commenting later, remarked, "If it didn't happen on film, it almost didn't happen."[4]

As far as the news director was concerned, the story was important if film were available to dramatize it, but worth only a mention without it. Certain stories lend themselves to certain media, and it is not at all strange that people who program the media should be influenced by this. Generally, situations that involve overt action and interpersonal confrontation are good stories for television. Stories that involve detailed information work better in print.

The amount of time available for preparation combines with the technical characteristics of a medium to affect the nature of the information presented as well as the manner in which it is presented. Books and motion pictures share few technical processes, but both allow more time for preparation than do newspaper or broadcast formats. As a consequence, books and feature films often deal with subjects in depth and with more authority than do the media that face a deadline every few hours. The greater length of books and films also provides more opportunity for authors and directors to develop subject matter with more artistic insight.

What the newspapers and broadcast stations give up to meet frequent deadlines, they gain in timeliness. They also appeal to a broader cross-section by presenting more varied subject matter within a single edition or broadcast.

[4]Robert Daley, "We Deal with Emotional Facts," *New York Times Magazine*, December 15, 1974, pp. 18ff.

Communication: Oil, Glue, and Dynamite

The presence of one medium influences the contents of the others. Television news has caused newspapers to depend less on timeliness. Between them radio and television have killed the old newspaper "extras" that were rushed to print and hawked in the streets. Newspapers have turned to more interpretive material and to exploiting the superior ability of print to transmit detailed information.

All these factors affect the kind of information that the media offer their audiences and the manner in which they present it. Thus they change the picture of the world that receivers would get if they were free to select and interpret the events to which they devote their attention.

Communication Versus Reality

Honest communication is an act of trust. Individuals and organizations find it hard to risk the dangers to self-preservation that frank talk requires. Some conversation is mainly ceremonial (the "How are you?" "Nice day, isn't it?" component of social chitchat) and even that may be guarded. But most communication involves a conflict between the status quo and change. Change frightens most of us because it appears to threaten our personality. We are like the university department chairman who was admonished for treating his faculty like a top sergeant breaking in army recruits. He responded: "Don't tell me to change. This is the way I am."

As individuals wear familiar habits like cherished old jackets, so social institutions cling to the friendly garb of accepted patterns.

But change is inevitable. Individuals grow through communicating, and social institutions adapt by exchanging information.

The patterns of individual and social development are controlled by the way individuals and groups communicate individually and through the media.

As John Dewey and Walter Lippmann reminded us, communication makes us effective to the extent that it helps us to understand and respond to the brute world of reality. Increasingly, the real world that affects us is beyond the reach of our own senses, and so we have to depend frequently on communication rather than observation to adjust our images of the reality in which we live.

What is true of individuals is true of groups and of institutions. Sometimes institutions investigate situations firsthand but usually they must rely on reports from others.

Each of us has some knowledge of what John Dewey called the "brute world." Some take shovels and spade the earth; some dig coal out of deep mines; some fell trees; and some care for animals. All of us have physical and emotional experiences that teach us about the world of people and objects.

But fewer of us do these things now than our ancestors did a hundred years ago. More often we operate machines that have the physical contact with the world. This mechanization itself removes us one step from reality. As the machines become more efficient fewer of us operate the devices that do the job. We find ourselves arranging for the work of the machines, keeping records of what they are doing, arranging for repairs, and filling out sheets that eventually result in people being paid to run the machines. More and more of us work with papers instead of the physical things they tell us about. Thus we find ourselves removed from firsthand contact with the world.

The increasing size of organizations may even rob us of firsthand contact with other people. As firms grow larger, a memorandum is likely to replace a conversation, and the company newspaper attempts to substitute for the human link that used to be provided by human contacts.

As we increase the size of our enterprises we require more organization, more manipulation of people and things, more paperwork, and more people working with papers—more reliance on secondhand information.

Decision-makers even more than others must deal with reports instead of firsthand contact. Persons who run very small stores cannot help but know nearly everything that goes on, but managers of department stores must rely for most of their information on secondhand reports from people who are interested in helping the managers to perceive themselves as efficient workers. For that reason they may not be told of errors in judgment that cost the store money. They may not be aware of an upsurge in customer complaints, and to get accurate information on pilferage and breakage they may have to make a special effort.

As enterprises become larger the firsthand knowledge of the decision-maker diminishes. The president of the United States, as executive head of one of the world's largest enterprises, faces more dangers than most persons of being underinformed and misinformed. This tendency has increased as the size of the government has increased, but it has been present for a long time, as this excerpt from Carl Sandburg's *Abraham Lincoln* illustrates:

> Among White House callers one day came John M. Thayer, a brigadier from Grant's army, who was for special reasons making a trip East. Fixing an earnest and somewhat quizzical look on Thayer, Lincoln asked, "Well, what kind of fellow is Grant?" Thayer replied that Grant was a real commander, popular with the army, making plans and throwing all his energies into their execution. Thayer said he had had opportunities to observe Grant during two years of service. "It has been

charged in northern newspapers that Grant was under the influence of liquor on the field of Donelson and Shiloh. The charge is atrocious, wickedly false. I saw him repeatedly during the battles of Donelson and Shiloh on the field, and if there were any sober men on the field, Grant was one of them."

"It is a relief to me to hear this statement from you," said Lincoln, "for though I have not lost confidence in Grant, I have been a good deal annoyed by reports which have reached me of his intemperance. . . . Delegation after delegation has called me with the same request, 'Recall Grant from command.' "[5]

A little later Sandburg describes Lincoln's plight in poetic language:

In the months between Fredericksburg and Chancellorsville, events swirled round the peculiar pivot where Lincoln moved, and put him into further personal isolation. So often daylight seemed to break—but it was a false dawn—and it was as yet night. When hope came singing a soft song, it was more than once shattered by the brass laughter of cannon and sudden bayonets preceding the rebel yell.[6]

The "splendid isolation" of the occupant of the White House came in for frequent discussion more than a century later. George E. Reedy observed it when he was press secretary to President Johnson and later articulated it in his book *The Twilight of the Presidency*.[7] Journalists discussed it frequently as President Nixon headed down the path to Watergate. Syndicated columnist Roscoe Drummond commented:

One small action which Mr. Nixon took a few days ago casts a revealing light on the most dangerous kind of isolation which builds up around a President in the hallowed, overrevered, overprotected environment of the White House.

And what was that action? You may hardly believe it, or believe it should have been necessary, but it was announced that the White House would now permit the Republican legislative leaders to determine occasionally the agenda of things they can discuss at their regular meetings with the President!

This is the most perilous, debilitating kind of isolation there is— isolation from the flow of candid, first-hand plain-talk exchange of views and counterviews.

That's what hardly any President gets and, evidently, President Nixon was shielded more than most.[8]

[5]Carl Sandburg, *Abraham Lincoln: The Prairie Years and the War Years*, combined ed. (New York: Harcourt, Brace & World, 1954), p. 369.

[6]Ibid., p. 370.

[7]George R. Reedy, *The Twilight of the Presidency* (New York: World Publishing, 1970).

[8]Roscoe Drummond, "President Nixon's Lonely Isolation," *Los Angeles Times* syndicated column in the Lexington, Kentucky, *Leader*, July 20, 1973.

During the Second World War General George C. Marshall had a suggestion as to how General Dwight D. Eisenhower might get better information from the African front, which Eisenhower was then commanding. Marshall told Eisenhower:

> In this sprawling theater, with demands on your time and attention all the way from Casablanca to Tunisia, you just can't get to all the places you might like to visit. You ought to have a man to be your eyes and ears. . . . an extension of your own faculties. Ideally, you'd have far more confidence in his information than in daily situation reports from the front.[9]

Decision-makers at high levels often have special sources of information, but they need them as protection against the dangers of isolation to which their positions condemn them.

The Media Intensify Information

As interaction with other people molds us in subtle ways, so does our use of the media. After we watch a light comedy on television we may tend to imitate the hero or heroine. We may decide our own social dilemmas on the basis of advice from Ann Landers to another hapless individual entangled in a problem similar to ours. Some of us may become a little more violence-prone after watching a gory film. While media impact is diminished because it removes us from firsthand reality, it does sometimes intensify the information it provides.

Media messages are intensified just because each member of the audience knows that many others are receiving the message at the same time. There is an old saw in the newspaper business that news becomes news when it is printed. It is true that a bit of information immediately assumes more importance the moment it is printed or broadcast. The fact that something is common knowledge will make it the subject of conversations, and people who are not in on it may feel ignorant.

Thus by emphasizing or ignoring an event the people who run the media exercise a considerable amount of power. It is the power to confer importance to information and status on individuals.

The media showed their strength in the Watergate scandals of 1972 and 1973. It is possible that the public could have virtually ignored the entire situation. President Nixon's landslide election in 1972 indicates that the

[9]Dwight D. Eisenhower, *At Ease* (Garden City, N.Y.: Doubleday, 1967), p. 260.

public was not much impressed by the implications of the break-in despite a considerable amount of national publicity about it. Given the initial public indifference, how did the story manage to dominate the news during the summer of 1973?

The answer is not too clear, but it is likely that the reporting of the *Washington Post* was the single most important factor that kept the story alive. Many other news media were content to let the story drop until the *Post* came up with a new development. Deep-digging *Post* reporters managed to keep the story alive until the Senate hearings came on television. Chairman Sam Ervin was projected as a latter-day knight with homespun Southern wisdom. When he and other senators clashed with well-known witnesses, headlines were made and all were locked in a kind of classic struggle.

This was a story of considerable public importance, but it might very well have died for lack of public interest if a strong newspaper had not assigned public importance to it by printing information about it. Since the *Post* is one of the dominant newspapers, the rest of the press gradually went along, adding their weight to the importance of the event. When the hearings opened and the clash of famous personalities made the story a television natural, the footlights came on and the nation was absorbed as it seldom has been before in a single great drama.

The Watergate story had much national importance, but this importance was recognized chiefly through the efforts of a small segment of the news media. It is reasonable to wonder what other situations of great national concern could achieve similar public attention through a combination of media persistence and dramatic action.

Similar to the ability to confer importance on information is the power to confer status on individuals. Citizens can earn status in their own communities if they can get the attention of the media. If their names and pictures appear regularly in a favorable context in the newspapers and if they are seen on telecasts, they may become prominent; if attention is showered on them, they become local celebrities. The same thing happens on a national and international level, although it becomes more difficult to achieve recognition at these levels. The process can work in reverse. If the media refuse to pay attention to a person it is nearly impossible to achieve public status except in the smallest communities where word of mouth may turn the tide.

Another advantage the media have in intensifying their impact is the fact that often they deal with great events. Few of us can observe earth-shaking events in person, so we rely on the media and come to associate the media with the magnitude of the events they report. It is easy when we see a broadcaster on the television news night after night to associate him or her with the greatness of the events described. Sometimes when famous television commentators have gone out to cover an event they have destroyed the event itself because bystanders besieged them for autographs and generally spent so much time admiring them that they forgot the event. It is worthwhile to remind oneself that newscasters, unlike reporters, may be little closer to the great events than is their audience— they are, after all, individuals sitting in a studio before a camera reading words usually written by someone else.

The importance of great events rubs off on the media and provides an aura of awe that assigns importance to media and their messages.

Technology provides firsthand experience for few but vicarious experience for many. Watching a moon walk, live and in color, is exciting, but it is still secondhand experience. It would be more exciting to be on the moon. But viewer interest is intensified by the knowledge that other people all over the world are watching the same event. Thus some of the media's disadvantage as a purveyor of information is compensated.

Oil . . .

Ann Landers and Abigail Van Buren help their readers face their problems just by showing them that others face similar ones. They also help keep society on an even keel by suggesting solutions that are socially acceptable. Much interpersonal and media communication has this regulatory function—it keeps the world running smoothly by helping individuals adjust to the reality of their lives. Much communication serves this purpose. The media encourage order by reporting the misadventures of those who transgress legal or social rules.

Glue . . .

Communication is the glue, too, by which social cohesion is maintained. The media gives strangers something to talk about, whether it is the doings of Rhoda or Phyllis, the views of Bella Abzug, or the price of oil. Over the years communication builds up and reinforces the ideas that hold a society together. Seminal documents such as the Constitution and the Declaration of Independence become a common heritage through communication. The result is not always so salubrious. Hitler held together a majority by preaching hatred of Jews and Communists and persuading Germans that they were oppressed by the terms of the Treaty of Versailles.

And Dynamite

But communication can rip society apart, too. Propaganda campaigns preceded the Russian Revolution of 1917 and Hitler's rise to the German chancellorship in 1933. Tom Paine's pamphlets helped fire the American Revolution. In the 1960's minority groups in the United States forced their demands before the public through dramatic actions that the media could not ignore, and American society was changed. Used purposefully and skillfully communication maintains the status quo or fosters change; holds society together or rips it apart.

Suggestions for Further Reading

Ardrey, Robert. *The Territorial Imperative*. New York: Dell, 1966.
  Reports studies of animal behavior that suggest hypotheses about human communication.
Birdwhistell, Ray L. *Kinesics and Context: Essays on Body Motion Communication*. Philadelphia: University of Pennsylvania Press, 1970.
  A readable, scientific report of knowledge in the field.
Fast, Julius. *Body Language*. New York: M. Evans, 1970.
  A popular version of kinesics.
Hall, Edward T. *The Hidden Dimension*. Garden City, Doubleday, N.Y.: 1966.
  A discussion of human behavior in relation to space, this book is full of insights about communication.
———. *The Silent Language*. Garden City, N.Y.: Doubleday, 1959.
  Explains differences in communication patterns in various cultures.
Lippmann, Walter. *Public Opinion*. New York: Harcourt, Brace, 1922.
  Dated in its examples, this work by an eminent journalist still provides much insight into communication as it affects public decision.
Pei, Mario. *The Story of Language*. Rev. ed. Philadelphia: J. B. Lippincott, 1965.
  An easily read account of the development of language.

2

Lifestyle and Mindstyle

Pick a ripe apple from a tree, look for worm holes, and eat it.

Or . . . go to the supermarket, buy a can of applesauce, open it, and eat it.

Pull an onion, dig a hill of potatoes, slaughter a steer, mix, add water and seasoning, cook, and eat it.

Or . . . go to the supermarket, buy a can of stew, open, heat, and eat it.

The quality of experience depends on the degree to which we accept the bounties of technology. We trade off experience for convenience.

For many the choice is easy: open the can; thaw the frozen dinner. Who wants to climb an apple tree? For others the choice is made by circumstances. How many apartment dwellers have an apple tree handy or a steer awaiting slaughter?

Technology eases life and adds variety and opportunity. But sometimes it controls people. Once a new technology is unleashed, the world is never the same again. The technology that produced the hydrogen bomb changed the world. The technology that makes birth control easy will probably do the same.

But the doubt lingers. Who or what is in charge, people or technology?

In advanced societies the focus shifts from the technology of things to the technology of information. The technology of things expands human physical powers. The technology of information extends human mental powers. Writing, the printing press, the telegraph, radio, and television have altered the way men and women think as well as the way they live.

Salvation or Damnation?

The central argument concerns all technology. "Technological determinists" argue that new technologies by their very existence control human destiny. Others respond that it is not the technology itself, but the way it is used that controls the world. The argument is endless; the truth, somewhere in between.

The technological determinists are of two schools. One holds that humankind will eventually use its own technology to destroy civilization and itself. Perhaps the hydrogen bomb will do the job. The other group believes that new technology will always save humanity from disaster and will eventually provide a utopia—never well defined, but always tantalizingly just across the horizon.

A leader among the determinists, Marshall McLuhan, considers communication so central to humankind that his major divisions of history— pretribal, linear sequential, and electric—are based on communication concepts. McLuhan's writing in the 1950's and 1960's seemed so revolutionary that they triggered outraged protest from some scholars and stout defenses from others. In the 1970's they seem less revolutionary, but they still provide insights available nowhere else. The title of one of McLuhan's books, *The Medium Is the Massage*,[1] sums up the creed of the determinists. No matter *what* messages are sent, he says, it is *how* they are sent that controls human response.

Undecided in his early writing whether to be optimistic or pessimistic in his determinism, McLuhan eventually opted for optimism, finding his own utopia in the "tribal village." Electric technology, he says, connects all humankind in a giant nervous system that in some vague manner will produce the new utopia—a world-scale tribal village.

The theories of the determinists are too extreme for most people to accept. People have always tried to control media technology, and most of this book is concerned with these efforts. In this chapter, however, we will examine the arguments of those who insist that control is impossible because the media technology inexorably determines its own effects.

[1]Marshall McLuhan, *The Medium Is the Massage* (New York: Bantam, 1967).

Lifestyle and Mindstyle

Two theories justify "media determinism." One assigns changes in communication processes as causes for other changes in society. The other holds that the effect of a message on a receiver is determined mostly by the human sense to which it appeals. For example, the same message might have different effects if it were directed to the eye through print or to the ear through the human voice.

A comparison of the oral versus the written tradition serves as a starting point for a consideration of the first theory.

The Oral Tradition

Before writing was invented the oral tradition flowered. Some see the oral tradition as a time of innocence . . . like the days in the Garden of Eden before Adam and Eve listened to the wily serpent. When humans depended on their voices to communicate and their feet to travel, these people feel, the world was kept on a scale comprehensible to the human mind.

The village, the tribe, or the city-state were the centers of community life. The world beyond the next mountain range was largely unknown. As darkness fell each night the world became smaller still as the tribe gathered around the fire for warmth and mutual protection.

Information and opinions were sent and received in face-to-face meetings. Common concerns were considered in public gatherings, and public celebrations marked times of good fortune.

Since records were carried in individual minds, the oral tradition required that people assemble to hear the accounts of their heritage. Elders were revered because they knew the myths and legends. Acquiring knowledge required memorization, so, while less of the past was preserved, it was better understood and more personally felt.

Since judges and rulers could not rely on written precedent, they had to search their memories for it. Since human memory is not always exact, laws and precedent were interpreted to fit the situation.

The way men and women communicate affects the way they think and the way they live. The change from the oral to the written tradition was a change in communication methods.

Harold Innis, the Canadian economic historian and student of communications, said that the oral tradition favored the preeminence of the church over other institutions of society. The church lives by celebration, the recital of the mass, the singing of hymns, the recitation of psalms and creeds, the giving and hearing of sermons. In an oral tradition the ecclesiastics are the keepers of the long tradition and the masters of the ceremonies by which they are preserved.

Greece and the Oral Tradition

Innis comes to grips with the conflict between the oral and the written tradition in his essay on "The Oral Tradition and Greece" in *Empire & Communications*.[2] "Greek civilization was a reflection of the power of the spoken word," Innis tells us, bolstering the point by quoting Socrates:

> I cannot help feeling, Phaedrus, that writing is unfortunately like painting; for the creations of the painter have the attitude of life, and yet if you ask them a question, they preserve a solemn silence, and the same may be said of speeches. You would imagine that they had intelligence, but if you want to know anything and put a question to one of them, the speaker always gives on unvarying answer.

The dialogues were an effort to preserve the power of the spoken word on the page, and Plato succeeded in this because of the "inconclusiveness" of his work.

> The power of the oral tradition persisted in his prose in the absence of a closely ordered system. . . . The life and movement of dialectic opposed the establishment of a finished system of dogma. He would not surrender his freedom to his own books and refused to be bound by what he had written.[3]

Music was essential to the oral tradition, extending its flexibility and increasing its emotional range. Music heightened the intensity of ceremonies and so united individuals in a common culture.

Despite the incursion of the written word into Greek culture, the oral tradition was so strong there that Greece avoided some of the results of the written word in later cultures. A professional group of scribes never gained power there, nor did the priesthood use the written word to gain control of education. The strength of the oral tradition in Greece slowed the development of written codes, which limited the latitude accorded judges in interpreting laws; but as literacy increased so did the demand that laws and judgments be published. The strength of the oral tradition permitted control of extreme forms of religious celebrations because it centered the wisdom of the past on the newer cults. "The Delphic oracle has no sacred book and with its maxims 'know thyself' and 'nothing overmuch' has been compared to a serious newspaper managed

[2]Harold Innis, *Empire and Communications*, rev. Mary Q. Innis (Toronto: University of Toronto Press, 1972).
[3]Ibid., p. 57.

by a cautious editorial committee with no principles in particular."[4]

By the second half of the fifth century B.C. the great strength of the oral tradition was giving way to the power of the written word. Laws were written in prose that began to have a recognized pattern, although its development was slowed by the Homeric epic pattern of the oral tradition. "Writing was beginning to destroy the bond of Greek life. In 470 BC Athens had no reading public, but by 430 BC Herodotus found it convenient to turn his recitations into book form."[5]

Innis regarded the fall of Athens and the execution of Socrates as the "great tragedy of the oral tradition."

The spread of writing emphasized the differences among the Greek city-states and hastened the end of Greek civilization. Sparta resisted longer than Athens by emphasizing music and crystallizing few laws into writing.

One senses a sadness as Innis chronicles the last great stand of the oral tradition. Perhaps the oral tradition is the only one that is able to withstand the tendency of every medium to build up a monopoly of knowledge that is exploited for a time, perhaps brief, by a ruling class, until the very monopoly encourages the rise of a competing medium which repeats the process.

Writing Favors Large-Scale Organization

Writing made possible the organization of social and political institutions on a larger scale than ever before possible. Orders could be sent over long distances, thus ensuring their delivery as intended and without trusting the memory of a messenger. Thus administration of an empire was considerably simplified. Writing also enhanced efficiency by making it possible to keep exact copies of the laws and other records.

Since long recitations and the services of minstrels and elders were no longer required to preserve information, the tendency was to minimize ceremony as the written word came into use. Instead of elders a new group came to power. These were the scribes. People who learned to read and write were assured of positions of influence and generally they became part of a governmental civil service.

The diminution of the importance of ceremony struck at the power of the church, and the long-range effect of the change was to elevate secular power.

[4]Ibid., pp. 73–74.
[5]Ibid., pp. 80–81.

Writing diminished ceremony in still another way. It opened the door for knowledge to become more linear and more personal. In an oral society, individuals who would be knowledgeable must attach themselves to the best teachers they can find where they will probably be members of a group of students. Learning, then, is a social experience. With the advent of writing, scholars can shut themselves up in a room and study the written word. In fact, to learn many things, they must be prepared to endure solitude. The same scholars, when they become productive, are likely to supply the fruits of their labor to fellow students in the form of articles. Thus, the persons who deal with the basic ideas of society are changed from social to solitary beings.

The opinions of those who celebrate the glories of the oral tradition raise the question as to whether the savants of the day might not have been well advised to decide whether writing should have been put into general use. No such examination was made, of course, the world then as now accepting at face value any technological innovation that came along. Good or bad, we have been dealing with the results ever since, as we have been dealing with the results of the invention of the automobile and the atomic bomb.

The contrast between the oral and written traditions illustrates the principle that the nature of communication in a society affects its structure, habits, and power patterns. Once the written tradition established itself, even variations in its technology changed society. The surface used is one of the technologies that affect society, in Innis's view. He separates media into two classes: time-binding and space-binding. Time-binding media are those that, like the oral tradition, teach a reverence for things of the past and tend to limit people to small geographic areas and small units of government. Space-binding media are the opposite. They encourage knowledge of other places and the growth of empires. They speed commerce and interaction among societies.

In studying the power patterns produced by the media, Innis theorized that certain media would favor certain groups. In an elaborate historical analysis, he recognized the church and state as the two dominant power centers during most of the period of his interest. Then he proceeded to examine historical data against his hypothesis that the time-binding media favored church control, and the space-binding media the development of secular empires. The books which resulted are not only examples of brilliant scholarship but also fascinating case studies of the use of historical data to substantiate a theory about power patterns in society.

Stone is a time-binding medium. It cannot be transported easily, it takes effort to chisel words on it, and so people tend to use words that they think will have lasting significance. And the material itself endures in time. The effect of words cut in stone is to preserve what already exists. People come to look at the monuments and they are reminded of the past glories of their society. This encourages the views of the traditionalists.

Each technology, Innis suggests, creates a "monopoly of knowledge." This monopoly sets up forces that strive for a new medium in opposition that destroys the earlier medium and in turn acquires its own monopoly of knowledge. Thus each civilization contains the seeds of its own destruction, seldom recognized by the participants.

In considering Innis's hypothesis we will first examine the technology that produced writing surfaces.

The Search for a Surface

One of the earliest technological concerns after the invention of writing was a development of a suitable writing surface. Stones were plentiful in many areas and labor was cheap, so one solution was to carve letters on stone. This tended to control verbosity, but did little for long-distance communication. Clay, another early writing surface, was more easily marked than stone, but no more easily transported.

The Egyptians found the first portable writing surface. Papyrus, a long-stemmed plant that grew in the Nile valley, was the answer. The stems were placed in layers under pressure to produce a coarse, paperlike material. Papyrus served Egypt and the Roman Empire well. Light and portable, it carried orders from Rome throughout the Mediterranean basin, and it was in such good supply that it formed the basis of libraries and led to the practice of reproducing books by dictating to a group of scribes. Slaves were used as copyists and the strihoi, a unit of fifteen or sixteen syllables, became the standard measure of the work of a copyist for establishing the price of manuscripts. Another effect of making records of public proceedings was that speakers, notably in the Roman senate, began to consider the wider effects of their words.

Egypt had a good thing in papyrus manufacture for a time, maintaining it as a state monopoly until the pharaoh pushed his advantage too far and forced his competitors to invent a substitute. Fearing that the library at neighboring Pergamum would surpass that at Alexandria, the pharaoh forbade the use of papyrus in Pergamum.

Technology came to the rescue of the resourceful citizens of Pergamum, who experimented with the hides of animals as a replacement for papyrus. By about 190 B.C. they had perfected the processing and it became apparent that parchment was superior to papyrus. It was more permanent as well as more flexible. It is still used for some official charters and diplomas. A fine quality parchment is called vellum.

Papyrus, because of government monopoly and control, had tended to favor the secular power of Rome, but by the eighth century its use was declining in favor of parchment, which was more suited to the production of large books. Since parchment could be produced over a larger area and in an agricultural economy, it tended to favor decentralized administration and the monastic world. Parchment helped build up a powerful religious element in western Europe, and so, following Innis's theory, it invited competition to the new monopoly of knowledge that it had helped to create. That competition came from paper.

The Chinese Invent Paper

The Chinese had long been restless with the limitations of the silk and bamboo surfaces on which they were writing. Ts'ai Lun, minister of public works, found a solution by inventing paper in A.D. 105. He found that a cheap and satisfactory surface could be made by pounding hemp and certain other plants and treating them chemically. Some variation in the content of the brew was permissible. Old fishnets were sometimes thrown in. Fortuitously for the Western world, some Chinese paper makers were taken prisoner and their Turkish captors encouraged them in their work. By about A.D. 800 a paper industry was established in Baghdad. The Crusades and the Moorish conquest of Northern Africa provided the contact that spread the knowledge of paper-making to Europe.

The spread of paper-making throughout Europe in the thirteenth century eventually broke the monopoly of knowledge held by the monasteries and, combined with printing, changed the power patterns of society.

Paper Strengthens Secular Concerns

A plentiful supply of paper speeded up commercial development since it provided a record of transactions. More important, paper answered a need for publication of the vernacular. Already a split between the monks and the rest of the population had developed over language. The ecclesiastics had held their grip over religious doctrine by using Latin. Plentiful and cheap paper made it possible to publish in the language of the common people, thus threatening the monopoly of the church.

Writers in the vernacular were attracted to feudal courts and they were encouraged in their work. Charlemagne set about preserving ballads of the common people in their own language. Alfred the Great gave impetus to the secular, vernacular movement:

> Therefore, it seems better to me, if it seems likewise to you, that we turn some books which are most needful for all persons into the tongue which we can all understand; and that you act . . . to the end that all the youth now in England of free men who have the wealth to be able to apply themselves to it, be set to learning so long as they are no use for anything else, until the time when they can read English writing well; let those afterwards be instructed in the Latin language.[6]

The church fought back. Clerics preached in the vernacular but continued to write in Latin. The universities were building up their own monopolies of knowledge and so challenging the power of the church. The University of Paris added to church literature, but, since it was outside of Rome, the kings of France used it as a weapon against domination by the Papacy. The songs of the troubadors and the poetry of Dante, Petrarch, Boccaccio, and Chaucer turned the tide to the vernacular. Monks were outnumbered by lay copyists. It was estimated that the city of Paris had ten thousand lay scribes by 1450.

Eventually even the monasteries reluctantly gave up expensive parchment in favor of cheap paper. The church's monopoly based on parchment gave over to secular dominance and the widespread use of paper. A monopoly of knowledge built on a medium that emphasized the virtues of time and tradition gave over to a new monopoly based on a medium that emphasized control of space.

Paper and books printed in the vernacular also emphasized nationalism. A common language was a powerful bond, and books printed in the vernacular hastened the developing national loyalties.

Printing

Printing added another technological factor to the written word. It accentuated the movement to publication in the vernacular and so increased the tendency of the written word to favor nationalism. In the separate kingdoms that were developing in Europe the kings increased their domination over religion by encouraging the publication of religious as well as lay books in the common tongues. Printing developed more slowly in France than in other countries of Europe, probably because of the financial interests of publishers in the works of copyists. Censorship

---

[6]Ibid., p. 131

by the church in France was broken because France exported cheap paper to neighboring countries where it was turned into printed books forbidden in France. These were then smuggled back across the border.

Innis reports that Great Britain's experience with the printing press had great influence on the Colonies.

> Restriction on the press was paralleled, but the expansion of literary activity in Great Britain, which had served as an outlet to political repression, overwhelmed the colonies and compelled concentration on newspapers. . . . The agitation against restrictions was carried out with more success than in Great Britain, in part by revolutionary spirits who had emigrated to avoid repression.[7]

In general, the Innis view is that printing intensified the monopoly of knowledge that, inherent in any medium, is particularly pernicious in the written word. One expression of this print monopoly is exploited, he says, by textbook publishers: "A large textbook subject to revision at suitable intervals can be profitably exploited at the expense of works of scholarship."

Books, Newspapers, and Radio

The communications media affect the society in which they function, but they are also shaped by society and technology. Innis held that newspapers developed early in America because Colonial writers were overwhelmed by the literary tradition of England and, instead of competing with it, turned to a new form—newspapers.

In a circular process, American newspaper enterprise was transplanted to Britain and turned that society's emphasis from time to space. Because of language and technological differences newspapers did not achieve such a dominant position in Germany, so the stage was set for a battle between the opposing "monopolies of knowledge." Innis sees World War I as a struggle between societies dominated by books and societies dominated by newspapers.

Media differences also had an influence in bringing about World War II. This time the battle was between newspaper-dominated and radio-dominated societies. Hitler's power as a speaker was legendary, and some of this magnetism was transmitted by radio. German society was shaped by radio even before the war began, although British and American leaders failed to capitalize immediately on the new technology:

[7]Ibid., pp. 156–157.

The loud speaker had decisive significance for the election of the Nazis. Regions dominated by the German language responded to the appeal of the spoken word inviting them to join a larger German Reich. The Second World War became to an important extent the result of a clash between the newspaper and the radio. In the conduct of the war the power of the mechanized spoken word was capitalized in the English-speaking world, notably by Churchill and Roosevelt. Russia had an enormous advantage in the difficulties of language and its impermeability to German propaganda.[8]

The competition between established and new media is illustrated by the influence of British publishers who managed to see that initially broadcasting was entirely a government monopoly and thus did not compete with newspapers for advertising.

The Word in Sound and Print

Innis, as we have seen, argues that media affect society because of their ability to enshrine information in time, or their ability to spread it rapidly over space. Others argue that the effect of the media is principally determined by the sense to which they appeal. Walter J. Ong sees important differences between communication by sight and communication by sound.

The word is primarily a spoken thing, Ong says, but writing transposes it to space.[9] Writing forces us to assimilate information with the eye rather than the ear. Ong notes that a spoken word is an event, a happening that dies as soon as it is completed. The written word, a symbol for the spoken one, lives, not only in space, but also in time. Although the spoken word lasts only a moment, it strikes the listener with force and provides a dynamic experience. The written word is passive.

Writing carries less of the personality of the sender and permits more control of the message by the receiver. Ong quotes J. C. Carothers: "Few people fail to communicate their messages and much of themselves in speech, whereas writings, unless produced by one with literary gifts, carry little of the writer and are interpreted far more according to the reader's understanding or prejudice."[10]

Ong emphasizes the ceremonial nature of sound: "Sound unites groups

[8]Ibid., p. 165.
[9]Walter J. Ong, *The Presence of the Word* (New Haven: Yale University Press, 1967).
[10]J. C. Carothers, *Culture, Society and the Written Word*, quoted in ibid., p. 115.

of living beings as nothing else does. There is some relationship between resort to sound and socialization. . . ."[11]

Sound brings people closer to reality. "Sound situates man in the middle of actuality and in simultaneity, whereas vision situates man in front of things and in sequentiality." And again: "At a given instant I hear not merely what is in front of me or behind me or at either side, but all these things simultaneously, and what is above and below as well. . . . Sound thus situates me in the midst of a world."[12]

Assimilating information by sight is different from assimilating it by sound, and the nature of the medium used has something to do with the way we accept information and probably with the way we think about it.

McLuhan's theories are built on similar ideas. He views all technology as extensions of human beings. Clubs and rocks are extensions used in battle and so is the atomic bomb. A communications medium that appeals to the ear is an extension of the ear; a visual medium is an extension of the eyes. McLuhan holds that the written work, in its appeal to the eye, has dulled our other sensitivities, and that written words turn people into linear thinkers. Readers follow the word and sentence patterns that are arranged in logical, sequential order and they learn to think in the same way. Taking in information through the ear is an entirely different process, which produces an "all-at-once" effect and involves us in firsthand experience in a manner impossible for the printed media.

"Linear thought" has become the trademark of the Western world and accounts for the material achievements of Western civilization. But writing and printing and the era of linear thought that they helped produce are over, in McLuhan's opinion. The computer, the very triumph of linearity, combines with "electric technology" to produce a new environment. The speed of electric communication and the speed of the computer re-create the "all-at-once" environment of the ear of the oral tradition.

The new speed and involvement require the participation of both eye and ear, and the combination may produce an equivalent of tactile experience. The media, by their manipulation of the senses, produce rich or dull communication experience. The blessing of the new all-encompassing media seems to be that they provide experience equivalent to that felt by people before writing was invented.

McLuhan emphasizes how the media manipulate the senses:

> The phonetic alphabet reduced the use of all the senses at once, which is oral speech, to a merely visual code. Today, such translation can be effected back and forth through a variety of spatial forms which we call the "media of communication." But each of these spaces has

[11]Ong, *Presence of the Word*, p. 122.
[12]Ibid., pp. 128–129.

unique properties and impinges upon our other senses or spaces in unique ways.[13]

There is little doubt that humans process information differently, depending upon the sense through which it is received. At the same time, the mere intervention of any mechanical device will change the nature of the experience. Face-to-face conversation is sure to be more intense and more "participatory" than communication through any mechanical device. The telephone, for example, is part personal, despite its electrical circuitry. Telephone conversations provide instant feedback, something that is not available in most media communication. This allows responses similar to those of face-to-face talk. One person can interrupt the other to disagree, to seek clarification, or to add support. Some of the side-channels that add information in ordinary talk are left intact in telephone talk. Tonal cues, hesitations, and nonverbal sounds such as laughs and groans all tend to add "naturalness" to a telephone conversation. These cues do not come across with the accuracy and ease of firsthand conversation, but they carry much information, especially if the persons talking on the telephone are well acquainted.

Lack of visual information, on the other hand, sets a telephone conversation apart from a face-to-face visit. The information conveyed by facial expressions and body movement is lacking. So is information about the situation in which the other person is speaking. A person who knows the other party to a telephone call well may sense an "artificial" quality about the conversation. Often this is because the other person is in the presence of someone else and may not talk as frankly as he or she would in private. Individuals who use the telephone professionally may take advantage of the lack of visual channels. Telephone salespersons may be trained to read their pitch to make it sound like a regular conversation. One young saleswoman was thrown into confusion and hung up when the stranger she had called inquired: "Are you reading that?"

Less personal feeling is built up in a telephone call, so it is easier for either party to terminate it. The mechanical act of hanging up the instrument is easier than walking away from another person. One man has even refined the art of ending a telephone call abruptly. He breaks the connection while he himself is talking on the theory that the other party will not be offended because nobody will believe that anyone will hang up on himself.

Thus even telephone conversations, probably the most natural of media-mediated communication processes, differ because of their mechanical nature. It seems reasonable to surmise that all media-

[13]Marshall McLuhan, *The Gutenberg Galaxy* (Toronto: University of Toronto Press, 1962), p. 45.

mediated communication affects individuals differently just because of the mechanical or electrical intervention.

McLuhan popularized the idea of audience participation in the media through the words "hot" and "cool." In the McLuhan idiom "hot" refers to a medium that is low in audience participation, "cool" to one that is high. Hot media, such as books, carry much information and require less participation; while cool media, such as television, carry little information and require more participation.

McLuhan sees television as participatory partly because the picture is built on a pattern of lines so dots are left on the screen that the viewer unconsciously fills in. This "mosaic" pattern heightens the sense of audience participation, McLuhan argues, because of the effort required to fill in the dots. This argument is vitiated by consideration of the mechanical nature of a motion picture projector. The film provides the illusion of motion by projecting a series of still pictures at the rate of twenty-four per second. As the frame changes in the projector, a shutter closes the aperture, leaving the screen blank. The process occurs rapidly, but it might be argued that the viewer has to fill in the blank screen in the same way that the television viewer has to fill in the dots on a television screen. Despite this similarity, McLuhan classifies motion pictures as less participatory than television, and sees a motion picture as shown on television as radically different from one projected by conventional means.

Diverging Roads

Innis and McLuhan make many of the same assumptions and often their roads are parallel. McLuhan acknowledges Innis's contribution to his thinking: "Innis was the first person to hit upon the process of change as implicit in the *forms* of media technology. The present book is a footnote of explanation to his work."[14]

Nevertheless, there are differences even in beginning premises. Innis presents many illustrations of factors other than eye and ear appeal that affect the reception of media messages. Simple availability of a medium and the habits of the agency that controls the supply or channel are two of them. McLuhan tends to ignore factors other than the sense to which the medium appeals and the degree to which an audience participates.

Innis is more deeply impressed by the value of the oral tradition and consequently more distrustful of the technologies by which that tradition was replaced. In his earlier writings McLuhan shared this view, but later he changed his mind.

[14]Ibid., p. 50.

The disagreement becomes most obvious in consideration of the effects of the electronic media. Innis believes radio and television extend the process already started by writing and printing: they strengthen nationalism, emphasize space over time, and minimize concern for values.

McLuhan's views are opposite. He considers radio and television as a part of an electric technology that also includes the electric light, the telephone, and all electric circuitry. This electric technology will, he thinks, form a web of nerves that will connect everyone in the world and turn the planet into a "tribal village." If we are able to understand the nature of our opportunity quickly enough, he hints, we can gain back some of the advantages of an oral civilization and benefit from the "wholeness" of a world society.

McLuhan himself points up his difference with Innis in his introduction to a reprint of Innis's *The Bias of Communication*. McLuhan says Innis is untrue to his own method in attributing to radio the same effect as print—extending spatial penetration at the expense of time.

> After many historical demonstrations of the space-binding power of the eye and the time-binding power of the ear, Innis refrains from applying these structural principles to the action of radio. Suddenly, he shifts the ear world of radio into the visual orbit, attributing to radio all the centralizing powers of the eye and of visual culture.[15]

It could be argued that Innis did not live to see the effects of television (he died in 1952), but he had ample opportunity to consider radio. McLuhan seems to base his belief on the idea that a medium that appeals to the ear is necessarily time-binding. As we have seen, while Innis makes this distinction in comparing the oral and written cultures, he believes other factors can modify the impact. Hindsight in the 1970's would indicate that, so far, the Innis thesis has more validity than that of McLuhan.

Communications scholar James W. Carey endorses Innis's view of the effect of the electronic media, although he supports it on slightly different grounds. McLuhan's ideas, Carey says, fall into the pattern of earlier utopian thinkers; his work is actually an extension of ideas first expressed in the mid-nineteenth century.[16] Carey praises Innis's scholarship and methodology and supports it with the observation that the modern media have increased their control over space by decreasing signaling time (the time between the sending and receiving of a message). Carey says nothing

---

[15]Marshall McLuhan, introduction to 1968 printing of Harold A. Innis, *The Bias of Communication* (Toronto: University of Toronto Press, 1951).

[16]James W. Carey, "The Politics of the Electronic Revolution: Further Notes on Marshall McLuhan" (Paper presented at the Association for Education in Journalism convention, Lawrence, Kansas, 1968). A more accessible source of Carey's ideas on McLuhan is his article in the *Antioch Review* listed at the end of this chapter.

of the human sense to which a medium appeals. It is not at all certain that Innis would have followed the same logic, but both concluded that radio leads to increased emphasis on space and empire.

Innis and McLuhan eventually come to quite different conclusions. McLuhan predicts a utopian society as a result of the near instantaneous speed of the electric media and their effects on the senses. Innis has no such belief in a better society through any single medium, but seeks a method by which space-binding and time-binding media can be balanced to provide an orderly, if not utopian, society.

Communication Patterns and Lifestyle

The questions raised by Ong, Innis, and McLuhan are of the first magnitude. They center around the query: What are the effects of our methods of communicating on our life patterns and our society?

Some investigators have approached the same great problem by peeling off one tiny piece at a time. This is the method favored by social scientists who set up laboratory experiments under controlled conditions. They may investigate such questions as whether an attitude is changed more effectively if arguments are put in order ABC or BCA; or how the effect of a persuasive document is changed if an authoritative source is cited or omitted. Much ingenious and well-designed research of this nature is done every year, and gradually it is increasing our understanding of our own communication process. When it is well controlled it has the authority provided by rigorous method.

Observations on a grand scale such as those of Innis can never achieve the rigor of the controlled experiment, but they have their place nonetheless. They provide insights that can be refined into theories and hypotheses to be tested in experiments and controlled observation.

Whatever their methods, communications scholars have established a direct link between the way humans communicate and the kind of society they build. The linking process is dramatically demonstrated historically by comparing the oral with the written society, but the process goes on continuously. The results are easier to observe in a related technology, transportation.

Widespread use of the automobile created the urban sprawl that surrounds most American cities. Streetcar and railroad lines had encouraged development in given areas with specific identities. Automobiles allowed people to settle anywhere within a wide radius of the city, and the easy transportation encouraged larger building lots. The resulting sprawl made it difficult to provide sidewalks, sewers, water, and other utilities, as well as police and fire protection. In retrospect it is easy to see how the automobile changed the lives of Americans, although there is no record of anyone predicting the changes very far in advance.

As transportation technology changes physical living patterns, communication technology changes the patterns of mental activity and social interaction. Political campaigning is radically different because of radio and television. The old-fashioned political rally does not attract the crowds it used to because people are sitting home watching television. Candidates have responded by slipping their appeals directly into the homes on television and other media. Along with this change have come side effects on the political process. Since media advertising requires much money, a premium is put on campaign funding. Since the production of effective thirty- and sixty-second radio and television spots is a specialized business, advertising people have become indispensable. Some fear that candidates are elected through the quality of their advertising rather than through any inherent virtues of their own. Even nonadvertising television material has its dangers. Perhaps television debates put too much of a premium on the good looks and easy small talk of a candidate.

The dangers are many and some of them are imagined, but the point is that a drastic change in the media has caused a drastic change in one of America's favorite pastimes—politicking.

American lifestyles have been changed in other ways by the transportation-communication trade-off. Telephone calls illustrate this trade-off. If you have a telephone you can chat with friends and conduct a great deal of business without leaving your home or office. Thus the telephone saves many gallons of gasoline, wear and tear on automobiles, and horrendous traffic jams. The Bell system has exploited the convenience of the telephone in its slogan advertising the "Yellow Pages": "Let your fingers do the walking."

As communications media become more sophisticated the transportation-communication trade-off will be more apparent. More people will be able to stay home and handle jobs that now require interaction with others in an office. Geographic location will be less important for many businesses. An insurance firm justified moving its headquarters to Florida on the grounds that, "If you have a postage stamp it doesn't matter where you are." In the future it will be increasingly true that it does not matter where you are so long as you can plug into the coaxial cable.

But the media shape society in more subtle and critical ways. Media have a strong influence on how individuals and groups interact.

Patterns of family living change with the media. One of the characteristics of the period of the "generation gap" of the 1960's was the tendency of teenagers to withdraw to their rooms to listen to rock radio. Such withdrawal was fostered by some radio stations that programmed material for the young audience. The result was sometimes a breakdown of more traditional patterns of family interaction as separate members lived in their own cocoons served by their own media.

A similar splitting of elements of society occurs between the better educated and the less educated. Highly educated individuals tend to obtain their information from newspapers, magazines, and books, while the less highly educated rely more on television and radio. As it becomes economically feasible for more media to survive, we may see society split along nontraditional lines; and as media become increasingly international, loyalties to a nation-state may give way to loyalties to special interests to which the media can cater.

As media fragment traditional social groupings, they create new ones, but these are likely to be smaller. Many small groups with diverse interests will make it more difficult for any single element to dominate a society as the church and state did at one time. As the groups become smaller and more varied, the media that can build the largest audiences may dominate society.

Computer technology, too, can create new power centers through the amassing of information. Computers can combine public and private files to create a new control point. The possibilities were demonstrated when Congressman Barry Goldwater, Jr., of California and his administrative assistant went to a computer installation in California. To demonstrate the capabilities of the system the operater punched in the number of the assistant's driver's license. In moments the computer amazed both men by cranking out a detailed dossier on the assistant.

In the course of their activities many public and private organizations keep records on individuals. Department stores know a good deal about their charge customers. Schools keep records on students, sometimes including statements of unsubstantiated opinion. Police departments keep records on persons arrested, regardless of whether the arrests led to convictions. Credit bureaus amass much personal information. The Army Intelligence Division bulges with files. Local, state, and federal offices have reasons to keep their own records.

While such personal information was resting in file cabinets in offices and store rooms scattered around the country it was not too dangerous. Its sheer volume made it too unwieldy. But the computer changed all that. As more and more records are stored on computer tapes it becomes more convenient to pull out the information. The speed of the computer combined with the habit of various agencies of sharing data have constituted a new and ominous center of information. The FBI files in Washington are the best-known example. The FBI shares information with police departments all over the country. Since the FBI and local police departments often cooperate with other governmental and private agencies, the dossiers of individuals, many of whom never have been arrested, keep multiplying. Nearly every application form that an individual is required to fill out requires the Social Security number. This goes into the computer along with the rest of the information, and it becomes the key by which computer systems put together in moments a file on an individual from diverse sources.

Such ability to command instantaneous personal information about a horde of one's fellow citizens is a potential source of power, but even more important are the potential positive uses of the computer. We will consider later how the general public can benefit from the computer's unmatched ability to store and dispense information.

Another new source of power through information is being created by the combination of electronic and space technology. Satellite relay makes it possible to broadcast to home receivers all over the world. Although the equipment has not been mass-produced to do this, some governments are worried that foreign nations will find a way to dominate the attention of their citizens. Satellites would provide an avenue for such cultural invasion far superior to conventional radio waves. Technologically it is possible for any nation with adequate resources to position a satellite so that it could broadcast directly to the homes of the citizens of any other country. Reception would be clearer than present international radio now provides, and jamming would be more difficult.

The fear of such propaganda is so great that a proposed pact to establish international freedom for such broadcasting was defeated in the United Nations. Obviously, the same general forces are at work as those that forbade importation of books into England in the early days of printing. The rulers of nations see their authority as directly depending on their maintaining control of information.

The media affect society, but the converse is true, too. Society affects the media. Often it is not possible to know whether a change in the media brought about a change in society or the order was reversed. The process is circular, and often the changes appear to be simultaneous.

As we have seen, Ong, McLuhan, and others emphasize the effect of the communication input on the "sensorium" (the total impulse receiving mechanism of the human body). They perceive great differences in the impact of a bit of information, depending on which one of the senses receives it. With his economist's eye, Innis found much of media-society interaction explainable in the availability of materials and inventions. Printing could not be an important factor until paper was invented and in plentiful supply.

But there are other factors, too, as facsimile transmission illustrates. In the early 1940's facsimile transmission of newspapers became a practical alternative to delivery by newspaper carrier. For publishers the advantages were great. They could do away with their large and expensive presses, and they eliminated in one step a problem that has plagued newspapers for a long time—how to get the paper to readers rapidly and regularly. Advantages to the readers were correspondingly appealing: they were freed from reliance on a sometimes erratic newspaper carrier, and they could receive fresh news only a few minutes after it arrived in the newspaper office.

Despite what seemed to be compelling arguments and efforts of several newspapers, facsimile delivery of newspapers did not come about. A reason may have been that consumers were unwilling to buy receivers and publishers could not make the transition from a heavy investment in presses to a heavy investment in receiving equipment. This seems unlikely, however, since facsimile receivers would have cost less than television sets.

Other factors were at work, and Innis's logic provides one point of departure. Perhaps there was not enough force to build up an opposition to the current "monopoly of knowledge." Publishers stood to benefit from the change, but it was not a necessity for their profitable survival. Perhaps the counteracting force was already present in another form. By the early 1940's radio was beginning to provide competition for newspapers in dispensing news, and it was speedier than either newspapers or facsimile.

Still another factor of more central importance was involved. Innis's theory assumed that the opposition to "monopolies of knowledge" would build up in the fringe areas surrounding the monopolized territories. Thus he saw opposition to the monopoly of knowledge held by scribes and copyists at the University of Paris coming from Germany and Holland where printers were producing books to compete with the written copies of the Parisians. Perhaps by the 1940's new communication technologies were so expensive that they could be developed only in countries where there was already a monopoly of knowledge because these were the richer nations. Under such conditions competition from new technologies and new groups must come from within the societies already monopolized. This changes the nature of the competition and makes it more difficult, but not impossible, for a new medium to enter the arena.

It also shows that media technology is not always the controlling factor. Other elements sometimes use the media to dominate society, leaving the media as passive elements. For example, facsimile may have gone unused simply because the forces that might have seized it to compete with newspapers were otherwise occupied. Radio was already in competition with newspapers, and television was already visible. With the opportunities to develop other new media, the elements in society that might have exploited facsimile never got around to doing so.

Assessing media effects on our minds and lifestyles is difficult because each of us is constantly affected by the process under study. It is becoming increasingly clear that the differentiation between "media" and "environment" is an artificial one. We are all a bit like the little girl who learned to distinguish pictures of cows, horses, and dogs, but could not recognize them when she saw the actual animals. For most of us, as for her, the media environment is the real environment. As such it continuously affects our minds and our lives.

Suggestions for Further Reading

Innis, Harold. *Empire and Communications.* Revised by Mary Q. Innis. To-
    ronto: University of Toronto Press, 1972.
    *Difficult reading, but a scholarly exposition of the author's view of how com-
    munications media affect power patterns in society.*
Carey, James W. "Harold Adams Innis and Marshall McLuhan." *Antioch Review*
    27 (Spring 1967): 5–39.
    A widely quoted comparison and explanation of Innis and McLuhan.
McLuhan, Marshall. *The Gutenberg Galaxy.* Toronto: University of Toronto Press,
    1962.
    McLuhan's views on the effects of printing.
———. *Understanding Media.* New York: McGraw-Hill, 1964. (A paperback edi-
    tion was published by Signet Books in 1966.)
    *A fairly comprehensive expression of McLuhan's views and more readable than
    some of his works.*
Ong, Walter, J. *The Presence of the Word.* New Haven: Yale University Press,
    1967.
    An exploration of the differences between the spoken and the written word.

3

Today's Media in Frozen Frame

Looking at today's communications media is something like watching a television picture of a football game—it is hard to follow the action because it moves so fast. Television's resourceful producers provide some marvelous help to a befuddled viewer by replaying a bit of the action in slow motion and by "freezing a frame" at a critical moment of play. These devices help in understanding what has happened, although often new action has begun before the speedy electrons have frozen the old.

We will be doing the same sort of thing in this chapter as we examine the rapid changes in the media. We will look briefly at a replay of the action that made the media what they are today. As in football, change is rapid and hard to follow. A slow-motion view of the past will help to understand previous plays in the communications game so that we stand a better chance of predicting those that are ahead. When we come to the last freeze frame, "the media today," it will already be history. But a replay and an occasional freeze frame will help us to use hindsight to sharpen foresight.

Our replay begins with books, moves to other printed media, then continues on through radio and television to the computer and satellite.

The Book: An Early Medium

When humans were content to leave their written records on rocks communication technology was simple. The essential material was a smooth rock; the essential tools a chisel and a hammer. As a need to preserve longer manuscripts was recognized, new formats were needed. The scroll, that standby prop of Sunday school plays, was the first answer. It consisted of a long sheet of papyrus equipped with a roller at each end. But the scroll was cumbersome and did not work very well with parchment.

The next step in the evolution of the book was the codex, which consisted of several sheets of parchment assembled into gatherings that were then sewn together.

But format was only part of the problem. As the Middle Ages gave way to the Enlightenment more and more people learned to read, and the demand for books exceeded the capabilities of the monks and clerks who hand-copied each new volume. Clearly, better production methods, new technologies, were needed.

An early answer to the need for more reading material in Europe was xylography, the printing of books from woodcut blocks. It is believed that the earliest printed book in Europe was made in this fashion. The best-known examples of xylographic books were made in the Netherlands, but others were produced in southern Germany. The techniques of copying and block-printing were merged in some early works as the illustrations were printed from blocks while the words were hand-copied. The block-printed books were mostly religious and often profusely illustrated. One book, illustrating the Ten Commandments, consists of ten woodcuts and printed verses. The illustration for the ninth commandment shows a woman standing by her husband, but flirting with a finely dressed admirer nearby. To her the devil whispers:

Thy spouse is old and very staid
Take this one who is better made.

Meanwhile an angel tries to damp the admirer's enthusiasm with this warning:

Covet not thy neighbor's wife
Or thou'lt lose both soul and life.[1]

Xylography was only a short-term answer to Europe's burgeoning demand for reading material, and it fell to Johannes Gutenberg to reinvent a system the Chinese had tried out centuries earlier—printing from movable type. The Chinese abandoned it because the large number of Chinese symbols made it impractical, but it was made to order for the twenty-six-letter alphabet. Gutenberg desired that his works should resemble the handwritten copies of the monks, so he designed many alternate forms of letters and ligatures that combined two or more letters. In all, he produced 290 symbols. For each, Gutenberg and his workers had to cut a steel punch that was struck in a copper block to produce a matrix. The actual type was cast in these matrices with an alloy that Gutenberg produced after much experimentation.

After three years of work, probably in 1456, Gutenberg and his assistants completed the elegant Forty-two line Bible, one of the landmark events in the history of communications. The two hundred copies printed did not constitute mass production by today's standards, but they demonstrated the great potential printing from movable type held for mass media, for the few to reach the many.

The Gutenberg Bible and later printing could not have been achieved without the growth of technology. Paper at last was being manufactured in Europe, centuries after its invention in China. Gutenberg himself had studied the science of metallurgy and was a skilled artisan. The wine press was at hand and ready to be adapted by an imaginative mind to the art of printing.

The technology was ready for the creation of a new medium of mass communication, but technology alone was not enough. During Gutenberg's lifetime and shortly before it universities were springing up all over Europe. The universities of Paris and Bologna were founded in the thirteenth century. The next century saw the start of universities in Prague, Vienna, Heidelberg, and Erfurt. Others opened in Gutenberg's time.

The book is one of the great tools of formal as well as informal education, and it is not strange that printing spread rapidly. Literacy was increasing and more people had the opportunity to study in universities and lower schools. By the end of the fifteenth century forty thousand different books had been printed in Europe and it is said that 10 million individual copies were in print.[2] Presses were opened in Mexico in 1539; in Peru in 1554; and in Cambridge, Massachusetts, in 1639.

[1]Heinrich T. Musper, "Xylographic Books," in *The Book Through Five Thousand Years*, ed. Henrik D. L. Vervliet (New York: Phaidon Publishers, 1972), p. 342. Reprinted by permission of Praeger Publishers, Inc.
[2]Helmut Presser, "Johannes Gutenberg," in Vervliet, *Book Through Five Thousand Years*, p. 354.

The printing and publishing of books has continued to be essential to the spread of education. As the level of education has risen, more and more people have come to rely on books as a primary source of information. The literary tradition of America, as in the rest of the world, depends on the ability to produce and circulate books in large numbers. The revolution signalized in Gutenberg's fifteenth-century print shop in Mainz has produced many forms of printing. In the development of civilization none has been more important than the book.

Book publishing today is a major industry as well as a significant cultural force. Total receipts of publishers in 1972 was 3.18 billion dollars, up 88.5 percent from a decade earlier.[3]

With at least a hundred new titles or new editions published every day of the year in the early 1970's, book publishers were providing much variety to the American reading public. As Table 3.1 shows, while the number of new titles is increasing, the rate of increase appears to be leveling off. With each new publication a financial risk, publishers are taking a more careful look at manuscripts submitted. Still, the number of new titles ensures tremendous variety in subject matter. Serious subjects predominate, with the largest single category, sociology and economics, accounting for 6,565 of the new titles or new editions in 1973. Fiction, with 3,688, and science, with 3,714, ranked second and third in new or newly revised books.[4] Table 3.1 shows the number and percentage increase in new titles from 1950 to 1973.

Table 3.1 New Books Published in the U.S. / 1950–1975

	New books published	Increase	Rate of increase
1950	11,022		
1955	12,589	1,567	14.2%
1960	15,012	2,423	19.2
1965	28,595	13,583	90.5
1970	36,071	7,476	26.1
1973	39,951	3,880	10.8
1975 (projected)	42,538	2,587	6.5

Source: Adapted from *Statistical Abstract of the United States*, 1974, p. 510.

[3]*Bowker Annual*, 1974, p. 169.
[4]Ibid., p. 194.

Reading depends on literacy and on the willingness of the public to make the effort required to buy or borrow a book and read it. Books have historically been a tool for education as well as pleasure, and they have appealed, as they do today, to the more highly educated. Part of the reason for this is the book-reading habit that is often instilled throughout the years of formal education. Table 3.2 shows the stable pattern of use for college textbooks in the United States from 1963 to 1972. The column at the right indicates the slight variation in volumes sold per college student throughout that decade.

The future of the book in its current form is no more secure than that of any other medium, but it has some inherent advantages over other media. As a fairly permanent form it provides communication over time—it stores information well. In addition, it allows for the development of a subject matter at length and in depth in a manner unmatched by other media.

Technology makes it possible for publishers to overcome one of the great disadvantages of the book format—the fact that it may be years between the germination of the idea for a book and its actual publication. The *New York Times* book production division has produced books in weeks instead of months or years, thus making of the book a journalistic medium. For many books such speed could be a disadvantage since a

Table 3.2   College Textbook Sales in the U.S. / *1963–1972*

	Total copies (in thousands)	Students enrolled (in thousands)	Copies per student
1963	42,535	4,495	8.49
1964	49,835	4,950	9.00
1965	57,590	5,526	9.39
1966	68,110	6,055	9.96
1967	70,720	6,348	9.89
1968	76,765	6,928	9.90
1969	80,380	7,299	9.82
1970	81,720	7,920	9.23
1971	82,015	8,387	8.80
1972	81,914	8,220	8.97

Source: Adapted from *Bowker Annual*, 1974, p. 174.

longer preparation time allows the development of perspective through prepublication criticism and rewriting. Longer preparation time, too, is necessary if the book is to be an individual, rather than a group project.

The Newspaper: A Different Use of Print

With early printers preoccupied with the publication of Bibles, hymnals, psalters, and other books, newspapers were a long time in coming. In the early seventeenth century some of the hand-copied European newsletters resorted to printing. Called *corantos*, they were a step in the evolution of the newspaper. They followed by nearly a century and a half the introduction of printing to England by William Caxton in 1476.

In Boston on September 25, 1690, Benjamin Harris published what he planned as the first issue of *Publick Occurrences*. But Harris had neglected to obtain permission in advance and the Massachusetts governor and council ordered it suppressed at once. The *Boston News-Letter*, generally regarded as the first Colonial newspaper, was begun by John Campbell in 1704. The first daily newspaper in English, The *Daily Courant*, had appeared in London in 1702, published by "E. Mallet."

Although both newspapers and books rely on printing technology, they are basically different media. While books entertain with fiction or inform and instruct through development of their subject matter, newspapers rely on the events of the day. Newspapers entertain with sports news and comics, but their main function is to report the events, ideas, and situations of the day. To do this job newspapers require a different format from that of books—a format that allows for quick assembly and last-minute changes.

Most books are designed to be read through, but newspapers attract their readers by providing something of interest to people with widely varying tastes. Few people outside the profession even pretend to read a newspaper through. Headlines provide a guide for scanning, and each reader can open the paper and read what his or her fancy dictates. Such a format provides an entirely different reading experience from that of a book.

While a book leads logically from point to point as it develops its subject, the newspaper simply masses together whatever the editors think will attract their readers, with some guidance as to the editors' opinion of a story's importance provided by the size of the headline and position on the page. Thus a single newspaper page can describe a kaleidoscopic collection of events, held together only by the logic of time.

Newspapers developed from two sources: the newsletters designed to serve the needs of merchants, shippers, and bankers; and from the pamphlets hawked on the streets of London and Boston, usually to protest the actions of the House of Commons or of the governor and his council. With this heritage, newspapers were more practical and political documents than were the early books, which, as we have seen, were more concerned with religious subjects. Newspapers came into existence because their publishers felt a need to comment and were bold enough to speak their piece. Over the years, newspapers have assumed a role as a more general medium of information, but their start as the observers, reporters, and critics of government still shows in their news and editorial pages.

While the technology for printing newspapers was basically the same as that for printing books, social needs and political aspirations did not provide the opportunity for newspapers to develop until centuries after the book.

Newspapers sought a wider audience than that of books, and so newspapers awaited the growth of literacy. In the 1830's in New York Benjamin H. Day sensed that the time was right to expand newspaper circulation. He founded The *New York Sun* on the theory that many people who did not read a newspaper could be induced to do so if the contents were sensational and the price cheap. He filled the *Sun* with whatever was shocking, relying heavily on humorous accounts of police court cases, and he sold the paper for a penny. His success was almost instantaneous; his competitors began to catch up with the *Sun's* circulation only after they imitated its content and style.

Thus Benjamin Day caused a communications revolution by realizing that social and economic conditions were ready for a radical departure in the media. He also brought to the fore an ethical dilemma that has been plaguing the media ever since. How far should the media go in tailoring their product to the lowest common denominator of interest to attract the largest possible audience? We will return to this problem later in the book.

For many years after Day's great discovery the newspaper was the one great mass medium in America. Today, newspapers are still one of the most pervasive media, although the number of daily newspapers and their total circulation appear to have hit a plateau. Between 1950 and 1974 the number of dailies fluctuated between a low of 1,748 in 1970 to a high of 1,774 in 1973, with no discernible pattern. The number in 1950 was 1,772; in 1974 it was 1,768.

Circulation is declining in relation to population. In 1974 the 1,768 dailies had a combined circulation of 61,877,197, or 293 copies per thousand population. As Table 3.3 shows, the number of copies of daily newspapers per thousand population hit a peak in 1945 and has declined since then. The decline, while slow, is a matter of deep concern to all students of the media. Some have shrugged it off as so small as to be unimportant.

**Table 3.3   Daily Newspaper Circulation and Population in the U.S. /
1900–1974**

	Circulation (in thousands)	Population (in thousands)	Copies per 1,000 residents
1900	15,102	76,094	199
1909	24,212	90,492	266
1920	27,790	106,466	261
1925	33,739	115,832	291
1930	39,589	123,077	322
1935	38,155	127,250	300
1940	41,131	132,457	311
1945	48,384	133,434	363
1950	53,829	151,868	355
1955	56,147	165,069	340
1960	58,882	179,979	327
1965	60,358	193,526	312
1968	62,535	199,399	314
1969	62,060	201,385	308
1970	62,108	203,806	305
1971	62,231	206,212	302
1972	62,510	208,230	300
1973	63,147	209,844	301
1974	61,877 (Sept. 30)	211,265 (June 1)	293

Sources: U.S. Bureau of the Census, *Statistical Abstract of the United States*, 95th ed. Washington, D.C., 1974, pp. 5, 508; U.S. Bureau of the Census, *Historical Statistics of the United States, Colonial Time to 1957*. Washington, D.C., 1960, p. 500; U.S. Bureau of the Census, *Historical Statistics of the United States, Continuation to 1962 and Revisions*. Washington, D.C., 1965, p. 69; *Editor and Publisher International Yearbook*, 55th ed., 1975, p. 6.

Others see it as foreshadowing the death of the newspaper. There is as yet no well-supported explanation.

Circulation is stabilizing, too, when compared on another critical measure—copies per household. As Table 3.4 shows, this index has declined since 1950, when 1.26 copies were sold for every household in the United States.

Thus, although daily newspapers have increased their total circulation nearly every year since 1900, the population has increased more rapidly, and so newspapers are reaching a smaller portion of the population.

Another indication of the level of acceptance of the newspaper is the size of each issue. Table 3.5 shows the increase in newsprint consumption by newspapers from 1950 to 1973. During the same period the average number of daily newspaper pages per issue increased at a fairly steady rate from 36 to 59. The average number of pages of Sunday newspapers increased from 112 to 182.

In the mid-1970's the number of daily newspapers appeared to have stabilized, circulation was declining slightly, and the total number of pages had reached a high. The newspaper industry was healthy, but not expanding.

The total number of newspapers at first glance exaggerates the variety of newspaper sources available to the average reader. In 1974 the 293 dailies published in cities of over 100,000 population constituted 17 percent of

Table 3.4 Daily Newspaper Circulation Per Household / 1950–1974

	Circulation (in thousands)	Households (in thousands)	Copies per household
1950	53,829	42,857	1.26
1960	58,882	53,021	1.11
1970	62,108	63,450	.98
1971	62,231	64,778	.96
1972	62,510	66,676	.94
1973	63,147	68,251	.93
1974	61,877 (Sept. 30)		

Sources: *Editor and Publisher International Yearbook*, 55th ed., 1975, p. 6; U.S. Bureau of the Census, *Statistical Abstract of the United States*, 95th ed. Washington, D.C., 1974, p. 39; U.S. Bureau of the Census, *Historical Statistics of the United States, Colonial Times to 1957.* Washington, D.C., 1960, pp. 242–244, 500; U.S. Bureau of the Census, *Historical Statistics of the United States, Continuation to 1962 and Revisions.* Washington, D.C., 1965, p. 69.

the total dailies in the country and had 64 percent of the total circulation. The other 83 percent of the dailies were published in places of 100,000 or less and accounted for only 36 percent of the total circulation.[5] Thus residents of large urban centers often still have to settle for one newspaper. This points to two trends: first, the concentration of population in great urban centers; and second, that even such large centers are not much more likely to supply residents with a choice of two local dailies than are cities of less than 100,000 population.

N. W. Ayer and Son, Inc., estimates that in 1971 the United States had 8,888 weekly newspapers, 412 semiweeklies, and 232 newspapers published three times a week or at other nondaily intervals. This gives a total of 9,532 nondaily newspapers in the country. Circulation figures for the weekly newspapers as a whole are difficult to find, for many of these papers do not belong to the Audit Bureau of Circulation, but the 7,553 weeklies on the list of the American Newspapers Representatives, Inc., had a

Table 3.5   Paper Consumption by Newspapers / 1950–1973

	Total consump-tion[a]	Advertising consump-tion	Percentage advertising consump-tion	Other consump-tion	Percentage Other consump-tion
1950	5,521	3,279	59.4%	2,242	40.6%
1955	6,173	3,827	62.0	2,346	38.0
1960	6,800	4,148	61.0	2,652	39.0
1965	7,851	4,750	60.5	3,101	39.5
1970	9,071	5,579	61.5	3,492	38.5
1971	9,569	6,017	62.7	3,579	37.3
1972	9,852	6,345	64.4	3,507	35.6
1973 (prelim.)	9,880	6,471	65.5	3,409	34.5

Source: Adapted from *U.S. Bureau of the Census, Statistical Abstract of the United States,* 95th ed. Washington, D.C., 1974, p. 509.

[a]In thousands of short tons.

[5]From data in *Editor & Publisher, International Yearbook,* 55th ed., 1975, p. 9.

total circulation of 31,997,341 for an average circulation of 4,236. Across the country this would give the weeklies a circulation of 158 per 1,000 population, considerably lower than that of the dailies, but still an indication of a thriving industry and an important medium of communication.

The average number of pages of weeklies is smaller than that of the dailies, and there is some agreement that, because of their smaller size and highly localized news, the weeklies are better read than the dailies. Certainly in many communities they exert a dominant influence and provide an important advertising medium.

Part of the weekly's influence depends on the personality of the owner. Most communications media are so large that only the very wealthy or large corporations can aspire to own them. The weekly newspaper and small radio stations and magazines are the exceptions. It takes money to own them, but a capable person, if he or she is willing to sacrifice, can aspire to such ownership. In the weekly newspaper field there is a long tradition of personal journalism. Weekly publishers can satisfy a desire to express their individuality, if they do not get too far out of tune with their readers. Often a certain amount of personal liberty appears to make good sense from a business point of view. Readers may be accustomed to the idiosyncrasies of their editor and look forward to the paper for that reason.

The weekly can be a personal expression for the reader, too. Since the weekly covers a small geographical area and relatively few people, the editor can report local events in readers' lives that would go unnoticed in even a small daily. The kind of events covered varies with the size of the paper, but some papers still report Sunday afternoon callers. To outsiders such information may seem so trivial as to be banal, but to the people involved it is a recognition of the dignity of everyday affairs.

Daily and weekly newspapers sometimes display great differences, but they share a common format and perform essentially the same function for their readers; that is, keeping them informed about current affairs.

The Magazine: Versatility in Print

As we noticed earlier, magazines came onto the scene in England and America at about the same time as newspapers. Like newspapers, they are periodicals, that is, they are published at regular, stated intervals. Most newspapers are published daily or weekly; magazines usually are published weekly, monthly, or quarterly.

A few magazines still try to interest every potential reader. *Reader's Digest* is the best remaining example of the general-circulation magazine. Its circulation of 17.75 million is the largest in this country. In addition, it has 11.5 million in its twenty-four international editions. *TV Guide*, with a circulation of about 17.7 million, is a close second. Despite *TV Guide*'s massive circulation, it still can be classed as a special-interest magazine. Its appeal is to television viewers.

Some illustrious general circulation magazines, including *Colliers, Life,* and *Look,* were killed by changing audience habits and economic factors. The *Saturday Evening Post* went through a metamorphosis that left it a very different publication from the one that dominated the weekly field in the early part of the century. The demise of these and other general circulation magazines indicates a major change in the habits of Americans.

It appears likely that the most successful magazines of the future will be those that appeal to a special audience. The special interests of readers may be based on geography (for example, *Southern Living* and *Sunset*), but more often the appeal is to an intellectual area, a field of knowledge, or a hobby. Some of the appeals are quite limited, as in magazines directed to cat fanciers, growers of African violets, or leatherwork hobbyists. Others such as news weeklies are directed to very broad groups and their efforts are aimed at reaching large circulations. Editors of intellectual monthlies such as *Atlantic* and *Harpers* know that their audience is limited despite valiant efforts to enlarge it.

Of economic importance are the trade journals and house organs. Trade journals are designed for persons interested in a certain industry or group of industries. These include *Editor & Publisher* and *Broadcasting*, which relate to the communications industry. House organs are published by businesses or other groups to appeal to employees, customers, or both. These magazines seldom appear on the newsstands, but in total they make up an important part of the magazine industry.

Another kind of subsidization may come from scholarly groups or clubs, which meet part of the costs of publication from members' dues. Examples from the communications field are *Journalism Quarterly*, *Public Opinion Quarterly*, and the *Journal of Communication*. These contain articles, often written by members of the sponsoring organization, that are of interest to the group. Usually these magazines do not pay the authors for articles. The writers are academicians or others for whom the prestige of publication is a negotiable asset.

The difference between magazines and newspapers is not always sharply drawn. Frequency of publication, as we noted, is one factor. Another is content, including subject matter and viewpoint toward it. For some magazines, such as the news weeklies, the subject matter may be as varied as the newspapers, but most confine themselves to a specialty.

Magazines are more likely than newspapers to express an overt viewpoint toward their subject matter. This is done in two ways. Some magazines will publish only writers who express a single viewpoint, although they permit shading within that general framework. *Ramparts*, for example, represents a liberal viewpoint; *National Review*, a conservative one. Other magazines may not espouse a general tone for the magazine, but encourage writers to express their own views. *Harpers* and *Atlantic* tend to follow this pattern, although regular readers can detect an overall editorial direction.

Type and quality of printing may distinguish between newspapers and magazines. Normally magazines, with less frequent deadlines, can produce higher quality layouts and use superior printing methods. Magazines also are likely to have covers, while newspapers do not. These distinctions are not conclusive either. Sometimes publications that have most of the characteristics of magazines will look almost exactly like newspapers. They may also be the same size as tabloid newspapers. *Variety* and *Billboard*, publications of the entertainment industry, have characteristics of both newspapers and magazines.

As in any enterprise, support spells continued existence or oblivion for magazines. The larger portion of most magazines' income comes from advertising. The money received from subscriptions or newsstand sales produces only a fraction of the cost of producing the magazine. A few magazines have been started by wealthy individuals who poured money into the enterprise for a prolonged period. Some publishers of serious magazines have complained that the public is so accustomed to paying only token amounts for their magazines that a serious publication without a large amount of advertising cannot succeed.

It is certain that for most magazines not supported by scholarly or fraternal organizations, it is critical to find an audience that is also a logical consumer group. *Popular Photography* and *Modern Photography* appear to have combined these successfully. Camera hobbyists are fond of indulging in the shop talk provided by the editorial contents and they tend to be free spenders in buying equipment and new gadgets. Thus advertisers and customers are brought together, presumably to the profit of the sellers and the publishers and the joy of the hobbyists.

Although hard figures are difficult to find because of the large number of separate magazines and the difficulties of definition, it is clear that general magazines have been declining, while the specialized ones tend to be successful. Publishers say that much depends on luck in achieving success in magazine publishing. The factors are so subtle that there is no foolproof way of conducting research that will provide accurate predictions.

Printing as a Leveler

Newsletters and direct-mail advertising illustrate the flexibility of print. With mimeograph and multilith making print available to more people for more uses, it can even be used as a personal medium. People who send their friends Christmas letters describing the year's activities are using printing as a personal medium. Most Americans are familiar with the way Tom Paine helped fan the American Revolution with *Common Sense* and other pamphlets. These tracts, short of being books because of their length and the manner in which they were printed, constituted an early form of personal journalism.

Despite the widely varied forms in which printing appeared, the profound effect of printing on civilization was caused chiefly by these three media: books, magazines, and newspapers. After the first use in Europe of movable type by Gutenberg the power and influence of printing increased until it became one of the great forces behind the Industrial Revolution. As literacy increased, the benefits of reading were available to commoners as well as aristocracy. The equalizing tendency of print was increased as free libraries became available.

The Film Industry

The dominance of print lasted well into the twentieth century, but in hindsight it is possible to see the birth of a challenge in 1877. In that year in Menlo Park, New Jersey, Thomas A. Edison invented the phonograph. Edison added the other ingredient of modern motion pictures twelve years later when, with his associate W. K. L. Dickinson, he perfected the kinetoscope. This device provided a peep-hole through which a person could see the illusion of a motion picture on the surface of a lens. Although it did not "throw" the image on a screen it is considered the parent of later motion picture machines. Inside the box an electric motor ran a fifty-foot loop of film between a light and a revolving shutter. The projection of motion pictures on a screen did not take place until Thomas Arnat perfected his vitascope, which was first used at the Cotton States Exposition in Atlanta in September 1895. Motion pictures were first projected on a theater screen on April 23, 1896, in a music hall on Herald Square, New York City.

When sound was added to motion in *The Jazz Singer*, starring Al Jolson, in 1927, the silent film era ended and a new communications medium was born. The Warner Brothers studio, the maker of *The Jazz Singer*, and the other studios could thank Lee DeForest, the first man to record sound on film, for their continued survival.

But sound and even color were not adequate innovations to support Hollywood's big-spending studios and lavish star system in the flamboyant way of life they had early adopted. Court action in 1946[6] took away from the Hollywood studios much of their control over the industry and a rich source of revenue. It required the studios to divest themselves of the theaters they owned throughout the country and to eliminate the "block booking" practice by which the studios had required independent theater operators to take the entire product of a studio in order to show the few grade A films.

This financial blow to film studios was scarcely equal to the punch delivered by the television industry. As people bought receivers and began to sit at home to watch the small screen, attendance at motion picture theaters dropped to about half what it had been in the early 1940's, and audiences became more selective. Table 3.6 gives an idea of the financial decline of the industry from 1950 to 1969. While total revenues of the industry increased, the percentage of money spent on motion pictures relative to other services declined.

The film studios adapted to their financial decline by belt-tightening and by providing material not available on television screens. Many of the famous production lots were sold, others were closed, and superstars became fewer and less lavishly pampered. Films for distribution to movie theaters became more shocking in their displays of violence and sex.

Table 3.6 Motion Picture Revenue as a Part of Total Services Expenditures / 1950–1969

	Total services expenditures (in millions)	Motion picture revenue (in millions)	Percentage of total services expenditures
1950	$21,786	$ 866	4.0%
1955	31,131	979	3.1
1960	44,480	894	2.0
1965	64,076	1,205	1.9
1969	95,288	1,438	1.5

Source: Adapted from U.S. Bureau of the Census, *Statistical Abstract of the United States*, Washington, D.C., 1972.

[6]United States v. *Paramount Pictures* (334 U.S. 131) 1946.

Eventually, some of the studios suffered the ignominy of selling their old feature films to television and becoming production agents for their rivals.

Broadcast Sound Without Pictures

Many scientists contributed to the technology that produced radio and eventually led to television. In 1865 British physicist and mathematician James Clerk Maxwell used mathematical models to predict the existence of electric waves. Two decades later German physicist Heinrich Rudolf Hertz, following Maxwell's theory, produced electric waves and studied their nature. A young Italian, Guglielmo Marconi, experimented with available equipment and in 1895 succeeded in sending a message for about a mile. By increasing the power of his transmitter and improving the sensitivity of his receiver Marconi kept increasing the transmission distance. In 1901 he sent a message for two thousand miles across the Atlantic from Poldhu in Cornwall, England, to St. Johns, Newfoundland. Voice transmission was made possible by the work of Ambrose Fleming and Lee DeForest. Fleming patented a two-element vacuum tube in 1904, and two years later DeForest constructed a three-element "audion" tube.

Ship-to-shore transmissions and military communications were among the first uses of the new medium. Marconi developed British naval communications and volunteered his services to his own country, Italy, when it joined in World War I.

Sydney W. Head, professor of communications at Temple University, describes some of the early stations:

> Although KDKA's 1920 Harding-Cox election program is usually cited as the historical beginning of broadcasting in America, a number of other stations claim the honor. KQW-San Jose (California) first broadcast in 1909 and ran a regular schedule in 1912; Station 2ZK-New Rochelle (New York) broadcast music regularly in 1916; a Detroit amateur station, 8 MK (later WWJ), began regular broadcasting over two months before KDKA's maiden broadcast. . . . At least a dozen stations still in operation date their beginnings from 1920 or earlier. But the fact remains that KDKA was the first commercially licensed standard broadcast station listed in the United States Department of Commerce records.[7]

[7]Sydney W. Head, *Broadcasting in America*, 3rd ed. (Boston: Houghton Mifflin, 1976), pp. 112–113.

A Long Island real estate firm sponsored the first commercial broadcast over station WEAF in New York in 1922, the year the station was founded by AT&T. WEAF was also part of the first network.

Soon more than a million receivers were in operation and stations were springing up across the country. Radio's almost instant popularity produced many local celebrities in addition to national heroes such as Amos and Andy, Jack Benny, Fred Allen, and Fibber MaGee. Soap operas flourished in the afternoons and comedy and variety programs at night. Milton Cross with his Saturday afternoon broadcasts of productions at New York's Metropolitan Opera House became a weekly fixture for many families. Radio's entertainment and limited cultural offerings soon became established patterns; its role in news and public affairs programming was another matter.

Newspapers were quick to use the facilities of radio to distribute news for publication. On March 30, 1903, the *London Times* carried a dispatch from New York slugged "By Marconigraph." The *New York Times*, the *Chicago Tribune*, and other U.S. newspapers received news on their own receivers from stations at Lyons and Bordeaux in France and from Nauen, Germany. Publishers valued radio as an aid in news-gathering, but saw it as a competitor in distributing news directly to the public. Publishers who bought radio stations soon found themselves in the middle of a dispute.

The Associated Press for a time denied service to broadcasters, even prohibiting AP member papers from broadcasting news reports on their own stations. The AP restrictions were hard to enforce, especially after the *Chicago Tribune* announced plans to air the returns in the Coolidge-Davis election of 1924. The haggling continued through the late 1920's. The AP and publishers made minor concessions, but no genuine resolution was reached.

It became obvious that one fear of newspaper publishers was that radio would use news to lure away advertising that would otherwise be placed in newspapers. During a 1925 meeting the American Newspaper Publishers Association issued a statement that "direct advertising by radio is likely to destroy the entertainment and educational value of broadcasting and result in the loss of the goodwill of the public."[8]

The same commercial concerns were still on the publishers' minds in 1933 when a newspaper industry group made another small concession to radio news. A press-radio bureau was to be formed to supply two five-minute broadcasts each day to radio stations with the proviso that they would be used without advertising sponsorship. Another part of the agreement was that CBS and NBC would suspend the feeble news-gathering attempts they had begun. A further restriction provided that the morning

[8]Alfred M. Lee, *The Daily Newspaper in America* (New York: Macmillan, 1937), p. 561.

news summary would not be read before 9:30 A.M. (hours after the morning newspapers were available) and that the evening summary would not be read before 9 P.M. (hours after the evening papers had been delivered).

Such restrictive practices encouraged the formation of press services for the broadcast media. By 1935 there were at least four such services: Radio News Service of America, Transradio Press Service, the American Newscasting Association, and the American Broadcasters' News Association, a profit-sharing organization. Some of these bought foreign news reports from such established agencies as Agence Havas of France and Reuters of England.

Some of the broadcast press services began selling their products to newspapers after the *Athens* (Georgia) *Times* led the way in 1935. This danger to the established newspaper agencies and the growing tendency of radio to find and report its own news caused the United Press and International News Service to make their service available to radio without restrictions as to advertising sponsorship. The Associated Press softened its restrictions on members who owned radio stations, and eventually all three press services were supplying news to radio stations. These actions killed off the special radio news services, although Transradio provided some lusty competition for a period.

Thus the battle to decide whether radio was to be allowed to provide a news service for the public was settled by competitive jockeying between newspapers and radio, not with any special consideration of the best interests of the reading and listening public. What appeals were made to principle seemed to be motivated more by special interests than by any grander considerations. The California Newspaper Publishers Association resolved "that by Federal enactment a start be made to return to the people the air channels now used by commercial interests, similar to the plan now in effect in England."[9] The small dailies of the Inland Daily Press Association asked

> that the Federal Communications Commission be requested to protect the listeners on all news broadcasts and preserve the true news value by requiring all subject matter under the title of news to be broadcast only as unsponsored editorial service from the station itself to listeners in the "Public Interest, Convenience, and Necessity."[10]

Despite these futile protests radio established its legitimacy as a purveyor of news. Local stations built news departments to offer competing information sources in many cities served by only one newspaper. The networks began to supplement press association reports by sending their own correspondents to the scene of breaking news. During the Second

[9]Ibid., p. 570
[10]Ibid.

World War radio demonstrated its versatility and timeliness. Edward R. Murrow's broadcasts from London for CBS during the siege set high standards for drama and authenticity.

After the Second World War television arrived and swiftly displaced radio as the most important in-home entertainment medium. David Halberstam used CBS as an example to show just how rapidly this change occurred:

> Before 1948 the CBS television network was virtually nonexistent. By 1951 it comprised 62 stations, and 16 million American homes had television sets. By 1952, CBS had 74 stations broadcasting to 21 million homes, and in 1954, the year CBS became the largest advertising medium in the world, its programs were broadcast over 202 stations to 32.5 million homes, or to roughly two thirds of the families in America.[11]

In the face of this assault on its audiences radio was forced into new directions. Instead of remaining a general-purpose medium, stations changed their formats to emphasize music, news, and sports. Radio made a strong recovery by accommodating itself to motorists, teenagers, sports fans, and people who wanted a background sound.

In 1950, 47 million sets were used and by 1957, another 38.5 million had been installed in automobiles. By 1960, 150 million sets were in use. The radio Advertising Bureau estimated that in January 1975, 401.6 million sets were in use in the United States, 291.2 million of them in homes and 110.4 million out of home—many in cars.[12] In late 1975 the Federal Communications Commission reported that 8,010 radio stations were in operation in the United States. These consisted of 4,459 commercial AM, 2,752 commercial FM, and 799 educational FM stations.[13]

Broadcast Sound with Pictures

The technology that produced radio gave television an early advantage. One important discovery not related to radio was made in 1817 when Baron Jöns Jakob Berzelius of Sweden discovered the element selenium. It was not until the 1870's that scientists discovered a unique quality of selenium—its ability to conduct electricity when exposed to light. This led to the development of the photoelectric cell (the electric

[11]David Halberstam, "CBS: The Power and the Profits," *Atlantic Monthly*, January 1976, p. 58.
[12]*Broadcasting Yearbook*, 1975, p. B-154
[13]*Broadcasting*, January 12, 1976, p. 45.

eye) and filled an important need in television transmitters. It was in the 1870's, too, that Sir William Crookes developed an early version of the cathode ray tube, which he called the Crookes tube.

A German, Paul Gottlieb Nipkow, built a crude mechanical television system in 1884, but a practical electronic system was not developed until the 1920's. In 1925 Charles Francis Jenkins, an American, and John Logie Baird, an Englishman, working independently, hit upon the idea of combining electronic technology with photography and a scanning disc. Vladimir Kosma Zworykin of the United States contributed to the development of the iconoscope, which codes the picture in the television camera, and the kinescope, which displays the picture in the receiver. Thus technological advances of more than a century were the basis of the all-electric television system in use today.

In 1928 the General Electric station, WGY in Schenectady, New York, began broadcasting three afternoons a week. The National Broadcasting Company opened an experimental station in New York City, and the next year the Columbia Broadcasting System started regular broadcasts on its new station, W2XAB, in New York City. Commercial telecasting, begun in 1939 in New York City, was discontinued with the start of the Second World War. When television was reintroduced at the end of the war it rapidly caught the fancy of the public, attracted established entertainment stars, and created new ones of its own.

By the end of 1975 there were 929 television stations in the United States of which 700 were commercial and 229 educational.[14] About 64.8 million homes, roughly 95 percent of the total number, had at least one television receiver, and more than 37 million, or 54 percent of the homes with televisions, were equipped with color receivers. Average total viewing time per home per day was estimated at six hours and twenty minutes. It was obvious that a great new mass communications medium was on the scene.

Table 3.7 gives an idea of the number of television receivers sold in the United States since 1950. The burst in the decade from 1960 to 1970 is partially accounted for by the availability and popularity of color sets. In 1960 only 2 percent of the sets sold in the United States were color receivers. This rose to 24 percent in 1965 and 48 percent in 1970. Of domestic receivers manufactured in this country in 1970, 57 percent were color.

One of the reasons that television could move ahead so rapidly was that it was preceded by radio. Not only did radio fight the long battle with newspapers to establish broadcasters as legitimate media of news and public affairs as well as entertainment, but it established advertising as the revenue base for broadcast media. Network organizations that had served radio gradually shifted over to television. Even the nature of the

[14]Ibid.

programming came ready-made to television. It took over the format of radio's soap operas, game shows, comedy and variety hours, and even some of the news shows and stars. As television attracted the mass evening audience it relied on formulas already tested in radio. It was the radio industry that had to adjust to its new and lower status. Radio changed and survived, but as quite a different medium than it was in the 1930's and 1940's. The shift in functions and patterns of use from radio to television dramatically illustrates the power of new technology to provide exciting new experiences for audiences and a revolution in communication habits.

Cable and Pay Television

No sooner does technology provide the means of a new medium of communications to threaten the old than it retires to a laboratory to create the means for another innovation that threatens the new giant. So it is with television. Dominating the mass media in the mid-1970's, television began to feel the threat of a still newer medium—this one, cable television, a combination of television's own technology with cable and satellite relay systems. Cable television is also called community antenna television (CATV) and broad-band communication. The latter term refers to cable's unmatched ability to provide a variety of

Table 3.7   U.S. Sale of Television Receivers / 1950–1973

	Total sales (in thousands)	Change (in thousands)	Percentage change
1950	7,355		
1955	7,758	+ 403	+ 5.5%
1960	5,829	−1,929	−24.9
1965	11,447	+5,618	+96.4
1970	12,220	+ 773	+ 6.8
1971	14,921	+2,701	+22.1
1972	17,084	+2,163	+14.5
1973	17,367	+ 283	+ 1.7

Source: Reprinted, with permission, from 1975 *Broadcasting Yearbook*, p. B-154.

services. It is this versatility that causes nervous twitches among television executives. Cable started as a system to provide clear reception for viewers whose signal was weakened by their distance from transmitters or by mountains or other obstructions. Cable operators, with their superior antennas, frequently provided additional channels, and some enterprising ones added services of their own, such as constant weather information and a news service. The last was achieved simply by focusing a camera on a wire service printer. These crude efforts were enough to make the point that cable's many channels could turn it into an all-purpose communications carrier.

The "communications revolution" predicted by many media specialists included two-way service. This would allow utility companies to read gas and electric meters. Viewers could shop at home, register their reaction to programs, order library materials, and even vote in nationwide political polls.

The aspects that disturbed proprietors of television stations was cable's ability to bring in many channels and thus threaten the audience for each station. It stands to reason that if ten channels are available, the audience for each of the ten is likely to be smaller than if only three are available. Since the amount a station can charge for advertising is directly related to the size of its audience, a proliferation of channels is likely to hit a station owner in the pocketbook.

The broadcast television industry kept watch as early systems grew. They began in the late 1940's when small concerns were formed to pick up signals in areas where reception was poor, amplify them, and supply them to the receivers of householders willing to pay a fee for the service. Charges were as low as five dollars a month plus an installation charge that averaged about twenty dollars. The two decades from 1950 to 1970 were years of rapid growth. In 1950 about 70 systems served about 14,000 customers. In 1970 the number of systems had increased to more than 2,400 and they served more than 4 million customers. By 1973 nearly 6 million households received their television programs over cable. It is no wonder that CATV was seen as one of the great growth industries.

But growth had slowed by the mid-1970's. After finally getting permission from the Federal Communications Commission to move into the big cities, cable entrepreneurs found unanticipated problems in wiring them. The problem spelled the need for venture capital and that was difficult to get in the recession atmosphere of the time. The Federal Communications Commission, after successfully asserting its power to regulate cable, was slow to develop codes and thus delayed the growth of the cable industry.

Satellite transmission was another area of uncertainty in the mid-1970's. Satellites offered the possibility of adding variety to the television fare of the American public, but there was some question that it might be used only as an additional transmission belt by which common carriers, such as American Telephone and Telegraph Company, would augment their land lines and cables. Direct satellite-to-home broadcasting furnished dreams of program enrichment and at the same time threatened, established stations that might find their signals less popular as a result of added variety. On the international scene the same technology posed threats to governments that were afraid to expose their citizens to ideas from other countries. Satellite signals might ignore national boundaries. Such economic and political considerations are the subjects for later chapters.

Paramedia Agencies

Around the media has grown a complex of related activities that serve the media and are served by them. The radio and television networks, for example, supply programs and advertising revenue to affiliated stations. They have assumed much importance because they control a large proportion of the programming of television stations. Most television stations depend on the network news programs to supply the bulk of their national and international news. This has enhanced the networks' influence and has subjected them to a special kind of scrutiny.

Like the networks, the press services that supply newspapers and radio and television stations with most of their nonlocal news have achieved much importance in the processing of information for the public. The Associated Press and the United Press International are the chief news agencies in the United States. Other less complete services with a smaller number of clients are the *Los Angeles Times–Washington Post* Syndicate, the *New York Times* Service, and the Copley news service. Other syndicates supply less timely information called feature material. These include the columns (interpretive, how-to-do-it, and personal advice, for example), comics, crossword puzzles, and similar fare.

The major press services come as close to being pure information agencies as any other agency. They seek out information, evaluate it, and distribute it to the organizations that form the final link to the ultimate audience. The AP and the UPI have been strong forces in the development of the concept of news and in the selection of news sources as well as the style in which news is presented to the public. They are distinguished by the large scale on which they operate, by the completeness of their coverage, and by their ability to report breaking news in almost any part of the world. The AP is a membership organization; the papers and stations served elect representatives to the board of directors, which is the ultimate policy body. UPI regards its customers as clients to whom it sells service for a fee. Both arrangements make the press agencies responsive to the desires of the media, for they have no other source of revenue.

Advertising agencies, too, are critical in their impact on the media. These are organizations designed to serve the needs of manufacturers and others who want to use the media to sell their goods or ideas. The men and women who work in the advertising agencies study the goals of their clients, recommend advertising policies, plan campaigns, create print or broadcast advertisements, and place them in the media. Traditionally, they take their fee from media as a percentage of the cost of running the advertising. Since the agencies often have much discretion on which media are used by their clients, they are important to publishers and broadcasters who depend on advertising revenue. Sometimes they have determined the content of programs sponsored by their clients, although this has become less common as higher rates have compelled several advertisers to share programs. The people who control the agencies link the media and the advertisers. Since much local advertising, especially in newspapers, is placed without the aid of agencies, their influence is less important with the more local media. But with network television and magazines the agencies can be a strong influence.

Another group of organizations that rely on the media and serve it are the research firms. These organizations provide information on which decisions are made to advertise in one medium or another, whether a program is canceled, or even whether a new publication is started. For the printed media the research firms determine readership and reader preference and study buying habits of readers. Assessing the size and nature of the audience is even more critical for the broadcast media because they do not have circulation figures. As the various media battle each other for the advertising dollar, research findings become issues that influence the way in which billions of dollars are spent.

Public relations specialists compose another group that is dependent on the media. Their success depends on their ability to attract favorable public attention to their clients, and to do this they must use the media. Since success for many enterprises depends on acceptance by a large number of people it is no wonder that effective public relations counselors are in demand. Many organizations have no one with such a title, but they are almost sure to interest themselves in what kind of attention they receive from the media. Government agencies, labor unions, and private-interest groups as well as businesses all feel the need for a "good press" or a "favorable public image." The interrelationship between the media and politicians is particularly subtle since politicians need the press to publicize their efforts to get elected and, once elected, they have something to say about media regulation.

The Information Industry

Information industry is a term that has come into vogue to refer to the activities that have to do with the production and transfer of information. Used in its broad sense it includes point to point transmission by mail, telephone, telegraph, or radio as well as the mass media. Perhaps the single most effective agent in producing a unified concept of the industry has been the digital computer.

The computer's unifying effect results from its ability to store, sort, and present information with ultra high speed and accuracy. The applications for saving human time and energy are boundless. For example, the voluminous testimony of the 1973 Watergate hearings of the U.S. Senate was stored in a computer and cross-indexed so that staff workers could find out all that was said on any given subject. A query using the key "White House horrors" will elicit a speedy outpouring of everything that every one of the witnesses or committee members said on that subject.

The computer has many other applications, but it is this ability to store, index, and retrieve information that relates it to the media most directly. It might, for example, change the whole nature of the library. Books may soon be fed into a memory bank, indexed, and printed out or displayed on a cathode ray tube as library patrons request. Quite conceivably it will be unnecessary to print the books at all. If one thinks of the library as connected with every household by one of the cable television channels, our picture of libraries (and librarians) changes dramatically. Perhaps we will not go to libraries at all, but simply sit at home and key in requests to the computer that *is* the library.

If the computer offers the possibility of making such a drastic change in a bedrock feature of our culture like the library, it is no wonder that proprietors of other media are poking at the newcomer with long sticks before embracing it. The computer offers real operating economies to many businesses, including the communications media. Newspapers, particularly, are finding it of great help in updating their operations. No one questions the value of this use of the computer. The questions about its use as a central depository of information focus around the profound impact it may have on the media and the marketing system. There is also a legitimate question as to whether its convenience will make it impossible for us to use it widely without violating the right of privacy.

We will consider these problems later when we make an effort to peer into the future of the media. The important thing for us to notice at this point is that new technology, including the computer and new modes of transmission such as cable and satellite, tends to increase the interdependence of the media and will certainly change the nature of the competition among them.

Suggestions for Further Reading

Barnouw, Erik. *Tube of Plenty.* New York: Oxford University Press, 1975.
  A popular history of broadcasting with emphasis on the development of television.

Bogart, Leo. "The Future of the Metropolitan Daily." *Journal of Communication*
  25 (Spring 1975): 30–43.
  A study of newspaper circulation with suggestions as to how newspapers can hold their audiences in the age of television.

Emery, Edwin. *The Press and America.* 3rd ed. New York: Macmillan, 1967.
  A standard history.

Head, Sydney W. *Broadcasting in America.* 3rd ed. Boston: Houghton Mifflin
  Company, 1976.
  A comprehensive one-volume history of radio and television in the United States.

Kirschner, Allen, and Kirschner, Linda. *Film.* New York: Odyssey Press, 1971.
  Readings covering many aspects of motion pictures.

Madison, Charles. *Book Publishing in America.* New York: McGraw-Hill, 1966.
  A history of publishing written by an insider.

Metz, Robert. *CBS: Reflections in a Bloodshot Eye.* Chicago: Playboy Press, 1975.
  A readable history of CBS.

Mott, Frank Luther. *Golden Multitudes.* New York: Macmillan, 1947.
  A history of best-selling books and some philosophy about what made them popular.

Tebbel, John. *A History of Book Publishing in the United States.* Vol. 1, *The Creation of an Industry, 1630–1865.* Vol. 2, *The Expansion of an Industry, 1865–1919.* New York: R. R. Bowker, Vol. 1, 1972; Vol. 2, 1975.
  A detailed history.

———. *The Media in America.* New York: T. Y. Crowell, 1974. (New American
  Library published a paperback edition in 1976.)
  A readable media history projected against a background of social change.

A glance back at
Part One
and ahead at
Part Two

Humans try to match their conceptions of reality with reality itself by taking in information directly from their environment or by receiving messages from others. Words have been forged into language systems through which simple ideas and complicated abstractions can be shared.

The transfer of a message requires a sender, a receiver, a symbol system, and a channel. In face-to-face communication sound and sight carry the message and no mechanical intervention is needed. As people felt the need to communicate over distance and over time, they developed media. Stone was an early medium, but through technology it was replaced by more versatile materials: papyrus, parchment, and, finally, paper. Over the years technology provided ways of using paper and other media more efficiently to send messages. The printing press, film, radio, and television have all multiplied human communication power.

Scholars have concluded that communication technology alters the meaning of messages and that a change in technology used in communication may profoundly affect patterns of power within society. One characteristic of modern media communication technology is particularly significant for its role in social change—the ability of one source to send the same message to thousands or millions of people at the same time. This puts the sender in a particularly sensitive role and makes each receiver relatively ineffective in controlling the messages from the media.

As we looked at the growth of the media in Chapter 3 it became apparent that the media communication business is large—in its economic significance and in its power to influence society. Various segments have traditionally assumed certain roles. For example, the newspaper informs while the film entertains and provides artistic experience. The computer provides links among the media and, combined with satellites, is likely to become a new communication medium.

Society has invested the information suppliers—the people who run the media—with special privileges so that they can carry out their job, but it has exacted special obligations, too. Those privileges and obligations are the subject of Part Two.

TWO
Special Privileges at a Special Price

4

The Implicit Contract

In the media-rich United States, broadcasters and publishers are always seeking an audience. Billboards urge us to turn to channel 9 on our television or number 99 on our radio dial. Our mailboxes are loaded with offers to subscribe, often at cut rates, to magazines. Newspapers "sample" us by leaving free copies on our doorsteps then sending a solicitor around to sell a subscription.

At the receiving end there are always people seeking the information and entertainment the media provide. Americans respond happily to the constant invitations they get to see a film, watch a television program, listen to the radio, or read a newspaper, magazine, or book. The question for most is not whether to attend to the media, but which ones to attend to and for how long.

How the media fit themselves to their audiences and the audiences to their media fascinates students of communication behavior as well as media managers. Individuals seeking information may be active or passive in their pursuit. That is, they may seek out media that provide the information they want or they may attend to whatever media are the most convenient. The media, on the other hand, must be active seekers of an audience if they are to survive.

The media bring themselves to the attention of their intended audiences in various ways. College textbooks reach students largely through the intervention of teachers, who recommend or require their reading. Publishers send their representatives and their advertisements to faculty members, seeking to persuade them to adopt a given textbook. Trade books, those designed for a general audience, come to the attention of potential readers through book reviews, advertising, radio and television talk shows, or displays at book stores and libraries. Motion picture theaters rely on reviews in other media, advertising, and word of mouth to draw patrons through their doors.

The details vary from one medium to another, but the essential process is the same. The producers and sellers of media use whatever channels and appeals seem most appropriate to reach the audience they seek. A circulation manager trying to sell subscriptions to the New York Times would use quite a different approach from one selling Playboy.

The offer to provide information and its acceptance constitute an implied contract: the publisher or broadcaster promises a certain kind of material and the receiver agrees to pay whatever charges are asked and to give his or her attention. The contract is easily terminated, especially by a radio or television audience, which can end the arrangement with the change of a dial.

In selecting content the media manager must always stay within limits of opposites: the content cannot be too dull or too shocking, too familiar or too novel, too difficult or too easy, too risque or too staid—the boundary adjectives cover many fields. Generally, the larger an audience sought the narrower the bounds must be. Newspapers, radio, and television usually try to engage the attention of all the people within their geographic range. This is one of the reasons they tend to be less daring in presenting sexually explicit material that tests the community's tolerance for formerly taboo subject matter. The testing of these social boundaries is left to films, novels, and magazines—media that typically seek to gather an audience by appealing to a few like-minded individuals from many communities.

Sometimes the implicit contract is of such long standing that it is maintained without anyone giving the matter any thought. A weekly newspaper may be such an accepted part of the community that no one questions its role. The editor's habits in providing material have synchronized with the community's felt needs. But let the editor radically change the content or a new owner and editor take over and alter it (perhaps even by so small a move as switching support from one political party to another), and the readers may decide the contract no longer holds. To achieve a lasting audience, a station or publication must perform the services that, consciously or unconsciously, the public expects of it. When they are successful, magazines and newspapers become regular, expected visitors to many households and broadcast media become part of the lives of many individuals.

Content selection is not the only way in which the media must live up to audience expectations. They must respect certain amenities in their reporting and in the manner in which they present information. Information of a private nature should not be published unless there is a clear public need for it, and sources of information must sometimes be protected. We will consider the legal controls in Chapter 5, but here we will be concerned with the ethical aspects—the self-restraint the media demand of themselves. Thus the matter of living up to audience and public expectations involves the selection of content, the manner in which it is treated, and the conduct of reporters in gathering information. We will start with a consideration of content selection.

Supplying Audience Needs

The supplier of any goods or services must identify a need and design the product to fill it. So it is with the media. In selecting information the editor or program director acts on hunch, intuition, comments of friends, and sometimes on systematic analysis of the information and entertainment needs of the people he or she is appealing to. Imitation and habit play a powerful role. However it is done, the media manager must provide a mix that will attract an audience large enough to finance the operation.

Each vendor of information and entertainment must define his or her own area of coverage. The content of a village weekly will differ markedly in style and content from a metropolitan daily, but both may be successful publications. Many persons may read both papers. A magazine for stamp collectors is different from one for political scientists, but both perform a useful function. A rural radio station's sound is likely to be much different from that of a big-city station, but when each performs its expected role it will attract an audience. Much of the skill of media management centers on determining the subtle mix of substance and style that will hold an audience.

Most media supply material designed to inform and to entertain. Often the two are clearly separated, but sometimes the distinction is blurred. Sports is "news," but it is about events that are entertainment. The same events, when broadcast live, are considered entertainment. Talk shows include information, but their intent is to entertain. Front-page feature items that are amusing but contain little information are entertainment.

The newsperson's name for them, "brighteners," makes their purpose clear. Magazine articles are frequently skillfully contrived blends of information and entertainment.

Often there is no good way to distinguish between the two because it depends on the reaction of the audience. The same material may be useful information to one person, but simply amusing or terrifying to another. An account of a crime wave is highly informative to people living in and near the city involved, but it will be merely entertaining to readers and listeners three thousand miles away who need to take no special precautions and cannot do anything about it anyway. Part of the skill of the media is to present important information in an interesting manner. Rudolf Flesch, who has written books on readable writing, suggests that such simple devices as use of personal pronouns and proper names enhance the interest value of a news story.

News of government is such a staple that it serves as a good example of the manner in which tradition and common sense can combine to define a content area. Early pamphleteers in England and the Colonies used the print media to report and often to covertly criticize their governments. The habit thus started, and reinforced by the obvious need for the people to know what their governments are doing, it has brought about agreement between newspaper editors and their readers that the newspaper is obligated to supply such information. The implicit agreement is so strong that it is seldom mentioned unless readers feel that the newspaper has failed in its obligation or a government official feels the paper has been too aggressive in ferreting out facts.

In the process of determining the nature of the content and the manner in which they will treat it media managers must decide on the audience to be served and then analyze the needs of that audience. The audience sought by most newspapers and television stations includes rich and poor; old and young; Democrats, Republicans, and Independents; black and white; urban and rural dwellers. Such an audience requires a considerably different selection and treatment of information from that of a publication that seeks to attract a specialized group.

Specialized magazines usually extend their geographic area in order to attract a large enough audience with special interests to make a profitable readership. Radio stations frequently specialize by trying to appeal to teenagers, lovers of fine music, or Country & Western addicts. Even some large newspapers specialize to some extent. The *New York Times* would be a considerably different newspaper if it tried to appeal to every resident of Manhattan. Instead it cultivates an audience of above-average affluence and interests and has been successful enough that its influence extends far beyond the boundaries of its city and state.

Once the decision as to the audience sought and the general nature of the content has been made, the medium assumes responsibilities to its audience and to others.

One prime responsibility is to define its subject matter so that readers can have some sound expectations as to the completeness of the report they are receiving. For a small-town newspaper this is often defined by tradition and accepted without discussion by the editor and the readers. Readers can probably assume that they are being informed of all the deaths, fires, and armed robberies. Through tradition and mutual trust the editor has an implicit contract with his or her readers. Readers should be able to assume that they are getting a complete report. Occasionally there will be pressure on an editor to leave out something that he or she normally would report.

Police news is a common focus of pressure. When a prominent person is arrested, public knowledge of the event may be more embarrassing than the penalty exacted by a court. If a newspaper or radio station normally reports drunk-driving arrests, then readers or listeners have the right to assume that they are getting a complete report. If the editor's son or the son of an important advertiser is arrested, the editor falls short of the responsibility if he or she fails to report it. One editor, himself arrested for drunk driving, called his paper and ordered that it be reported on page one. He clipped the story and kept it on his desk and thereafter showed it to anyone who had the temerity to ask that an arrest report be kept secret. Many newspapers and stations, often because they lack the space or time, do not report routine arrests, and they have no obligation to do so. However, if they customarily report such arrests, they have the responsibility to show no favoritism.

The responsibility to define an area of coverage, systematically explore it, then report objectively whatever turns up, seems simple when explained in terms of a police arrest record, but it develops gray areas rapidly. Covering a state legislature is an example. The editor of a mining journal looks for legislation that will affect mining and has a responsibility to report any such bills. No such simple guideline exists for the editor of a publication or station directed to the general public. So many bills are introduced in most legislatures that it is impossible to even list them all, and nobody would read the list if it were printed. Out of all the bills proposed the legislative correspondent has to select a few which he or she deems most interesting and important to the audience.

What criteria shall the correspondent use? It is easy to say he or she should report those that are of the most importance to the largest number of people. This is valid, but it involves so many value judgments that sensible persons would be almost sure to disagree if they had to rank the identical list of bills. The herd instinct usually evens out differing judgments so that all the media play up the same bills and often the same statements about them. Another factor leading to uniformity is that organizations with public relations skill can bring massive attention to bills they support or oppose, thus affecting legislative reporters' accounts.

Sometimes success in getting an important bill through depends on secrecy and this, too, can often be contrived. Thus a citizen may be deprived of knowledge of a potentially important bill because a reporter did not discover and evaluate the situation.

Reporters fail to live up to their responsibility to their audience when they fall into either trap—of providing too much or too little information about a bill because some highly skilled lobbyist is pulling wires behind the scenes.

The responsibility is clear enough. Reporters need to muster the best set of criteria they can in deciding what information to relay to their audience and they need to stick to these criteria despite pressures and despite the human tendency to report what all the other correspondents are reporting.

Sometimes the best that a general medium of information can do is act as an early warning system for its readers. With a wide variety of information needs among a large heterogeneous readership or listenership, reporters may have time or space only to mention that a situation exists with an indication as to where more information is available. This is the theory underlying the listing of court decisions, records of deeds, and applications to the zoning commission.

Perhaps the greatest danger to the responsibility of a communications medium to its audience is the reporter or editor with a cause. Causes are commendable for individuals, but a mass medium with a cause loses its ability to respond to the needs of its audience. As a promoter of a cause a reporter or commentator substitutes his or her own information needs for that of the audience.

During the heyday of the Hearst newspapers William Randolph Hearst espoused the cause of antivivisectionism and heavily involved the staffs of his newspapers with this issue. The result was that a vast amount of space was devoted to describing experimentation with dogs, whereas many readers of the Hearst papers were so deeply trapped by poverty, overwork, and miserable living conditions that they had hardly enough energy to devote to their own affairs. It was, in short, the substitution of Mr. Hearst's information needs for the ones to which his newspapers should have been paying attention—those of the readers.

The adoption of causes by the media sometimes leads to another surrender of responsibility to the audience. Quite frequently in the excitement of promoting a favored cause a news medium will seek to appeal to the chord that will provide the quickest response. This is always emotional and it leads public discussion away from the plane of reason. Some of Mr. Hearst's reporters became quite skilled in soliciting sympathy for animals undergoing laboratory experiments, but such emotion does not provide a reliable setting for discussion of public issues. What is more, it puts the public in the habit of deciding with its feelings instead of its reason. When politicians engage in such practices we call it demagoguery. When communications media do it the practice smells no better.

An appeal to reason instead of emotion is one way in which the media can live up to another responsibility to their audiences—keeping the discussion at the highest level to which the audience will respond. As we expect a friend to appeal to the best in us, we can ask no less of our communications media. As the media degenerate into name-calling and irresponsible assertions, society heads in the same direction. The media, by their pervasiveness and their control of public information channels, set the tone for most discussion, private as well as public.

To live up to their primary responsibility to their audiences the media must be loyal to some other groups, too. Among these are persons who supply information secretly.

Responsibility to Sources

Individuals who supply information to the media in confidence are the beneficiaries of a special loyalty from journalists. Often these informants would be damaged if their identity were disclosed. The role of the informer is not a popular one, but reporters, like police officers, have encouraged people to tattle by guaranteeing them secrecy.

Newsmen and women justify this practice by arguing that many individuals have information that should be published in the public interest, but are afraid to disclose it for fear of retaliation by some individual who will be damaged by the disclosure. A common example is a low-level government official who knows of corruption in the agency in which he works. He is naturally reluctant to denounce his boss publicly—the boss's means of retaliation are all too apparent. Sometimes a person who has witnessed a crime fears for her life if she is identified as the source of information about it.

Accepting and publishing information from individuals who refuse to accept responsibility for it has odious connotations. The only justifiable support for the practice is that sometimes the public interest is served.

Law enforcement officers use parallel arguments in defending their own use of informers. Typically their reward system is more effective than anything newspeople can offer. Law enforcement officers may promise immunity from prosecution for a crime in return for information. Sometimes they will allow a prostitute or a bookie to work undisturbed in return for information about criminal activities that are more obnoxious to the police.

Legal concerns become pertinent when material disclosed in the press is involved in a lawsuit. Courts have the power to force disclosure of information relevant to pending cases, and many reporters have been called to testify before a court or a grand jury. About half the states have "confidence laws" (sometimes called "shield laws"), which provide that reporters do not have to reveal the sources of information given them in confidence, but such laws are often narrowly interpreted by the courts. Reporters have spent time in jail when they refused to reveal their sources.

But it is the moral, not the legal responsibilities that concern us here. The question is whether it is responsible practice to accept and publish information that cannot be attributed to its source.

The arguments against such practices are quite compelling. Frequent use of unattributed or unverifiable information undermines confidence in the media. Listeners or readers are free to speculate that the reporter made up the tale. While this is seldom true, it is dangerous to provide the opportunity for a lazy reporter to mask poor fact-finding methods.

A strong argument against frequent use of unattributed information is that it provides an opportunity for vindictive people to embarrass others. Occasionally someone volunteers information to the press out of a strong conviction that the public interest is being thwarted. With the opportunities for inefficiency, lethargy, and corruption this is often true. On the other hand, a worker who feels he or she has been mistreated or has some other reason for being piqued may simply disclose information to get even.

Government, particularly the federal government, has been plagued with news leaks. This is logical enough because the government has been the target of good reporters ferreting out flaws in government operations. Officials themselves have contributed greatly to the leaks by acting arbitrarily and unreasonably in trying to keep too much information secret. While nearly everyone admits that a certain amount should be kept secret for purposes of national security, it is apparent that many officials have used secrecy as a means of covering up their own errors and malfeasance. Such intolerable uses of governmental secrecy are bound to lead to breaches of security.

Criticism of news leaks appears to be a fixed procedure for our presidents. In the administration of John F. Kennedy, FBI agents were used to investigate news personnel. President Lyndon B. Johnson expressed vast displeasure at newspeople who published information he would have preferred to keep secret. In the administration of Richard M. Nixon the extent of presidential action was exposed when congressional committees learned that taps had been placed on the telephones of high officials to determine the source of leaks.

Leaks from congressional committees also caused concern, as this news story shows:

> **Washington**—Leaks of confidential material from the House Judiciary Committee's impeachment inquiry were denounced by high admin-

\ istration officials yesterday as showing the committee is "out of control."

Vice President Gerald Ford and presidential counselor Dean Burch met with newsmen yesterday and attacked leaks from committee members during the past week as irresponsible, motivated by desires to impeach President Nixon, and justification for the President's refusal to turn over subpoenaed tapes of presidential Watergate conversations.

Their criticism was directed at statements by some committee members last week who said evidence examined by the committee showed that Secretary of State Henry Kissinger "initiated" wiretaps on some of his staff members when he was national security adviser to the President in an effort to stop leaks. This prompted Kissinger to threaten to resign unless his name is cleared.

Committee Chairman Peter W. Rodino, D-N.J., also deplored the leaks. At a closed committee session and again at a press briefing, he emphasized the need to protect confidentiality of sensitive materials and to retain public confidence in the committee's work.[1]

The story demonstrates the way leaks are often used by officials and others to further a purpose. It also illustrates the difficult decisions that face media people when such material becomes available. Faced with the knowledge that their audience has a right to know the sources of information, editors must decide whether a particular item is so important that ordinary rules can be abrogated. Disregard for such caution elevates the methods of the gossip columnist to the front page or the nightly news broadcast.

Protecting the Right Most Valued

In 1890 the *Harvard Law Review* published an article by Louis Brandeis and Samuel D. Warren arguing for a "right to privacy."[2] The two Boston lawyers held that excesses by the press required recognition of an individual's right to be let alone. Later, when he was a justice of the United States Supreme Court, Brandeis called the right of privacy "the most comprehensive of rights and the right most valued by civilized men."[3] Since then the courts have considered much litigation on the sub-

---

[1]"House Panel Criticized About Leaks," *Louisville Courier-Journal*, June 13, 1974, p. 1 (from dispatches by the *Los Angeles Times–Washington Post* Service and the *New York Times*).
[2]4 *Harvard Law Review* 193 (1890).
[3]*Olmsted v. United States* 277 U.S. 438, 478.

ject and more than half the states have adopted rules or legislation relating to it.

Like many legal questions, this one is also a philosophic and moral one. Essentially it comes down to the problem of defining the point at which information becomes a legitimate matter of public interest and discussion. An individual's personal habits and activities are his or her affair unless they can be shown to involve the public interest. Tradition and law have combined to loosely enforce this concept.

Tradition and law combine again to identify some of the points at which private actions automatically become a public concern and therefore legitimate items of news. A man's drinking habits are his own concern unless they cause him to run afoul of the law. If he is arrested for driving while intoxicated or for public drunkenness a legal record is made, which can be reported. The financial affairs of a small business proprietorship are not ordinarily matters of public concern. This changes if the owner files for bankruptcy, leaving a legal record, or when the concern decides to "go public" and offer stock for sale to the public. The Securities and Exchange Commission requires public disclosure of a considerable amount of information in order to protect potential buyers of stock. A person's wealth is usually considered to be his or her personal affair, but it becomes a matter of public record and news interest when a will is probated after that individual's death.

Another factor that determines the public importance of private habits and actions is the prominence of the individual involved. Men and women prominent in public affairs or entertainment find that their privacy is less respected than is that of others. Since the media find that their audiences are interested in personal information about prominent people, they seek it out. The general view is held that, once people push themselves into prominence, they give up some of their right to be let alone. When Gerald Ford assumed the U.S. presidency in 1974 the media described his habits of getting his own breakfast—hardly information of great concern, but the media acted on their principle that even trivia about important persons is newsworthy.

Often people are willing, even eager, to surrender their right to privacy. Certain kinds of success depend on fame or at least notoriety. One way to achieve this is to encourage the publication or broadcast of trivia about individual idiosyncrasies. Once public figures or entertainers have achieved status as newsworthy individuals the situation is likely to reverse. They no longer need the publicity engendered by such items, but the media still seek it out. After all, the media have helped to build them into public figures, so it is only natural that they should continue to seek out such information. Thus President Ford finds it impossible to maintain much privacy when he goes on a skiing vacation in Colorado; the press speculates endlessly about the activities at San Clemente even though former president Nixon is no longer in public life; and Frank Sinatra occasionally brawls with the press about items he considers intrusive.

A nagging question for the media and the public is the extent to which private infirmities of individuals are matters of public concern. For example, if a public official has a drinking problem should this be reported? Interpretations of the libel law help, but questions of responsibility persist. In libel cases the turning point sometimes centers on whether the private habit causes undesirable effects on the official acts of the person involved. If it had no adverse effect on the public it was none of the public's business.

But ethical more than legal questions plagued reporters considering how much they should tell about the drinking problem of Congressman Wilbur Mills of Arkansas. Mills, as chairman of the House Ways and Means Committee, was for years one of the most powerful men in the United States. Washington correspondents gradually built up Mills's reputation as a sober, responsible tax expert whose idea of a fine evening's entertainment was to curl up with the latest edition of the federal budget. These same correspondents were aware, too, that gradually the chairman's habits were changing: that Mills increasingly showed an inclination to forego evenings with the budget for evenings at nightclubs and that he appeared to be developing an addiction to alcohol.

The question: Were the chairman's changing habits a legitimate subject for news stories? The correspondents remained silent until, predictably, an incident involving the law triggered a flood of publicity. Mills was a passenger in his own car late one night in 1974 when it was stopped for speeding. Another passenger was Fanny Foxe, a stripper whose antics at the Tidal Basin that night provided highly interesting copy. Powerful individuals are often protected by public agencies, and the incident might not have come to public attention were it not for an alert cruising television newsman who responded to a vague message on the police band. Once at the Tidal Basin he recognized the newsworthiness of the incident. It is a commentary on the system of news values that Congressman Mills's affliction became public knowledge only after a relatively minor incident legitimized the situation as far as the news media were concerned.

When does an individual's income become a suitable subject for public discussion in the media? At one time such material was considered out of bounds when it concerned public figures. However, mounting distrust of public officials is focusing attention on their sources of income. President Nixon's tax problems in 1973, when he was found to owe nearly a half million dollars in back taxes, had something to do with the change in attitude. Frequently the initiative for such disclosure has come from the public figures themselves. It is not unusual for an elected official to call a press conference and disclose the contents of his or her tax return. Kentucky Congressman Joe Graves went a step further and, after announcing the figures to reporters, told them that a copy of his return would be on file in the Lexington, Kentucky, courthouse, where his constituents could inspect it at will.

General disclosure of such matters is becoming more common. Salaries of public employees in the past have often been kept private, even though legally public, through a gentleman's agreement. The records were not opened to the public or excuses were found to make it very difficult for a person to examine them. Newspaper editors generally went along with this policy and politely did not insist on the right to inspect the records. General concern and consequent newspaper response have begun to change that, with records generally more conveniently accessible and some newspapers publishing the higher, more interesting salaries.

In 1973 members of the Alabama legislature tried to force disclosure on the disclosers. The legislature passed and Governor George Wallace signed a bill that required that any reporter covering the legislature should be required to file a statement of his or her income. A court declared the law unconstitutional, but the trend toward more general disclosure of information of this nature persists. It appears to be a matter of legitimate public concern, for example, to know whether the publisher of the daily newspaper is also the owner of radio and television stations in the same city, or whether he or she has other local investments.

The business community and government go to considerable trouble to keep private income confidential. The records of the Internal Revenue Bureau are supposed to be sealed, even from inspection by other branches of the government. Corporations often regard their lists of stockholders as private information. Even a Senate subcommittee under Chairman Lee Metcalf of Montana was unable to get a very satisfactory response to requests for names of the thirty largest stockholders of various corporations. Retail businesses are particularly reluctant to disclose such information. Fairly typical responses to Senator Metcalf's request came from Ralph E. Bowers, vice president and secretary of Marshall Field & Company:

> We consider our list of stockholders and their holdings to be confidential and believe we are obligated to protect this confidentiality in the absence of some legal requirement to release the information.[4]

And from J. B. Jackson, president of J. C. Penney, Inc.:

> Our Company has always regarded information as to the ownership interests of particular stockholders of the Company as privileged and

[4]*Disclosure of Corporate Ownership*, report of the Subcommittee on Intergovernmental Relations, and Budgeting, Management, and Expenditures of the Committee on Government Operations, U.S. Senate, U.S. Government Printing Office, Washington, March 4, 1947, p. 314.

> confidential since it concerns the private affairs of the stockholders.
> Accordingly, the Company does not furnish to third parties infor-
> mation concerning the identities of particular stockholders or the
> numbers of shares held by them, except when required by law. . . .
> Although we presume that your request is for furtherance of a public
> interest, we feel that we must adhere to our position of not voluntarily
> furnishing the information in any instance.[5]

Despite such philosophy on the part of many business leaders, much information is available to intelligent and energetic reporters who are given
time to ferret it out. Reports of the Securities and Exchange Commission
and of the Federal Trade Commission carry many specific details that, if
generally known, would help the public to evaluate the business and industrial enterprises that serve it. Federal Communications Commission
files and reports are filled with useful information about the telecommunications industry. Annual reports of corporations are another source.
Often the newsworthy information in these materials is surrounded by a
welter of routine facts, so filtering it out requires diligence. Reporters also
need a thorough understanding of their field. Although such information
is not produced cheaply or easily, the news media are increasingly finding ways to bring it to public attention.

Income and personal habits of private individuals are regarded as matters that the media should not disclose—unless, of course, they affect the
public welfare.

The last proviso often requires newsmen and women to make difficult
decisions. Reporters sometimes build up personal friendships with the
individuals whom they cover. This makes it difficult to disclose damaging
information, and frequently a reporter has to decide whether he or she is
withholding such information to protect a friend or because the public interest is not being affected.

When such damaging information is once reported about newsworthy
individuals the entire force of the media may be brought to bear on it.
This happened in the Watergate case of 1973 and 1974, when the press
provided exhaustive coverage of shortcomings of President Nixon and
his administration after the initial break by the *Washington Post*. It happened, too, in the presidential election campaign of 1972 after it came to
public knowledge that the Democratic vice-presidential candidate,
Senator Thomas Eagleton of Missouri, had once undergone psychiatric
treatment. Various reporters had the information, but refrained from publishing it until they were sure the story was thoroughly documented.
After a columnist based in Washington did put the information in print,
all the media pounced on it, and on Senator Eagleton. Once it became

---

[5]Ibid., p. 315.

clear that the public was worried about the implications of a nervous breakdown and psychiatric care, Senator McGovern dumped Senator Eagleton from the ticket.

The responsibility of the press was clear. Once the information about Senator Eagleton's psychiatric treatment was established as accurate it assumed public importance. If one aspires to such high office as the vice presidency one must be willing to subject one's mental as well as physical health to public inspection. Senator Eagleton explained his original lack of disclosure on the grounds that he thought it unimportant. Any reporter could have told him differently, and one is forced to the conclusion that the senator was either naive or secretive.

Thus publication was appropriate. While Senator Eagleton may have felt that his psychiatric treatment was not relevant to his candidacy, it became rapidly apparent that the public could not be convinced that this was so. The media here exercised their responsibility in throwing the matter into the public arena for public decision.

More questionable was columnist Jack Anderson's decision on the basis of uncertain evidence to report that Senator Eagleton had been arrested on a charge of driving while under the influence of alcohol. Here is an exchange on that matter between the senator and Anderson from a CBS "Issues and Answers" program on July 30, 1972:

> Mr. Anderson: I think this is the occasion that I ought to take to face you. This is the first time we've had a chance to face though I did place calls, both at your office and in Los Angeles twenty-four hours before we used the story.
>
> Senator Eagleton: I'm sorry. We didn't get the notes on it, Mr. Anderson, but I'll take your word for it.
>
> Mr. Anderson: Of course. We placed calls and there's a record of the calls, but this is the first time I've had a chance to face you and I . . . I do owe you an apology. I've always told my reporters, Senator, that a fact does not become a fact for our column until we can prove it. Now I violated my own rule, and I want the nation and you to know I violated it.

A little later in the program:

> Mr. Anderson: Well, Senator, I would like nothing better than to dispose of this issue right here and now, and I wish that I could retract completely the story and say there's nothing to it. I cannot in good conscience do that.
>
> Senator Eagleton: You can't! I . . . I . . . well
>
> Mr. Anderson: I . . . I . . . I apologize to you for publishing a premature story. I apologize for publicizing documents that I have not seen and have not verified and in this age of Howard Hughes hoaxes

I'm acutely conscious of the fact this . . . these documents could be forgeries. . . .

Senator Eagleton: Well, I'm willing to cooperate, but I don't quite get the apology and then the no-retraction business. I take it you're saying the story should not have been aired in the first place.

Mr. Anderson: Absolutely.

Senator Eagleton: . . . and because you didn't see the identifiable data that would support such a story. . . .

Mr. Anderson: I should never have used it.

Mr. Anderson's position at that point was that, while he should apologize for disclosing the information prematurely, he could not retract it until he had evidence that it was untrue. The next day Senator McGovern removed Senator Eagleton from the ticket, so the issue became unimportant for most of the American public. It is generally agreed that a candidate for high public office must expect public scrutiny of aspects of his or her life that would otherwise be private. The Eagleton incident illustrates the speed with which careless reporting can do immense and unnecessary damage to a person's reputation. It underscores that the right to privacy is more than a right. It implies an obligation on the part of the media that goes beyond legal requirements. Without giving up its duty to keep the public informed, the media must be diligent in protecting individual reputations from unnecessary damage.

The U.S. Supreme Court is showing an increasing tendency to protect the right of individuals to privacy. In 1967 the court denied damages to a plaintiff because he failed to prove that an alleged false report was printed with knowledge that it was false or with "reckless disregard of its truth."[6] In 1974 the Court for the first time upheld an award for invasion of privacy based on a news story in a newspaper.[7] The Court based its decision on evidence that the writer of an article in the *Cleveland Plain Dealer* Sunday magazine published "knowing or reckless falsehoods" that made a West Virginia woman and her son suffer mental distress and humiliation.[8] Earlier privacy cases against newspapers more often involved material appearing in advertisements.

News and Social Stability

A decision to print or withhold information may involve, not the legitimacy of public concern, but whether publication will irreparably

[6]*Time, Inc. v. Hill,* 385 U.S. 374 (1967).

[7]"Newspaper Must Pay Award for Invasion of Privacy," *Editor & Publisher,* December 28, 1974, p. 13.

[8]*Cantrell v. Forest City Publishing Co.,* 419 U.S. 245 at 253 (1974).

damage the nation, or some other unit that demands loyalty. Such was the U-2 incident of May 1, 1960.

At the time U-2's, high-flying and speedy planes, were being used on regular spy missions over Russia. Equipped with sensitive cameras, they were the means by which the U.S. government monitored missile developments and other Russian activities deemed of critical importance to the United States. Since such action is contrary to international law, nobody admitted it, although it was known to high officials in the U.S. government, to the Russian government, and to some American journalists.

Eventually, on May 1, 1960, the Russians knocked down a U-2 piloted by Francis Gary Powers. The Russian government announced with appropriate indignation that it had caught an American plane flying illegally over Russian territory and spying. The U.S. government denied the U-2 was spying, but said the plane must have gotten off course. President Eisenhower gave the American cover story in a press conference.

For those reporters who knew that U.S. planes had been spying from the air, a fine question arose. Should they report what they knew to be the truth or should they support their government and report deadpan what the president and other U.S. officials said publicly? The questions came down to whether their basic loyalty was to their government or to the facts of the case (the truth?). President Eisenhower took them off the hook. Apparently he had no stomach for this kind of international dialogue. In a move that must have caused amazement on both sides of the Iron Curtain, he announced that his previous statement had been wrong and that the U-2 had been spying on Russia.

A similar problem arose for newspeople shortly after John Kennedy took office as president. The United States had been assisting some Cuban exiles who were preparing to invade Cuba and depose Premier Fidel Castro. Information about the situation spread around Washington, although the government refused to confirm U.S. involvement. *New York Times* reporters put together a comprehensive story, and the paper was prepared to give it front-page display. President Kennedy called the *Times* publisher to ask that the story be withheld in the national interest, and the request was granted. The invasion turned out to be a fiasco and the new Kennedy administration was discredited. President Kennedy later said he wished the *Times* had ignored his request.

Such are the dilemmas that face responsible newsmen and women. To whom do they owe their primary loyalty? Certainly they have a responsibility to print honest information. When is that responsibility subordinate to the need to support one's government?

This is a problem of a free society in competition with closed societies. The Russian government or the Russian publicist is not faced with such a decision. Since it is not necessary to keep the public informed no problem arises. In an open society the government and press always work with the knowledge that informing the public also means informing the enemy or potential enemy.

The question comes down to a decision as to how critical it is that certain information be kept from another government. Some secrets are legitimate. Information on the deployment of guided missiles cannot be made public without jeopardizing public safety. The tendency of government is to hide more than it should. The delicate responsibility of the media is to keep the layer of secrecy as thin as it can be without damaging security.

To Titillate or Inform?

One of the responsibilities of the media is to report in the proper perspective. The charge of sensationalism may refer to selection of material or to the manner in which it is treated. Some information is by its nature sensational. In New York City tabloids of the 1920's and 1930's regaled their readers with accounts of shady goings-on among the prominent and lurid crime among the undistinguished. The "best" story was one that combined sex, violence, money, and prominent people. Such gossip always seems to have a high degree of interest, but the average New Yorker of those days could not have found much value in knowing of orgies that transpired behind the brownstone fronts of the East Thirties and Forties or on secluded Long Island or Westchester estates.

Sometimes apologists for the tabloids would make the point that the hordes who read them were largely semiliterate. Was it not better for them to be reading the tabloids than not to be reading at all? To some extent they were right. Those newspapers did contain some information, simply presented, of a serious nature, and many persons developed the newspaper reading habit through their daily adventures with the tabloids.

The tabloids selected sensational material, and they treated it in a sensational manner, thus doubly insulting their readers.

Responsibility in Gathering Information

Another area of ethics concerns the methods reporters use in collecting information. Is it, for instance, ethical to trick a person into giving information by using loaded questions? Is it all right to threaten people who have information you need? Should a newspaper or broadcaster pay for information obtainable in no other way? How much effort should be spent in verifying information? Is one source enough? Two? Three?

At one time police reporters were quite adept at tricking people out of information. This technique works well with the person who is arrested and already confused and frightened. Loaded questions will sometimes do the job. Any question that suggests the answer is loaded. Even such a conversational gambit as, "It's a nice day, isn't it?" is loaded, although innocent.

Less innocent are loaded questions asked of a person accused of a crime. These may include such probes as "Why did you do it?" "How much did you get?" "Where did you hide the stuff?" Each one implies the larger answer, that the suspect is guilty, and each one is an effort to trick an admission out of the suspect. That such questions are sometimes used by detectives and trial lawyers is not much of a defense for their use by reporters.

Threats, too, have forced information out of unwilling informants. One early training film had a reporter telling a source on the telephone that he was "at headquarters." This was literally true, since the reporter, assigned to police headquarters, was making the call from that location, but the implication, that he was a police officer, was untrue. Since impersonating a police officer is a crime, the hint that the reporter is an official is unfair to the source of information. It is likewise unethical for a reporter to fail to reveal that he or she is a reporter seeking information for broadcast or publication.

Should a news medium pay for news? Many people are opposed to the practice. They hold that newsworthy information should be available to the people through the media and that paying for it is likely to cause public figures to withhold information until they can profit from it.

Verification of information by the media is not unlike the process by which individuals evaluate the information they receive, although it should be more rigorous. Each of us, when confronted with new information, evaluates it against at least three criteria: whether it is innately reasonable, whether it fits in with other information we have, and whether the source of information is reliable. If it fails to pass such tests we may dismiss it. If it meets our criteria we may use it as the basis of a decision or we may pass it along. If we are naive we accept much information uncritically; if we are sophisticated we apply the tests more rigorously than most others. If the information is spicy or exciting we face the temptation to pass it along even though we are not convinced of its accuracy.

So it is with the media. For them the need to test new information before passing it along is even more critical than for the individual because the media affect many people. The temptations are great for the media, too. After all, newspeople are in the business of supplying information, and if they are first with it their efficiency is demonstrated. So the impulse is to broadcast or publish information without adequate checking in order to beat the opposition. Fortunately, media people have built up an immunity to this temptation.

This immunity has its limits. Sometimes haste or laziness compounds errors. The National Advisory Commission on Civil Disorders criticized the media for accepting uncritically statements from law enforcement officers during the 1967 race riots:

> The press obtained much factual information about the scale of the disorders—property damage, personal injury and deaths—from local officials, who were inexperienced in dealing with civil disorders and not always able to sort out fact from rumor in the confusion. At the height of the Detroit riot, some news reports of property damage put the figure in excess of $500 million. Subsequent investigation shows it to be $40 to $50 million.[9]

Carl Bernstein and Bob Woodward, in describing their coverage of the Watergate affair for the *Washington Post,* told of the concern for accuracy displayed by executive editor Benjamin C. Bradlee, metropolitan editor Harry Rosenfeld (since named national news editor), managing editor Howard Simons, and city editor Barry Sussman. This excerpt tells of a meeting called to consider a story that H. R. Haldeman, the top presidential aide, was one of the individuals who controlled funds used for political espionage:

> During that 7:00 P.M. meeting, just before the deadline, Bradlee served as prosecutor, demanding to know exactly what each source had said.
> "What did the FBI guy say?" Bradlee asked.
> The reporters gave a brief summary.
> "No," Bradlee said, "I want to hear exactly what you asked him and what his exact reply was."
> He did the same with Deep Throat, and the doorstep interview with Sloan.
> "I recommend going," Rosenfeld said.
> Sussman agreed.
> Simons nodded his approval.
> "Go," Bradlee said.
> On the way out Simons told the reporters he would feel more comfortable if they had a fourth source.[10]

The Watergate story was difficult and carried such important overtones that any error would have been highly dangerous for the *Post.* But the

---

[9]*Report of the National Commission on Civil Disorders* (New York: Bantam, 1968), p. 364.

[10]Carl Bernstein and Bob Woodward, *All the President's Men* (New York: Simon & Schuster, 1974), pp. 179–180.

habit of checking, rechecking, and demanding more than one source is not unusual in the newspaper and broadcast industries. It is one way in which reporters and editors protect themselves, the reputations of those they are writing about, and the credibility of their profession.

Maintaining Credibility

A responsibility of the media to themselves and to their society is to maintain their own credibility. To be effective they must be believable and believed. If the public does not trust the media it has nowhere else to turn for information about public affairs. In the mid-1970's there was evidence that people were losing trust in the media as well as in many other institutions of society.

In achieving believability the appearance of rectitude is almost as important as rectitude itself. For the media this appearance is maintained by guarding the quality of their product and the conduct of their staff.

Since truth is an abstraction that means different things to different people, the media can scarcely claim that their content is always truth. But they should be able to claim accuracy. This requires that their content reflects verified facts and that when information is speculative the audience should be told that it cannot be verified. While there are legitimate questions of proper selection and emphasis of content, there should be no questions as to the reliability of specific information, and the public should be able to believe that the media represent its interests.

This happy situation does not exist for all citizens and all media, as one interviewer for the Kerner commission reported:

> The average black person couldn't give less of a damn about what the media say. The intelligent black person is resentful at what he considers to be a totally false portrayal of what goes on in the ghetto. Most black people see the newspapers as mouthpieces of the "power structure."[11]

Such an attitude reflects inadequate coverage of black neighborhoods as well as the inability on the part of white reporters and editors to understand the viewpoint of black people. The commission recommended, as one way to remedy this lack of confidence, the training and hiring of more blacks to work in the media.

Literal factual accuracy assumes less importance in the minds of some proponents of the "new journalism." This expression has been used to

[11]*Report of the National Commission on Civil Disorders*, p. 374.

cover a variety of writing and reporting styles, but all provide freedom for a writer to approach a subject in his or her own way. Often new journalism uses a very personal approach and attempts to involve the emotions of the reader. In the hands of experts like Tom Wolfe and Gay Talese the method is powerful. Often fiction techniques are used to heighten the reality, as we shall see when we consider new journalism in more detail in Chapter 10. It is important that readers understand the methods being used so that media credibility is not diminished.

Guarding Against the Appearance of Evil

Favorable attention in the media is like money in the bank. Many organizations cannot exist without public favor and the shortest route to public favor is through the media. Many organizations buy advertising time and space. Still others seek attention in news and entertainment segments. Sometimes their efforts to gain such attention lead them to offer disguised bribes to people who control content. These may range from fancy hats to the fashion editor, to expensive lunches, liquor, or even part-time jobs that require little work.

Some media organizations have rules that require their staff to refuse part-time jobs with any branch of the government, political parties, or even civic agencies. The theory is that the reporter might, perhaps unconsciously, be influenced in his or her regular work by such activities. The same worry has led some newspaper managements to forbid their employees to run for public office, even the school board. Other newspaper managements feel that such participation in public affairs is good for reporters.

Sports coverage raises ethical problems. Managements of major sports clubs are often willing, sometimes eager, to pay the expenses of broadcasters and writers who accompany the team on road trips. Some colleges and professional sports clubs insist on the right to name the announcer who broadcasts their games. Some clubs pay the announcer.

Writers and broadcasters who may influence the purchase of products are likely to receive favors and gifts from manufacturers. Since writers for women's and family pages frequently report on new products, they are particularly subject to this temptation. The attempt to influence the writer is clear enough—otherwise the manufacturer has no reason for presenting the gifts. Some writers accept all presents and say that their work is not influenced thereby. Others return all except those of trifling value on the grounds that, whether they are influenced or not, it will be suspected that they are. Some media units require that all gifts be returned to the sender.

Since news organizations tend to regard themselves as the guardians of morality in high places they need to take every precaution to avoid any chance that they themselves can be suspect.

Like reformers, newspeople must constantly remind themselves that in even the highest of causes the end does not always justify the means. Reporters must frequently make decisions where there are no rules and only their own sense of rightness to be appeased. Another illustration from the Watergate saga of Bernstein and Woodward makes the point. In trying to get a line on the activities of G. Gordon Liddy they needed to trace some calls to Liddy from Miami.

They tell of Bernstein's reservations about trying to get confidential information from someone he knew in the telephone company office:

> Bernstein had several sources in the Bell system. He was always reluctant to use them to get information about calls because of the ethical question involved in breaching the confidentiality of a person's telephone records. It was a problem he had never resolved in his mind. Why, as a reporter, was he entitled to have access to personal and financial records when such disclosure would outrage him if he were subjected to a similar inquiry by investigators?
>
> Without dwelling on his problem, Bernstein called a telephone company source and asked for a list of Barker's calls.[12]

Deciding when the end justifies the means is not a problem that plagues media workers alone, but they have to face it more often than most people. Like Bernstein, many reporters never settle it.

For all media workers and owners ethical behavior and the look of honesty are critical, for they cannot do their job without the confidence of the public.

Ethics and Law

The implicit contract between audiences and media, like all things implicit, requires faith on both sides. Most of the work in maintaining such faith falls on the media. They must select useful and interesting material and present it in an acceptable manner, all the while protecting the right of individuals to privacy and preserving the basic values of their society. Such a task assumes in the men and women who run the media a maturity of judgment and self-restraint required of few other professions. In deciding such ethical questions, editors and news managers operate in a gray area in which they can find logical reasons for various courses of

[12]Bernstein and Woodward, *All the President's Men*, pp. 35–36.

action. Those who control entertainment content have even more subtle problems. Whose ideas of morality should they project? The answers, of course, reflect the convictions of media decision-makers and of the many forces that play upon them.

In Chapter 5 we will consider an area in which decisions are governed by a clearer set of rules—statute law and court decisions. As ethical questions merge into legal ones, media decisions are sometimes easier, but they are never very easy. It is in the area of the ethics and law of communications that society forges many of the understandings by which it survives.

Suggestions for Further Reading

Commission on Freedom of the Press. *A Free and Responsible Press*. Chicago: University of Chicago Press, 1947.
Better known as the "Hutchins report," this report presents the findings of a distinguished panel.

Johannesen, Richard L. *Ethics in Human Communication*. Columbus, Ohio: Charles E. Merrill, 1975.
A consideration of ethics in various situations.

Kittross, John M., and Harwood, Kenneth, eds. *Free and Fair*. Philadelphia: Association for Professional Broadcast Education, 1970.
Readings on radio and television access to courts and on the fairness doctrine plus texts of broadcasters' codes of ethics.

Levy, Leonard W., ed. *Freedom of the Press from Zenger to Jefferson*. Indianapolis: Bobbs-Merrill, 1966.
Contains the classic statements relating to freedom of the press in early America.

MacDougall, Curtis D. *The Press and Its Problems*. Dubuque, Iowa: Wm. C. Brown, 1964.
Ethical problems of newspapers and reporters.

Nelson, Harold L., ed. *Freedom of the Press from Hamilton to the Warren Court*. Indianapolis: Bobbs-Merrill, 1967.
A companion book to that edited by Levy (listed above), this volume contains many later documents of importance.

Press Freedoms Under Pressure. New York: Twentieth Century Fund, 1972.
A report and recommendations on press freedom. It includes the Supreme Court Pentagon papers decision.

Report of the National Advisory Commission on Civil Disorders. New York: Bantam, 1968.
Chapter 15 considers the role of the press in riot situations.

Rivers, William, and Schramm, Wilbur. *Responsibility in Mass Communications*. Rev. ed. New York: Harper & Row, 1969.
A lucid presentation of ethical problems of the media.

Schulman, Robert, "Anatomy of a Decision," *The Quill*, November 1975, pp. 22–25.
How Louisville, Kentucky, newspapers and broadcasters used guidelines in attempting to keep the city calm in a busing crisis.

5

The Limits
of Freedom

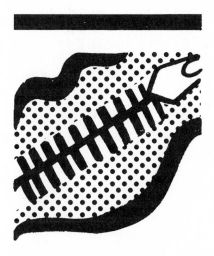

    Power centers in society are always wary of other agencies that deal in information. Individuals who gain authority are invariably intelligent enough to see that information and power go together. Government leaders instinctively seek to control their critics, whether they are outspoken individuals or media systems.

    Plato early learned the fate of those who presume to question the wisdom of the mighty. Serving in 368 B.C. as tutor to the heir apparent to the throne of Sicily, Plato went beyond his teaching duties to criticize the Sicilian government. The elder Dionysius, ruler of Syracuse, thereupon arranged to have the philosopher sold as a slave. Ransomed by a friend, Plato escaped back to Athens and founded the Academy. Even after this experience Plato advocated censorship.

Information Is Power

    People who have good information and good sources of information are more successful than others. The bettor who has a good tip on the horses (provided it really is good) is more likely to come away from the track money ahead. The investor who keeps abreast of the market is more likely than others to make money. The candidate who learns what is on the minds of the voters increases the chances of winning political office.

In the same way governments need information. Czar Nicholas of Russia and Louis XVI of France were deposed partly because they misjudged the mood of their subjects. Good information might have helped them to save their governments and their lives. The same need is implicit in democratic governments. Those who rule through "the consent of the governed" must try to understand the desires of the public.

Persuasion is necessary even in a totalitarian regime. A dictator cannot provide a police officer for every citizen, throw everyone in jail, or execute every citizen or banish a total population to Siberia. People must be persuaded to obey the laws. When persuasion fails to do the job it is often strengthened by a show of force, and so it becomes subtle or blatant coercion. The presence of a patrol car every few blocks tends to keep traffic more orderly, and tales of torture by a secret police tend to keep a population in line. So the power of a government to "persuade" its citizens is reinforced by the show of force (the presence of a police officer) and by occasional demonstrations of its application (a police officer pulls a driver over to the curb).

Thus persuasion and coercion are among the basic devices used in the exercise of power. Other devices are punishment and reward. These are often used in combination, as when a mother rewards a child with candy for being good, but punishes with a spanking or withdrawal of affection if a child is bad. Persuasion is often used in combination with both. The line between threat and persuasion is indefinable, but depends primarily on the manner in which a bribe or threat is presented and in the power position of the person doing the persuasion. For example, a police officer is likely to be more successful in "persuading" a loiterer to move along than a private citizen would be. Somewhere along the crooked line between threat and persuasion is morale. Morale is high when people comply with accepted behavior patterns because they feel rewarded. Morale is low when they comply out of fear of reprisals.

Communication is intrinsic to the use of power. The most efficient exercise of power is through persuasion. A mother or father may avoid a public scene by persuading a child to refrain from shouting in church rather than spanking him. A supervisor fires a worker only as a last resort, after first trying to persuade the worker to follow standard procedures. However, persuasive power is enhanced by the power position of the persuader. The persuasiveness of both parent and supervisor is strengthened because they can administer punishment or offer rewards. The "personal style" of an administrator is determined largely by the manner in which that person mixes a system of punishments and rewards with persuasion.

The same is true of government: a totalitarian regime tends to rely on force and threat of force to control its population; a democratic government relies more on persuasion and reasoning.

With persuasion a central device for exercising power, the channel through which the persuasive message is carried becomes of interest to individuals and governments.

A parent has instantaneous communication channels through which to practice his or her persuasive powers. "Be quiet or I'll spank" may be all that is needed. The message is quickly given, instantly received, and its effect is noted at once.

The communication channels for government are longer. Every government except the smallest has to rely on media to carry its persuasive messages. Plato was concerned with this problem when he urged that a city-state should contain no more citizens than could be gathered within the range of a human voice. Primitive tribes may still meet this practical standard, but as nations grow larger their dependence on communications media increases accordingly. It is no wonder that political leaders view the media with interest and sometimes with alarm. The media provide the channels by which governments exercise their powers. The people who control the media may become arbiters of power—in reality, separate power centers. That is why the relationship of government to the media is such a critical one. We shall examine that relationship in different types of governments and consider the methods by which government seeks to control the media that provide information channels.

The Totalitarian Way

Totalitarian governments try to consolidate as much control as possible in the hands of the ruling elite. Agricultural and industrial production are in the hands of government, churches are banned, and communications media are run by agencies of the government or the ruling party. No country, not even Russia, has such complete control, but some approach it closely.

Competition from the media system is eliminated by the simple expedient of making it subservient to the government. For practical purposes the residents of such a state are told only what the leaders of government think they should know, so the media become publicity organs for the government. Kenneth E. Olson described this aspect of the Russian press and quoted Stalin and Khrushchev's views:

> The Soviet press . . . has developed a form of journalism totally different from anything in the western world. News is incidental, for the

chief function of papers is to serve as a collective propagandizer, agitator, and organizer for the Communist cause. Stalin spoke of the press as "the transmission belt between the party and the masses," and Khrushchev said, "Just as an army cannot fight without arms so the party cannot carry on its ideologic missions without the efficient and powerful weapon, the press. We cannot put it in unreliable hands; only the most faithful, most trustworthy and politically steadfast people, devoted to our cause."[1]

Born in revolution and in fierce competiton for the public ear, the Bolshevik government, in one of its first moves, ended the opposition press. Censorship of all non-Bolshevik papers was decreed late in 1917 by the Council of Peoples Commissars. The secret police (the Cheka) was empowered to arrest offending editors. In a few months all opposition presses had been silenced.

The vigorous anti-Bolshevik press was replaced by propaganda papers whose efforts were coordinated under the Gozizdat, a bureau of the Commissariat of Education. Over the years the policy of strict government or party control has been maintained.

Pravda (Truth) is the organ of the Soviet party. Directed from Moscow, it is printed there and in many other Russian cities. It expresses the view of the party and serves as the guide for other Soviet publications. It is also followed by foreign journalists in Russia as the best indication of party and governmental policy. It circulates to Communist leaders and to the ruling elite all over Russia.

Izvestia, published by the Kremlin, is the second paper in the country. It, too, is printed in various Russian cities. It has a more popular image than *Pravda* and concerns itself more with the actual operation of the government and with foreign affairs, presenting a less theoretical approach than *Pravda*.

Under the leadership of these two publications, various ministries publish papers for their special groups. These include *Krasnaya Zvezda* (Red Star), aimed at the armed forces by the defense ministry; *Gudok* (Whistle), for railway workers by the transportation ministry; and *Selskaya Zhizn* (Rural Life), by the ministry of agriculture. The Central Council of Trade Unions, the Union of Soviet Writers, and the All-Union Committee of Physical Culture all have their special publications. Communist youth, a special target of Soviet propaganda, are the intended audiences for *Komsomolskaya Pravda*, *Pionerskaya Pravda*, and nearly a hundred other publications.[2]

Also in Russia are newspapers for each of the fifteen republics, ministry

[1]Kenneth E. Olson, *The History Makers* (Baton Rouge: Louisiana State Press, 1966), p. 325.
[2]Ibid., p. 323.

papers at this level, and a local press. Thus an elaborate media organization pervades the Soviet Union. Editors may criticize certain aspects but never the system itself or major party decisions. Soviet journalists defend this system, even though, to the Western observer, it seems to provide a pure propaganda apparatus for the party and government. The Soviets say that the party and the government represent the people and that whatever the government does is in the best interests of the people, thus it would be absurd to allow the press to criticize the party or government. Their press is free they say, while the Western press is shackled to and subservient to the capitalistic system.

The press in Yugoslavia is a bit more independent than that in Russia. Newspapers are owned by the Socialist Alliance of the Working People of Yugoslavia and managed by councils of workers. The councils make most of the administrative and policy decisions, although stories concerning governmental policy and international relations are subject to government control. The Yugoslav papers carry a small amount of advertising. The revenue from this, plus the profits from printing other publications, allows some of the papers to operate without governmental subsidy.

In totalitarian societies the broadcast media are under even tighter control than the printed ones. Usually the government owns them and operates them directly as an arm of its propaganda or education ministry. The pattern is consistent, too, with the news agencies. For example, Tass, the Russian news service, is so much an arm of the government that its agents abroad are sometimes suspected of being spies.

Each totalitarian society has its own variations, but the general picture is clear enough. The government, which is synonymous with the ruling party, forestalls the development of political power in the media systems by making the distribution of information a governmental function controlled by administrators who can be counted on to follow government and party line. A different tradition has grown up in the Western world.

The Open Society and Information

Open societies encourage the expression of opinions by individuals and support a variety of media. Freedom of thought and expression are regarded as basic human rights. Along with these go the right to information on which to base opinions. Such philosophy requires that anyone can say, broadcast, or print anything so long as he or she is willing to take the consequences. This philosophy requires that the arena of discussion be kept wide open—that subjects can be banned only for the most pressing reasons and that information of public interest can be kept secret only in times of grave emergency. It is with defining the pressing reasons and grave emergencies that much of communication law in the Western world is concerned. It is also the concern of this chapter.

Traditionally four types of information have been designated as undesirable and punishable under the law: defamation, the damaging of another's reputation; blasphemy, material that tends to bring God or religion into contempt; obscenity, lewd or disgusting sexual material that offends community standards; and sedition, material that may incite violent overthrow of the government. These are designed to protect individual rights, to maintain community standards of morality, and to protect the government from violent overthrow. As we saw in Chapter 4, the right of privacy has gained some recognition in the twentieth century on the theory that individuals have the right to be left alone unless their activities become matters of legitimate public concern. Freedom to publish or broadcast is sometimes curtailed when information about a trial or other criminal proceeding would violate the rights of an individual or interfere with the orderly processes of the courts.

The tendency of most governments has been to enlarge these forbidden areas and to increase the variety of situations that are judged to be violations. The tendency of the media has been the opposite: to narrow the definitions of actionable material and so decrease governmental control over areas of public discussion.

This is a continuing war in the United States. The skirmishes and battles are fought in the courts, the state legislatures, the Congress, and in the office of the president. The battles began in the early days of the Republic and have continued to the present. They will not end, although the arenas, the players, and the methods will vary. It is a war between two powerful and strongly opposed forces. There are periods of relative calm and periods of intense fighting. The discord bubbles just under the surface continually, so that decisions in individual cases are reached on the basis of the most recent balance of powers. The manner in which this balance is maintained has much to do with the state of human liberty.

Subsidized Media

It is easy to think that the Communist bloc countries have a wholly owned, monolithic press system as opposed to one entirely in private hands in the Western countries. This is partly true, but the information systems of the Western democracies are so varied that any generalization is faulty. The printed media tend to be in private hands in the democratic countries, but the broadcast media are often publicly owned.

Even the United States, one of the strongholds of private media owner-ship, has a vast armed forces broadcast network and many television sta-tions licensed to public agencies.

In the United States the notion of private ownership of the media is well established. Journalists and pamphleteers were in the vanguard of the fighters for individual liberties. The framers of the Constitution had fought to overthrow what they regarded as an unjust government. Their suspicion of authority in general prompted them to dilute power in their new government by reserving whatever they could to the states. The Bill of Rights further diluted central power by safeguarding individuals in their rights to free expression and their attempts to seek redress from grievances.

With such an attitude among the founders of the United States there is little wonder that a press in private hands was assumed and that safe-guards to protect free communication were built into our basic charter. Here, as in England, there is a common understanding that government, as the great controlling agent of society, needs a monitor that is not under its control.

But a press free from government control did not necessarily imply an impartial press.

Political parties subsidized the press and paid some editors, and there were some scathing political diatribes in the early papers. The parties sometimes managed to channel public funds into the press. At the end of the eighteenth century the *Gazette of the United States,* edited by John Fenno, received funds from the Federalist party and printing contracts from the Treasury Department.[3] During the same period Jefferson's oppo-sition party gave Philip Freneau translations to do for the State Depart-ment to subsidize his work as editor of the *National Gazette.*

In most of Western Europe a successful commercial press has dwarfed the party press, as it has in the United States, but vestiges of control by political party or interest groups survive.

For example, in Norway the labor movement distributes the profits from some of its larger papers to subsidize the smaller ones. In Norway, too, the one Communist paper apparently receives party funds. Party papers in Finland are at least partially subsidized. Businesspeople as well as politi-cal parties subsidize some of the smaller papers.

Olson describes the situation in Italy:

> There are twenty-two [papers] which are political party organs and
> subsidized by parties. In addition . . . nine others are known to
> be supported by industries, and five are official voices of semistate
> organizations.[4]

[3]Alfred M. Lee, *The Daily Newspaper in America* (New York: Macmillan, 1937), p. 479.
[4]Olson, *History Makers,* p. 179.

The story is similar in Greece:

> Many papers still suffer from economic anemia. These are stronger dailies whose operations are profitable enough so that they can stand on their own feet, but a number of dailies get help from political parties, banks, or industrial firms whose views they espouse.[5]

While the pattern of independent ownership of newspapers is dominant in Western democracies, it is by no means universal. Governments outside the totalitarian countries seldom own or admit to owning newspapers, but political parties and even industrial groups sometimes have their own press.

Ownership of Broadcast Facilities

Ownership as a control device is used in broadcasting much more widely than for the printed media. Four general patterns of control emerge:

1. The government owns and operates the broadcasting system directly through an executive department established for that purpose. In addition to Russia, several other European countries use this system.

2. Broadcasting is operated through a public corporation or authority. The government retains final and full authority, but normally grants considerable autonomy to whatever buffer unit is established. Thus broadcasting is supposedly removed from political domination but is finally answerable to the people through the government. Britain, France, West Germany, and Belgium use this structure.

3. In a slight modification of the previous system, a government may set up a private corporation to run the broadcast system. The government may be the sole stockholder or may share ownership with private interests. Italy, Sweden, and Switzerland use this device.

4. Ownership is in private hands with a minimum of government control. The United States and Japan follow this pattern, although in both countries publicly owned broadcasting facilities are competing for audiences.[6]

---

[5]Ibid., p. 268.

[6]This classification is used in Burton Paulu, *Radio and Television Broadcasting on the European Continent* (Minneapolis: University of Minnesota Press, 1967), pp. 51–52. It is based on the work of Albert Namurois in *Problems of Structure and Organization of Broadcasting in the Framework of Radio-Communications* (Geneva: European Broadcasting Union, 1964).

Great Britain is worth special attention because it has produced what is generally conceded to be a superior broadcast service and because it allows coexistence of a public and a private system. The British Broadcasting Corporation (BBC) operates under Royal Charter and is licensed by the postmaster-general. It receives its revenue from a tax on receivers and is not permitted to carry advertising. From the early 1920's until 1955 the BBC monopolized radio and television in Britain.

In 1955 commercial television was introduced to Britain with the start of the Independent Television Authority (ITA). The ITA gains its revenue from leasing channels to private contractors who produce programs and sell advertising. Commercials are grouped at strategic breaks in the program and so are less of an intrusion than those in the American system.

ITA's lighter fare at first took about 70 percent of the British audience from BBC, but BBC fought back by establishing a second network, BBC-2, with a somewhat lower cultural level than original BBC programming. By 1972 BBC and ITV appeared to be splitting the British audience about half and half.[7]

In the 1970's commercial radio was introduced in Britain partly in answer to "pirate" radio stations that were siphoning off advertising by broadcasting into the country from ships lying just outside territorial waters. The Independent Broadcasting Authority (IBA) was established to oversee commercial television and radio.

Late in 1974 London's first two commercial radio stations, the all-music Capital Radio and all-news London Broadcasting, observed their first anniversary, with at least one on shaky ground financially. Radio Clyde in Glasgow and other new commercial stations apparently were doing better.

But the future of commercial broadcasting in Britain is not assured. In July 1974 a committee of the British Labor party urged that the party endorse the full nationalization of television and radio as well as government intervention in newspapers and motion pictures. The party took no stand, but Lord Annan, provost of the University College, London, was appointed to chair a committee to study the proposal. The government promised to extend the charters of the BBC and IBA until July 1979 to give the committee time to make its study.

As a public corporation the BBC is in a delicate position in airing criticism of the government, but it has followed a policy of arranging time for the government in power and also for members of the opposition. It has maintained an independent posture despite the powers that are assigned to the government. Among these are the right

> to appoint or dismiss BBC governors at will; revoke its charter for "reasonable cause," assign or withdraw radio frequencies and televi-

---

[7]Jack Gould, "What Public TV Can Be: 1. Britain's BBC," *Columbia Journalism Review* 11 (July/August 1972): 16.

sion channels; determine the amount of money payable by the Treasury to the Corporation; nationalize the BBC in an emergency; or revoke its license for unsatisfactory performance.[8]

Despite the freedom granted to the BBC, government ownership of the media is the ultimate control device. It is the system by which the government can most easily orchestrate the information that reaches the public. Not far behind as an effective control is licensing.

Licensing

One of the most odious and effective of governmental controls is licensing. Granting a license is simply giving a person permission to engage in a certain activity. It is made an offense to perform certain acts without a license. Many activities are thus proscribed, among them driving an automobile or practicing law or medicine.

Licensing has many advantages for the ruler. It lets him or her know who is engaging in certain activities or who aspires to. It allows a ruler to set certain conditions before a citizen is granted a license. Perhaps its greatest appeal is the convenience with which violators can be punished. It is relatively easy to establish whether a person driving a car possesses a license. If not, that individual is obviously guilty. Perhaps it is this convenience that has made licensing, over the centuries, one of the principal devices for controlling expression. Licensing of speech or of the media is particularly abhorrent to many people because it negates the basic civil liberty of free expression.

One of the earliest means of expression to be controlled by this device was the stage. The Greek comedians of the fourth century B.C. more than once felt the pressure of the licenser. The first mention of written licenses for acting in England appears to be in Queen Mary's proclamation on her accession in 1553. She forbade her subjects "to play any interlude" involving the controversial points of the Christian religion without "her graces special license in writynge for the same."[9] In 1574 Queen Elizabeth granted a patent to players of the Earl of Leicester, a favorite of hers, giving them the right to perform in all cities and towns of the realm. But she established the condition that the master of revels should pass on all plays before they were produced. The master of revels became a key figure in British stage censorship. He was frequently a person with literary ability and usually showed no concern about the moral implications of a play. He

[8]Paulu, *Radio and Television Broadcasting*, p. 63n.
[9]Frank Fowell and Frank Palmer, *Censorship in England* (London: Frank Palmer, 1913), p. 13.

was interested in eliminating anything that might cause dissatisfaction with the government or embarrassment to a friendly foreign power.

Licensing appears to have been accepted casually by Shakespeare, whose company was granted a patent to play in London and the provinces. This acceptance of censorship was transferred to the New World, with Pennsylvania providing more examples than the other Colonies. Governor Hamilton issued a license to a company of players in 1754, but public reaction caused the legislature to respond by passing a bill to suppress lotteries and plays. After more skirmishes the legislature repealed former provisions forbidding plays when it was faced with petitions signed by thousands of residents. Two officials were designated to approve performances in advance, and fines and imprisonment were prescribed for persons who presented plays without a license. The powers of censorship were confirmed by acts of 1851 and 1876, and in 1879 a new detailed act was passed. This required the mayors of first-class cities to act as censors.[10] Other Colonies also assumed the power to license plays.

Religious and secular officials were quick to see the dangers in printing after Johannes Gutenberg perfected it. The obvious solution was censorship, and the first books from Gutenberg's press attest that they were printed by authority. Licensing became the common way of controlling printing. Two modern historians describe the situation a century after the invention of printing in these words:

> All countries censored books; Protestant authorities labored to keep "papist" works from the eyes of the faithful, and Catholic authorities took the same pains to suppress all knowledge of "heretics." All bishops, Anglican, Lutheran, and Catholic, regulated reading matter within their dioceses. In the Catholic world, with the trend toward centralization under the pope, a special importance attached to the list published by the bishop of Rome, the papal Index of Prohibited Books. Only with special permission, granted to reliable persons for special study, could Catholics read books listed on the Index, on which most of the significant works written in Europe since the Reformation have been included.[11]

Power to license, exercised by representatives of the pope in early England, was assumed by the crown after the Reformation. The bishops still issued the "imprimatur" or permit to print, but now they issued it in the name of the king instead of the pope.[12]

---

[10]Described by Justice Sulzberger in his opinion in *Oellers to Use of Commonwealth v. Ritter*, 5 Pa. District Reports 149 (1896).

[11]R. R. Palmer and Joel Colton, *A History of the Modern World*, 3rd ed. (New York: A. A. Knopf, 1965), p. 87.

[12]Thomas Pitt Tasswell-Langmead, *English Constitutional History* (Boston: Houghton Mifflin, 1919), p. 753.

The king's court, the Star Chamber, was the agency through which the crown exercised most of its control over printing in the 1500's and 1600's. In the ordinance of 1586 the Star Chamber provided that the government must be kept informed of all presses in operation and forbade printing except in London, Oxford, or Cambridge. The Archbishop of Canterbury and the Bishop of London were to decide how many printing presses were needed; and no new presses were to be established until the number in use fell below this figure. The number of apprentices was limited. The Stationer's Company, a group of publishers and booksellers, was given responsibility for day-to-day enforcement of the act. The Stationers were authorized to search for and seize books printed contrary to the act and to seize presses and type used in their manufacture.

An ordinance of 1637 was far more elaborate, and it prescribed the licensing policy that lasted continuously until 1694. The act forbade publication or importation of unlicensed books. Law books were to be licensed by the two chief justices and the chief baron; historical and political works by the secretaries of state; books of heraldry by the earl marshall; and "all other books, whether of Divinitie, Phisicke, Philosophie, Poetry or whatsoever" by the Archbishop of Canterbury and the Bishop of London. All books were to bear the name of the author and printer.

The same ordinance attempted an indirect control of content by limiting the number of presses and regulating the affairs of those who operated them. Only twenty printers were allowed. None of them could have more than two presses, except one who had been a master or upper warden of the Stationer's Company, who could have three. No one was permitted to build a press or cast type without giving notice to the Stationer's Company. Only four type foundries were allowed. A seven-year apprenticeship was required and the number of apprentices was limited. No books printed abroad in English could be imported, and all incoming books were to be landed at the Port of London.

Parliament's victory over Charles I destroyed all the machinery for press control because it depended directly on the crown and the courts of High Commission and Star Chamber, which were abolished. In the resulting free-for-all unlicensed printers began pirating titles that had been reserved for members of the Stationer's Company, many of whom were facing ruin. In answer to a petition from the Stationer's Company, Parliament passed the act of 1643, which reactivated much of the Star Chamber ordinance of 1637, but lodged enforcement power in Parliament instead of the crown.

Apparently this act, like its predecessors, was not very effective, for in 1647 Parliament took note of the

> many Seditious, False, and Scandalous Papers and Pamphlets daily
> printed and published in and about the Cities of London and

Westminster and thence dispersed into all parts of this Realm, and other parts beyond the Seas, to the great abuse and prejudice of the People, and insufferable reproach of the proceedings of the Parliament and their Army. . . .[13]

Later acts stiffened the penalties further. No house or room was to be rented to a printer without notice to the Stationer's Company. Notice was required from any persons making parts for printing presses.

Tinker as it would with licensing during the next fifty years, Parliament did not find a satisfactory enforcement procedure. In 1692 a minority of the House of Lords wanted to discontinue licensing, but could not persuade a majority. The licensing act was continued for two more years. During that period the arguments against licensing were circulated widely, and when it came to considering renewal again in 1694, members of Commons produced eighteen reasons for discontinuing it. All practical, the reasons ignored the constitutional principle involved. They were based mostly on logical contradictions in the act itself and on arguments that it did not accomplish its purpose. For example, custom house officials were ordered to open packages of books only in the presence of members of the Stationer's Company, but, asked Commons, how did officials know there were books in the packages until they had been opened? Likewise, smiths were forbidden to undertake iron work for a printing press without notice to the Stationer's Company, but how was a smith to know that a particular piece of iron work was for a press?

The Lords were convinced, for licensing of printing passed out of existence in England in 1694. Tasswell-Langmead, an English constitutional historian, commented:

> It is a noteworthy fact, and a striking example of the predominance of the practical as compared with the theorizing spirit in English politics, that this emancipation of the press . . . attracted scarcely any attention at the time; and was justified by commons . . . without any reference to the great principle involved, and solely on the question of detail concerning the abuses and inconveniences incidental to the censorship.[14]

Censorship in America

Licensing in the Colonies followed the patterns of the mother country. The first printing press in English-speaking America was estab-

---

[13]C. H. Firth and R. S. Raith, eds., *Acts and Ordinances of the Interregnum, 1642–1660*, 3 vols. (London: His Majesty's Stationery Office, 1911), 1: 184.
[14]Tasswell-Langmead, *English Constitutional History*, pp. 756–757.

lished at Cambridge, Massachusetts, in 1639. Its first book, *The Freeman's Oath,* was published that year. Twenty-three years later the general court of Massachusetts prohibited all printing unless previously approved by the licensers named in the act. These men were General Daniel Gookin and the Reverend Mr. Mitchel of Cambridge.[15] Apparently licensing remained a live issue in Massachusetts. The general court reversed itself the following year, setting the press "at liberty as formerly," but re-established censorship in 1664.

Licensing persisted for a time after it had been abolished in England, but gradually it fell into disuse. That it was still a threat to printers is indicated by an incident in 1700. Bartholomew Green of Boston was asked to print a pamphlet in answer to a recent book by the Reverend Increase Mather, president of Harvard College. Green declined to print the pamphlet until it had been approved by the lieutenant-governor. In defending his refusal he published a handbill saying:

> the piece being also Controversial; I concluded it would be altogether inconvenient for me to Print it upon my own head without asking advice; for which I referr'd myself to the Honourable William Stoughton, Esq.; our Lieutenant Governor. . . . Nor was it a new thing to show Copies to the Lieutenant Governor in order to their being Printed. . . .[16]

Massachusetts was not the only Colony to experience licensing of expression. Isaiah Thomas preserved what has become a famous quotation showing the prevailing attitude of those in authority in the late 1600's. Sir William Berkeley, governor of Virginia, wrote:

> I thank God that we have not free schools nor printing; and I hope that we shall not have these hundred years. For learning has brought disobedience and heresy and sects into the world; and printing has divulged them and libels against the government. God keep us from both.[17]

On February 21, 1682, printer John Buckner was called before Governor Culpepper and his council in Virginia and censored for printing the laws of 1680 without the governor's permission.

The unfavorable opinions toward printing in Virginia seem to have stifled it there. There is no record of printing in the Colony from 1682 until about 1729. Until 1766 there was only one printing plant in Virginia

---

[15]Isaiah Thomas, *The History of Printing in America,* 2 vols. (Albany: Joel Munsell, 1874), 1: 59.
[16]Ibid., 1: 423.
[17]Ibid., 1: 330.

and, in the words of Isaiah Thomas, that "was thought to be too much under the control of the governor."

As a proprietary province Pennsylvania was not quite so much under the direct control of the crown as Massachusetts. The governor was appointed by the proprietor (originally William Penn) rather than by the king. Licensing was seldom employed in Pennsylvania, but the lives of printers were made difficult by other controls. Pennsylvania was unique among the Colonies in that the powerful position of the Quakers allowed them to exert what amounted to a licensing power.

William Bradford, the first printer in Pennsylvania, felt the sting of Quaker licensing. The minutes of the Society of Friends for the quarterly meeting of April 10, 1687, show that Bradford was ordered to "show what concerns Friends or Truth before Printing, to the Quarterly Meeting of Philadelphia; and if it requires speed, to the Monthly Meeting."

Even before printing got a start in New York the crown expressed its desire to keep it under control. The royal instructions to Governor Dongan, dated May 29, 1686, have this provision:

> And for as much as great inconvenience may arise by the liberty of printing within our province of New York; you are to provide by all necessary Orders that no person keep any press for printing, nor that any book, pamphlet or other matters whatsoever be printed without your especial leave and license first obtained.[18]

The Zenger Case

Substantially the same clause was included in the orders of several later governors, but it is not in the documents relating to the appointment of Governor John Montgomery in 1727. The instructions to Governor William Cosby, who came to New York in 1732, are not available, but it seems unlikely that they contained any broad power to license the press. Surely Governor Cosby would have relied on such power if it existed to silence John Peter Zenger's *New York Journal*. Instead Zenger was charged with seditious libel when his famous case came to trial in 1735.

Zenger was thrown in jail in 1734 after he allowed his *New York Journal* to be used by Colonial leaders James Alexander and Lewis Morris as the vehicle for attacks charging the Cosby administration with tyranny and oppression. While Zenger languished in jail for eight months, Alex-

---

[18]John R. Brodhead, *Documents Relating to the Colonial History of the State of New York*, 11 vols. (Albany: Weed Parsons, 1856–1861), 3:375.

ander, a lawyer, helped keep the *Journal* publishing and prepared Zenger's defense.

The chief justice, an appointee of Governor Cosby, disbarred Alexander, and Andrew Hamilton of Philadelphia agreed to argue Zenger's case. Generally recognized as the ablest attorney in America, Hamilton staged a brilliant performance based on Alexander's brief. He admitted that Zenger had published the material alleged to be libelous, but urged the jury to assume the power to decide whether the material was actually libelous. The jury, already partial to Zenger, was persuaded by Hamilton's highly emotional arguments, even though British law and most precedent gave the judge power to determine all but the fact of publication.

Hamilton's victory did not set a legal precedent in America, and it was not until 1792 that the Fox libel law officially gave British juries power to determine whether published material was libelous.

Printing was introduced later in the other Colonies and there is little evidence of licensing. Although there is no clear-cut termination of licensing in the Colonies, sentiment had crystallized by the time of the Revolution. The constitutions of every one of the new states contained a guarantee of a free press. This invariably meant "freedom from censorship" or "prior restraint." Under this doctrine authorities cannot require that material be submitted to an official for approval before it is printed, but a publisher is not absolved from punishment for forbidden material after publication. (See Figure 5.1.)

The Pentagon Papers

Despite a long tradition in the United States that favors freedom from prior restraint, the issue is not settled. The Pentagon papers case of 1971 resulted in an uncertain victory for the press. The case began when Dr. Daniel Ellsberg turned over copies of classified documents to the *New York Times*. The papers had to do with U. S. entry into the Vietnam War, and the *Times* editors concluded that it was in the public interest to print them. A U.S. district judge issued a temporary restraining order at the request of the government. When that same judge refused to issue a permanent injunction the case went to the court of appeals and eventually to the Supreme Court.

The Supreme Court ordered the injunction lifted, but the reasoning of some of the justices did not provide much comfort to advocates of a free press. The nine judges offered nine opinions—a remarkable indication of the confusion surrounding the issue. Views ranged from Justice Black's unequivocal defense of the right to publish to others that the question hinged on whether the government could prove that publication posed a threat to national security. Justice Black declared:

I believe that every moment's continuance of the injunctions against these newspapers amounts to a flagrant, indefensible, and continuing violation of the First Amendment. . . . In my view it is unfortunate that some of my Brethren are apparently willing to hold that the publication of news may sometimes be enjoined. Such a holding would make a shambles of the First Amendment.[19]

In his dissent Chief Justice Burger criticized the speed with which the Supreme Court had acted and suggested that, if more time had been taken, a different decision might have been reached:

Of course, the First Amendment right itself is not an absolute, as Justice Holmes so long ago pointed out in his aphorism concerning the

Figure 5.1 Censorship Precedes Publication

If government intervention in publication or broadcast of questionable material precedes publication, it is censorship (prior restraint). In Anglo-American theory, censorship is seldom justified. Appropriate controls may be applied after publication, however.

[19]*New York Times* v. *United States*, 403 U.S. 713 at 714–715 (1971).

right to shout "fire" in a crowded theater if there was no fire. There are other exceptions. . . . Conceivably such exceptions may be lurking in these cases and would have been flushed had they been properly considered in the trial courts, free from unwarranted deadlines and frenetic pressures.[20]

Hair and Procedural Band-Aids

Alleviation of censorship was achieved earlier and is better established for the printed media than for the others, but stage, film, and electronic media have made considerable progress.

As we have seen, the stage passed through a period of strict censorship, but it has emerged as one of this country's most outspoken forms of expression. This has come about largely through a tacit acceptance of the idea that theater audiences are sufficiently mature to make their own judgments in matters of taste and political expression. The idea that the stage should be accorded some protection from prior restraint was cautiously sanctioned by the U.S. Supreme Court in 1975.

In that year the Court held in a 5–4 decision that the city of Chattanooga, Tennessee, had failed to provide adequate procedural safeguards when it refused to allow a performance of the controversial musical *Hair* in the civic auditorium. *Hair,* which included on-stage nudity, a liberal sprinkling of "street language," and simulated sexual intercourse, was on road tour in 1972 when the incident occurred. Having reviewed prior restraint in relation to other media, Justice Harry Blackmun, writing for the majority, said:

> The theory underlying the requirement of safeguards is applicable here with equal if not greater force. An administrative board assigned to screening stage productions—and keeping off stage anything not deemed culturally uplifting or healthful—may well be less responsive than a court, an independent branch of the government, to constitutionally protected interests in free expression. And if judicial review is made unduly onerous, by reason of delay or otherwise, the board's determination in practice may be final.[21]

While agreeing with the Court's conclusion, Justice William O. Douglas objected in a separate opinion to the implication that censorship might

[20]Ibid., at 749.
[21]*Southeastern Promotions, Ltd.,* v. *Conrad,* 95 S. Ct., 1239 at 1247–1248 (1975).

have been justified "by the simple application of a few procedural band-aids."[22]

Film: Early Control

As a medium appealing to a much broader spectrum of the public than the stage, film has a turbulent history of censorship in the United States. For many years censorship was justified by the courts on the ground that films are a business and an entertainment and therefore not worthy of First Amendment protection.

Even in their early days as peep shows, the movies packed in audiences. In the nickelodeons (the admission was five cents) patrons could see the early storytelling movies that followed *The Great Train Robbery* of 1903. By 1907 there were about five thousand nickelodeons of various size and decor in the country.[23] In Chicago alone there were 116 nickelodeons, 18 ten-cent vaudeville houses, and 19 penny arcades. These had an estimated daily attendance of 100,000.

It was inevitable that this great new phenomenon would attract the attention of reformers and editorial writers. A 1907 *Chicago Tribune* editorial said movies ministered to the "lower passions of childhood," that they were "wholly vicious," and that "there is no voice raised to defend the majority of the five-cent theaters because they cannot be defended. They are hopelessly bad."

But the movie houses stayed full. In the 1920's movie attendance reached 50 million a week and produced half a billion dollars a year in revenue. As the movies boomed so did the ardor of the censors. The 1920's were years of change. Economic prosperity allowed the excesses of the flapper age. Movies reflected and added impetus to these developments, which disturbed many. Since they were highly visible, movies got much of the blame.

Movies were not all that innocent. A certain willingness to pander to the audience is indicated by the titles of some of the films of these years: *A Shocking Night, Lying Lips, Luring Lips, Red Hot Romance, Flame of Youth, Virgin Paradise, Scrambled Wives, The Truant Husband, The Fourteenth Love, Her Purchase Price, Plaything of Broadway.*

There were demands for a federal censorship law, and when none was forthcoming, several states and cities passed their own. In 1907 Chicago became the first city to institute censorship of films. The chief of po-

---

[22]Ibid., at 1249.
[23]Murray Schumach, *The Face on the Cutting Room Floor* (New York: William Morrow, 1964), p. 16.

lice, who was named censor, soon had refused permits to two hundred pictures. Jake Block, operator of a number of nickel and dime theaters, deliberately exhibited *The James Boys* without permission to test the constitutionality of the ordinance. Block argued that the law discriminated against motion picture exhibitors, delegated discretionary and judicial powers to the chief of police, took property without due process of law, and was unreasonable and oppressive. The Illinois Supreme Court held that inasmuch as the ordinance applied to all motion picture operators alike it did not discriminate; that it did not delegate to the police chief discretionary or judicial powers, but laid down guidance when it told him to ban immoral or obscene films; and that it was a proper exercise of police power over public morals.[24]

Encouraged by this decision, many other cities enacted their own censorship. By 1940 more than thirty-two cities, among them some of the country's largest, were censoring films. The first state censorship law was passed by the Pennsylvania legislature in 1911. This statute established a board of three censors authorized to review all films to be shown in the state. They were empowered to pass all that were "moral" and "proper" and to ban those found "sacreligious, obscene, indecent," or such as tend, in the board's view, to debase or corrupt morals.[25] Ohio and Kansas passed licensing laws in 1913 and Maryland in 1916. New York established censorship in 1921 and Virginia in 1932. Also in 1932 Massachusetts ordered that only films "in keeping with the character of the day and not inconsistent with its due observance" could be shown on Sunday.[26]

In an unanimous decision in 1915, the United States Supreme Court held that motion pictures did not come under the free press protection of the First Amendment. The Court held: "The exhibition of motion pictures is a business pure and simple, originated and conducted for profit, like other spectacles, not to be regarded . . . as part of the press of the country or as organs of public opinion."[27] This almost casual dismissal of the motion picture's right to free expression was the final word of the Supreme Court on the subject for thirty-seven years.

With this endorsement, film censorship became an established practice. No additional state censorship laws were passed, but cities increased their activity, with an estimated ninety of them censoring films in 1950. The six states that regularly censored films had more impact than their number indicates. They were among the more populous states, with a popu-

---

[24]*Block* v. *Chicago*, 239 Ill. 251, 87 N.E. 1011 (1909).

[25]Pennsylvania Laws 1067 (June 19, 1911).

[26]Richard S. Randall, *Censorship of the Movies, the Social and Political Control of a Mass Medium* (Madison: University of Wisconsin Press, 1968), p.12.

[27]*Mutual Film Corporation* v. *Industrial Commission of Ohio*, 236 U.S. 230 at 244 (1915).

lation of 36.6 million in 1940. They also included nearly all of the nation's thirty-one motion picture distribution centers, most of which served cities outside their own states. Thus Maine, New Hampshire, Rhode Island, and Vermont would receive films censored in Massachusetts; Missourians would see those censored in Kansas; and Kentuckians and West Virginians were forced to abide by the restrictions imposed by Ohio censors. The censor boards were a major influence on the film makers, who tended to tailor their films to pass the requirements of states and cities with censors.

Most of the state censorship laws provided only general guidelines to their censor boards. Adjectives such as *obscene* and *indecent* leave much room for interpretation. Mrs. Lucy H. Love, secretary of the Pennsylvania Board of Censors, told how the board applied the laws:

> We keep an analysis sheet on each picture giving such details as the characters played by the first four or five actors (so called leads), number of killings, suicides, drinkings, etc.
>
> In Pennsylvania, the films are viewed with the following matters in mind. We make eliminations of new methods of crime, sabotage, propaganda, sex, cruelty to children, cruelty to animals, brutality, profanity, sacrilege, indecent exposure.[28]

Kansas adopted the most specific published guidelines. It barred

> ridicule . . . of any religious sect, or peculiar characteristics of any race or people or any public official . . . evil suggestion in the dress of comedy characters . . . loose conduct between men and women and, whenever possible, barroom scenes and social drinking . . . display of nude human figures . . . crimes and criminal methods . . . prolonged and passionate love scenes when suggestive of immorality . . . ridicule or facetious remarks about motherhood or scenes pertaining to childbirth.[29]

Licensing of expression declined in the United States in the years following the Block decision of 1909, although films were slow to benefit. In 1925 the Supreme Court took the first step in protecting freedom of expression from interference by the states.[30] This was reinforced by later decisions. In 1931 the Court reversed a decision of the Minnesota courts that would have allowed prior censorship of a newspaper on grounds that previous issues showed a tendency to publish illegal material.[31]

[28]Letter to Reta R. Vanderburgh dated March 27, 1944.
[29]Kansas Gen. Stat. (1935) #51.101–51.112.
[30]*Gitlow* v. *New York*, 268 U.S. 652 (1925).
[31]*Near* v. *Minnesota*, 283 U.S. 697 (1931).

The Second World War strengthened films as a free medium of expression. By order of President Franklin D. Roosevelt films were not subjected to war censorship; and Congress, in a price-control bill, exempted films from censorship as a condition of sale or distribution. During the war, too, the United States signed a resolution at an inter-American conference in Mexico City urging that controls on press, radio, and film be abandoned when the war ended.

The Miracle: Some Freedom

Finally in 1952 the Supreme Court reversed its earlier decision. In the *Miracle* case[32] the Court declared that "motion pictures are a significant medium for the communication of ideas" and thus protected by the free speech clauses of the First and Fourteenth amendments. The decision did not go all the way in freeing motion pictures from licensing, taking note of the possibility that movies, because of their vividness, can be a greater force for evil than other media. The Court held that this hypothesis might be "relevant in determining the permissible scope of community control, but it does not authorize substantially unbridled censorship. . . ." Thus limitations should be recognized only in exceptional cases and states should be required to demonstrate the need for special restraint in each case. A freer atmosphere was encouraged, but licensing was preserved.

In the ensuing confusion the scope of motion picture subject matter was considerably enlarged. In regard to a film version of D. H. Lawrence's novel *Lady Chatterley's Lover*, the Court held that a standard of "sexual immorality" that banned the depiction of adultery as a desirable way of life was a limitation to the free flow of ideas.[33]

Printed media had been largely free of licensing for years when the Supreme Court considered the question directly as applied to films in 1961. Times Film Corporation, a distributor of foreign films, decided to force the issue by refusing to submit a film, *Don Juan,* to the Chicago Board of Censors. Based on the Mozart opera *Don Giovanni,* the motion picture apparently contained no objectionable material. The company argued that the city could, if it wished, proceed against the film after it had been shown in public. Nevertheless, the board refused to grant a license that would have permitted the initial showing. Thus the licensing issue was directly joined.

[32]*Burstyn* v. *Wilson,* 343 U.S. 495 (1952). The case concerned Roberto Rossellini's film, *The Miracle,* which told of a simple girl who believed the stranger who raped her was St. Joseph. The charge was sacrilege.

[33]*Kingsley International Pictures* v. *Board of Regents,* 360 U.S. 684 (1952).

In a 5–4 decision the Supreme Court upheld the licensing power, rejecting the claim that the distributor had the right "to exhibit, at least once, any and every kind of motion picture." Writing the majority opinion[34] Justice Clark said that the company's view would result in stripping a state of power to prevent obscenity, which is not protected against prior restraint. Clark also returned to earlier arguments that motion pictures may have a greater capacity for harm than other methods of expression. Motion pictures, he said, are not necessarily subject to exactly the same rules governing other media.

In a dissenting opinion Chief Justice Earl Warren argued that the majority decision opened the door to unlimited motion picture censorship and possibly to censorship of all media. He was particularly concerned about the lack of procedural safeguards in the Chicago licensing system. An exhibitor could suffer irreparable damage because of the time consumed by litigation, he said, pointing out that the present case had taken nearly three years. Warren also objected that the majority opinion had made no effort to prove the greater impact of motion pictures over other media and said the point was irrelevant anyway. Even assuming greater impact the Court could not, under the Constitution, treat one medium differently from another.

In a separate dissenting opinion Justices Douglas and Black recorded their view that any licensing of films constituted an abridgment of the First Amendment.

The majority opinion in the *Times Film* case might very well have led to an increase in censorship, but the opposite actually occurred. Shortly afterward the courts of last appeal in Pennsylvania, Oregon, and Georgia held that motion picture censorship violated their state constitutions. Ohio and Massachusetts courts had previously banned censorship on the basis of the First Amendment.

The U.S. Supreme Court dealt a further blow to movie censorship in 1965.[35] While holding that prior censorship "may be permissible with respect to films which are demonstrably outside the scope of constitutional protection," the Court went on to express so many doubts about procedural safeguards that the work of the censorship boards was made almost impossible. Maryland's procedures were found to be inadequate because they did not provide prompt judicial review and because the review procedures favored the censor instead of the exhibitor.

This decision left the philosophical question of motion picture licensing unresolved, but it further weakened it in practice. Procedures were found inadequate in New York, Kansas, Virginia, and the city of Memphis, and legislative bodies failed to pass new legislation. In some other

[34]*Times Film Corporation v. Chicago*, 365 U.S. 43 (1961).
[35]*Freedman v. Maryland*, 380 U.S. 51 (1965).

jurisdictions, new legislation has been passed requiring speedy judicial review of refusals to license and putting the burden of proof on the censoring body.

More recent cases show an effort to comply with the principle that an exhibitor has a right to show a film until there is a judicial determination that it is obscene or otherwise illegal. *Heller* v. *New York*,[36] which came to the Supreme Court in 1973, is an example. Officers watched part of a film that was being shown in a theater, and then an assistant district attorney requested a New York criminal court judge to review it. The judge bought a ticket and watched the film in its theater showing. Immediately thereafter he signed a search warrant ordering the seizure of the film as evidence as well as three "John Doe" warrants for the arrest of the theater manager, the projectionist, and the ticket taker. (Action was dropped against the last two on motion of the district attorney.) The film, entitled *Blue Movie*, showed a nude couple in what the judge called "the ultimate sex act." In the trial three persons testified as expert witnesses for the exhibitor. They included a professor of sociology and a newspaper writer. The theater manager claimed not only that the film had redeeming merit, but also that the seizure of the film without an adversary hearing violated the Fourteenth Amendment.

Chief Justice Burger, writing the opinion of the Court, held that the seizure was justified when it was to secure evidence to be used in court. He said that if other copies of the film were not available, the authorities should permit the seized copy to be duplicated so that the showing could continue pending a decision. The case was remanded to the state courts for consideration of the substantive issue, whether the film should be judged obscene in the light of Supreme Court rulings in other cases.

Justice Douglas dissented on grounds that the New York obscenity statute violated the First Amendment. Justice Brennan, in a joint dissent with Justices Stewart and Marshall, held that the New York obscenity statute was too broad.

What Is Obscene?

The Supreme Court has been concerned with procedural protections but has shown little inclination to accord First Amendment protection to material regarded as obscene. In a 1973 decision Justice Burger said that "it is now well established that obscene material is not protected by the First Amendment."[37]

[36]413 U.S. 483 (1973).
[37]*United States* v. *Twelve 200-Foot Reels of Super 8 mm Film*, 413 U.S. 123 at 126 (1973).

In a dissenting opinion Justice Douglas stated, "I know of no constitutional way by which a book, tract, paper, postcard, or film may be made contraband because of its contents." He said the Constitution did not purport to give the federal government censorship or oversight into literature or artistic productions, save as they might be governed by copyright or patent laws. "The First Amendment," Justice Douglas wrote, "was the product of a robust, not a prudish age." The four decades that preceded it saw the publication virtually without government molestation of two classics of pornographic literature: William King's *The Toast* and John Cleland's *Fanny Hill*. This was an age, Douglas said, when Benjamin Franklin wrote his "Advice to a Young Man in Choosing a Mistress" and "A Letter to the Royal Academy at Brussels." Douglas wrote:

> The advent of the printing press spurred censorship in England, but the ribald and the obscene were not, at first, within the scope of that which was officially banned. The censorship of the Star Chamber and the licensing of books under the Tudors and the Stuarts was aimed at the blasphemous or heretical, the seditious or treasonous.[38]

The proper methods for controlling obscenity have troubled our best judicial minds for generations. Even more difficult has been the problem of defining what is obscene. The statutes are little help with this. Usually they simply add a string of adjectives like "lewd," "lascivious," and "pornographic." The courts, in their efforts to arrive at a workable concept, have considered four factors:

1. The likelihood that the material will incite sexual emotions in the receiver
2. The presence or absence of redeeming social value
3. The manner in which the material is advertised and the manner in which the potential audience is alerted as to the nature of the material
4. The extent to which the material is in accord with prevailing community standards

Through a long list of state and federal cases judges have addressed themselves to the problem of defining obscenity by various interpretations of these basic considerations. Invariably the results have been inconclusive—so vague, in fact, that a publisher or film maker has extreme difficulty in predicting whether a given passage will be considered obscene or pornographic.

In the line of cases two stand out: *Roth* v. *United States*[39] and *Miller* v.

---

[38]Ibid., at 134–135.
[39]354 U.S. 476 (1957).

"Our decision on pornography is NO!"   "... And YES ...!"

From the Louisville *Courier-Journal*, June 6, 1974. © 1974 The Courier-Journal. Reprinted with permission.

California.[40] Justice Brennan, writing the majority opinion in the *Roth* case, declared that the question of obscenity hinged on "whether to the average person, applying contemporary community standards, the dominant theme of the material taken as a whole appears to prurient interests."

In the *Miller* case Chief Justice Warren Burger prescribed the following test:

> The basic guidelines for the trier of fact must be: (a) whether "the average person, applying contemporary community standards" would find that the work, taken as a whole, appeals to the prurient interest . . .
> (b) whether the work depicts or describes, in a patently offensive way, sexual conduct specifically defined by the applicable state law, and
> (c) whether the work, taken as a whole, lacks serious literary, artistic, political or scientific value.

Those who find such statements vague and of little help in specific cases are in good company, as the frustrated disputes found in minority opinions attest. "Prurient interest" is itself a vague concept. Who is the "average person"? What is "patently offensive" to one person may be something different to another. Perhaps the most elusive concept of all is "contemporary community standards." In the *Miller* case the majority decreed a return to local standards on the ground that they would differ in different parts of the country. This is a valid idea, but not too helpful. The immediate question arises as to how large a community should be considered: New York State or New York City? Are Manhattan's standards different from those of the Bronx or Staten Island? Even if one could define the appropriate community there is no guidance as to how its standards shall be defined. Sometimes expert witnesses are called, but there is no real agreement as to who is the mythical "average person" and therefore the designated expert. If it comes down to a jury decision much will depend on the make-up of that particular jury.

It is no wonder that courts and the public are intrigued as well as plagued by the difficulties of maintaining community standards of morality in print and motion pictures. The problem increases when it is applied to the broadcast media.

Censorship of Broadcasting

The battles of print and film foreshadowed the troubles of radio and television. Advocates of censorship build a strong case. They begin

[40]413 U.S. 15 (1973).

with all the reasons for censoring print, add those that accrue to films because they may have more impact, then top those with the final clincher —that radio and television have to be licensed to avoid chaos in the radio spectrum.

An act of 1912 theoretically conferred upon the secretary of commerce the power to regulate frequencies of broadcasters, but when Secretary Herbert C. Hoover tried to penalize the Zenith Radio Corporation for using an unauthorized frequency in 1926 the statute was found ineffective. The Radio Act of 1927 succeeded in providing the necessary authority and included the provision that broadcasters should operate in the public interest. In subsequent amendments Congress has provided elaborate machinery in the Federal Communications Commission (FCC) for regulating the technical aspects of broadcasting. In addition to assigning channels to broadcasters, this includes regulating the strength of signal and other engineering aspects. These require a large staff and elaborate records, but they are not so onerous as the task, also assigned to the FCC, to monitor the requirement that broadcasters must operate in the public interest.

The theory that supports this requirement is clear-cut. The number of broadcast stations is limited by the capacity of the radio spectrum. This limits the number of possible stations, so use of a channel becomes a privilege contingent upon acting in the public interest. The license is renewed every three years and can be withdrawn if the station is not deemed to be operating in the public interest.

The Supreme Court put it this way in *Red Lion Broadcasting Co., Inc.* v. *United States*:[41]

> Because of the scarcity of radio frequencies, the Government is permitted to put restraints on licensees in favor of others whose views should be expressed on this unique medium. But the people as a whole retain their interest in free speech by radio and their collective right to have the medium function consistently with the ends and purposes of the First Amendment. It is the right of the viewers and listeners, not the right of the broadcasters which is important. . . . It is the purpose of the First Amendment to preserve an uninhibited marketplace of ideas in which truth will ultimately prevail, rather than to countenance monopolies of the market, whether it be by the Government itself or a private licensee.

In *Red Lion* the Court casts the FCC in a role that approaches the difficulty of walking on water. The FCC is to see that broadcasters do not interfere with the First Amendment rights of their listeners. At the same time the FCC is under pressure to ensure the First Amendment rights of the broadcasters.

[41]395 U.S. 367 (1969).

FCC regulations to ensure operation in the public interest require radio and television stations to present discussion of public issues and require that these issues be given fair coverage. If one side of a controversial issue is presented the station management is obligated to seek out other views even if none are volunteered.

In famous Section 315 of Chapter 47 of the U.S. Code, Congress requires broadcasters to provide equal time to all qualified candidates for a given public office if they provide time for any of the candidates.

This glance at a few of the regulations under which radio and television operate indicates the complexity of the task for broadcasters as well as the FCC.

Broadcasters contend that arguments based on the limited spectrum do not fit reality. Richard C. Wald, president of NBC News, noted at a Nieman panel discussion that actually there are fewer daily newspapers than broadcast outlets. He said:

> I don't think there are three cities that have competing daily newspapers, but there aren't three cities that don't have at least five competing broadcast organizations. In the city where I live, there are forty-two competing radio stations and seven competing television stations. There are three newspapers and they hardly compete.[42]

He argued that if broadcasting is regulated print media should be regulated in the same way:

> Many of the dangers of the First Amendment come from deciding that there ought to be a law that will set people straight by setting up outside agencies to dictate to the press what it is that ought to be done. Obviously in this case the outside agency is . . . the FCC. And it seems to be directed against television or broadcasting. . . . The fact of the matter . . . is . . . some believe that those rules that apply to broadcasting ought also to apply to the press. I do, too.

The Supreme Court took the opposite view in *Miami Herald* v. *Tornillo*,[43] as we shall see in Chapter 14.

Contempt and Free Expression

Among the inherent powers of Anglo-American courts is contempt. It is the power by which courts enforce order, require the attendance of witnesses, force testimony from witnesses, and enforce deci-

[42]*Nieman Reports*, June 1973, p. 13.
[43]418 U.S. 241 (1974).

sions. If a disturbance in court threatens to disrupt proceedings, the judge can quell it by citing the offender for contempt. If a person disregards a subpoena ordering him to appear in court he can be declared in contempt and arrested. If a defendant fails to pay a court-ordered fine she can be held in contempt and punished. It is a necessary power, for without it our courts could not function. Legislative bodies also exercise an inherent contempt power on the theory that they must be able to force disclosure of information as the basis for legislation.

Direct contempt is the power by which courts and legislatures punish for actions within their presence. If a witness refuses to answer a question, the court's direct contempt power can be used in punishment. *Constructive contempt* is the term for the court's power to punish for actions committed outside the presence of the court, but that the judge construes to be contemptuous. There has never been any serious questioning of the power of direct contempt, but the power of constructive contempt is less certain. It is well established in England but has frequently been questioned in the United States.

On March 2, 1831, Congress enacted legislation that provided that the contempt power should be limited to

> the misbehavior of any person or persons in the presence of the said courts, or so near thereto as to obstruct the administration of justice, or the misbehavior of any of the officers of the said courts, party, juror, witness, or any other person or persons, to any lawful order . . . of the said courts.[44]

The law was enacted in response to the action of U.S. District Judge James H. Peck, who had imprisoned and disbarred an individual for criticizing an opinion that was up for appeal. Thus the statute would seem to clearly disallow the power to punish contempt by publication. This is the power by which newspapers and broadcasters are sometimes punished for disseminating information or opinion that a judge rules prejudices a court proceeding.

This law was a model for state legislation, and by 1860 twenty-three states had enacted similar statutes. Nevertheless, during the last four decades of the nineteenth century and first four of the twentieth, both state and federal courts reassumed the power to punish for constructive contempt.

The Supreme Court itself sanctioned this interpretation in a 1918 decision,[45] holding that the expression "so near thereto" should apply to cause rather than actual physical proximity. In his vigorous dissent Justice Holmes said:

[44]28 USCA #1385.
[45]*Toledo Newspaper Co.* v. *United States*, 247 U.S. 402 (1918).

When it is considered how contrary it is to our practice and ways of thinking for the same person to be accuser and sole judge in a matter which, if he be sensitive, may involve strong personal feeling, I should expect the power to be limited by the necessities of the case "to insure order and decorum in their presence."

More than two decades later the Supreme Court accepted Justice Holmes's view in part when it applied the "clear and present danger test" to contempt actions. Previously it had held material to be contemptuous if it had a "reasonable tendency" to cause major evils.[46] This doctrine was further strengthened in 1946 when the court reversed a Florida decision that had held executives of the *Miami Herald* guilty of contempt for editorials that charged that judges were delaying convictions of criminal defendants through technicalities. This was held despite what were said to be gross inaccuracies in the editorials. The majority held that the danger to the administration of justice did not have the "clearness and immediacy" necessary for a contempt citation.[47]

Some state courts and lower federal courts indicate that the issue is not settled. It requires the balancing of the right to a free trial against the right of free expression. A basic tenet is that the defendant must be tried only on evidence submitted in court and only on the facts relating to the specific incident that brought about the indictment. Newspaper and broadcast media have been charged at times with so prejudicing a community against an individual that it became impossible for him or her to receive a fair trial.[48] To prevent this courts have used their contempt power to punish publication of a defendant's previous criminal record. A common procedure in England, this practice has gained some acceptance in the United States.

In the 1970's the stands of proponents of both sides moderated. The media tended to use restraint in reporting events surrounding arrests, and bar associations urged trial attorneys to keep their public statements to a minimum.

Disclosure of Sources

Another use of the contempt power has resulted in conflict between press and law enforcement agencies. This is the attempt by courts, grand juries, and legislative bodies to force reporters to disclose their

[46]*Bridges v. California*, 314 U.S. 252 (1941).
[47]*Pennekamp v. Florida*, 328 U.S. 331 (1946).
[48]Cases cited as illustrations are the trials of Richard Bruno Hauptmann in the Lindbergh kidnaping case in 1935 and of Dr. Sam Sheppard in the death of his wife in 1954.

sources of confidential information. The media argue that if they are forced to reveal sources their effectiveness will be curtailed because individuals will be reluctant to furnish information. The counter arguments from law enforcement agencies is that their work is hampered when anyone is provided immunity from the requirement to disclose information needed by officials.

The issue was far from resolved in the mid-1970's, although twenty states had shield laws granting varying degrees of protection from forced disclosure. In 1972 the Supreme Court ruled that the First Amendment does not provide such protection.[49] This decision intensified efforts to enact a federal shield law, and a number of versions of such a law were introduced in Congress. Even representatives of the press were not in agreement as to the desirability of such a law, with some leaders insisting that the only reliable protection was in the First Amendment; and that such a law would set a bad precedent, for what Congress could grant it might later decide it could take away.

The Media and Self-Regulation

Sometimes the media have attempted to temper governmental censorship by imposing limits on themselves. When a single station, magazine, or newspaper restrains itself to avoid governmental censorship no one can call it censorship. But the term *self-censorship* has been applied to attempts of industrywide organizations to control content and therefore avoid official censorship. The softer expression, *self-regulation*, is more exact because it recognizes that the control is essentially voluntary.

Voluntary though it is, the control can be strict and effective, as the film industry illustrated. The creation on March 11, 1922, of the Motion Picture Producers and Distributors of America, Inc. (MPPDA), was an answer to threats of censorship and attacks on film content by pressure groups. Will H. Hays, president of the organization, made that quite clear in a report twenty years later describing its genesis: "Constant threat of investigation and litigation afflicted the industry. . . . There was prospect that some 22 censorship bills would become law."[50]

Essentially Hays and his assistants interpreted the various censorship practices and the complaints of pressure groups such as the Legion of De-

[49]*Branzburg v. Hayes*, 408 U.S. 665 (1972).
[50]Will H. Hays, *The Motion Picture in a World at War*, Twentieth Anniversary Report of the Motion Picture Producers and Distributors of America, Inc., March 30, 1942, p. 22.

cency (a Roman Catholic group) to the producers. A code developed by the "Hays Office," as it came to be called, prescribed caution in handling bedroom scenes, crime, religion, and other sensitive areas, and it forbade explicit sex, profanity, and obscenity. Producers were required to submit every new film for review and to make changes if violations were found. Only then could the film receive the MPPDA stamp of approval, which authorized its showing in the theaters of America.

As court decisions opened the way for more freedom in subject matter the film industry added a new wrinkle to its efforts to reach an accord with interest groups. Under Jack Valenti, a successor to Will Hays, the MPPDA began in 1968 to classify films so that moviegoers would know in advance what to expect. This allowed producers to make films "for mature audiences" dealing more explicitly with sex and other subjects not considered suitable for younger, more impressionable audiences. Under the system that evolved films are listed in one of four classifications: G (general audiences), PG (parental guidance suggested), R (restricted, children must be accompanied by adult), and X (children forbidden). This latest accommodation between the industry and the interest groups appears to have worked better than some earlier attempts. It tries to put into effect the sound principle that people should be allowed to decide for themselves and their children the nature of material to which they wish to expose themselves.

Liked? No Way!

Trying to entertain many while offending few has driven broadcasters, too, to self-regulation. The National Association of Broadcasters (NAB) has developed elaborate codes, and networks and local stations have their own systems for controlling content.

The radio and television codes of the NAB contain admonitions about special responsibilities to education and culture and to the needs of children. They are quite specific about certain advertising practices, including the number of commercials within a given time. The television code, for example, provides that "in prime time the number of program interruptions shall not exceed two within any 30-minute program or four within any 60-minute program."[51] It also provides:

> In both prime time and all other time, the following interruption standard shall apply within programs of 15 minutes or less in length:

[51]*Broadcasting Yearbook*, 1973, p. D-36.

5-minute program—1 interruption;
10-minute program—2 interruptions;
15-minute program—2 interruptions.[52]

The code also provides that: "News, weather, sports and special events programs are exempt from the interruption standard because of the nature of such programs."[53]

The NAB code is formally accepted only by the stations that are members of the organization, and questions have been raised about the effectiveness of the organization's monitoring system. Although the NAB has never achieved a control over broadcasting comparable to that once exercised over film producers by the Hays Office it has helped to raise standards. It is also a convenient device through which the industry can demonstrate its good faith. For example, it cooperated when the networks accepted the urging of FCC Chairman Richard E. Wiley and established a "family viewing hour" during the 1975–1976 season. Under the plan the hours from 7 P.M. to 9 P.M. Eastern time were cleared of excessive sex and violence so that children could watch without danger of corruption.

One of the ironies of the family viewing period, like many good works, is that it attracted as much criticism as praise. It was ridiculed as an effort to appease those who would clean up television while really allowing more sex and gore later in the evening. Other critics asked about the children in the Midwest, where family viewing was scheduled from 6 to 8 P.M. They argued it was unlikely that many children were packed off to bed at eight. Perhaps the hardest blow came from a group of television producers, writers, and performers who filed suit charging that the family-viewing-time policy violated their First Amendment rights of free expression.

Each of the networks maintains an in-house censor. Herminio Traviesas, who heads NBC's section on standards, has a staff of forty in New York plus twelve "program editors" on the West Coast. Few question the right and duty of networks to control the content of their programs, but the job is not a popular one. George Schlatter, producer of the "Cher" show, said, "There's no way for them to be liked."[54]

Sometimes the censorship involves something other than sex and violence, as Newsweek reported:

> Recently, the comedy writers for CBS's "Cher" concocted a family-hour version of the nightly news, titled "All Good News." Characters playing Walter Cronkite, Eric Sevareid and Roger Mudd were supposed to appear wearing—respectively—mouse ears, a bunny suit and

[52]Ibid.
[53]Ibid.
[54]Newsweek, November 24, 1975, p. 85.

a tie that flashed "Miami." Decidedly unamused, CBS insisted that the idea be abandoned—and that's the way it was.[55]

Printed media, through normal editing procedures, maintain their own standards, but there has been little industrywide control for either newspapers or magazines. Any attempt to devise an industrywide control group is likely to be challenged as opening the door to violation of press freedoms, as we shall see in Chapter 14.

Media Freedom and Individual Liberty

As populations increase and cities and nations become more crowded our institutions increase in size. This is especially true of the two institutions that concern us here: government and the communications media. Government increases in sheer bulk—more people work for it, it spends more of society's money, and it affects each individual in more ways and more directly. The same is true of the media. As nations develop industrially and gain more population the number of media units increases and so does the time that each person devotes to the media.

As these two great institutions increase in size and pervasiveness they come in contact, and conflict, more frequently. We have examined some of the patterns by which this relationship is controlled. As we have seen, sometimes a government solves its problems relating to the media simply by taking them over. Licensing is another system by which these relationships are controlled. Still another is punishing certain media practices by use of the contempt power or other means. These are formally established patterns that are recognizable and thus frequently discussed.

Side by side with the formal, recognized patterns of direct control by ownership, licensing, or punishment is another system, which relies on rewards. The post office, through its second-class mailing rates, has encouraged the publication of newspapers and magazines. Often second-class material is carried at a loss, so it amounts to a federal subsidy. This is a reward system with a built-in punishment. Congress has provided that certain kinds of material cannot be carried at favorable second-class rates—thereby influencing editors to follow acceptable standards for content.

Many other informal reward and punishment systems exist. Sometimes an official favors a given reporter with exclusive information. The Nixon administration was accused of offering television stations the security of a

[55]Ibid., p. 86.

five-year instead of three-year licensing period in return for more favorable news treatment. The carrot-and-stick trick takes many forms.

But the reward-punishment system is not entirely one-sided. The media have their weapons, too. Favorable publicity is essential for a candidate for office or to get a program through Congress. By giving or withholding coverage the media exert powerful influence. In this chapter we have taken the traditional approach, studying some of the government controls over the media. It is helpful also to study the relationship in a different framework—to understand that government and media are two power centers that influence each other as they interact.

In a democratic society each claims to speak for the people. And each is instrumental in its effect; that is, both media and government exist to further the objectives of citizens, and ideally each would have no purposes of its own. Such an expectation is not entirely realistic, since most organizations tend to adopt policies that will promote their own survival and growth.

It is the citizen who ultimately wins or loses in the natural conflicts between media and government. As government control of the media becomes restrictive each citizen is diminished in the ability to make his or her own decisions. If the government absorbs the media or makes their work impossible the citizen loses the ability to function in the complex world, where most of the information he or she needs has to come through the media. On the other hand, if the media entirely dominate the government, or if they pursue their own interests rather than those of their audiences, the citizen is again left without a means to find the way through the maze of civilization.

So a workable society in which each individual has an opportunity to be a participant depends on a healthy government-press relationship. One of the great successes of the American system has been its ability to maintain an effective tension between these two great institutions. There have been excesses on both sides, but each time a reaction has set in early enough to balance the powers.

Since ultimate effectiveness goes to whatever institution can maintain the public confidence, the attitude of each individual is a factor. After the Watergate excesses of the 1970's public confidence in the government decreased and there was some increase in confidence in the media. Since government usually has the upper hand and since it is able to present a more unified policy and enforce it with police power, it is usually the greater threat to individual liberties. Many dedicated reporters have gone to jail for a principle, while few government officials have made the same trip for the same purpose.

At the same time a fat and contented press can be almost as effective an apologist for government excesses as a press openly kept by the government. In some ways it is more persuasive because it is less suspect.

The formal and informal practices by which the power relationships between government and press are maintained are critical ones that need constant re-examination. A press corps constantly at the throat of government can be destructive, but so can a too-friendly press. Health for the body politic consists in adjusting the rules so that the parties are wary of each other. Thus perhaps the public can keep media channels clear enough to safeguard individual liberties even as institutions increase in size and complexity.

Suggestions for Further Reading

Carmen, Ira H. *Movies, Censorship and the Law.* Ann Arbor: University of Michigan Press, 1966.
One of the standard treatments of film law.

De Vol, Kenneth, ed. *Mass Media and the Supreme Court: The Legacy of the Warren Years.* New York: Hastings House, 1971.
Considers control of motion pictures and printed media.

Gillmor, Donald M., and Barron, Jerome A. *Mass Communication Law: Cases and Comments.* 2nd ed. St. Paul: West Publishing, 1974.
One of the two leading texts in its field. The other, listed below, is by Nelson and Teeter.

Hachten, William A. *The Supreme Court on Freedom of the Press: Decisions and Dissents.* Ames: Iowa State University Press, 1968.
An analysis of Supreme Court decisions, emphasizing more recent cases.

Knightley, Phillip. *The First Casualty.* New York: Harcourt Brace Jovanovich, 1975.
Argues that truth is "the first casualty" of war.

Nelson, Harold L., and Teeter, Dwight L., Jr. *Law of Mass Communications.* Mineola, N.Y.: Foundation Press, 1973.
A comprehensive text.

Randall, Richard S. *Censorship of the Movies: The Social and Political Control of a Mass Medium.* Madison: University of Wisconsin Press, 1967.
Not easy reading, but a systematic presentation.

A glance back at Part Two and ahead at Part Three

In Part Two we considered the expectations that a democratic society generally holds for its communication media. To survive a newspaper, station, or other medium must somehow provide a service that meets the needs of a group of people who form its audience. The successful media hold their audiences by an adroit mixture of information and entertainment. Audiences tend to be fickle, and sometimes in trying to hold them the media provide a lean mixture—mostly froth with little substance.

One of the responsibilities is to keep the mixture as rich as possible: rich in information and worthwhile entertainment. Other responsibilities include avoiding unnecessary damage to the reputation of individuals, helping to maintain stability without choking off innovations, and, most important, keeping the information needs of the audience paramount to that of any special interest, even the owner's.

In Chapter 5 we saw how some expectations are made explicit and required by law. We saw that open and closed societies take different views toward their media. In totalitarian regimes control is strict, and often the government or the ruling party owns the media, the better to control them. In open societies the media are freer and more likely to be privately owned. Indeed, one of the marks of an open society is the ability of citizens to exchange ideas freely. Censorship has been applied to all the media. Broadcasters are perhaps most subject to censorship because a government can easily withdraw the privilege of using the air waves. Most of the Earth's population must still put up with media that are heavily censored or actually owned by government.

Many media regulate themselves to protect their image before the public. The movies are a prime example. An industrywide code has existed for many years. Early in its history it limited sexual and blasphemous content of films and other material that might offend community standards. More recently the film industry has provided a classification system by which moviegoers can be forewarned of content to which they might not wish to expose themselves or their children.

In Part Three we shall turn our attention to another aspect of content control that has received wide attention: the effect of ownership and advertising on the media.

THREE
Private Ownership and the Profit System

6

Who Owns
Our Media?

Any of us can own a newspaper—if we have enough money.
Any of us can start a television station—if we have enough money and can
get the FCC to assign us a channel.

Any of us can publish a magazine—and if we start small it may not take
too much money.

Beautiful! Since everyone is free to be a publisher or broadcaster the
First Amendment guarantee of free speech and press is secure.

So what is the hassle about ownership?

The laws of economics and the limits of the air waves keep reality from
squaring with our theories. The fact is that fewer and fewer owners are
controlling more and more of our media.

There was a time when itinerant printers could pack up their equipment and carry it to another town if they thought they might do better
there. The investment in capital was small. Even in those days it could not
be said that "anybody can start a newspaper," but the opportunity was
open then to many more individuals than now.

New and cheaper printing processes make ownership easier again. Small presses, even some "office machines," make it less costly to start a tiny paper from scratch. Talent and hard work, both applied with vigor, have made it possible for some people to get into the newspaper business without much money. But so far they are the exceptions. To buy an established weekly takes thousands of dollars, and it takes millions to start or buy a daily of any size. Even those with adequate cash find it difficult to build or buy a newspaper or broadcast station. Since the owners control the content of our media—what we know about the world beyond our senses—it is worthwhile to discover who they are.

Herbert Brucker, former editor and journalism professor, expresses the dilemma in these words:

> Today freedom of expression is limited not only by the fact that one has to command formidable capital before one can exercise it, but also by the fact that even the rich have few opportunities to acquire a newspaper. Newspapers are more and more being gathered into the hands of corporate monsters that own two or more papers. Even riches cannot buy them.[1]

The seeds of chain newspapering were spread early among American publishers. In addition to his Philadelphia publishing interests Benjamin Franklin, at one time or another, owned portions of newspapers in Charleston; Newport; New York; St. Johns, Antigua; and Lancaster, Pennsylvania.[2]

In the days when little capital was required to get into the newspaper business Franklin's forays into chain journalism caused little worry. Today it is different. When few can own a newspaper the motives of those chosen few are valid questions for public discussion. When supercorporations can own many media outlets it is expedient to inquire into the effects of such concentration of control.

The concerns about ownership come to three major questions:

1. Does chain or group ownership of the media constitute a threat to freedom of expression and the free flow of ideas?

2. Is there danger in allowing a single ownership to control different types of media—such as broadcast and newspaper outlets?

3. Can a single ownership effectively dominate the media voices in a single area?

Questions two and three are varieties of cross-ownership, the control of different types of media by a single organization. All the questions pose

[1]Herbert Brucker, *Communication Is Power* (New York: Oxford University Press, 1973), p. 331.
[2]Alfred M. Lee, *The Daily Newspaper in America* (New York: Macmillan, 1937), p. 31.

aspects of competition and could be summarized in the question: Is competition among the media sufficient to provide for the information needs of the public?

From the consumer's point of view the question becomes one of complementary use rather than competition. Do the various media, used together, provide the information and entertainment sought at a price that most people can afford? The question is not simply whether the public needs more units of any of the media, but whether the economic, ownership, and regulatory forces provide a satisfactory balance among the media units available to the public.

No definitive answer has been found to any of these questions, but the questions are useful in defining areas of concern. Sooner or later our society must come to some consensus on them. In the meantime, various governmental agencies take actions that represent the views of their administrators as to what the right answers are. In Chapter 3 we considered some of the ways that governments control the media. Here we will look at the patterns of ownership in the United States and at the ways the federal government and economic forces have affected those patterns.

Economic Forces Control Ownership

Group ownership, cross-ownership, and lack of daily newspaper competition are not brought about by sinister, plotting media owners who are trying to limit the spread of ideas. Rather, they are produced by the fact that the owners generally are guided more by business and economic considerations than by thoughts about the marketplace of ideas. The economic forces acting on the communications media are the same as those that act on the rest of American business, and these forces tend to produce higher profit margins for businesses that grow bigger. The natural result, for newspapers as well as grocery stores, is for two units to merge into one larger unit, and for the larger units to come together under common ownership. These are the economic forces that have given us regionwide and nationwide grocery chains, hotel and motel chains, and that account for the fact that our huge automobile production is almost entirely in the hands of four vast companies.

The economies of scale that help to produce these large concerns are also aided by the fact that once an organization gains size and control of economic resources it is in a position to exert some pressures against smaller firms—to compete by temporarily dropping prices below cost, for example, or to exert other pressures that may persuade a smaller company to allow itself to be swallowed up before it is killed off.

Our tax laws, too, favor growth in size for communications media and other concerns. If newspaper or station owners make a profit they have several choices as to what to do with the excess funds. They can plow them back into the business and provide better news coverage or better programming for their audience; they can take them out of the business as profits; or they can invest them in related business enterprises. Some of our media owners have taken the first course and given us great newspapers and fine broadcast programming; some have taken the second and made themselves and their stockholders wealthy; many have taken the third course, for the tax laws allow them to keep more of the excess funds if they are reinvested than if they are taken out as profit.

Given the decision to reinvest it is only natural that owners will look for enterprises in which they have some management skill. A hotel owner is likely to build or buy additional hotels, a grocer sitting on surplus is likely to invest in another grocery store, the proprietor of a carry-out chicken business is likely to start a chain of chicken stands. Likewise, publishers or broadcasters are likely to look for enterprises in which they feel some competence—another newspaper, another station, perhaps a magazine or a book publishing concern, something in what has come to be called the "information field."

The process snowballs. Good management provides a publisher with a surplus that allows him or her to buy another newspaper. Continued good management of two newspapers provides an opportunity to purchase a third newspaper. With increased profits from an increasing number of units, it soon may be possible for an organization to acquire not just one newspaper at a time, but another group. Eventually a company may own fifty newspapers, as the Gannett organization did in 1975.

Economists say there is some point at which the economies of large-scale business start working in reverse—when increased size becomes a liability instead of an advantage. Running a large number of newspapers or broadcasting stations spread across a continent puts a tremendous premium on management skills. Certainly, two of the early chains in the United States, Hearst and Scripps-Howard, showed little sign of expansionist tendencies in the early 1970's, although their size was already imposing.

Other growth patterns may emerge. Instead of expanding by buying more communications units, a concern may do as other businesses frequently do—diversify. This may result in a local publisher buying into other concerns in his or her own community. Such interlocking ownership is likely to make some people ask whether the newspaper can remain impartial when some of the publisher's other investments are imperiled by events in the news.

The same thing happens in reverse when some other entrepreneur, trying to diversify, buys up the newspaper or television station in town. The new owner inevitably faces criticism that his or her other, primary interests will not permit that person to be impartial in reporting events that affect those interests. When the new owner is a huge corporation the criticism, although it may be muted by fear, is sure to be intense. At one time the daily newspapers of Montana were owned by the Anaconda Copper Company, which was the state's largest industry. Problems of objectivity seem almost insurmountable under such circumstances.

The same arguments are sometimes used to question the ability of the Radio Corporation of America to provide an impartial news service through its subsidiary, the National Broadcasting Company, when the parent company derives much of its income from enterprises other than NBC. RCA is a large defense contractor for the U.S. government. Its holdings include Random House publishers, Hertz Rent-a-Car, RCA Victor Records, Banquet Frozen Foods, companies that retail furniture and drugs, and others that manufacture a wide variety of electronic equipment.

CBS, which is also a government defense contractor, has a variety of other holdings. These include Columbia Records; Holt, Rinehart & Winston publishers; CBS Films; a musical instrument manufacturing firm; and Creative Playthings, a toy manufacturing firm. Through its consumer publishing division it controls *Field & Stream, Road & Track, World Tennis, Cycle World, Sea, PV4,* and *Popular Library.*

Among ABC's holdings are portions of several foreign broadcasting companies, nearly four hundred motion picture theaters, a record company, ABC Films, *Prairie Farmer, Wallaces Farmer, Wisconsin Agriculturist, High Fidelity,* and *Modern Photography.*

The problem is common at all levels of communication. When a person receives information in a conversation he or she evaluates it partly by a consideration of the purpose the other has in providing the information. So it is with the media. Since the organizations controlling them have wide-ranging interests, it is wise for the receiver to be aware of those interests. A banker's motives may be pure when he advises buying a certain stock, but it is worthwhile to know whether he happens to be a director of the company involved. It is no aspersion on the motives of the networks to point out that they or their parent companies have other interests and that it makes sense for their audiences to be aware of those interests. It also makes sense to know what, besides the newspaper, a local publisher owns.

Individuals connected with large communications enterprises argue that the forces that have produced massive communications enterprises are not of their doing. Besides, they say, a newspaper or a broadcast station must be of a reasonable size and have financial security to do its job effectively. Sometimes this is achieved by group ownership (see Figure 6-1) and cross-ownership.

The argument has some merit. It is not difficult to point to newspapers that became more zealous as news reporters after they were allied with groups. It appears to be true, too, that some newspapers that might otherwise have died were revived when a chain owner purchased them and supplied a transfusion of new capital and management skill.

It is also easy to see that certain economies accrue to group ownership. Some traditional functions, such as purchasing and personnel, can be centralized. A group may improve news coverage by maintaining a bureau in Washington, something that most of its individual member papers might not be willing to afford. Skill in budgeting and other management techniques and development of new technology are made easier.

John S. Knight, editorial chairman of the Knight newspapers, explained some of the economic forces that lead to expansion of groups:

> Economics largely determines the number of newspapers [held by group owners], and . . . many local owners often sell to our large groups for reasons that are solely economic.
>
> Example: In many instances a newspaper owner faces the reality that upon his death, the estate taxes will be spectacularly high in these days of inflated values. He often, therefore, elects to sell his newspaper for cash and notes, or make a tax-free exchange of his stock for a listed and marketable security.

Figure 6.1 Chain Ownership Saves Staff Services

In single newspaper ownerships (left), each paper maintains its own staff services, including budgeting, personnel, and purchasing. A group owner (right) can use skilled personnel more efficiently by providing a central office that serves the needs of all the papers in the group. The group thus requires fewer, less skilled staff workers at each paper.

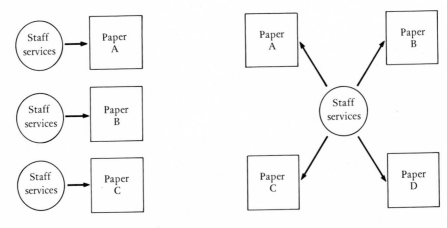

Who Owns Our Media?

Example: In the case of Knight, owners of newspapers in Miami, Detroit, Charlotte, Tallahassee, Macon and Philadelphia wanted to sell and indicated that they wanted to sell to us. In each instance, other than Chicago, these owners were dealing with no other party. In Chicago, where the test was "best qualified to carry on the traditions of the News," Knight was selected as the buyer of the *Daily News* by trustees representing the estate of the late Col. Frank Knox.[3]

Groups Tend to Expand

Economic forces fuel the acquisition philosophy of newspaper groups. Mr. Knight illustrates the philosophy of his group in a sentence from the letter previously quoted: "Sometimes there is either a need [or] a desire to sell, and we are always interested."

The same philosophy is expressed in three advertisements that appeared in a single issue of *Editor & Publisher*. Worrell Newspapers, Inc., in a full-page spread said: "We publish good hometown newspapers for good people in good communities in good states. Hopefully, some day, we can serve you and your community, too."[4] The "you" is obviously a publisher who might be considering selling a newspaper. United Media, Inc., took two-thirds of a page to briefly describe itself and then said: "We believe community publications are today's dynamic growth medium. We deliver information that really counts to people who really count. Come and join us. . . ."[5] Hammell Newspapers of Florence, Alabama, gave the clearest call of all. They said: "As a young and fast growing community company we are interested in expanding in newspapers and broadcasting anywhere in the country. Consider joining the club."[6]

With economic forces combining with aggressive buying policies it is no wonder that the number of groups and their average size are increasing in the United States. In 1972 fifty-three dailies changed hands and thirty of these landed in groups.[7] In the following year fifty-three dailies were sold and of these forty-eight went to groups or to other newspapers to form new groups.[8]

The trend toward common ownership is accelerated by the tendency for group to swallow group. Having previously absorbed the Macy news-

---

[3]John S. Knight, "In Defense of Group Ownership" (a letter), *Editor & Publisher*, June 2, 1973, pp. 6–7.

[4]*Editor & Publisher*, December 29, 1973, p. 15.

[5]Ibid., p. 27.

[6]Ibid.

[7]*Editor & Publisher*, December 30, 1972, p. 18.

[8]*Editor & Publisher*, December 29, 1973, pp. 24 ff.

papers centered around metropolitan New York, the Gannett organization merged in 1971 with Federated publications of Battle Creek, Michigan, thus adding seven dailies to the thirty-six it already owned. The stakes were large. In 1970 Gannett had netted 11.45 million dollars on gross revenues of 159 million dollars. In the same year Federated had net earnings of 2.67 million dollars on a 30-million-dollar gross.[9]

The tendency increased again in 1974, when seventy-nine dailies in the United States were affected by changes in ownership, nearly all of them enlarging existing groups or forming new ones. The *Washington Post* expanded its communications empire by purchasing the *Trenton* (New Jersey) *Times* and the Sunday *Times-Advertiser*, long held by the Kerney family. The Gannett organization sold the Newburg [New York] *Evening News* to the Canadian-based Thomson group. The biggest deal of the year was the merger of Knight's sixteen dailies with the Ridder group's seventeen, to produce the country's largest circulation group.[10]

W. H. James, publisher of the *New York Daily News*, predicts that the trend toward group ownership of newspapers will continue:

> We will see the now-growing newspaper groups expand and we anticipate new ones to be formed. . . .
>
> Many of the newspaper groups, based on a big city newspaper, will wish to acquire more smaller-city newspapers where profits as a percentage of sales, and growth potential are higher. They will further diversify into specialty magazines, other publishing ventures, and into forest products to insure their paper and fiber supply.
>
> The single family ownership, the personal newspaper proprietorships will decline, as high sales prices, personal estate problems and other factors make it desirable to sell.[11]

Given the economic forces present and the obvious zest for merger that animates many group owners, it is difficult to see how Mr. James can be wrong in his prophecy. Unless drastic forces intervene, the home-owned newspaper seems to be headed the way of the mom and pop grocery store.

The Size of Existing Groups

How far we are along that road already was underscored early in 1974 by Dr. Raymond B. Nixon, a student of newspaper ownership trends. Dr. Nixon reported that, as of January 1, 1974, 977 dailies in the United States belonged to a group. This was 54.9 percent of the 1,768 dailies in the country. Dr. Nixon reported that this constituted an in-

9*Editor & Publisher*, April 17, 1971, p. 96.
10*Editor & Publisher*, December 28, 1974, p. 22.
11*Editor & Publisher*, December 29, 1973, p. 14.

crease of 98 or 11.2 percent in group-owned dailies in three years. The groups are increasing in size and also in number. In 1910 the country's 13 groups held 63 dailies, averaging 4.7 dailies per member. By 1974 the number of groups had grown to 165 holding 977 dailies, for an average size of 5.9.[12] It remains to be seen whether the increased number of groups will offset the trend toward grouping.

The size of a newspaper group is indicated by the number of papers, total circulation, total assets, or revenues. Most commonly used are number of papers and circulation. In number of papers owned Gannett and Thomson led in 1976 with fifty each. They were followed by the Scripps League with thirty-six; Knight-Ridder, thirty-five; Donrey, thirty; and Freedom, twenty-five. When other factors are considered a somewhat different picture emerges, however:

Group	Total Circulation
1. Knight-Ridder Newspapers	4,790,467
2. Tribune Company Owned Newspapers	4,089,464
3. Newhouse Newspapers	3,518,673
4. Hearst Newspapers	2,745,264
5. Scripps-Howard Newspapers	2,505,601
6. Gannett Newspapers	2,314,668
7. Times Mirror Company	1,743,349
8. New York Times Company	1,701,525
9. Evening News Association	1,344,164
10. Robert McLean Newspapers	1,112,246[13]

It is not very clear what this overwhelming evidence of the increasing dominance of newspaper groups means to the reader. Almost uniformly, the management is careful to assure readers that the group-owned newspaper retains local autonomy in news and editorial matters. Some group owners stay almost entirely out of the local news operation, paying attention only to the business and financial aspects. S. I. Newhouse built such a reputation, and on occasion, it enabled him to buy newspapers that would not otherwise have been available. For example, after Mr. Newhouse purchased the *Birmingham News* in 1955, Major Clarence Hanson, Jr., publisher of the *News*, said, "The decisive reason [to choose Newhouse as a purchaser] was his established reputation for permitting his papers to be operated locally, and his assurances that the *News* would be so managed."[14]

[12]*Editor & Publisher*, February 23, 1974, p. 9.

[13]Ranking of U.S. newspaper groups according to the 1974 circulation of daily (Monday through Saturday) newspapers published. *Editor & Publisher International Yearbook*, 55th ed. (1975), passim.

[14]"On to Birmingham," *Time*, December 12, 1955, p. 81, quoted in John A. Lent, *Newhouse, Newspapers, Nuisances* (New York: Exposition Press, 1966), pp. 131–132.

While such assurances may be sincerely meant, changes are inevitable when a paper changes hands. Many group owners provide expert help to raise the quality of the newspapers they buy. This outside help usually improves the quality; it also affects the news and editorial judgment of the editors and reporters. If it did not there would be little point in providing it. On the other hand, some groups will install new business procedures to produce more revenue, but will keep hands off the news and editorial departments.

Often group ownership provides independence from local economic forces. If an advertiser tries to control the news content of the paper, he or she is likely to find that the management, confident in the strength of its ownership, refuses to surrender its prerogatives of deciding on news and editorial opinion.

While much has been said and written on the subject, there is little hard evidence to prove the advantages or disadvantages to the general public of group ownership. Often readers benefit from a wider selection of syndicated material and perhaps from the group's bureaus in Washington and the state capital. The paper may become more professional in its writing and editing. What is really lost is local autonomy—the knowledge that final control rests in the hands of an individual or group that resides in the community and is primarily concerned about the welfare of the community.

Highly concentrated press control in underdeveloped countries has sometimes led to indifference toward the press, as Raymond B. Nixon and Tae-youl Hahn point out:

> As for the trend toward press ownership concentration in the world today, we can say at this stage only that the press in underdeveloped countries is more concentrated than that of the developed countries. But this fact alone may suggest why the press in certain underdeveloped countries sometimes changes so quickly from control by a few private owners to control by a few in the government. For if only a few individuals are involved on either side, it really may make very little difference to anyone else.[15]

Group ownership of newspapers and the other communications media is of concern in many countries. In the late 1960's and early 1970's a study of Canadian media was sponsored by a special committee of the Senate of Canada. One of the conclusions of the detailed report was that: "In the newspaper field today, Canada has four or five large, expanding companies, making substantial profits, and seemingly intent on acquiring the dwindling remainder of independent newspapers."[16]

[15]Raymond B. Nixon and Tae-youl Hahn, "Concentration of Press Ownership: A Comparison of 32 Countries," *Journalism Quarterly* 48, 1 (Spring 1971): 16.
[16]*Words, Music and Dollars*, Vol. 2 of *Mass Media*, a study for the Special Senate Committee on Mass Media (Ottawa: Queen's Printer for Canada, 1970), p. 433.

Almost half of the daily newspapers in Canada were owned by three chains: Southam Press with 18.1 percent; F. B. Publications with 18.2 percent; and Thomson Newspapers with 8.4 percent. In addition, one group controlled four of the nine dailies and thirteen weeklies in Quebec; and K. C. Irving had acquired all the English language dailies in New Brunswick. The report noted some of the groups also had radio and television interests.[17] Dr. Nixon reported that in the same year 66.4 percent of Canada's 116 dailies were group owned.

These figures assume more significance when compared with ones reported by Nixon and Hahn[18] on the circulation of Canadian newspaper groups. The four largest ownerships in Canada control 52.92 percent of the circulation; the eight largest, 70.13 percent; and the twenty largest, 88.54 percent. Corresponding figures for the United States are 18.00 percent for the four largest groups; 28.34 percent for the eight largest; and 42.99 percent for the twenty largest.

In 1974 a New Brunswick Supreme Court found K. C. Irving, Ltd., and three associated publishers guilty of setting up a monopoly. The Irving group published all five English language dailies in the province, and the court held that their action constituted a monopoly designed to prevent or lessen free competition.

Justice Albany M. Robichaud affirmed that the five papers had complete editorial autonomy but held that danger of central control existed in that "the potential was always there to be exercised at any time, and the likelihood that such control be exercised was always present. It was never extinguished." He ruled that any arrangement lessening competition is illegal "even although it may not appear to have actually produced any result detrimental to the public interest."[19] Such a philosophy, sometimes expressed in the United States, too, raises questions about any concentration of media control.

Cross-Ownerships

Chain or group ownership usually implies the ownership of several newspapers or broadcast stations. It has most often been applied to newspaper groups. Cross-ownership means the ownership by a single individual or a group of different media, such as several newspapers, radio and television stations, and perhaps magazines. Cross-ownership has most often been a matter of concern when a single organization controls

[17]*Good, Bad, or Simply Inevitable?* Vol. 3 of *Mass Media*, a study for the Special Senate Committee on Mass Media (Ottawa: Queen's Printer for Canada, 1970), p. 433.

[18]Nixon and Hahn, *Concentration of Ownership*, p. 13.

[19]"Court Rules Irving Group in Canada Is Monopolistic," *Editor & Publisher*, February 2, 1974, pp. 15, 42.

all the newspapers and the dominant radio and television stations in a given community, thus giving a single management something approaching a monopoly.

Bryce W. Rucker depicts a gloomy picture of chain ownership of radio stations by newspapers as well as broadcast chains:

> Chain broadcasters control virtually all of the most powerful (50,000 watt) stations in the United States. Seven of the eleven clear channel AM radio stations not now designated for duplication are owned by chains: AVCO industrial complex, two; NBC, one; Palmer, one; religious organizations, two; and the Minneapolis *Star* and *Tribune* newspaper-broadcasting chain, one. Two of the four not chain-owned are owned by newspapers and another is licensed to an insurance company. Only KFI Los Angeles is owned by persons with no other mass media holdings or obvious special interest causes to plead.
>
> The situation is almost as bad with the other 50,000 watt day and night stations. Forty-seven of these sixty-two stations are in chain hands, of which the networks control twelve; newspaper-broadcasting chains, eight; industrial-broadcasting chains, seven; insurance-broadcasting chains, three; movie theater-broadcasting chains, one; and a church broadcasting chain, one. Of the fifteen maximum-power stations not owned by chains, newspapers control four; a labor union, one; industry, one; and a movie operator, one. Only six of the seventy-three full-time, 50,000 watt stations are independently owned.[20]

Professor Rucker also reported that groups owned 496 of the 1,602 FM stations, or 31 percent. In describing his findings about ownership of television stations, Rucker said: "No other local medium of mass communications in American history has become so chain-dominated as television . . . enterprising chain broadcasters have virtually taken over television. They now control 73.6 percent of all commercial stations."[21]

On the other hand, broadcast station ownership by newspapers decreased from 1945 to 1966, according to Christopher Sterling, who attributed the decline to a flood of new owners in the field.[22] In a later study sponsored by the National Association of Broadcasters, Professor Sterling found further evidence to support the trend. He reported that fewer than 7 percent of all broadcast stations in the hundred largest markets were controlled by a daily newspaper in the same market. (*Market* is the advertiser's word for a geographic area defined for selling purposes. In the United States it is often roughly equivalent to a metropolitan area.) Professor Sterling reported that group control of broadcast units peaked at 39

[20]Bryce W. Rucker, *The First Freedom* (Carbondale: Southern Illinois Press, 1968), pp. 189–190.

[21]Ibid., p. 193.

[22]Christopher H. Sterling, "Newspaper Ownership of Broadcast Stations, 1920–68," *Journalism Quarterly* 46 (Summer 1969), p. 233.

percent in the top hundred markets in 1940, but was down to 33 percent in 1967, the latest figures he reported. On the basis of his study, Sterling advised that additional controls by the FCC were "ill-advised, at least at this time."[23]

The facts, of course, are interpreted against one's preconceptions. It is unlikely that Professor Rucker was persuaded by Professor Sterling's cheerful analysis. Rucker marshals facts to show that the most profitable stations with the largest audiences and the highest advertising rates tend to be owned by groups or by newspapers or by both. Since newspaper publishers were in the field early, he says, they tend to own the more successful, established stations and the ones with profitable network affiliations.

The Federal Communications Commission has ruled that one group can own only seven television, seven AM, and seven FM stations, and that only five of the television stations can be the generally more profitable VHF stations. One of the results of this ruling is a constant "trading-up" process by which owners holding their maximum number of stations sell stations in smaller cities when they have an opportunity to buy stations in larger metropolitan areas with a larger audience, higher advertising revenues, and larger profits.

In general, the most profitable stations are VHF stations situated in the very largest markets and holding network affiliations. Rucker pointed out that, at the time he wrote, thirty-seven of the forty VHF stations in the ten largest markets were owned by chain broadcasters. The remaining three were licensed to newspapers in the same cities.[24] These ten top markets contain nearly 40 percent of all television-owning households, so the impact on listeners is tremendous, although ill-defined.

Network operators are in the business of supplying programs to stations. As such the networks are not licensed by the FCC, although it is obvious that they have great influence on the programs seen by television viewers. The networks are also station owners, with each network owning five stations. Of these fifteen stations, all but one are in the top ten markets of the country. They are thus tremendously profitable.

Rucker cited three cities as having total local media monopolies in 1967: Rock Island, Illinois; Zanesville, Ohio; and Temple, Texas. In each of these cities the same ownership had control of the only newspaper, the only television station, and the only AM radio station.[25] Guido Stempel pointed out that for two of them monopoly was not quite complete. Both Rock Island and Temple had competing FM stations.[26]

---

[23]"Newspaper-Broadcast Combinations Decline," *Broadcasting*, March 29, 1971, p. 92.
[24]Rucker, *First Freedom*, p. 196.
[25]Ibid.
[26]Guido H. Stempel III, *Effects on Performance of a Cross-Media Monopoly*, Journalism Monographs, no. 29 (Lexington, Ky.: Association for Education in Journalism), p. 4.

After a study of the media and their use in Zanesville, Professor Stempel concluded:

> The people of Zanesville were not well served by the media monopoly that existed there for 16 years. They used the media less and were less well informed than the people of the other two communities we studied. The news content of the Zanesville media seemed less comprehensive than that of the media of the other two communities.[27]

Stempel studied the content of the Zanesville newspaper and broadcast station compared to that of the media in similar cities. He also compared media use and public attitude toward the media and the level of information of public affairs of a sample of the public. The only test on which the Zanesville media did not suffer by comparison with those of the other communities was in public acceptance. The public seemed to be about as favorably impressed with the Zanesville media as the people in the other communities were with theirs.

The Stempel study is useful in forming further hypotheses, but it furnished insufficient evidence for generalizations about the effects of media monopolies or whether the monopoly was connected with the deficiencies he found. Until further studies are made the question remains open. The common-sense conclusion is that, as a matter of policy, the more variety that can be provided in responsible news and opinion, the better. Competition in information, like competition in manufacturing shoes, is likely to stimulate a better product.

Networks and News Services

Press associations and networks dominate the news that citizens receive from their local newspapers and broadcast stations. Smaller newspapers sometimes obtain their nonlocal news from a single press service, but larger dailies often receive the reports of both the major press associations, the Associated Press and United Press International, and are likely to subscribe to some of the supplementary services such as those provided by the *New York Times* and the *Washington Post–Los Angeles Times* syndicate. With several services and perhaps its own bureau in Washington, a large daily can tailor to some extent its national and international news to the needs of its local readers.

Television stations find it more difficult to perform the same service for

[27]Ibid., p. 29.

their audiences. National news programs provided by the networks are designed as units. While a newspaper can easily insert local material into a national story, it would ruin the flow of the network broadcast for a local station to attempt to do the same. News feeds by networks and other organizations can be taped and interspersed in local news programs, but so far editing procedures have not attained the flexibility of the print media. And few television stations have been willing to meet the high costs for personnel and production needed to match the slick quality of network news.

Thus the three network news departments have much control over the content of national and international news. Good production provides easy viewing, which helps to lull millions of people into thinking that they are getting an adequate diet of news from painlessly watching the television tube. More than half the people in the United States say that they are getting most of their national and international news from television. Such mass and easy access to the public consciousness raises the question as to whether three national networks can provide sufficient variety in news processing to supply the needs of a nation of 200 million people.

More national networks with more news departments would help, but prospects are not too good. Some attempts have been made, but launching a new network takes great resources, and the established ones are in a position to put some roadblocks in the way.[28] More stations with their own Washington bureaus is another answer and some progress is being made here.

Also of concern is the ownership of the networks. As public corporations they issue stock that is traded on the New York Stock Exchange and is widely distributed. Large holdings are necessary before an investor can exert influence on company policies. Bankers, as money managers, often are in positions of power. Senators Edmund S. Muskie and Lee Metcalf found that banks own 38.1 percent of CBS stock, 34.8 percent of ABC, and 6.7 percent of RCA.[29] Fears were expressed that large stockholders might have an indirect influence on news policies through influence over long-term hiring and firing policies, and that great corporations might seek to promote a bland image by insisting on noncontroversial programming.

The two major press associations in the United States, the Associated Press and United Press International, also exert much control over the nonlocal content of newspapers and broadcast stations. Newspapers have more flexibility in adapting wire service copy since they do not receive finished "programs" as television stations do from the networks and as some radio stations do from the networks and wire services.

[28]See Rucker, *First Freedom*, chap. 9.
[29]U.S., Congress, Senate, *Disclosure of Corporate Ownership*, 93d Cong., 2d sess., 1974, Senate Document No. 93–62, pp. 169, 170, 175.

Economic factors, too, provide more local control over the press services. While the networks receive no payment from affiliate stations for the news broadcasts, press services are paid by the local paper or broadcaster for the services they provide. The Associated Press, for example, serves about 3,000 broadcasters and 1,750 newspapers in the United States and gets about two-thirds of its domestic revenue from newspapers and one-third from broadcasters.[30] Their ownerships, too, make the press services more a creature of the local units than is true of the networks. The Associated Press is a membership cooperative, composed of the papers and stations it serves. It is nonprofit and exists on membership dues and levies for services performed. United Press International, which provides its services to clients for a fee, was formed when United Press, owned by Scripps-Howard newspapers, acquired Hearst's International News Service in 1958. The press services receive their share of criticism for dominating the news field, but, in general, they have been more successful than the networks in avoiding charges of bias. Part of the reason is that they are not owned by huge industrial conglomerates as are the networks.

Antitrust Philosophy and the Media

Perhaps as a result of the First Amendment, government controls over ownership of the media have been rather sporadic and often have appeared to have no central philosophy. Most of the control has been by the federal government under power granted by the Sherman Anti-Trust Act of 1890 and its successors and under the Federal Radio Act of 1927 and its successors.

The Sherman Act forbids "every contract, combination in the form of trust or otherwise, or conspiracy, in restraint of trade or commerce among the several states." It was the beginning of antitrust legislation, which was enlarged and amended in the Clayton Act of 1914 and later statutes. Designed to foster competition in business and to eliminate or restrain monopolies, the antitrust bills constitute landmark legislation that attempts to refine our concepts of the role of free enterprise in our society. Reflecting the scope and difficulty of the problems, the legislation remains uncertain in its effects, but its role in regulating the communications industry is beginning to take shape.

The antitrust laws have been applied to the communications industry primarily to eliminate practices that are deemed unreasonable restraints on trade or constitute unfair competition, and to limit the domination of

[30]"Wes Gallagher of AP: An Extensive Newsman," *Broadcasting*, July 9, 1973, p. 57.

Who Owns Our Media?

one owner over the media of an area. Recently there are indications that the Antitrust Division of the Department of Justice is considering the effects of chain ownership. Owners of both print and broadcast media, along with chain owners, are particularly vulnerable.

A suit against the Associated Press decided by the Supreme Court in 1945, while it did not involve ownership considerations directly, served as a precedent in later actions. In its decision the court found the AP in violation of the antitrust laws because its bylaws (1) prohibited member newspapers from furnishing news of spontaneous origin to nonmembers, and (2) empowered members to block applications for membership by competitors. Associated Press membership (which gave access to its news reports) was sufficiently important, the Court felt, that lack of it might put a newspaper at a competitive disadvantage and so constitute an unreasonable restraint of trade. Readers of nonmember papers, too, would be placed at a disadvantage, the Court noted, because they might not receive the wide range of news afforded by the Associated Press.

Writing the majority opinion, Justice Black answered the argument that applying the Sherman Act to the Associated Press was an abridgment of the constitutional guarantee of a free press. His words have been quoted frequently: "Surely a command that the government itself shall not impede the free flow of ideas does not afford non-government corporations a refuge if they impose restraints upon the constitutionally guaranteed freedom. Freedom to publish means freedom for all and not for some."[31]

The immediate result of the decision was to require the Associated Press to admit the *Chicago Sun* to membership and provide it with the same service given to the long-time AP member, the *Chicago Tribune*, which was competing with the *Sun* in the morning newspaper field in Chicago. The long-term result was to serve as a precedent for the entry of the Department of Justice into cases involving the distribution of news as well as ownership and business practices of newspapers.

Another important application of the antitrust laws to the media world occurred early in 1950 when the government brought suit against four executives of the *Lorain* (Ohio) *Journal*, charging that they had conspired to restrain trade when they refused to accept advertising from some local concerns that also advertised over radio station WEOL and in the *Lorain Sunday News*, competing media.[32]

Local businesspeople testified that they had been forced to discontinue advertising with competing media in order to continue using space in the *Journal*. The government also showed that the *Journal* had previously bought out a competing newspaper, the *Times-Herald*, for $300,000. Seventy thousand dollars of this was for the newspaper, the balance for an

---

[31]326 U.S. 1, 19–20.
[32]92 FS 794 (1950).

agreement by publishers of the *Times-Herald* that they would not start another paper in Lorain for five years. The government also introduced testimony by the president of WEOL that the *Journal* refused to publish the WEOL program schedule, even as paid advertising.

The court held that these acts, taken together, proved that the *Journal* was in restraint of trade, and that requiring the paper to accept WEOL's advertising did not constitute an infringement of First Amendment rights. The court recognized the newspaper's right normally to control the nature of the advertising it printed, but held in this case that the rejection of advertising was not due to the offensive nature of the material "or even because the prospective advertisers were not the sort of persons with whom they wished to deal. Their refusal to deal was based solely on a desire to force these advertisers not to continue to enter into relations with another available mode of communications."[33]

The concept of the geographical market enunciated by the Supreme Court in *Brown Shoe Co.* v. *United States*[34] provides some insight into the approach to ownership problems by the attorneys in the Antitrust Division of the Department of Justice. The geographic market is the area involved. In the antitrust cases so far, the government has concerned itself mostly with single cities or metropolitan areas. The effect of the AP decision has direct national implications, but the Lorain and Mansfield applications concern competition within a narrow area. This is true in more recent cases.

For example, in *Times-Picayune* v. *United States*[35] the government charged that the Times-Picayune Company, which owned morning and afternoon dailies in New Orleans, dominated the newspaper market to the disadvantage of another afternoon paper, the *Item*. The government was unsuccessful in breaking up the Times-Picayune Company's combination, but the goal was clear enough—to increase competition at the local level. The government was successful in a similar attempt in Kansas City in 1957.[36] Here, the Kansas City Star company was forced to sell its radio and television stations and to eliminate its policy of forcing advertisers to buy space in both morning and evening papers in order to get an ad in either one. Cross media ownership was a factor here as well as domination of the newspaper market and forced advertising rates. In this case the effort by the government was limited to a local market. In 1967 the government again defined the market locally when it brought and won a suit to require the Times-Mirror Corporation of Los Angeles to sell its recently

[33]92 FS 794, 801.
[34]370 U.S. 324.
[35]345 U.S. 594.
[36]*U.S.* v. *Kansas City Star*, 240 F 2d. 643.

acquired and neighboring *San Bernadino Sun*.[37] Since the *Times* had been competing with the *Sun*, the lessening of competition was quite obvious. But again, the effort by the Justice Department was felt on the local level. The *Sun* was eventually sold to the Gannett group, which has wide national holdings, without objections by the Department of Justice.

Another publishing arrangement that has attracted the attention of the Justice Department is the joint operating agreement. (See Figure 6.2.) Newspapers in a few cities have formed separate corporations that, typically, attend to all the business and mechanical functions such as printing, circulation, advertising, and promotion. The news and editorial departments are kept distinct. Profits are split in accordance with an agreed upon ratio.

Such agreements were in effect in twenty-two U.S. cities in 1968 when the Justice Department brought suit to break up one of them, Tucson Newspapers, Inc., which provided printing, advertising, and circulation services for the city's two dailies, the *Tucson Daily Citizen* and the *Arizona Daily Star*. Tucson Newspapers, Inc., was wholly owned by the two newspapers. The case reached the United States Supreme Court in 1969 on appeal. Justice Douglas, writing the majority opinion,[38] held that the arrangement violated antitrust laws because it involved price-fixing, profit-pooling, and market control.

The majority opinion denied the applicability of the failing-company

Figure 6.2   Joint Operating Agreements

Under a joint agreement, two newspapers jointly own a third company, which performs all the functions of both papers except for news and editorial work. The joint operating company collects revenues, pays expenses, and distributes profits according to an agreed-on formula. The shared operations save money for each paper, but have raised questions about the ability of the papers to remain truly independent.

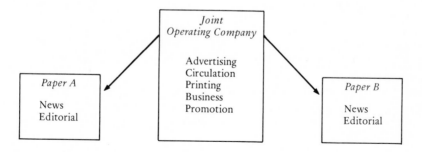

---

[37]274 F. Supp. 606.
[38]*United States v. Citizen Publishing Co.* 394 U.S. 131 (1969).

defense, a doctrine sometimes used previously to make exceptions to the antitrust laws when one of the companies involved in such an arrangement was in such financial straits that failure appeared to be inevitable. In the Tucson case the court found no evidence that either newspaper had been in imminent danger of failing when the agreement was reached, although the profit picture for both was considerably enhanced by the arrangement.

The decision caused consternation among the publishers involved in the other twenty-one joint operating arrangements, and considerable pressure was brought on Congress to pass legislation excepting them from the antitrust laws. Not all publishers favored the legislation; several smaller ones argued that it would make it possible for large publishers to so dominate a market that smaller papers might be squeezed out, and that added difficulties would be placed in the way of anyone trying to start a new venture.

Nevertheless Congress passed and President Nixon signed the Newspaper Preservation Act of 1970. In the opening section Congress made this declaration of policy:

> In the public interest of maintaining a newspaper press editorially and reportorially independent and competitive in all parts of the United States, it is hereby declared to be the public policy of the United States to preserve the publication of newspapers in any city, community, or metropolitan area where a joint operating arrangement has been heretofore entered into because of economic distress or is hereafter effected in accordance with the provisions of this chapter.[39]

The effect of the act was to legitimize the operating arrangements already consummated as of July 24, 1970, but to require the prior written consent of the attorney general before any such new arrangement could be made.

In 1971 the publisher of the *San Francisco Bay Guardian*, Bruce Brugman, contended in a suit that the Newspaper Preservation Act was unconstitutional because it violated freedom of the press in unfairly encouraging a monopoly. Brugman argued in the suit that a joint operating arrangement between the *San Francisco Chronicle* and the *San Francisco Examiner* gave those papers an unfair competitive advantage, and enabled them to cripple competition. Profit-sharing, joint advertising rates, and common printing operations were cited as putting the *Guardian*, a monthly publication with 17,000 circulation, at a competitive disadvantage.

The federal judge refused to declare the act unconstitutional, holding that it does not constitute a violation of freedom of the press. The opinion

[39]15 U.S.C.A. 1801.

called the act "merely a selective repeal of the antitrust laws. It merely looses the same shady market forces which existed before the passage of the Sherman, Clayton and other antitrust laws."[40] A higher court review of the law's constitutionality did not result from the suit because the *Guardian* settled in 1975 for about $500,000.

The net effect of the act was to bring into the open controversies between some of the large publishers and smaller ones competing in the same area or around its fringes. Diluted as they now are by the Newspaper Preservation Act, the antitrust laws seem unlikely to have much effect in stemming the tide of newspaper monopolies.

The FCC and Patterns of Ownership

The Federal Communications Commission is required by law to license radio and television stations, so it inevitably has some influence over ownership patterns. The question of how much influence it has and should have and the nature of the influence is obscured in a muddy sea of conflicting philosophies. A brief glance at the history of radio regulation shows why the sea is so murky.

In 1927 the radio spectrum was becoming sufficiently cluttered that it was impossible in some areas for a station to stay on a given frequency and get its signal out. A new station might use the same frequency or one so close that interference made listening impossible. The broadcasters turned to the logical agency, the federal government, to ask for some means of orderly assignments of frequencies. The result was the Radio Act of 1927, which created the Federal Radio Commission with authority to assign frequencies and grant licenses. Under this act and the Communications Act of 1934, which succeeded the 1927 act and created the Federal Communications Commission, the Commission was "*directed* to grant licenses *only* if the public interest will be served."[41] It is apparent that the Federal Communications Commission is required to take some interest in ownership of broadcast media.

In hearings that preceded the 1934 law, the National Association of Broadcasters indicated its acceptance of the idea of licensing in the public interest in these words:

> It is the manifest duty of the licensing authority in passing upon the applications for licenses or the renewal thereof, to determine whether

[40]344 F. Supp. 1155 (D.C. Cal. 1972).
[41]Walter B. Emery, "Government's Role in the American System of Broadcasting," *Television Quarterly* 1 (February 1962): 8 (emphasis in original).

or not the applicant is rendering or can render an adequate public service. Such service necessarily includes broadcasting of a considerable proportion of programs devoted to education, religion, labor, agricultural and similar activities concerned with human betterment. In actual practice over a period of seven years, as the records of the Federal Radio Commission amply prove, this has been the principal test which the Commission has applied in dealing with broadcasting applicants.[42]

Thus required to consider the public interest as well as channel availability in granting licenses, the Federal Communications Commission needed to develop a set of criteria to guide it in determining what constitutes public interest. This determination has been made with only indifferent success.

The pressure under which the FCC sometimes has to work may be one of the reasons it has not been very successful in formulating a consistent policy. The right to use a VHF channel in a metropolitan area can be worth a fortune, so pressure is inevitable in the FCC's decisions. In the early days of radio, when there was less concern about concentration of media ownership, the FCC paid relatively little attention to other media holdings of applicants for channels. Newspaper publishers often argued that their experience in publishing made them familiar with community needs and gave them the resources to manage successful stations. As it became apparent that more and more media outlets were being dominated by fewer and fewer owners, the FCC began to pay more attention to the effects of media concentration.

FCC rules block huge chains by prohibiting single ownership of more than seven television, seven AM radio, and seven FM radio stations. No more than five of the seven television stations can be VHF. Single ownership of more than one television station in the same city is blocked, but one party has sometimes gained control of a television station and AM and FM radio stations in the same city.

Cross-ownerships of broadcast and newspaper properties in the same city have usually been protected by the FCC's practice of giving preference to the current licensee when licenses come up for renewal. Since newspaper publishers had been early purchasers of television stations, their interests were thus protected. That is why the case of WHDH in Boston caused shock waves among owners. The dispute over channel 5 in Boston dragged through FCC hearings and federal court procedures for more than a decade—from the late 1950's through the end of the 1960's. In the end the channel was taken from the company that had operated it since 1957 and given to a challenger. This was the first time that the

[42]Report by Federal Communications Commission, *Public Service Responsibility of Broadcast Licensees*, March 7, 1946, p. 10. Quoted in Ibid., p. 8.

Who Owns Our Media?

FCC had failed to renew the license of an operating television station.

Diversity of ownership was a strong factor in the decision, as the FCC made clear in its ruling:

> Diversification is a factor of first significance since it constitutes a primary objective in the Commission's licensing scheme. . . . When compared with Charles River and BBI [the other applicants for the channel], WHDH manifestly ranks a poor third because of its ownership of a powerful standard broadcasting station, an FM station, and a newspaper in the city of Boston itself. While it is true that the existence of numerous other media in Boston in which WHDH has no ownership interest may not be ignored and does somewhat diminish the weight to be accorded the preferences to Charles River and BBI on local diversification, nonetheless those preferences are quite significant here. A grant to either Charles River or BBI would clearly result in a maximum diffusion of control of the media. . . . A new voice would be brought to the Boston community. . . . We believe that the widest possible dissemination of information from diverse and antagonistic sources is in the public interest.[43]

The District of Columbia Circuit Court of Appeals upheld the FCC decision in the Boston case and cited precedents for the proposition that "the Commission does not exceed its powers in seeking to avoid rather than foster a concentration of control on the sources of news and opinion."[44]

The WHDH decision encouraged a flurry of challenges to station ownerships over the country. These were not successful in changing the ownership of any stations, but they resulted in some compromises by which station owners agreed to provide programming sought by groups that were challenging the license. Station owners were eventually reassured by a statement from the FCC that its policy was, in general, to favor the present licensee unless a competitor was clearly superior. Commissioner Robert E. Lee, dissenting in the WHDH decision, stated the arguments for giving preference to a current licensee:

> To hold otherwise would permit a new applicant to submit a "blue sky" proposal tailor-made to secure every comparative advantage while the existing licensee must reap the demerits of hand-to-hand combat in the business world, and the community it serves, in which it is virtually impossible to operate without error or complaint, if for no other reason than there are insufficient hours in the broadcast day with which to satisfy all the desires of the public.[45]

[43]16 FCC 2d 1 (1969). Quoted in Donald M. Gillmor and Jerome A. Barron, *Mass Communications Law* (St. Paul: West Publishing, 1969), p. 737.

[44]444 Fd 841 (1970). (1971 supplement), p. 278.

[45]16 FCC 2d 1 (1969).

One of the effects of the decision was the stilling of a media voice in Boston. The *Boston Herald-Traveler,* which had been in joint ownership with WHDH, was closed. The newspaper had been losing money for years and had been kept alive with infusions from the company's broadcast properties. In the first half of 1973 the WHDH Corporation reported a net profit after taxes of $300,000 from its AM and FM stations. In the corresponding period a year earlier, when the company had operated the newspaper and television station as well as the radio stations, it had taken a $400,000 loss. As sometimes happens, profitable broadcast properties had been used to keep alive a financially weak newspaper. Sometimes multimedia owners do the opposite: sustain broadcast stations from newspaper profits. Thus joint ownership sometimes increases the number of media voices.

In 1970 the FCC announced that it was considering a rule that would prohibit cross-ownerships of media in the same city. That is, an owner could hold no more than one broadcast unit in the same city. Owners who held a television station, an AM station, and an FM station in the same city would be required to sell two of the properties within five years. In the following year the FCC announced its proposed rules would not exclude common ownership of an AM and an FM station in the same market. This change was prompted by doubts that FM stations could make a go of it in some cities without support from an AM station. The FCC appeared to be genuinely trying to increase the diversity of ownership, but it was uncertain about the result of such a rule.

Commissioner Nicholas Johnson took a dark view of the change, commenting: "The Commission has today boldly confronted the problem of the growing concentration of the mass media. . . . It has responded by shuffling sideways, taking one timid step forward, and turning tail and running backwards."[46]

Whatever the merits of the proposed rule, it caused so much and such varied reaction that action was delayed for years. Finally, in July 1974 the FCC listened to individuals representing the media and other organizations in three days of oral arguments. Then the commissioners settled back to consider that testimony and the twenty-four volumes of written testimony it had collected. When the announcement of the rules came in January 1975, it was an anticlimax.

In the future, the FCC announced, it would bar sales of stations that would result in common ownership of a newspaper and any kind of broadcast station in the same city. At the same time, all but sixteen of the existing cross-ownerships were approved. The sixteen ownerships singled out for dissolution were all in small cities. Apparently they were regarded as more threatening to diversity in programming, the criterion that

[46]FCC Dkt. no. 18110.

the FCC said was its primary concern. Of the sixteen combinations to be dissolved, seven were of newspapers and television stations, and nine of radio stations and newspapers.

Several of the owners of newspaper-broadcast combinations that were ordered dissolved complained that the action was capricious and discriminatory, and they indicated that they would seek waivers of the rule. The FCC suggested that waivers might be issued if owners could prove undue economic hardship or that competing information services were available to residents of the areas concerned.

Perhaps the only certainty about the rule was that it would be challenged. In addition to criticism from owners ordered to sell parts of their properties, the rule was criticized from the other side on the ground that it did not go far enough in breaking up media combinations; that it was, in fact, so timid in taking on the media giants as to be useless. The National Citizens Committee for Broadcasting, which had urged the FCC to break most of the cross-ownerships, filed notice of intent to appeal in the U.S. court of appeals in Washington within an hour of the FCC announcement.

The Department of Justice indicated that it, too, might take action in court since the FCC rules did not go as far as Antitrust Division attorneys had urged.

The unusual nature of the rule, the criticism surrounding it, and the fact that several members of the FCC itself expressed dissatisfaction with it all indicate that the issue is not closed.

Cross-Ownership and CATV

Little attention has been paid to the ownership of cable antenna systems until recent years because the industry has been small compared with television and newspapers. The National Cable Television Association reported in 1974 that 8 million homes (12 percent of those with television receivers) were subscribers to a cable system.[47] Most of these subscribers are in rural areas or on the edges of metropolitan areas, and the chief benefit they derive is better reception or the ability to receive more channels than would be available with a home antenna.

Sometimes called broad-band communications because of its ability to carry many channels, cable is possibly the all-around communications medium of the future. In the "wired nation" concept it will connect homes with central switching points to provide access to information and entertainment from many different sources. Since it has the capability of two-way communication, subscribers may be able to select those parts of

[47]Les Brown, "It Takes a Good Memory to See Cable TV's Future," *New York Times*, March 10, 1974, sec. 6, p. 6.

the news report they want, or to see material stored in libraries, or to order a film screened on their video tube. When cable is combined with satellite communications and digital computers, the possibilities for information exchange are endless.

It is likely that the ultimate consumer will have to pick up the tab directly by paying for installation, a monthly fee, and for whatever special services are not supported by advertising.

Such a versatile and glamorous medium was certain to raise fears in the hearts of owners of television stations. (See Figure 6.3.) Their profits come from selling an audience to an advertiser. The larger the audience the higher the rate. If there are only three, four, or five channels available, the audience for each one may be relatively large. If twenty or fifty channels were available, the audience for each channel would obviously be smaller. Such audience fragmentation and advertising budget fragmenta-

Figure 6.3   Audience Fragmentation: A Broadcaster's Nightmare

The circle at the left represents the potential audience. Most broadcasters would like to gain the whole pie, but they have to settle for a piece of it. Some broadcasters fear that with the coming of the multichannel cable, the audience will split even further, so that no single medium will have an audience large enough to attract massive advertising support.

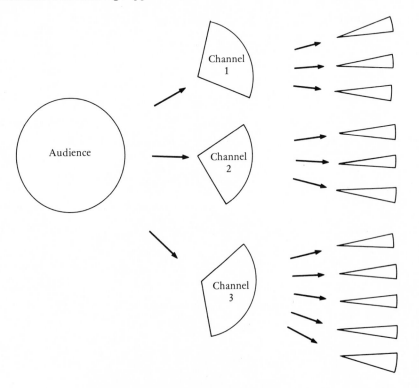

tion, its logical accompaniment, have led many television station owners to lay what roadblocks they could in the way of cablecasting. The FCC has been torn between its desires to protect existing media voices, including television stations, and its commitment to encourage as many diverse sources of information as possible.

For a time the FCC had protected television stations by forbidding the development of cable systems in the hundred largest markets, but when that ban was lifted on March 31, 1972, cable operators eagerly applied for franchises. Two large cable concerns, Teleprompter and Sterling, were franchised to serve Manhattan. They found they could not sign up as many subscribers as they had anticipated, and they were beset by shakedown attempts from apartment building superintendents, vandalism, and the pirating of their service. Other companies found the going rough in other big cities. Some operators concluded they did not yet have enough to offer city viewers to make them willing to pay the bill. They could select programs from several channels and other entertainment outside the home that was unavailable to residents of country areas. Consequently growth in the early 1970's was slower than anticipated.

In its efforts to promote variety in media voices, the FCC forbade network ownership of cable systems. It also refused to allow television stations to own cable systems in their home cities. The FCC was less decisive in its view toward ownership of a cable system by a radio station in the same city. Members were attentive to two arguments: first, since there are many more radio than television stations, ownership by radio would not seriously limit the diversity of viewpoints; and second, that some radio stations, particularly daytime only and FM stations, could use resources from the radio stations to program a cable channel. The counter argument was that, since both radio and cable are more local media than television and compete for the same advertising dollar, it is desirable to keep them separate to increase the competition in ideas and advertising.

Telephone companies were also forbidden to own cable systems in areas where they had the telephone franchise. They frequently managed to profit from cable by charging a rental for the use of their poles.

Cable still seems likely to fulfill at least part of the all-encompassing role foreseen for it. It is taking longer to develop than expected partly because other media, particularly television, see it as a major threat and have been able to impose roadblocks. There is no doubt, however, that the combination of cable, satellite, and computer technology will eventually provide as great a change in our news and entertainment habits as did the growth of television. The applications of the new technologies will affect social habits and power patterns in our society.

This bright future for cable is supported by a report of the President's Cabinet Committee on Cable Communications in 1974, which recommended that cable be permitted to develop like books, magazines, and newspapers with as little federal regulation as possible; and that cable become a common carrier available to all, as is telephone service.

Diversity in the Future

A few things come clear from a discussion of the problems of ownership of media. Perhaps most salient is that the FCC and the Justice Department are committed to the idea of preserving all possible diversity in ownership and that the courts regard this as a constitutional goal. We have taken little time to consider the role of Congress, but it is safe to register a strong undecided vote from that quarter. Congress is much influenced by the media owners who would like as little interference as possible. In establishing the FCC, Congress seemed to provide it with power to regulate concentration of ownership, at least the courts have so interpreted the legislation. In passing the Newspaper Preservation Act in 1970 Congress gave lip service to the idea of diversity of ownership, although it is doubtful that this legislation genuinely forwarded that objective. Again, after the WHDH decision, Senator John O. Pastore, chairman of the Senate Subcommittee on Communications, introduced a bill that would have made it difficult for the FCC to make another similar decision. It was panic legislation introduced at the behest of broadcasters. When it met vigorous protest, the bill was withdrawn.

Another clear indication from studying the material is that economic trends tend to create group ownership. Business efficiency, the increasing size of all our institutions, government tax policy, and the desire for expansion of present proprietors all indicate that the trend to fewer ownerships will continue unless the public and the government intervene. In the future some combination of satellite, cable, and computer technology may drastically change the situation so that small units become economically feasible, but that is not presently in sight.

Many of the problems of media ownership are still ahead of us. The FCC has declared itself the proper agency for the regulation of cable television. The ownership and operation of satellites with its international complications is a vast project that requires government cooperation.

Some have argued that the only way to preserve a marketplace of ideas in a world of fewer and fewer media ownerships is to separate ownership from control of content. As we have seen, multimedia owners often attempt to do this. Corporate structure is adaptable enough so that employees could become owners and policy-makers for their newspaper or station, but such experiments are in their infancy. Cable television, with many channels and the possibility that an owner could simply lease the channels at a fee, without a direct interest in or responsibility for the content, seems to offer the best possibility for separating ownership from control of content. Access laws, discussed in Chapter 14, might offer the same possibility.

Perhaps the most startling conclusion is that we really know very little about the effects of ownership patterns on the content of the media and on the reaction of the audience. It is an area ripe for research, but a difficult one, both because it is highly charged emotionally and involves large financial stakes and because we have hardly begun to consider what methods of fact-finding will work.

Suggestions for Further Reading

Brucker, Herbert. *Communication Is Power*. New York: Oxford University Press, 1973.
A consideration of ownership patterns with suggestions for alternatives.

Linton, Bruce A. *Self-Regulation in Broadcasting: A Three-Part College-Level Study Guide*. Washington, D.C.: National Association of Broadcasters, 1967.
Discusses industry codes.

MacCann, Richard Dyer. *The People's Films: A Political History of U.S. Government Motion Pictures*. New York: Hastings House, 1973.
An analysis of government attempts to use film to affect public opinion.

Mayer, Michael F. *The Film Industries*. New York: Hastings House, 1973.
A business guide including a consideration of legal controls.

Posner, Richard. *Regulation of Advertising by the FTC*. Washington, D.C.: American Enterprise Institute for Public Policy Research, 1973.
Treats one important aspect of advertising control.

Quinlan, Sterling. *The Hundred Million Dollar Lunch*. Chicago: J. P. O'Hara, 1974.
The story of the complicated WHDH case in which owners of the Boston Herald-Traveler lost a television channel. Part of the book uses new journalism techniques.

Rucker, Bryce W. *The First Freedom*. Carbondale: Southern Illinois Press, 1968.
A critical account of media ownership patterns in the United States.

Seiden, Martin H. *Who Controls the Media?* New York: Basic Books, 1974.
Material generally supports the theory that present ownership patterns provide sufficient diversity.

7

Advertising and the Media

Who pays for the information and entertainment that the media regularly shower on the American public? Who meets the payroll of broadcast and print news departments? Who funds the technology that brings information to the public?

What control does the person or organization that foots the bill have in deciding what information is collected and to whom and in what manner it is distributed?

Should the reader of the morning newspaper be concerned about who is paying the cost of the information he or she is getting? Should the viewer of a televison public affairs program worry about where the money to finance it came from? Should you, the reader of this book, ponder the motives of the person who wrote it and the publishing house that commissioned and produced it?

These questions are the concern of this chapter. It is important to remember that the question "Who pays the bill?" is really asking: "Who is sufficiently interested to provide the labor and resources to distribute information?" Presumably the people who gamble their resources on any project have some return in mind.

First Goal: Earn a Profit

The commercial media work for profit. They are a part of the private enterprise system in the United States, and if they do not produce a profit they will die. Candid media people will say that the first objective of a newspaper or a broadcast station is to make money. If this sounds hardheaded, it simply reflects one of the facts of economic life. A newspaper that does not produce a profit fails, and it is futile to discuss the ethics of a dead newspaper.

The death of an unprofitable paper or station may be slow, but it is almost inevitable. For many years, the Bingham family of Louisville, Kentucky, took the losses of radio station WHAS-FM along with the compliments of members of the community who enjoyed the serious music the station programmed. Barry Bingham, Jr., has recounted that he would answer favorable comments about the station's programs from business friends with the suggestion that they buy an advertisement on the station. The answer often was: "Oh, no. I don't want to clutter that good sound with ads. I like it just the way it is."

The end result was that in the summer of 1975 the format of the station was changed to emphasize news. Presumably the managers of Bingham enterprises hoped that Louisville business firms would be less reluctant to clutter the new format with commercials, which would help the station to pay its own way. The station, with its program of serious music, had continued to exist because profits from other enterprises were used to meet the annual deficit. Few owners can or will continue such losing media indefinitely.

To profit, and thus to live, the media must collect payments from the two groups who benefit from their services—the audience and the advertisers. By answering information and entertainment needs of a certain group a publication or a broadcaster attracts an audience. Having attracted an audience, the media manager can then go to companies that have something to sell to that audience and offer space or time at a given rate. To put it crudely, the advertising salesperson "sells the audience" to an advertiser.

Revenue Source: Audience or Advertisers?

Some media depend on their audience to pay all costs and thus provide the profits that will keep them alive. Book publishers, motion picture and legitimate theaters, record companies, some magazines, and pub-

lishers of special information services rely on their readers and audiences
as their sources of income. At the other end of the spectrum, radio and
television stations collect no money directly from their audience, but rely
on advertisers completely. Most newspapers and magazines collect
money from their readers in subscriptions or street sales, although for
most well over half their income comes from advertisers. Table 7.1 shows
the sources of revenue for different media.

There are many variations on these general patterns. During one phase
of American history many newspapers relied on contributions from political parties. The parties provided funds in return for favorable treatment.
Such practices are now considered unethical. Book publishers normally
depend on buyers of their books, but occasionally a publisher will use alternate financing. Sometimes this takes the form of finding authors who
are willing to pay the costs of publishing what they write. Although such
a publisher is derisively referred to as a "vanity press," Walt Whitman
and Thomas Carlyle among others who eventually became highly regarded initially paid to have their works published. Sometimes someone
with a special interest will sponsor a book. During congressional hearings
on Nelson Rockefeller's accession to the vice presidency it was revealed
that the Rockefeller family had provided money to ensure publication of a
not-too-friendly biography of Arthur Goldberg when Goldberg was run-

Table 7.1 Sources of Media Revenue

*The two major sources of revenue for U.S. media are audiences and ad-
vertisers. X's indicate principal sources for each of the media. Occasionally the patterns will differ. For example, motion picture theaters and
cable systems sometimes collect income from advertisers. Other revenue
sources may be grants from government, political parties, interest groups,
or even individuals.*

	Audiences	Advertisers
Radio		X
Television		X
Newspapers	X	X
Books	X	
Magazines	X	X
Films	X	
Cable	X	

ning against Rockefeller for the governorship of New York. Nelson Rockefeller apologized for the action and his family seemed none too happy about its involvement, but the publisher escaped criticism. It is everyone's right to say or publish what he or she wishes within the boundaries of libel and other after-publication restrictions. It may be that when books are published under special financial arrangements, consideration for the reader requires that this information be supplied.

Individuals and groups with special viewpoints to support may finance publications, and occasionally a wealthy individual will contribute sums to create an "endowed press" or to back a play.

Publisher-Advertiser Symbiosis

For many years newspapers were the medium that generated discussion about the effects of advertising on news and editorial policy. Prominent advertisers were sometimes credited with controlling editorial policy and even for keeping out of the paper stories that would damage them. The prototype story concerned a newspaper that did not report an elevator accident in a large department store that was also a large advertiser. Given many newspapers and the different timbre of their publishers and editors, such incidents must surely have occurred, but they are less important than other influences produced by advertising.

The more sophisticated arguments pointed out that newspapers, local manufacturers, and department stores are all, by local standards, large enterprises, and that their proprietors are wealthy individuals; therefore they think alike about political and economic issues. This think-alike tendency is increased by the social structure. The wealthy form a social circle and reinforce each other's opinions when they meet at the country club and other expensive places of amusement. The advertising tie-in between newspapers and other establishment enterprises simply reinforces the already existing bond. It was this situation that, as Raymond Clapper put it, "has resulted in the majority of newspaper editors and publishers thinking not at the dictation of business groups, but as part of the business group."[1]

As the argument ran in the 1940's, some were more blunt than Clapper. Kenneth G. Crawford, Washington writer for *PM*, put it this way:

> I can honestly say that I have never seen an advertiser try to dictate editorial policy. That is, I have never seen an advertiser walk into the office, pound the editor's desk, and demand that a piece of news either

[1]Raymond Clapper, "A Free Press Needs Discriminating Public Criticism," in *Freedom of the Press Today*, ed. H. L. Ickes (New York: Vanguard Press, 1941), p. 92.

be printed, or suppressed. In the offices where I have worked, an advertiser who tried it, even if he were a big advertiser, would more likely than not have been thrown out. Almost no responsible newspaperman will admit, even to himself, that the advertisers who pay the heavy freight have anything to say about the operation of the railroad.

The reason the advertiser seldom tries direct dictation is that the editor has anticipated his demands. Editorial policy was what the advertiser thought it should be before the advertiser quite knew what he thought. The editor and the advertiser think alike, but the editor thinks faster.[2]

Many newspaper people of the era of Clapper and Crawford had visions of the "adless newspaper." This would be a paper whose costs were paid entirely by the reader. In the early 1940's such a newspaper was being attempted. Ralph Ingersoll had recently founded *PM* in New York City. It accepted no advertising, adopted a hard-hitting style of investigative reporting, and became, probably, the newspaper most talked about by newspaper people. Ingersoll wrote that he tried to create a newspaper

that will succeed or fail exclusively on its ability to satisfy the man who has an interest in knowing the truth rather than the man who has a stake in suppressing it—the advertiser, the politician, the special pleader. . . . I devised a commercial formula—a cost-and-price structure—so that if a quarter of a million people wanted such a paper they could support it directly by the nickels they paid for it every day."[3]

PM's Experiment

PM attracted some scoffers, many of whom delighted in pointing out that readers missed advertising so much in the paper that *PM* adopted the practice of summarizing ads in other papers and printing them free as a public service. Other newspaper people were more friendly. Nelson P. Poynter, owner of the *St. Petersburg Times*, commented:

Such newspapers [as *PM*] are needed as a check on our conventional press. If a few such newspapers can succeed in a few larger fields, new facilities in syndication and printing will bring their basic national and international features to other fields where young men with small capital can start adless papers of their own.

They need not compete directly with omnibus newspapers, nor

[2]Kenneth G. Crawford, "The Press—Half Slave and Half Free," in Ickes, *Freedom of the Press Today*, pp. 97–98.

[3]Ralph Ingersoll, "A Free Press—for What?" in Ickes, *Freedom of the Press Today*, pp. 140–141.

jeopardize their profits. But they can compete for reader interest, reader respect, reader confidence. This is competition which will benefit the public, competition which the founding fathers sought to preserve in the constitutional guaranties.[4]

PM never achieved adequate support from its readers and eventually it died, failing to provide the model for other publishing ventures that Nelson Poynter had envisioned. With the demise of *PM* went most serious consideration of publishing a major newspaper in the United States without advertising.

Founded in 1922, *Reader's Digest* held forth for more than thirty years without advertising. Finally, in 1955 it began to sell advertising space after a survey indicated that 80 percent of its readers would prefer seeing advertising instead of paying ten cents more per copy for the magazine.

Newspapers, magazines, and broadcasters are tied in through advertising with the system of mass distribution of goods that is essential for mass production and the economies that result from it.

Arguments for Advertising

A strong argument for advertising is that it provides an economic base that enables a newspaper, magazine, or broadcaster to provide better service for its audience. A well-financed newspaper can afford to hire more reporters to describe the local scene, and to subscribe to more press services and syndicate offerings to provide variety and depth in national and international news. It may be able to establish its own bureau in Washington or abroad to give a local slant to news of nonlocal origin. Each of the three U.S. television networks maintained Saigon staffs of more than forty persons during the Vietnam War, and the total television industry's costs for covering that war are estimated at 50 million dollars. A healthy communications industry is necessary for routine and special coverage of world affairs.

Television's advertisers pay the enormous fees expected by prominent performers and thus allow the viewer to see stars who normally perform only in expensive nightclubs in the larger cities.

Another argument favoring advertising is that the business firms that advertise are so many and varied that media proprietors are independent of any of them. Their job is to attract an audience and in so doing they cannot afford to concern themselves with the interests of anyone except

[4]Nelson P. Poynter, "Checks and Balances to the Fourth Estate," in Ickes, *Freedom of the Press Today,* p. 217.

the reader or viewer. It is simply good business to put the interests of the audience first, for this is how to attract an audience that will in turn attract advertisers. In this way the interests of everyone concerned are best served. The audience gets the information and entertainment it desires; the advertiser is able to reach many people automatically; and the media proprietor serves the public and collects a good profit.

This argument is often true. A well-financed newspaper or station can be independent of any of its advertisers. So long as it serves the best interests of the audience, advertisers will need it more than it will need them. Success in many businesses depends on the ability to reach many persons with a selling message at a reasonable price. Some businesspeople have brought suit against newspapers on the ground that being excluded from advertising columns is discriminatory and cripples a business so that it cannot survive.

It is the timid publisher or station owner who raises questions about the validity of the argument. Some publishers, recognizing the large sums that advertisers are spending with them, feel it is only natural to provide some extra services. These may take the form of copy in the paper extolling the virtues of home renovation, for instance, and listing the businesspeople (invariably advertisers) who can provide the service. Special sections devoted to travel are filled with stories describing the joys of vacationing in some far-off haven and, not so incidentally, with advertisements from hotels, airlines, travel agents, and others who profit from people who take such vacations.

Whether a publisher condones such activities from timidity or an excess of zeal to maximize profits, readers are entitled to wonder whether the newspaper is putting their interests foremost or considers them as statistics to be "sold" to anyone who can meet the advertising rates.

PM's discovery that readers wanted to know what is being advertised offers some powerful support for the argument that advertising provides readers and listeners with information they need and want to know. When prices rise consumers read the supermarket advertisements more carefully to see that they are getting the most possible for their grocery dollar. One attorney's wife persuaded her husband that they should subscribe to the local paper when she proved she saved more than the subscription cost by redeeming coupons at the supermarket. Newspaper ads, by publicizing prices, probably keep the competitive pricing system going and certainly help the consumer get the most for every dollar. If newspapers and broadcast stations did not provide a means of advertising, some substitute system would have to be dreamed up. The "throwaway" publications or "shoppers," which sometimes consist of nothing but advertising, underscore the point. If the public finds them interesting, then there must be a high level of interest in advertising.

Closely tied to this argument is the point that advertising is a necessity to keep the economy running. If products are not advertised and sold, then factories lay off workers, there is less money spent in payrolls, still fewer goods bought, more factories close, and a recession or depression develops. It is clear that advertising creates desires and provokes people into buying things they probably would not otherwise purchase. So advertising is one of the great forces in the United States that keeps the industrial economic system functioning. It is far cheaper to sell through advertising than to rely entirely on salespeople.

This argument is so cogent that it sometimes leads to a false set of priorities. Perhaps an advertising specialist cannot be faulted for regarding the mass media as one great medicine show designed to attract the public into the tent so that the barker can give the sales pitch. After all, that is the job of advertising specialists, but the people who run the media need broader motives.

Exploitation Versus Service

Some television managers have adopted the advertiser's jargon so that they call the area in which their signal is received their "market." Thus we hear of the Pittsburgh market or the Detroit market. If the media are going to carry advertising, it is reasonable that they should be able to extol their virtues to the people who buy the space and time. At the same time, one can hope that the distraction of providing a channel to a group of potential advertisers does not get too much in the way of a media proprietor's vision of an audience to be served. The difference is between exploiting an audience and serving it.

Perhaps the most telling argument against advertising in the mass media is that it forces media proprietors into efforts to maximize the size of their audience, and it makes survival more difficult for the media that are not first in advertising in their circulation area.

The well-known tendency of the networks to program against each other illustrates the struggles to attain the largest audiences. This practice has two identifiable results, both disadvantageous to audiences. First, it results in the networks scheduling their strongest programs against their competitors' strongest programs, thus depriving viewers of the opportunity to watch the top of the line in both or all three networks. Second, it promotes imitation. When a program does particularly well in the ratings, the other networks produce similar programs. Thus the networks break out in rashes of detective programs one season, doctor programs another, and so on through the gamut.

Both practices limit the variety available to the viewer and stifle the creative instincts of producers. They result from the natural instincts of network executives to be "first" in the ratings, but this urge is tremendously increased by the economics of advertising.

Newspapers' survival conditions are affected, too, by advertising practices. Advertisers, quite naturally, try to get maximum exposure of their messages at minimum cost. Once a newspaper achieves the largest circulation in its area it is able to offer advertisers greater circulation than its competitors at a lower cost per thousand readers. In cities where there is more than one newspaper many individuals will read two or three papers. If the same advertisement were inserted in all these newspapers it would be waste, or "duplicated," circulation from the point of view of the advertiser, who is likely to choose to buy space in only the paper with the largest circulation. This practice is so widespread, in fact, that the largest circulation newspaper in an area can count on a considerable amount of national advertising that will not be available to its competitors. Since advertising produces well over half the revenue of most newspapers, this advantage for the largest circulation newspaper may be of enough importance to put the competitors out of business.

Thus, while readers may be quite willing to support a second newspaper in a community, the economics of advertising is such that being in second place in circulation, perhaps by only a few thousand, may be a fatal blow. The economics of advertising is part of the reason for the demise of a number of newspapers with large circulations, but not the largest in their community.

No one can expect a company to spend money in advertising to keep a newspaper solvent. The only justifiable reason to buy advertising is to sell products. While an advertiser cannot be blamed for the paucity of cities with more than a single newspaper, the advertising system itself is a factor. With readers habituated to paying only about a third of the cost of the paper, circulation revenue will not meet expenses.

The net effect is that the economics of industry and advertising rather than the information needs of the public have become the determining factor in the number of daily newspapers available in any community. Newspapers depend on advertisers for their lives.

Public Acceptance

In other media, too, most people would rather accept advertising and take their cheap or "free" media. Many people say they like advertising in the media.

As Figure 7.1 shows, the public tends to accept advertising, although the degree of acceptance appears to vary from one medium to another.

Surveys of radio and television audiences consistently show listeners and viewers are tolerant, even appreciative of advertising. Tables 7.2 and 7.3 show the trend.

For practical purposes, the way many of the media have developed, it is not a question as to whether advertising will be a major source of support, but rather what the influence of advertising is. Not all publishers are happy with this fact, but most adjust to it. Ralph Ingersoll, founder of the adless *PM*, became the owner of advertising-supported papers after the fall of *PM*. In 1975 the fourteen dailies owned by Ralph Ingersoll and Associates had a total daily circulation of nearly 400,000.

Magazine publishers, too, have complained that the necessity to win the largest possible circulation has caused magazines to sell themselves so cheaply that readers are unwilling to pay a reasonable part of the cost. Cut-rate subscription offers may result in an actual loss to the publication because the advertisers may not be interested in those subscribers, and increased advertising rates may not meet the cost of producing and dis-

Figure 7.1 How People Feel About Advertising

In 1975 advertising in newspapers was regarded with most favor, advertising by direct mail with the least favor. The data comes from a nationwide probability sample of 1,803 persons taken by the American Association of Advertising Agencies.

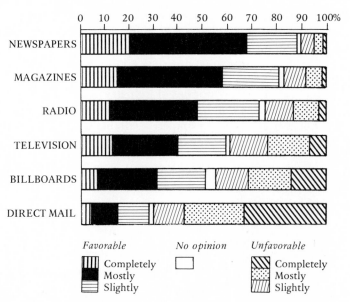

From *Editor & Publisher*, March 29, 1975, p. 12. Reprinted with permission.

tributing the magazine. *Saturday Evening Post, Look,* and *Life* were limiting their circulation in their last days.

The ultimate in advertiser support is reached by the so-called controlled circulation publications that are distributed free to readers. Neighborhood "shoppers" fall into this class, as do some magazines that are sent free to persons in a position to make buying decisions of importance to the advertisers. For some of these publications, free circulation is a beginning step intended to demonstrate the publication's value to readers before they are asked to subscribe. For others, it is a way of life.

Table 7.2   Views Toward Television Commercials / 1963–1974

Views expressed in answer to the question "Which one of these four statements comes closest to describing how you feel about commercials on television?"

	Nov. 1963	Nov. 1964	Jan. 1967	Nov. 1968	Jan. 1971	Nov. 1972	Nov. 1974
I dislike practically all commercials on TV	10%	10%	11%	13%	11%	14%	12%
While some of the commercials on TV are all right, most of them are very annoying	29	26	26	25	24	27	28
There are some very annoying commercials on TV, but most of them are perfectly all right	31	35	33	35	38	32	35
The commercials on TV seldom annoy me—in fact, I often enjoy them	24	23	21	22	24	24	23
DK/NA	6	6	9	5	3	3	2

Source: Based on a series of nationwide surveys conducted by the Roper Organization, Inc., for the Television Information Office. Adapted from the Roper Report, *Trends in Public Attitudes Toward Television and Other Mass Media, 1959–1974.* New York: Television Information Office, 1975. Reprinted with permission of the Television Information Office.

What is a reasonable amount of support from the advertisers, on the one hand, and from the readers on the other? Allen H. Neuharth, president of Gannett Newspapers, asked that question at the 1973 meeting of the Associated Press Managing Editors Association in Orlando, Florida. He titled his speech, "Is Your Newspaper Worth a Cup of Coffee?" The suggestion was that newspapers had failed to increase the price to readers to match the price of other goods and services. Paid circulation has traditionally been more highly regarded than free by newspaper and magazine management. The feeling is that the readers are more likely to take a publication seriously when they pay directly for it. Also, the editorial and news staffs are more likely to put the readers first if the readers pay more.

The audiences of broadcast stations might gain more control over programs if they paid the bill for the service directly. That is the argument for proponents of pay television. Cable television makes it technically feasible to charge viewers for programs. The large number of channels available on cable systems also make it possible to provide variety. Therefore, a small group of viewers might be able to meet the costs of a program they wanted to see. As we noted in Chapter 6, the commercial networks and stations have opposed pay television for the obvious reasons that audiences would be smaller and so of less interest to advertisers.

Three major media have been able to survive mostly without advertising support: books, motion pictures, and the stage. It is significant,

Table 7.3   Desirability of Television Commercials / 1963–1974

Views expressed in answer to the question "Different people have all sorts of things, both good and bad, to say about TV commercials—for example—that they are in poor taste, that they are informative, that they are amusing, that there are too many of them, etc. Now, everything considered, do you agree or disagree that having commercials on TV is a fair price to pay for being able to watch it?"

	Nov. 1963	Nov. 1964	Jan. 1967	Nov. 1968	Jan. 1971	Nov. 1972	Nov. 1974
Agree	77%	81%	80%	80%	80%	81%	84%
Disagree	14	10	9	10	10	14	12
DK/NA	9	9	11	10	10	5	4

Source: Based on a series of nationwide surveys conducted by the Roper Organization, Inc., for the Television Information Office. Adapted from the Roper Report, *Trends in Public Attitudes Toward Television and Other Mass Media, 1959–1974.* New York: Television Information Office, 1975. Reprinted with permission of the Television Information Office.

too, that these media depend less or not at all on the periodic appeal that bolsters the audiences of newspapers, magazines, and broadcasters. Newspapers rely on the newspaper reading habit and try to establish themselves as regular friendly visitors. Magazines do the same. Radio and television rely on weekly situation comedies, daily talk shows, and soap operas to keep the audience tuning in. Broadcasters have the additional pull of presenting familiar personalities. Personalities on news programs and hosts of variety shows as well as radio disc jockeys may become surrogate friends who encourage a continuity in viewing patterns.

While some of these factors work for the nonperiodic media, the regularity of contact is uneven and less pronounced, so that there is more of a gamble involved. Certainly some people have a movie-going habit, a play-going habit, or a book-reading habit. But that is different from a habit of tuning in a certain program at a certain time every day or week or reading the newspaper at a certain time each day. Moviegoers may go to a film theater to see a certain favored star, and book readers may buy the work of a certain author, but those habits still lack the regularity of appeal offered by the periodic media.

For this reason each offering by a book publisher, a film company, or a theater producer is a gamble. Although this arrangement provides less security, it encourages originality. Lack of advertising income, while it may cause financial worries, does provide freedom from advertising restraints. The nonperiodic and nonadvertising media have come in for their share of criticism, but they are more likely than the others to experiment and provide variety in content. They also supply material of interest to relatively small audiences.

In sum, advertising has strengthened the financial position of the media it uses, but it has taken away some of the adventure and variety found in the media that put their chips on each new book, play, or film offered to the public.

The Middlemen of Advertising

Advertising agencies are the middlemen between the media and the industries that spend billions each year in them. Professionals in the agencies advise the companies that advertise, plan campaigns for them, produce the advertisements, and decide what media will carry them. Activities in the agencies are vital to the media and to the public.

As they plan campaigns, agency people suggest whether television, radio, newspapers, magazines, direct mail, or some combination of these will be used. Furthermore, they usually select what specific network, station, or publication will carry the advertising. Thus their good will is important to the media that depend on advertising. Much media research is designed to discover information that will impress the agencies.

The public's direct stake in agency activities comes from the agencies' control of commercial content of the media. The vast number of advertising messages that reach the public have important social effects, as we shall see later. Consumers of the products advertised are affected, too, by the quality of the ethical decisions made in the agencies, for these have much to do with the honesty and fairness with which products are presented to the American public.

Most national and a considerable amount of the local advertising, especially in the broadcast media, is handled through agencies. There are about four thousand such agencies in the United States, ranging in size from tiny operations to such giants as J. Walter Thompson, which places nearly a billion dollars' worth of advertising every year. The people who work for these agencies perform many marketing services for the advertisers they represent, but essentially they prepare and place selling messages. For this service they receive a percentage of the charge by the paper or station for carrying the advertising. Normally they buy time and space and pay the bills for the advertiser, subtracting their commission as the money passes through their hands.

Regulation of Advertising

As one of the most visible of business activities, advertising is frequently scrutinized for its honesty, and it has come under formal and informal regulation. Considering the nature of early efforts to sell nostrums of all sorts, it is surprising that regulation came so late. Early American newspapers are full of advertising for miraculous medicines which were said to cure everything from "frightful dreams" through "stinking breath" to "the body decay'd lean."

One of the earliest industry efforts to police advertising was sparked by *Printer's Ink,* an advertising trade publication. In 1911 its editor presented a model statute and urged its adoption by all state legislatures. Revised in 1945, the model bill has been enacted, sometimes with variations, in forty-five states. It makes false advertising a misdemeanor. Endorsed by Better Business Bureaus, it has undoubtedly been useful in keeping potential Shylocks from using the media to defraud, but it has never produced a great volume of cases.

The federal government was slow to regulate advertising, but now its agencies are the principal means of control. By far the most influential agency in this regard is the Federal Trade Commission. Other federal agencies involved in the regulation of advertising in interstate commerce are the U.S. Postal Service, the Federal Communications Commission, the Food and Drug Administration, the Securities and Exchange Commission, and the Alcohol and Tobacco Tax Division of the Internal Revenue Service.

The U.S. Postal Service

The Post Office Department (now the Postal Service) became concerned early with deception in direct-mail advertising and in ads in periodicals carried at favorable second-class rates. Patent medicines and their fantastic claims were tolerated for extended periods, but eventually they led to the first systematic clean-up efforts. Fly-by-night operators found the mails a convenient device for their schemes and frequently they moved from one post office address to another, one jump ahead of the postal inspectors.

Fraud charges involving religious movements are among the most difficult for they involve freedom of religion as well as freedom of the press. *United States* v. *Ballard*[5] furnishes a good example. The charge was that literature was sold and distributed, funds solicited, and memberships sought in the "I Am" movement "by means of false and fraudulent representations and promises." It was charged that Guy W. Ballard had pretended to record the words of the "ascended masters," including Jesus and other religious figures.

When the mail fraud charge went to the jury in district court, the judge limited the issue to a decision on the basis of whether persons accused were sincere in their beliefs. If jury members believed the accused were sincere they were instructed to bring in a verdict of not guilty. The jury brought in a guilty verdict. On appeal the circuit court held that the judge had erred in limiting the issue only to the sincerity of Ballard and his family.

The Supreme Court reversed the circuit court, but still remanded the case for further proceedings in the district court. In a dissent, Justice Jackson stated aptly some of the dilemmas that face a court in religious issues, whether or not they involve advertising. He commented:

> There appear to be persons—let us hope not many—who find refreshment and courage in the teachings of the "I Am" cult. If the members of the sect get comfort from the celestial guidance of their "Saint Ger-

[5]322 U.S. 78 (1944).

main," however doubtful it seems to me, it is hard to say that they do not get what they pay for.

Jackson argued that the principal wrong done by false prophets is not financial, but the "mental and physical poison" that they sow. The Constitution, however, put that beyond the reach of the prosecutor, "for the price of freedom of religion or of speech or of the press is that we must put up with, and even pay for, a good deal of rubbish. . . . I would . . . have done with this business of judicially examining other people's faiths."[6]

Throughout the history of the United States the Post Office has been one of the valves generally encouraging, but sometimes inhibiting the flow of advertising and other information. Traditionally the Post Office has encouraged the circulation of newspapers and magazines through favorable second-class rates, often transporting them at less than cost to provide a wide dispersal of information among citizens.

Once a publication begins to depend on the use of second-class rates to distribute copies, the possibility of removal from this status or even an increase in the rates becomes a threat to the publication's survival. Magazines are particularly dependent on the mails for distributing their copies, so any change in second-class rates affects their budgets. The chief organization of the magazine industry, the Magazine Publishers Association, keeps an eye on rate changes and their effects on magazines. One magazine specialist, Robert Root, underscored the importance of second-class rates: "The hard publishing fact is that advertising and subscription costs, as visualized today, simply cannot bear the full distribution costs, along with ever-mounting production costs."[7]

Thus the removal of second-class rates can be a control device on a magazine or newspaper. In addition, the statutes make it a crime to mail obscene material.[8] Thus the Post Office has two control devices: (1) the threat of removal of second-class privileges, and (2) penalties in a criminal action. To the publisher the Post Office is another watchdog to be appeased; to consumers the Post Office represents another buffer that affects the information and ideas that they receive.

The Federal Trade Commission

One of the first moves of the federal government in the control of advertising came with the passage of the Federal Trade Commission Act of 1914. The commission established by the act was designed at first

[6]Ibid., pp. 94–95.
[7]Robert Root, *Modern Magazine Editing* (Dubuque, Iowa: Wm. C. Brown, 1966), p. 429.
[8]18 U.S.C.A. 1461.

to police competitive practices outlawed by the antitrust laws, but it now spends most of its time regulating advertising. Its original purpose was underscored by court decisions that limited its power to control advertising to cases in which competitive businesses were injured. In 1937 the U.S. Supreme Court extended the FTC's power to include cases in which the consumer was the aggrieved party, and in the following year the Wheeler-Lea Admendment enacted the provision into law.

Thus armed, the FTC has become the most important regulatory agency for advertising. It monitors advertising in interstate commerce and receives complaints from consumers and others. It has fairly complicated hearing procedures to determine whether an advertisement is false or misleading. It has three kinds of remedies against objectionable material. These are voluntary agreements from advertisers to end the undesirable advertising; cease and desist orders that force compliance but are subject to court review; and publicity. The last alternative has been quite effective.

One of the tests of an advertisement is literal truth, but even material that passes this test may be found to give a false impression when taken as a whole. Such material requires subtle decisions—especially in television advertising where the combination of eye and ear channels provide for communication through implication.

The Federal Communications Commission

Through its licensing power and mandate to keep broadcasters operating in the public interest, the Federal Communications Commission has sometimes become involved in the regulation of advertising. One of the critical issues is whether advertising should be held to the same standards of fairness as news and public affairs broadcasting.

New York lawyer John F. Banzhaf brought the issue to a head in 1966. He wrote to the FCC complaining that station WCBS-TV in New York was airing cigarette commercials without allowing time for ads in rebuttal describing the harmful effects of smoking. This, he insisted, constituted a violation of the fairness doctrine, which requires broadcasters to cover both sides of controversial issues.

The FCC brushed aside WCBS's defense that it had over a period of years broadcast programs describing the health hazards of smoking and ordered the station to provide time for rebuttal advertising. This began the "counter commercials" that annoyed broadcasters and cigarette manufacturers alike until cigarette advertising was ruled off the air by Congress.

The FCC was also involved in another delicate area of regulation: advertising that urges political action or otherwise tries to influence social change. In 1970 the Business Executives' Move for a Vietnam Peace complained to the FCC that Washington radio station WTOP refused a series of one-minute paid commercials protesting the Vietnam War. WTOP based its refusal on a claim that it had already fulfilled its duty under the fairness doctrine by broadcasting varied views on the subject.

A few months later the Democratic National Committee (DNC) sought a judgment from the FCC holding that "a broadcaster may not . . . refuse to sell time to responsible entities, such as DNC, for the solicitation of funds and for comment on public issues."[9] The FCC rejected the complaints of both the Business Executives for a Vietnam Peace and the DNC. The cases were combined when they were appealed to the Circuit Court of Appeals for the District of Columbia. The court overruled the FCC, 2–1, observing: "Even if broadcasters were to succeed in presenting a full spectrum of viewpoints and partisan spokesmen on non-advertising time, their reaction of *total* initiative and editorial control is inimical to the First Amendment."[10]

When the case came to the Supreme Court on appeal, the lower court decision was reversed 7–2.[11] Justice Warren Burger, writing for the majority, put much stock in the argument that it is the duty of the broadcaster to present all the important views involving public issues, and that it is the duty of the FCC to remove a station's license if it fails to do so. Justice Burger put his faith on the already established procedures for requiring broadcasters to provide variety of viewpoints in public affairs programming. The lower court's decision would have added another force to the fray—a force that could be initiated by any person or group with enough money to produce commercials and buy broadcast time. Burger cited the refusal of Congress to make broadcasters into common carriers of information. Although they are responsible for balanced reporting of views on public issues, they are not required to provide access to anyone who wishes to discuss an issue. The essential right, he held, belongs to the public, and it is the right to be informed. This right is paramount to the right of any individual or group to speak out on broadcast facilities.

Justices William O. Douglas and Potter Stewart concurred with the majority decision in separate opinions. Douglas cited growing threats to liberty. Stewart held that the lower court decision would require the government to exercise controls over the media. He said:

> This is a step . . . that could eventually lead to the proposition that private *newspapers* "are" government. Freedom of the press would then be gone. In its place we would have such government controls upon

[9]412 U.S. 94 at 98.
[10]450 F. 2d 642 (1971).
[11]412 U.S. 94 (1972).

the press as a majority of this Court at any particular moment might consider First Amendment "values" to require. It is a frightening spectre.[12]

Justice Brennan, in dissenting, maintained that the majority decision offered a safe haven to broadcasters who try to avoid controversy. The decision, he said, permits broadcasting of commercials dealing only with products or noncontroversial concerns.

Issue Advertising: An Overview

Broadcasters are not required to accept advertising concerned with issues in order to fulfill their obligations to present all sides of matters of public concern. Presumably a broadcaster who accepts advertising on one side of a controversial issue would be required to accept commercials representing other views of the same issue. As the appeals court remarked, the initiative in public affairs programming might be transferred partially from the broadcaster to whatever organizations had interest enough and money enough to buy commercials.

As far as newspapers are concerned, the issues are clear-cut. A privately owned paper is not required to take advertising it considers undesirable so long as the exclusion is systematic and does not constitute part of a pattern that violates the antitrust laws. This makes it possible for newspapers to censor motion picture advertising and to reject advertisements that are considered to be in bad taste or that would tend to victimize a paper's readers.

Most newspapers accept political and issue advertising on the grounds that such material is in the public interest. The New York Times, for example, has stated editorially that it considers it a duty to keep its columns open to "those who wish to express a particular point of view, no matter how widely divergent it may be from our own."

The courts have held that college newspapers in state-supported institutions do not have the option of rejecting issue advertising. The theory is that the paper, even though it is published by students, is an organ of the state institution and thus an arm of government. The same logic has been used to require public transit authorities to accept issue ads in stations and cars.

It is clear enough from this discussion that commercial advertising is not protected as free speech under the First Amendment. The Supreme Court upheld that view when the issue came before it.[13] First Amendment

[12]412 U.S. 94 at 133.
[13]Valentine v. Chrestensen, 316 U.S. 52 (1942).

protection was granted to issue advertising, however, when the *New York Times* was sued for libel in connection with material run in a paid advertisement concerning civil rights. The court disposed of the question with this statement: "That the Times was paid for publishing the advertisement is as immaterial in this connection as is the fact that newspapers and books are sold."[14]

Other Federal Regulatory Agencies

The Securities and Exchange Commission (SEC) requires detailed information before securities can be offered to the public. It can stop the sale of any stock that is misrepresented in material filed with the SEC or in the prospectus that is used to interest prospective buyers.

The Alcohol and Tobacco Tax Division of the Internal Revenue Service monitors liquor advertising to prevent false statements, and it has enforcement powers.

The Food and Drug Administration (FDA) oversees labeling and branding of food, drugs, and cosmetics to prevent false statements. By agreement with the FTC, which has similar powers, the FDA generally limits its jurisdiction to labels, leaving advertising to the FTC.

Self-Regulation

Since advertising has been a ready tool for every fast-buck artist as well as legitimate businesspeople it is inevitable that many people would attempt to use it to exploit the gullible. Because it takes only a few good drubbings for even the most naive to henceforth mistrust advertising, the legitimate business suffers from every fake who advertises. This has brought about a good bit of self-regulation in the industry.

The media themselves tend to be blamed directly or indirectly by victims of fraudulent advertising and by a decline in confidence in advertising in general, so they tend to be careful to ensure the truth and fairness of the advertising they run. Large stations and newspapers have specific standards of advertising acceptance and staffs to see that they are adhered to. Magazines do the same.

Gay Talese tells a bit about how the *New York Times* advertising censors work:

[14]*New York Times v. Sullivan*, 376 U.S. 254 at 265–266 (1964).

> In the ad [for Coppertone] is a big tawny photograph of Raquel Welch
> in a bikini, a *Playboy* pose that raised the eyebrows but not the objec-
> tions of *The Times'* Advertising Acceptability department, which has
> become more liberal in recent years. These men . . . reject advertise-
> ments dealing with fortune-telling and horoscopes, miracle medi-
> cines, and speculative investments in mines, and they generally tone
> down the wording in ads to avoid overstatement. . . . They disallow
> nudes in ads except in the case of children, but they will permit the
> scantiest of bikinis in ads for tropical islands and suntan lotions and
> soap—*The Times* . . . now accepts the fact that women have navels.[15]

The rules that govern the work of the *Times'* censors cover several
pages. They are meant to root out advertising that is fraudulent, over-
stated, or immoral. With the advent of sexually explicit motion pictures,
many newspapers have put their artists to work airbrushing clothes on
actresses pictured in the ad copy, while editors change the wording to
make it less shocking. Some motion picture companies have responded
by preparing two sets of advertising. If a risque ad is rejected a more moderate version is instantly available.

Better Business Bureaus receive complaints about advertising, and
through negotiation and threat of legal action, they keep in check the activities of unscrupulous advertisers. In a form of self-regulation the
American Association of Advertising Agencies (the 4A's) cooperates with
a national bureau that monitors advertising, investigates complaints, and
brings pressure on advertisers found remiss.

The rise of consumer groups has increased the sensitivity of businesses
and enforcement agencies to flaws in advertising. Sharp criticism from
Ralph Nader[16] and the American Bar Association[17] has made the FTC
stricter in its enforcement procedures. The credibility of advertising is as
important to the media that carry it as to the advertisers themselves.

Advertising as a Social Force

The criticism of advertising centers around two central factors:
advertising as a waste, and advertising as an undesirable influence on
the public.

[15]Gay Talese, *The Kingdom and the Power* (New York: World Publishing, 1969), pp.
77–78.
[16]Edward F. Cox, Robert C. Fellmeth and John E. Schulz, *"The Nader Report"* on the Federal Trade Commission (New York: R. W. Baron, 1969).
[17]The Report of the American Bar Association to Study the Federal Trade Commission,
1969.

The first criticism follows a line of reasoning that at first appears to be logical enough. The costs of advertising are high; they are paid by companies that make a profit from selling goods to the public; the cost of advertising is added to the selling price of the goods; therefore, advertising increases the costs of goods and services. Proponents of advertising counter this criticism by arguing that although advertising does cost money and that the cost is added to the price of goods and services sold, this cost is negligible compared to any other method of selling in volume. The price of salespeople to accomplish the same sales volume would be prohibitive. In fact, they argue, advertising is essential to the volume sales that make possible mass production that in turn allows for low unit price. Volume sales not only allow for low production costs, but allow for a low mark-up on each item, thereby keeping prices down.

The advocates of advertising have the better argument. Goods in abundance can be achieved only by mass production, and marketing and advertising make this possible. Advertising is a phenomenon of a society of abundance. When goods are scarce there is no need to advertise. In an affluent society there is need for a means of informing consumers about the options open to them, and advertising performs that function.

As to the undesirable social effects of advertising, it is not easy to reach a conclusion.

One of the principal arguments under this heading is that advertising creates wants. Furthermore, the argument implies that these wants so created are materialistic and thus debasing. It is doubtful that critics include among the undesirable advertising that which advocates regular church attendance, or notices of concerts or public affairs lectures—activities that are deemed to be socially desirable. Advertising promotes these activities as well as the purchase of expensive liquor, luxurious gas-eating automobiles, and tickets to topless-bottomless nightclub shows. Presumably the criticism concerns the advertising urging activities that are considered unacceptable.

The criticism of advertising seems to imply that all goals of advertising are somehow socially unacceptable. If the creation of all new wants and needs is undesirable, then preachers should be removed from their pulpits and statesmen silenced. Advertising people counter this argument by working on the old maxim that today's necessities were yesterday's luxuries. Central heating and air conditioning were not seen as a "need" a few generations ago, but few of advertising's critics denounce them now.

But some of the criticism of advertising is justified. Too often advertising turns the public's attention to frivolities, to time- and energy-wasters. Too often it develops a need for a large automobile with so much power that energy is wasted and the atmosphere sullied.

Advertising is often criticized for urging the public to believe that there are simple solutions for complex problems. Are you ignored by the opposite sex? Perhaps our patented pimple remover, waist shrinker, bust builder, smile brightener, breath purifier, shyness eradicator, will do the job. Simply send in the coupon and enclose your check. . . .

Successful advertising often does sell the hoped-for results of its products rather than the products directly. Thus we find a happy world of beautiful people finding in the sponsors' products simple solutions to complicated problems. Many observers have noted the peculiar dichotomy of the news media. Events of the real world, usually grim, march up and down one set of columns, while adjacent to them is pictured the hoped-for world of pleasure, success, and peace, all to be achieved through the use of given products.

There is no question about it. Advertisers do use oversimple sales pitches. The need to seize attention quickly, project an unambiguous message, and leave a distinct impression requires simple messages. That is the nature of advertising and one of its dangers. In repeatedly hammering home the idea that happy solutions to complex problems come from bottles, stereo sets, or glamorous clothing, advertising may strip some people of the ability to face a reality that often requires time, work, and agony to achieve an accommodation with the world.

Most criticisms of advertising center around the methods used and sometimes the frivolity of the goods sold. The methods debase the public, critics say, and make people less capable of facing their problems. Advertising people could do some things to meet such criticisms, but the objections will never be completely erased. Some restrictions would make selling impossible, and some of the criticisms seem to be founded on a vague feeling of unease with mass production and mass selling rather than with advertising per se. If advertising is seen as corrupting the world it is more likely that the ultimate villain is buried deeper in the system. While the United States retains its present system of free enterprise, advertising will be a part of it. It can be improved in its emphasis and method, but it is a necessity in some form.

Advertising and the Media

Advertising was an early component of American as well as British newspapers. The *Boston News-Letter* of December 10, 1730, for example, carried ads for butter, books, velvet, corks, empty bottles, and clothes from Europe. A store took space to announce a new address; a debtor denied that he had absconded; and the owner of a stolen sloop sought to recover it. John Peter Zenger, famous for his struggle with Governor Cosby, was the first American newspaper publisher to run display advertising. It appeared in Zenger's *New York Weekly Journal*. Magazines followed the lead of newspapers.

Advertising was more critical for radio. Early stations were maintained by manufacturers of receivers as an inducement to the public to purchase sets. Once the idea of commercial messages proved profitable, advertising took over as a means of financing broadcasting, despite protests from then Secretary of Commerce Herbert C. Hoover and inventor Lee DeForest. Television took over radio's commercial patterns as it took over many of its programming ideas.

Why do books remain free of advertising material? One reason certainly is that they lack the periodic schedules of newspapers and magazines. Advertisers cannot count on regular space or time every day, every week, or every month. Neither can they count on a guaranteed audience size. Newspapers and magazines, with circulations ascertained and warranted by the Audit Bureau of Circulations, can deliver a known audience. Radio and television can do almost as well after new programs in the fall or spring schedule have found their audience and viewing patterns have been predicted. The size of the readership of any new book is a guess, and few advertisers are willing to share the gamble a publisher takes with each new title. But this has some advantage for the publisher. Since readers have always had to pay the full cost of the books they buy they never got in the habit of expecting to pay one-third or less of the actual cost as they do when they buy newspapers or magazines.

Like books, motion pictures have neither a periodic appeal nor a guaranteed audience and so they have never attracted the advertising sponsorship given broadcasters, magazines, and newspapers. Their start as peep shows probably had something to do with it, too. Peep-show proprietors collected nickels from patrons who came in from the street to watch the low comedy or cheap thrills provided. People attended in sufficiently large numbers to provide a profit, but the kind of people attracted did not have a great deal of money to spend, so advertisers were not too much interested in trying to win them as customers. Just the same, advertising is still a staple of some movie houses—particularly in smaller cities and towns where promotional material may take from five to fifteen minutes of a program. The income derived in this way keeps some theaters open.

What has all this to do with the content and effects of the media? The answer is speculative.

Sometimes advertisers have influenced the media directly. This control was obvious in the great days of radio when an advertiser would buy an entire program. "Buying" it often meant that the advertising agency would plan the program, hire the stars, oversee production, and buy the specified time for its airing. The network served merely as the conduit connecting the advertiser with the audience. This sometimes led to the stars becoming identified with the products avertised. Thus comedian Jack Benny opened his radio show in the early days with the words: "Jello again, this is Jack Benny. . . ." A manufacturer of auto lubricants sponsored "Horace Heidt for Alemite," and so it went.

Star identification with products did not disturb too many critics until the 1970's. Then protests from pressure groups stopped the practice in many children's programs of having the star do the commercial. The children were so easily influenced by the performers, some people felt, that such practices amounted to exploitation.

Sponsored newscasts posed a special problem. Sponsor pressure was usually negative and veiled. It took the form of withdrawing as a sponsor if the content or the newscaster were considered undesirable. At the other extreme some news commentators interrupted their comments to enthusiastically deliver the commercials. Boake Carter was an early example of the practice that has been carried into the mid-1970's by Paul Harvey. Most reputable newscasters resist doing commercials on the ground that it might possibly appear to prejudice their credibility as a newsperson. "Today," NBC's highly successful soufflé, mixes hard news, comment, interviews, banter, and banality. At first it required its performers to double as news and entertainment personalities as well as product pluggers. Some of the individuals considered for the "host" roles have been said to turn it down despite the large salary offered because they did not want to do the commercials.

Their stand is reasonable. Even the appearance of mixing the news and advertising functions reduces the credibility of the performer. When Tom Brokaw became host of "Today" in 1976, NBC relaxed the requirement.

What effect has advertising had on the information media of the United States? We can make only general estimates. As we have seen, advertising has intensified the media's natural drive to maximize the audience, which sometimes is accomplished by debasing the content.

The media that are not supported by advertising tend to offer more variety and to appeal part of the time to minority as well as majority audiences. The quality of their product is not always higher. Motion pictures, unsupported by advertising revenue, have sought to hold and increase their audiences by pornography and other displays not generally regarded as uplifting. Some novels appear to be designed only to sell books and movie rights to the profit of the author and publisher. It is not possible to generalize about quality of content of the media supported by advertising as compared to those depending entirely on their audiences.

Media and their advertisers depend on each other, support each other, and often could not live without each other. But their marriage is one of tension.

Edward Corlett, one-time publisher of a Copley newspaper in Joliet, Illinois, described this publisher-advertiser tension in these words:

> If an advertiser finds out that he can get things in a paper, or keep things out, why you are going to be in misery every day of your life.
>
> If there was an item of news that I regarded as harmless, something that didn't matter whether it ran or not, and an advertiser came in and asked me not to run it, I would tell the editorial department to run it for just this reason—the advertiser would go out and brag about it, claiming he kept the item out, and then the advertisers get a regular job aiding the editor right along![18]

In a 1938 memorandum to some of his staff Henry R. Luce described his view of Time, Inc.'s relationship with advertisers:

> We do not want to be subsidized by anybody. . . . But if we have to be subsidized by anybody, we think the Advertiser presents extremely interesting possibilities. We believe we can be subsidized by the Advertiser by giving him value for value received and without compromising more than a small fraction of our journalistic soul. The small fraction we are frankly willing to sell for a price.[19]

That "small fraction" Luce was willing to sell marks the tension that always exists between the manager of an information medium and advertisers. How the manager handles that friction has much to do with the stature and credibility of the station or publication.

A *Minneapolis Star* writer found evidence in 1975 that some newspapers are giving in to advertising pressure, citing two examples. The first consisted of a quotation from a letter by a reporter on another, unnamed Midwestern paper to a friend: "No longer is it hinted that I should write stories about companies that will draw their advertising. I am now instructed to do so." The other example concerned a photograph and a banner line in the *Hartford Courant* announcing holiday auto sales. Reportedly, the story said, the announcement was suggested by the newspaper's advertising manager.

Things were better in Minneapolis, the article continued. The *Star* suffered a decline in auto ads after the paper published articles on car-repair services. The paper also received an "implied threat" to withdraw advertising after an unfavorable story about a food product. Robert W. Smith, publisher of the Minneapolis dailies, said: "I would guess that the

[18]Walter S. J. Swanson, *The Thin Gold Watch* (New York: Macmillan, 1964), p. 205.
[19]Robert T. Elson, *Time, Inc.* (New York: Atheneum, 1968), p. 357.

Star's consumer reporting alone has cost us a couple of hundred thousand dollars in lost ads."[20]

The critical influence of advertising comes, not from casual interference in editorial matters, but in the degree to which advertising commits, consciously or unconsciously, the editorial policy to a view of the medium's audience as a commodity to be sold rather than people who must be understood and informed.

[20]Peter Ackerberg, "Advertisers Bark, But Have No Bite on News Coverage," p. 9 of a reprint from the *Minneapolis Star* of articles on the news media in the Twin Cities that ran in that paper from August 25 through September 6, 1975.

Suggestions for Further Reading

Buxton, Edward. *Promise Them Anything: The Inside Story of the Madison Avenue Power Struggle.* New York: Stein and Day, 1972.
   A frothy account of advertising agencies.
Divita, S. F., ed. *Advertising and the Public Interest.* Chicago: American Marketing Association, 1974.
   Papers from a conference that covered FTC rulings, consumerism, and other aspects of advertising.
Freedom of Information in the Market Place. Columbia: University of Missouri, School of Journalism, Freedom of Information Center, 1966.
   Report of a conference on advertising and consumerism.
Hinckle, Warren. "The Adman Who Hated Advertising: The Gospel According to Howard Gossage." *Atlantic Monthly,* March 1974, pp. 67–72.
   Presents the idea that most advertising promotes nonessentials that compose only a small part of the gross national product.
Key, Wilson Bryan. *Subliminal Seduction: Ad Media's Manipulation of a Not So Innocent America.* Englewood Cliffs, N.J.: Prentice-Hall, 1973.
   A discussion of subliminal messages in advertising.
Mandell, Maurice I. *Advertising.* 2nd ed. Englewood Cliffs, N.J.: Prentice-Hall, 1974.
   Part I considers history and control of advertising and its relation to society.
Moskin, J. Robert, *The Case for Advertising.* New York: American Association of Advertising Agencies, 1973.
   A defense of advertising.
Preston, Ivan L. *The Great American Blow-up: Puffery in Advertising and Selling.* Madison: University of Wisconsin Press, 1975.
   An exposition of exaggeration in advertising.
Sandage, C. H. and Vernon Fryburger. *Advertising Theory and Practice.* 9th ed. Homewood, Ill.: R. D. Irwin, 1975.
   Early chapters provide background and theory.
Welles, Chris. "The Numbers Magazines Live By." *Columbia Journalism Review* 14 (September-October 1975): 22–27.
   Questions the validity of some of the research that attempts to measure magazine audiences.

A glance back at
Part Three
and ahead at
Part Four

In Chapter 6 we considered one of the most controversial aspects of the media in the United States—the extent to which ownership, particularly chain or group ownership, affects the way the media do their job. Although various governments own media units, particularly educational stations, the media generally are privately owned in the United States. This is defended generally on the theory that it is the only workable alternative to government ownership. Most of the criticisms of private ownership center about the question as to what, if any, limits should be placed on the number of media units that a single individual or group may own. We saw that the Federal Communications Commission limits the number of stations that can be held by a single owner, but that there is no corresponding limitation on the printed media. The FCC and the Justice Department have limited the number of media units that can be held by a single owner in the same community. The goal has been as much diversity of ownership as possible. As in other businesses, economic forces push in the opposite direction, toward fewer owners controlling more units. There is some hope that technology will lower the cost of ownership and so attract more individual owners.

Chapter 7 examined another economic question about the media—whether their dependence on advertising has any adverse effects and whether advertising itself is a useful social force. Only a cursory glance told us that advertising is an essential component of a free-enterprise, industrialized society. Advertising is necessary to sell goods in the large quantities required to support mass production and the economies it allows.

In the United States the question has settled down to deciding, not whether advertising should be allowed, but the extent to which it should be regulated. Advertising material is subject to much more control by government than the other content of the media, and First Amendment protection is not generally extended to it. Various government agencies are active, and advertising agencies and the media themselves provide self-regulation.

Among advertising's virtues is that it finances the media, sometimes lavishly enough that they can afford to provide high-quality content and can spend large sums to report major events like wars and national elections.

In Part Four we will consider how the media translate revenue from advertisers and audiences into content such as entertainment and the solid information that makes the democratic system function.

FOUR
Content and How It Is Selected

8

News, Information, and Reality

Stories rocketed around the world when President John F. Kennedy was assassinated in Dallas, Texas, on November 22, 1963.

News? News of the highest order.

Why? Because it combined the elements that make a great news story: drama, conflict, physical action, human interest, and importance. The people involved were already well known, and the lives of millions were affected. The event was unexpected and therefore all the more interesting.

The indicators of news value are unmistakable when they combine as they did in the Kennedy tragedy. No reporter could fail to recognize the news value of such a story.

In most other events and situations, news values are not so clear-cut. Usually the news is not dominated by a single, overwhelming story, so more judgment is required of the newspeople who decide what will be told to media audiences. Work habits of news organizations determine not only what events and situations they report, but also the manner in which the information is presented.

We will discuss news values and the habits of news organizations, but first we need to consider news as a special kind of information.

In Chapter 1 we viewed information as a mysterious something that links individuals to the world outside their skins. Information, we saw, comes to us through our senses, either firsthand from direct contact with the world, or secondhand through another person or a system that relays information from areas outside the reach of our senses. The world may be beyond our physical reach because of space or time limits. We cannot see, hear, or feel what is going on in another city; neither can we see, hear, or feel what was going on in the time of Plato. We have some idea of what is going on in other cities because our news media tell us; and we have an inkling of what went on in Plato's time because the historical media tell us.

News is information, but special information. Special because it links us not to all reality, but to certain aspects of it. In deciding what events to report, media people determine what these "newsworthy" aspects are. Media can easily control *what* they will report. Determining *how* they will report it is more difficult. The difficulties stem from differing concepts of reality.

Since human experience is unique, each of us has our own concept of the world. If ten individuals have knowledge of a certain situation, each of the ten will have a somewhat different concept of the reality of that situation. Each may understand that his or her own concept only approximates reality, but each must act on his or her own concept.

The news media seek to provide information that will help individuals in their audience to feel closer to the reality of certain events and situations.

What events and situations and whose sense of reality?

Varied Forces Center on the Media

The media have tight control over what events and situations they select for scrutiny, but only a loose control over the sense of reality they apply.

We will consider the second problem first. Composed of many individuals and complex technology and influenced by many forces, the news media are a kind of trading post where various concepts of reality try to prevail. We have seen that the media owner and the advertiser affect the attitude projected toward a situation, the concept of reality that is transmitted.

But economic controls are only part of the picture. Each reporter, each editor, producer, or camera operator has a part in selecting the concept of reality that will be broadcast or printed. A camera angle can change one's concept of a situation, as Orson Welles demonstrated in the film *Citizen Kane*, where low camera angles made people seem bigger than life and fostered an eerie mood. Does the camera move into a close-up of nervous tapping fingers of a subject being interviewed? Artistic, maybe, but also a control on the viewer's perception of reality. In a still photograph the moment when the shutter is released can make the subject look foolish or profound.

Television reporters who do the remote "stand-up" accounts of events can control the tone of the report that reaches the viewer. One news director admitted that he often disagreed with the interpretation of his reporters, but said it was difficult to do anything about it. He said that television reporters tend to regard themselves as "personalities" when they get on camera and resent any criticism of their approach to stories.

The technical aspects of the media have their impact, too. It is easier to change written copy for print than a radio or television news reporter's account on film or tape, so the editor is more likely to be influential in the printed media. Bulky cameras and recording equipment have limited the ability of television to keep pace with radio in on-the-spot coverage, although new lightweight cameras are now available. It was such equipment that allowed station KNXT in Los Angeles to bring to millions of viewers a powerful live drama in May 1974. The event dramatized the way broadcasters' ability to report events instantaneously has profoundly changed the controls they can apply.

Live Coverage Provides Drama

Live cameras and microphones transmitted color pictures and the sound of bullets as four hundred police officers surrounded a house in south-central Los Angeles where members of the Symbionese Liberation Army were holed up. The drama was intensified because it was suspected that fugitive heiress Patricia Hearst was inside. It turned out that she was not, but her parents, watching at their home near San Francisco, did not know it at the time. The drama of the event was heightened for viewers all over the country by the publicity that the SLA had received over an extended period after its members kidnaped Ms. Hearst.

Live broadcast of such dramatic events provides television with a new way of structuring reality for its viewers. Bill Eames, news director for station KNXT, said that newspeople in the studio were as amazed as their viewers by the possibilities of "real-time" coverage of events as demonstrated by the Los Angeles incident. He gave his views of the effectiveness of such coverage in these words:

Small children are locked into television in a way adults seldom understand because they believe that what they are seeing is going on at the same time. They are caught up in it. It is real to them.

Real-Time coverage does this for the adult. It is happening right now—no film, no video tape, no delays, no editing. There is always dramatic tension in any live report because anything might happen.[1]

Such coverage often puts news reporters in physical danger, and frequently it endangers their efforts to structure reality in the way they would like to. The writer reporting the affair for *TV Guide* described some of the dangers that make it difficult "to do a good job of reporting" in live coverage. Among the dangers are those of broadcasting false information and rumor; of broadcasting "inflammatory, slanderous, obscene" material; of being "used" to create an event simply by telecasting it live; of exaggerating a story in the excitement of live coverage; and of giving simplistic accounts of complicated occurrences.

The Media Structure Reality

The "dangers" just reported are instructive, for they provide a view of the control that news reporters feel they should exert in structuring reality for their viewers. Offhand, one might think that leaving cameras and microphones open at the scene of a dramatic news event would bring the viewers as close to the event as they could get without joining the reporters to duck the bullets. But in the Los Angeles shoot-out the television editors thought they had lost control of the story. They believed they should be able to screen out "inflammatory, slanderous, obscene" material. Television newspeople are trained to do this for good reason. Stations are not supposed to be broadcasting such information. Just the same, the practice alters the concept of reality that the audience receives. Newspeople also see their role as requiring them to interpret the scene for the viewer. They should not, they believe, exaggerate a story or provide a simplistic account of it. In other words, they should interpret the story in some fashion that places it in perspective. Whose perspective? Obviously, that of the station, its news department, and of individual reporters, although this is seldom admitted. (See Figure 8.1.)

The values reflected in these dangers as seen by newspeople reflect normal standards of news judgment and a desire to avoid superficial, if dramatic, coverage. Just the same, they illustrate how a set of values structures the picture of reality provided by the news media. The control of content normally exercised by a television reporter is further exemplified by *TV Guide's* comments:

[1]Joe Saltzman, "It's Live—and It's Terrifying," *TV Guide*, March 15, 1975, p. 6.

The more complex the story, the more danger there is of doing a superficial job of reporting.

A picket line is a good example. On video tape or film, the reporter would talk to those on the line, would interview union leaders, a union family at home, management officials, public officials, show an empty plant, and develop a polished story that covers all angles. In Real-Time coverage, the reporter goes to the demonstration and reports on it, doing it all ad-lib over one static picture from one location.[2]

The methods suggested for developing a "polished story" are familiar to any viewer of television news. It shows how a television reporter typically goes about structuring reality for viewers. The point is, reality very

Figure 8.1 Editing the News
An untidy environment is cleaned up as journalists impose some order on it so they can report it. Question: How accurate is the orderly version?

[2]Ibid., p. 10.

seldom comes in the form of a "polished story." As a population dependent for most of our information on the news media, all of us are deeply influenced by the structure of events that the media provide. Conscientious news reporters and editors shape their reports as they attempt to tell what an event means. For many stories such shaping is necessary. When a city council sets next year's tax rate, for example, some background is needed before a citizen can understand it. Obvious questions are how it compares with last year's rate and what caused the changes. What background questions are asked and how they are answered have an effect on the way a piece of information is received.

Naturally enough, few newspeople go around talking about "structuring reality." They talk about good stories, putting things in perspective, supplying background, providing balance, and reporting in depth. Since we are interested in tracing what information becomes news and how this relates to reality, it is important to examine the manner in which newspeople decide what to print or air and how they put it into perspective.

What actually gets into the news stream is determined by many things: the energy and intelligence of reporters; the habits of public officials; the interests of the public as seen by journalists; the traditions of the society; and sometimes by the sheer accident of a record falling into a reporter's hands, or by the intuition through which he or she puts two apparently isolated bits of information together and comes up with a clue on a situation that needs to be reported.

News organizations are large, somewhat varied, and institutionalized. This means that they form habits that they seldom question, but that determine the nature of the material they present for public attention. Moreover, news organizations regularly examine their own news reports alongside those of their competitors.

Patterns Repeat

These two factors—the institutionalizing of news-gathering habits and the constant attention to and sometimes mimicry of competitors—mean that the news reports tend to be repetitive. That is why one is likely to be exposed to reports of the same events whether one watches the early evening newcasts of ABC, CBS, or NBC, and why the front pages of newpapers across the country often feature the same news. The tendency toward sameness is further increased by the reliance of networks, stations, and newspapers on the two major news services, the Associated Press and United Press International.

Local news will have a surface difference, but journalistic habits produce an underlying sameness here, too. Local news staffs cover the same sources, so they report the same type of information. Police news is a staple. In small cities a person's arrest is almost sure to be noted in the paper. In the larger cities the volume of arrests is so great that it is not practical to report an arrest unless it involves another newsworthy characteristic, such as a widely known name. Courts, meetings of public bodies, and appearances by celebrities are reported by most of the media.

Newspeople see each other at national and regional meetings, they read each other's newspapers and watch each other's broadcasts, so it is not strange that they have the same ideas about what constitutes news. Neophytes in the profession are more often taught by example than by precept. The old-fashioned expression "a nose for news" is out of style now, but there is still in the profession more of a tendency to "feel" what is newsworthy than to analyze logically whether an event is worth public attention. The feeling is based on experience and contact with others.

Consumers of the media need to understand the values, habits, and limitations of news organizations in order to comprehend the messages these organizations send. As a person evaluates the report of a neighbor who has seen a fire down the street by considering the neighbor's ability to observe accurately and report honestly, so one evaluates the media. One aid to understanding is knowledge of news values. We listed some of these values at the beginning of this chapter. Now is the time to consider them in more detail. First: interest value.

The News Must Be Interesting

Tradition, instinct, and imitation are the chief governors of news value. An inherent first consideration is whether something will interest an audience. Even teachers with a captive audience in a classroom cannot depend on the importance of their material to accomplish their purposes. If they do not make it interesting, or at least palatable, to the students, it will have no effect on them. An individual faces the same necessity in a conversation. If he or she fails to interest the other party, the conversation ends. A speaker, too, must interest the audience or be ineffective. This common necessity sometimes causes teachers to become performers, conversationalists to become strident, and speakers to indulge in off-color jokes.

Media face the same problem. Even serious news has to have enough interest value to catch an audience and so provide a profit and enable the medium to survive. The media have toned down considerably since the days of yellow journalism when stories were sometimes invented to attract an audience. One phase of responsibility is refusing to give in to the drama of an event just to attract an audience. That is part of what the reporters were saying about the Symbionese Liberation Army shoot-out. Something like, "We shouldn't put it on the air live just because it is sure to attract an audience." The temptation to do just that is great. Competitors were reported to be angry that they had been beaten out by station KNXT on this "once-in-a-lifetime achievement." One competing reporter said: "Next time I'll be there first no matter what." The drama of the event as it was presented live made it big news. Drama frequently enhances the news story.

Drama Provides News

Elements of drama present themselves in various disguises, but they are part of nearly every news item. The tattered remnants of drama are recognizable in even the most hackneyed news stories. Stories of fires and homicides are likely to get into the news. They appear so often that they become monotonous and one of the reasons they are so frequently reported is that newspeople are in the habit of regarding these events as newsworthy. And the habit developed for a good reason—originally such stories were full of drama. If they appear dull now it is because journalists, having found a rich vein of drama, are slow to give it up. Occasionally a new twist revitalizes such a story. Sometimes it is a macabre twist, as when a Florida television commentator won national, though posthumous, publicity in 1974 by seizing a pistol and shooting herself before live cameras.

Journalists find drama in events that involve physical action or conflict or, better yet, both.

Wars are great news events. They involve conflict and great physical spectacles—ships and airplanes in movement, bombings, raids, and any number of men and machines in violent physical activity. Strikes and street confrontations have the same appeal, although on a smaller scale. Physical action is what produces the drama of hold-up stories, auto accidents, plane crashes, and Easter egg rolls on the White House lawn.

Drama is provided, too, by events that put human forces against each other or against disaster or disease. Drama that combines physical action and human conflict is usually recognized as highly newsworthy. Courtrooms are full of such drama, as playwrights like John Galsworthy and producers of Perry Mason episodes are aware. News reporters tap the same mine of drama. Since their accounts report actual events they have added impact. Conflict occurs in legislative bodies, even in PTA meetings. It is a staple of news.

Fortunately for the news reporter in search of an audience, drama and physical action are easily found. Street riots, prison breaks, wars, border incidents, saloon brawls, and husband and wife spats all make for the magic combination of picturesque activity and human conflict that intensifies the drama. Incidents in profusion are available for reporting.

Some People Are Newsmakers

Another habit of the news media is to report the activities of certain persons without consideration as to whether these activities have any significance. A president can get national publicity by stumbling momentarily in disembarking from an airplane, but an average citizen could break her skull without attracting notice in the news—unless she did it in a spectacular manner. A governor can be sure of statewide notice by making an utterly fatuous statement, but a small businessman is lucky to get the attention of his wife with a lucid analysis of a statewide problem.

Media people implicitly classify certain individuals into a group of newsmakers. These persons can get public attention whenever they want it—and receive it often when they do not desire it, or deserve it; whereas other individuals often cannot make the news even by hiring a publicity agent.

Who are these "newsmakers"? Their selection represents the habits and traditions of newspeople and the news business. They are the motion picture stars, the politicians, the prominent businesspeople, and labor leaders who have dealings with the press. Some persons achieve this status simply because of their position. A college president is a local newsmaker on arrival in town, and so is the head of an important business. Most newsmakers, however, are created by the news media themselves, often with the help of a public relations specialist. One fairly bland New York State legislator managed to earn statewide publicity for a considerable period after he acquired a press secretary with a talent for inventing pungent, quotable statements on legislative business. When placed in the legislator's mouth at press conferences, the phrases were quoted widely by reporters hungry for bright material. If an individual has been in the news a great deal there is an assumption that he or she belongs there. The media, bedazzled by their own creations, turn to them at every opportunity. This process has been labeled the *status-conferring function* of the media.

Prominent places receive more coverage, too. An event that occurs in a large city is more likely to be reported than one that occurs in a small village. More news reporters are likely to be on hand, but that is not the whole reason. There is an assumption that an event is more interesting if it happens at a place already known. Show business benefits from this. Before it turned seedy, New York City's Broadway and Forty-Second Street was seen as a glamour spot. The focus shifted to Hollywood and Vine, although the decline of the major studios has dimmed that image, too. Washington, as the stage for great events and the home territory for many reporters, frequently captures media attention.

Timing Determines News Value

Timing is one of the most intriguing aspects of news. Being the first to get a bit of information before the public is regarded as a major achievement, even if the edge lasts only for a few minutes or a few hours. Much of the lore of early newspapering concerns new techniques to be first with the news. These have included carrier pigeons, steamboats, the telegraph, and radio. Much technological development has resulted from this competition. A more fundamental consideration involves news values. What does the element of time have to do with the decision as to whether a given bit of information is worthy of being transmitted at all?

Time, more than any other aspect, makes it clear that news is a relative, not an absolute, concept. A given bit of information may be newsworthy at one time, worthless at another, since it will be competing for attention with an entirely different set of other potential news stories.

As an individual's own sensory system selects messages from the environment for transmission to the brain, so the news media select messages from their larger environment for transmission to their audiences. When many possible events are available to be reported, each single event has less likelihood of being transmitted.

More events occur simultaneously in large communities than in small ones, so each one has less chance of being reported. Small-town residents can expect to see their names in the local weekly paper once in a while, but if they move to the city the big daily there will probably never mention them.

The same thing occurs in the larger environment of world affairs. An event of great drama and consequence that is covered by all the news media will result in other events being overlooked. The Watergate story of the early 1970's had all the qualities of a great news story—drama involving important people in high places and great issues. The media gave it such thorough treatment that it crowded many other stories out of the news—particularly out of the broadcast news and off the front pages of newspapers.

In other words, events that would have been the source of important news stories in normal periods were simply ignored or put in the back of the newpapers where they received considerably less attention. One interesting game is to speculate on what stories would have been brought to national attention if Watergate had not occurred. This will always be a matter of conjecture because there is no record of the stories that were not reported.

This is just one of the ways in which time affects the news stream. In their eternal quest to be timely the media sometimes give important events little attention simply because they have already been reported by a competitor. Occasionally the desire to update a story (find a new angle that has not been emphasized) will result in emphasis on minor elements.

Importance Enhances News

The importance of an event or situation is, of course, a criterion of news value. Importance is estimated on the basis of the number of people affected and the degree to which the event affects them. On a local level an accident is more likely to be reported if it results in serious injury or death than if only minor injuries were involved. It is also more likely to be reported if a number of persons are involved rather than only one. A war is newsworthy on the basis that it affects many people in important ways.

A logical question is why anything that is not important should get into the news stream. The answer lies in the nature of media audiences. Too often readers and listeners will ignore or tune out information about foreign trade, a bill in Congress to change the corporate tax structure, or a city hearing on zoning. All these matters are important, for they will affect the lives of many people. Yet they are often complicated, and so difficult to understand and boring. The media would lose much of their audience if they reported only important matters, no matter how dull. When importance combines with drama, as in the Kennedy assassination, newspeople have no problem. But usually they must eternally struggle to make the important interesting and to judiciously lighten their fare with dramatic, but less important, information. (See Figure 8.2.)

"Human Interest"

Often the material that leavens the serious content of the news report is "human interest." This is material that appeals primarily to the emotions. While it may be a part of a serious story, it may also be trivial. It may be funny or sentimental or both. It may be the bright sayings of children or the saucy remark of a drunk to the police court judge. A generation ago some newspapers hired "sob sisters" to interview unfortunates charged with murder or other serious crimes to dredge up whatever pathos was available.

Today human interest is often injected into serious stories by interviewing persons or families affected by social disorders such as strikes or unemployment. Television is particularly effective in presenting such human interest material.

Many other elements enter into a decision as to whether an item is newsworthy. Editors study their audiences to find their special interests. Cities with populations of foreign extraction, for example, may demand more emphasis on stories from the homeland. An event is more interesting if it occurs close to home. There are also cycles of interest in certain types of information. For example, a series of hotel fires around the country is likely to touch off local stories about the comparative safety of hometown hotels.

Newspeople Rely on Public Records

The public-record system produces news, and sometimes it seems that information is deemed newsworthy just because it becomes part of the public records. Such information includes births, deaths, mar-

Figure 8.2   The Important Versus the Interesting
Problem: how to interest an audience even when an important event (left) lacks the drama of a more sensational event (right).

riages, divorces, land transfers, actions in bankruptcy, and arrests. For the journalist this is easy reporting. The information is accessible in a public office; it is usually privileged so that the reporter is safe from a libel action if the reporting is accurate. Moreover, since it is recorded by a public agency and hallowed by tradition, it is easy to think that it is important. As Walter Lippmann pointed out, many individuals go through life and come to the attention of the public through the news media only three times: when they are born, when they marry, and when they die. A person may conduct a successful business for years without being injected into the news stream, but the moment the business fails and the owner files for bankruptcy the event is reported. A mark has been made at the point where the public-record system crosses the reporting traditions of the news media.

Often public records provide tips that can be developed into dramatic news stories. More often they serve as supplements in reporting the more important stories.

Reporters are the victims of their own preconceptions and their own habits in their use of records. News tradition in many cities says that police blotters, court records, and property deeds should be inspected and reported every day. Many other records go unnoticed because they are not part of the traditional reporting pattern. Legislative documents containing information of public importance frequently go unreported unless there is another event that propels them into the news. At one time newspapers in New York State put on a concentrated drive to open certain records for inspection by reporters. Finally the legislature agreed, but with the stipulation that reporters using the documents should sign so that a record could be kept. A year later a committee chairman who had led the drive reported to the New York Society of Newspaper Editors that only three reporters had used any of the documents.

Events Versus Situations

What are the results of this set of news values?

One is that the media tend to cover events more often than they report situations. Events signalize situations and so they are often important bits of information, but usually knowledge of an event is useful primarily because it helps to clarify a situation.

For example, a prison riot is an event of importance and it deserves thorough news coverage. Even more important than the riot itself is the situation that caused it. If the media encourage the public in their habit of ignoring what goes on behind prison walls not very much will get done to improve prison conditions in time to avert the riot. The very lack of coverage of the situation in prisons may lead to riots, for the prisoners are aware that violence is one way to get public attention. Perhaps they are sometimes driven to violence because they believe that is the only way to draw public attention to what they see as intolerable conditions.

Evidence for this view is the frequency with which prisoners try to convert prison violence into a chance to state their case. Early in 1974 when prisoners in an Alabama prison gained control of a cell block, one of their demands was that they be allowed to talk with Harold Martin, editor and publisher of the *Montgomery Advertiser* and *Journal,* who had won a Pulitzer Prize for revealing corruption in the Alabama prison system. Later that same year one of two convicts who were holding hostages in the cell block of a Washington, D.C., court building was talking on the telephone with a *Washington Post* reporter when the hostages escaped.

Labor strikes often appear to occur without warning, as picket lines form or violence occurs. The strike, too, is simply an event that signalizes a situation that had been developing over a long period. Negotiations are reported more often than they were a few years ago, but still more situation coverage would help take the uncertainty out of industrial life.

The Watergate story is an example of an event that brought a situation to public attention. Perhaps the situation would not have reached its dangerous climax if the media had been more alert in covering the unsavory events of the presidential campaign of 1972. If public attention had been given to the "dirty tricks" and other sabotage of that campaign perhaps they would have subsided without reaching so disastrous a climax.

Another result of journalistic preference for reporting events is that the public is put at the mercy of people who understand how to create events. A public relations expert, charged with the job of persuading people of the virtues of drinking milk, may stage what historian Daniel Boorstin has called a "pseudo event." In such instances, the imagination of some publicists seems to be limited to beauty pageants. The pictures and accounts of untold hundreds of milk queens and other shapely queens who grace newspaper pages and television screens attest to the success of this technique.

Beauty contests are only one kind of "event" that is staged to get a message across. We have seen that prison riots may be planned for the same purpose. The prisoners might prefer a beauty pageant to draw attention to their plight, but they are limited to the grim resources at hand.

On the political level some have charged that President Nixon's summit conferences and his dramatic trip to China were staged primarily to demonstrate to the country that their chief executive was on the job in foreign affairs despite some minor misadventures at home.

The habit of event coverage may allow the media to ignore situations until they are in the crisis stage, and it sometimes forces groups pleading special causes to stage dramatic, even violent events to gain public attention. If situations could come to public attention before a major confrontation were reached, it would be easier to achieve the inevitable compromise.

Media manipulation was one of the skills of the Symbionese Liberation Army, which kidnaped Patty Hearst. Tapes carrying the voice of Ms. Hearst were sent to Bay Area stations, which aired them and so gave a public platform to the tiny group that made up the SLA. Walter Cronkite of CBS, Harry Reasoner of ABC, and John Chancellor of NBC all deplored this "use" of the media by the SLA.

A related difficulty with event coverage is that it puts the initiative into the hands of the people who are the sources of news rather than leaving it with the editors and reporters.

An individual who understands the news values and folklore of the media can often manipulate the news stream to his or her own advantage. Some individuals do this by gaining access to a "forum" and then taking advantage of it. Since the news media habitually give coverage to an individual who has established himself or herself as a source, one good way to gain a forum is to win election to the Senate or some other high office.

Most senators can get coverage in their own state any time they want to expend the energy. Many have managed to extend the forum so that they get national coverage whenever they voice an opinion. The value of the Senate as a national forum is demonstrated by counting the number of candidates for the United States presidency who have come from the Senate. President Nixon and three of the four immediately preceding presidents had seen service in the United States Senate, and President Ford was a veteran of the House of Representatives.

Senator Joseph McCarthy of Wisconsin made use of his position as senator and of the press during the Eisenhower administration, making reckless charges of Communism against government employees, especially those in the State Department. Usually the charges were not substantiated, but newspapers of the day printed them because they were dramatic, important if true, and because they came from a senator. Largely disregarded was the question of the damage done to individuals because of unsupported charges.

The press has made a substantial start in the direction of situation coverage. In-depth reporting is one answer; some aspects of the new journalism are another. Both methods give reporters time and encourage them to investigate the aspects of a situation rather than simply writing what someone announces about it.

Newspapers are moving to situational coverage partly in response to the competition from radio and television. Radio is unmatched as a medium for getting simple information rapidly to large numbers of people; television is unmatched in its ability to provide realistic coverage through film or live presentation.

Outdistanced by other media in these two important aspects of news, newspapers have little choice except to exploit the areas in which they function most efficiently: providing detailed coverage and interpretative material. Radio and television cannot carry the detail that is available in almost any newspaper, so the citizen who wants depth must turn to newspapers. Since newspapers have less need to compete now on the basis of timeliness, it is obvious that they have more time to report the revealing detail and to put the information in perspective.

Many newspapers are taking only partial advantage of this opportunity. Often a paper will run interpretative, in-depth articles from press services on national and international affairs, but still rely basically on spot news locally. Since newspapers usually are better staffed in the news department than the local radio and television stations with which they are competing, they have the best opportunity to provide the thorough local coverage that every community needs.

Together, the news media provide the picture of the community which most people hold. For nearly everyone there is no alternative to accepting the picture painted by the media as the closest they can come to reality.

When News Is Created

But how does the media picture compare with reality?

In his autobiography Lincoln Steffens told how, when he was a reporter in New York City, he and a reporter for a competing newspaper "started a crime wave." Even in the early part of the century the daily police files in New York were heavy. There were so many arrests for small crimes that no newspaper could begin to report them.

Steffens and his competitor solved the problem by surveying the files each day, taking a few of the more interesting crimes, and writing stories on them. Often they agreed on the material selected and both they and their editors were content. One day, however, Steffens's competitor printed the story of an incident that Steffens had ignored. Steffens's editor, following the traditional practice of reading the opposition newspaper, saw the story and demanded of Steffens why he had not been a good enough reporter to get it.

Steffens retaliated by printing several more items than usual the next day, making himself look good and his competitor look bad. This started a battle, with each reporter escalating each day until the papers were so full of crime news that readers were demanding to know what the police were doing about the "crime wave."

Theodore Roosevelt, then the New York City police commissioner, came under criticism, but he ended the mounting crime wave handily. He simply called both reporters into his office, telling them that he knew what they were doing and that they had to stop. Steffens and his competitor agreed to return to their previous system, and the crime wave was over.

The story supports the assumption held by some social scientists that the news media create an environment that has little relevance to the reality of the world. Certainly the media distort the world, but almost any reporter or editor would argue that the distortion is minor.

The range of selection is large and the events and situations that can be described in the media are few. Media managers select what to report largely on the basis of habits and traditions of the trade. These habits provide the criteria by which the "hard news" is selected.

A Healthy News Mix

Every conscientious newspaper and radio and television station tries to report the actions of government as they affect citizens. Each one tries to give some indication as to the amount of crime in the community, and each tries to report those things that are unusual enough to merit attention.

Perhaps it is this last effort that subjects the media to the criticism that they provide only "bad" news. It is true that some newspapers and newscasts sound like tales of disaster. One hears stories of petty crimes, accidents, natural disasters, and other unpleasant aspects of life. Perhaps the weather report is thrown in. Rain, ice, smog, and fog may only deepen the gloom.

Such news reports reflect the penchant of some news organizations to follow the police report. This is convenient and it does give a clue as to the state of affairs in the community. Just the same, the police usually are involved in the unpleasant side of life and to report all their activities sometimes is like chronicling the daily routine of a morgue attendant. The question raised by Lincoln Steffens's story is appropriate here. How much of this news does the public need?

As the reporter answers this question he or she makes decisions that do create a "pseudo environment" for readers and listeners. If none of the police news is reported, a false impression of the community is created. If so much is printed that other news is crowded out, the picture thus created is false, too. Many other, more palatable events are occurring in the community.

A news organization mixes news from many sources, but it cannot control the mix the way a food processor can mix elements to provide a crisp cereal with guaranteed minimum daily requirements of vitamins needed for health.

A healthy news mix is just as important as a healthy vitamin mix, but we do not know what the healthy mix is, and most reporters and editors would feel that they were tampering with the news stream if they tried to arrange one. Still, by the sources they cover, the selections they make, and the proportions they provide in the daily news report they are controlling the picture of the world created for their audiences.

The Media Have Options

To some extent the editors, writers, and producers are held to rigid limits by their own traditions and by the expectations of their audiences; but to a surprisingly large degree they are free to present whatever information they wish.

There is no question that some events are newsworthy. For example, when President Nixon made his famous trip to China in 1972 and provided an opportunity for reporters to enter China after many years of exclusion, no argument that the president was using the trip to present a favorable image to the public before election could change the fact that it was newsworthy. The same held true when President Ford made a similar pilgrimage in 1975. When a governor signs a law that affects every driver of an automobile, a reporter would have to be blind not to recognize a news story. The same is true when fire destroys a downtown building.

But there are many other situations in which there is little consensus about the news value of an event. In such situations a news organization has options. For example, when a social justice group was planning a march in one city the newspaper ignored it after one brief mention. When a local ecology group battles the Army Corps of Engineers to force the corps to cancel construction of a dam that will flood an historic area, the news media often play a critical role in the outcome. If the paper thinks the issue is newsworthy it can provide a flood of publicity, which is likely to rally support to the ecology group. If the media play down or ignore the story the engineers are likely to go ahead with the construction. Their funding and bureaucratic support will probably decide the issue.

If a school board needs to persuade the public to vote a bond issue to provide a new building, the media are a critical factor in the campaign.

The journalist must make his or her own decision so often that the old editor's remark, "News is what I say it is," is more truth than joke.

Skillful presentation can make almost any news story appear to be important and interesting. Furnished with interesting news items that seem to be important few readers or listeners will complain about the fare they are getting. They may accept a light feature story or picture on the front page of their newspaper every day because they have no idea as to what would replace it.

The complaints that do reach the managers of the news stream often have to do with favorite personages or causes that are treated in ways that the listener sees as unfair.

Packaging and Media Power

Much of the media's power to dictate the selection of news comes from the manner in which information is presented. One of the arts of news presentation is to command the attention and interest of the audience. Any successful news organization has writers, editors, photographers, and producers who can stimulate interest by the manner in which the material is presented. A television newscast is carefully prepared with a mixture of material, variety in length of items, and spacing of stories with different visual stimuli and audio impact. Newspapers, too, are carefully designed to be attractive formats for presenting whatever it is that the editors and reporters have decided is the news for that day. (See Figure 8.3.) The art of presentation sometimes receives as much attention from the media as the harder one of selection. Newspeople have come to talk about their job as "packaging" the news in attractive form.

Figure 8.3   Packaging the News
Same news—different packaging.

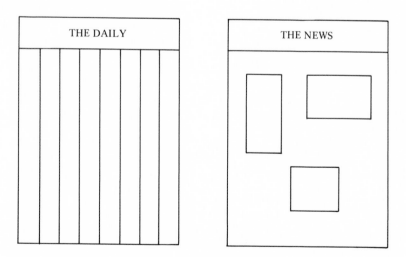

Perhaps they should spend more energy on deciding what it is they should be putting in the package. As we have seen, the public has become less enchanted with its media in the 1960's and early 1970's. This disenchantment is sufficient to cause one to wonder whether, were the Constitution and Bill of Rights being written today, freedom of the press would be singled out for special protection.

Certainly this protection was not granted so that some individuals can use the media only to make money. It was designed to serve the needs of the many who receive the news.

In their lack of definition of news do the media risk abrogation of the special privileges by which they live?

What elements should go into a redefinition of news?

The principle is clear enough: the information provided should be the information most necessary to the audience sought. Many news organizations have promised this, but have provided only tidbits of solid information while serving up large portions of titillating trivia.

A redefinition of news should not put too much stock in statements that the "professional judgment" of a seasoned editor is the only answer. These may paralyze the reasoned process of finding out what people want and need to know. The fact that a network news broadcast has a large audience does not prove that the public is getting what it needs—or even what it wants. The network newscasts are so similar that the decision to tune in one over the other is made on a preference for the personality of the newscaster or on some other trivial basis. The fact that a newspaper is delivered to 95 percent of the households in its circulation area proves little. Often the citizen's choice is to subscribe to this paper or no local paper. In broadcast and print the public has so little opportunity to choose between real alternatives that it is illogical to assume that acceptance means enchantment.

Social scientists are providing tools in increasing number for discovering the desires and needs of the public in news fare. Advertisers have grown accustomed to using similar tools for measuring the effectiveness of their sales messages. It is time that more broadcasters and newspapers began to adapt and apply the same powerful tools for measuring what their readers want rather than simply for testing the appeal of the package they provide.

Similar methods are becoming available for reporting different "news" than the traditional. Observation techniques can systematize reports about the public in ways that were not possible a few years ago. Content analysis can reveal the meaning of a document or a series of documents more exactly than even careful reading will do. Sampling methods make it possible to report to the public information about itself that is not available now. It is possible to report attitudes on local issues with sufficient precision to point up potentially dangerous situations before they erupt into violence or hard disagreements that will make compromise more difficult.

Traditional reporting methods, too, can be directed toward need. The news still should be presented in attractive packages. However, the test will come, not on the package, but rather on the utility of its contents.

News Consumers and News Values

Initiative needs to come, too, from the consumers of the media. Understanding the values and habits of their media is one way in which audiences can use their media more effectively. Another way is to tell their editors and news directors what they like and dislike about the news presented. Such information, regularly and systematically presented by individuals and groups, could have a telling effect on media news habits.

Closing the News-Reality Gap

News is not reality. But news carefully and intelligently presented, and carefully and intelligently received, can help a receiver to bring his or her thinking closer to reality. The media present an institutionalized version of reality. As every individual has his or her own version of reality, so does every unit of the media.

The media need to study the needs of their audiences, and readers and listeners need to study the habits of their media. Out of such mutual exploration can come an accommodation that will enable the media to select and present information that will bring their audiences closer to the world of reality.

Suggestions for Further Reading

Boorstin, Daniel J. *The Image: A Guide to Pseudo-Events in America.* New York: Harper & Row, 1964.
A discussion of the nature of events that make news.

Davis, Elmer. "The Need for Interpretive Reporting." In *The Press in Perspective,* edited by Ralph Casey, pp. 50–67. Baton Rouge: Louisiana State University Press, 1963.
Discussion of the news form by one of America's most thoughtful commentators.

Frome, Michael. "Freedom of the Press—for Those Who Own One." *The Center Magazine* 8 (July/August 1975): 12–24.
Author tells of his dismissal as conservation editor for Field and Stream, which he ascribes to his tough environmental stand.

Fulbright, J. William. "Fulbright on the Press." *Columbia Journalism Review* 14 (November-December 1975): 39–45.
Urges restraint and less emphasis on personalities in the news.

Powers, Ron, and Oppenheim, Gerald. "Is TV Too Profitable?" *Columbia Journalism Review* 11 (May/June 1972): 7–13.
Discusses revenues in the television industry in relation to amount spent for news and public affairs programming.

9
Politics and the Media

Politics is the process by which people win or lose power, and by which nations decide to wage war, where new highways shall run, or who shall pay taxes. Politics pervades governments.

In the United States politics has been a preoccupation of the media from the start. A Boston printshop was the staging area where the idea of the American Revolution was nurtured. It was political comment in the *New York Weekly Journal* that led to the famous trial of John Peter Zenger in 1735. Early newspaper publishers were constantly defending themselves against charges by legislatures or governors that they were overcritical of the government or divulging forbidden information.

Since politicians make the basic decisions that control social and economic change, it is small wonder that the media feel it is their duty to report political activity. Politics manifests itself in all organizations and in many forms. Here we will discuss politics in relation to public decisions and government. This is the point where public opinion and public policy meet and where it is easiest to study the role of the media in social change.

Politics is most easily observed and most fully reported in the Western democracies, such as the United States, England, and France, where popular election of government officials requires at least a minimum public discussion of candidates and issues. But politics exists in every form of government. Politicians are as necessary in reaching public decisions as speculators are in making a market work. Without speculators markets would be dead because the mechanism for reflecting price fluctuations would not work. Without politicians the marketplace of public issues would wither for the lack of committed partisans. In closed societies, politics and politicians may go underground, but they will continue to exist as long as the desire and need for change continues. They are less observable, but they are no less real. Leaders must gain at least a minimum of public acceptance for their programs or else they will face revolution. This accounts for the great pageants of Hitler's Germany and for the speed with which new dictators move to take over the instruments of public communication. The politicians in closed societies must also sell themselves and their ideas to a king, dictator, party chairperson, or whomever fills the role of final decision-maker.

Communication and Public Decisions

The interlocking of the communications process with public decision-making is vividly illustrated by comparing the role of the media under a dictatorship with that under a democracy. Under a totalitarian regime the managers of the public media become the apologists for the head of state. Dictators exercise this control in different ways and with varying success, but it is often apparent that the media are reinforcing the government by persuading the public to follow the leaders' wishes, or by threatening calamities if government programs are not accepted. Government secrecy is perhaps the most powerful weapon, because it cannot be detected by an uninformed public. Underground media and a word-of-mouth "opposition press" express discontent, but the wry and bitter jokes whispered over a coffee counter are no match for the control over information that comes from domination of the media.

The concept of freedom of information has achieved enough acceptance that even those governments that live by suppressing it like to pretend they support it. Apologists for dictators have argued that, since the government is the people, anyone circulating information that the government desires to suppress is acting against the interests of the people. The public interest and freedom of the press are served, according to this theory, by accepting whatever limitations the rulers, in the name of the people, impose. To a Western ear this is tortured logic.

Ex-justice William O. Douglas has effectively argued the opposite view: that any interference with the circulation of ideas or opinions is an insufferable impediment to freedom. This line of reasoning, based on John Stuart Mill's theory that in a free marketplace of ideas truth will drive out error, puts no prior restraints on the right of individuals, or media, to say anything, true or false, with whatever motives, good or bad.

The press, particularly in the United States, has always been fascinated by government and often repelled by it. The Revolutionary press fanned distrust of British government into revolt at the birth of the United States. Once a new government was established the press had to tolerate it, but it never got over the habit of distrusting those in authority. Politicians who championed the press praised it profusely until their ascendance to power. Once in power, they often attacked the press as a nuisance or even as subversive.

Given their inherent antagonisms it is not strange that media and government have, in recent times, been the principal contestants for public favor and the power that goes with it. But this was not always true. Power centers of Greek and Roman civilization and of medieval times were the church and state. The battles between the Papacy and the kings of France, England, and Italy during the Middle Ages show that the power centers of society were again church and state.

In an increasingly secular society the church has lost influence, and other power centers have risen. The Industrial Revolution saw the rise of the merchant prince. In the late 1800's the railroad barons and the steamship barons were said to control the New York State legislature. Certainly their influence in Congress was powerful. With Congress dominating a series of usually lackluster presidents, the way was open for businesspeople to make the decisions that were critical to society.

Some of Charles Dickens's novels were protests against social conditions in England of his day. Lincoln Steffens, Ida Tarbell, and other muckrakers voiced similar protests in the United States. With government help workers in American industry found that organization provided them with an argument to which entrepreneurs had to listen—the strike. So for a time labor vied with business and government as one of the great power centers.

As labor gained concessions the views of its leaders moved closer to those held by the industrial establishment, and to some extent it became part of the power structure that is subsumed under President Eisenhower's term, the *military-industrial complex.*

The President and the Media

When President Franklin Roosevelt came to power in 1932 the badly shaken economy forced him to drastic action. Business had failed to provide economic security for either its workers or its investors, so the federal government had to step in. As the federal government acted decisively to meet the nationwide emergency, it became dominant in areas formerly assigned to state governments, and it assumed increased powers over business. Clearly the federal government was the power center of the country.

The same series of events also had an effect on the distribution of power within the government itself. The initiative for the dramatic changes of the 1930's came from the office of the president. Congressional power withered as Congress lost the initiative and the president became dominant.

Both of these trends—increased federal power and enhanced prestige of the presidency—were speeded by the Second World War. Through our history the stresses of war, with the need for quick decisions on grave questions, have led to increased power for the president since he, as an individual, can act faster than the legislative body.

Franklin Delano Roosevelt set the tone for the activist presidents who followed. As the power of the office increased, it attracted men fascinated by power—the kind who were likely to, and did, strengthen it still further.

Thus it was circumstances and personalities that, by the middle of the first administration of Richard M. Nixon, had left the United States presidency the transcendent center of power in the United States. Congress, which was poorly staffed compared to the president and was frequently unable to marshal an effective majority, offered no effective counterbalance. By failing to take initiatives and by crying for presidential action rather than taking action on their own, many members of Congress abetted the power takeover by the presidency.

For a time the country's communications media seemed disinclined or unable to challenge presidential power. Some of the reporters who covered the federal government sensed what was happening and tried to make the public aware of it. These reporters were thwarted for a time by the peculiar dynamics of the media-government relationship and by the skill with which the administration exploited it.

The president or a strong state or local executive is by no means powerless in controlling the content of the media. The press has no choice except to report the words and activities of the president. How could it be otherwise? The president is the most powerful person in the country. He usually has a large following, and what he says and does affects, often very directly, the life of every resident. The press, by intense coverage of the occupant of the White House, helps to build him to bigger dimensions. Although this makes him even more newsworthy, the press has no alternative. Ignoring the presidency would be abdicating the watchdog function of which the press is rightfully proud.

Technology, too, works to the advantage of the president. For the same reason that the media must cover presidential news, radio and television usually provide time for the president whenever he requests it to address the public. The natural persuasive power of the president in seeking time is enhanced because he appoints the members of the Federal Communications Commission, which regulates broadcasting.

The President Has Direct Access

In exercising his privilege of addressing the public directly, the president can command attention to himself and his programs in a setting that he largely controls. From Franklin Roosevelt on, presidents have been aware of this power. The electronic media have thus provided the chief executive with a means of reaching the public without filtering the message through the minds and typewriters of the working press.

It was the administration's desire to keep the president's electronic access unfiltered that led to the battle over "instant analysis" during the first Nixon administration. Spiro T. Agnew, then vice president, opened the battle with a speech on November 13, 1969, in Des Moines, Iowa. He came directly to the point:

> Tonight I want to discuss the importance of the television news medium to the American people. No nation depends more on the intelligent judgment of its citizens. No medium has a more profound influence over public opinion. Nowhere in our system are there fewer checks on vast power. So, nowhere should there be more conscientious responsibility exercised than by the news media. The question is, Are we demanding enough of our television news presentations? Are the men of this medium demanding enough of themselves?
>
> Monday night a week ago, President Nixon delivered the most important address of his Administration, one of the most important of our decade....
>
> When the President completed his address ... his words and policies were subjected to instant analysis and querulous criticism. The audience of seventy million Americans gathered to hear the President of the United States was inherited by a small band of network commentators and self-appointed analysts, the majority of whom expressed ... their hostility to what he had to say.[1]

[1]"Transcript of Address by Agnew Criticizing Television on Its Coverage of the News," *New York Times*, November 14, 1969, p. 24.

For the present, it is enough to remember that the administration thought the question important enough and felt its position strong enough that it raised the issue. Obviously the president and his advisers prized the power to go directly to the people through the electronic media, and to do it in a way that provided the barest minimum of interpretation or analysis by news reporters or commentators.

The presidential campaign of 1972 provides another example of the president's power to use the press in his own way. President Nixon created events that were extremely newsworthy and put him in a favorable light. While not patently political, his trip to China strengthened him as a candidate. It combined picturesque drama made to order for extensive television coverage with the aura of great events—our president opening relations with a vast, mysterious, formerly unfriendly country. In addition to making events, the president addressed the nation directly over radio, a medium that he preferred for a sober discussion of issues. His logic apparently was that radio is better suited than television for speech presentations of any significant length. The president's campaign managers also provided "surrogates" who would answer the other candidate's charges, allowing the president to seem above partisan issues and preoccupied with the great affairs of his office. President Franklin Roosevelt had used many of the same techniques, having gone through an entire election campaign without once mentioning publicly the name of his opponent. If he felt called upon to refute a point he relied on a phrase that became famous: "There are those who say. . . ." "Those" referred to the opposition candidate, and having quoted him in this roundabout way, Roosevelt proceeded to contradict him.

The technique worked well for both Roosevelt and Nixon, but it did not always lead to a fruitful discussion of public issues. The opposition candidates found themselves putting in grueling days of travel, speaking, and handshaking and yet making less impression on the public than the incumbent who, by comparison, appeared to be taking his ease in the White House.

People within the Nixon administration apparently were so confident after the landslide election of 1972 that they decided the moment was right for the executive branch to establish its dominance over the media as it had over Congress.

Theodore White, an astute observer, expresses the opinion that the administration might have achieved dominance over the press for itself and future presidencies if it had not been for the Watergate scandals.[2] In the ensuing confrontation the president fought for public acceptance of his version of events as opposed to that presented by Congress and the media.

[2]Theodore H. White, *The Making of the President, 1972* (New York: Atheneum, 1973), pp. 284–285.

"Out, damned spot! out I say!"

From the Louisville *Courier-Journal*, September 18, 1973. © 1973 The Courier-Journal. Reprinted with permission.

In their victory the press and Congress preserved public confidence in the media and avoided dominance by the presidency. The victory was fraught with danger for everyone involved. It raised the question as to whether the press could win such a massive battle without overkill. A future battle of such dimensions could destroy credibility in all our institutions and make it impossible for our society to survive.

The Watergate affair and the battle for public confidence that followed raise the most fundamental questions about the relationship between press and government. We do not have definitive answers to any of the questions, although there are plenty of opinions. Raising the questions at least puts the problem in better perspective.

Some Fundamental Questions

In stark and simple form the questions run like this: How is power won or lost? Who are the protagonists? Who has what power? What are the rules for handling it? To whom is the accounting made? Who makes the rules? Who is the referee? What are the skills? The weapons? What is the pace of ideas and issues? Who decides what we talk and think about? What does it take to get action? Who makes the decisions?

The questions sound simplistic when set out so starkly, but their answers describe how power is maintained in any society that depends on popular will. In any such society the media occupy positions of vast importance. They may not be entirely antagonistic to the governing elite, but if some elements of the media are not critical, the democratic process fails.

This kind of discussion makes the media sound much more monolithic than they actually are. Newspapers, radio, and television range through most of the shades of political belief from ultraconservative to ultraradical. They also present a wide variety on another dimension. Some are placid, timid, and almost blindly willing to accept what anyone in authority tells them, whereas others are inclined to question every word from a government official. In the Watergate scandals the political hue of the media was not important. What was needed was a bold press. That was what it took to cling to the Watergate story in its early days. The Watergate revelations, as they rose to a crescendo, did unite the press and gave it a monolithic power seldom displayed.

The interaction of the printed and electronic press may have been the final factor that allowed the press to win its victory. When the *Washington Post* ran into a dry spell in finding new stories about the Watergate scandals, public interest began to wane. The combination of a Senate hearing with live nationwide television coverage turned the tide of public apathy. There is some question whether or not newspaper coverage by itself could have raised the level of public interest to the pitch that it reached months after the story had originally been reported. Television was well suited to transmit the drama of the hearings and thus fan public interest, which led to a thirst for more articles in the newspapers and eventually to an erosion in public confidence in the Nixon presidency.

In covering the presidency, as in covering other areas of public information, reporters are constantly faced with the problem of determining the proper distance they should maintain from the source. A reporter's value is determined by his or her ability to obtain information. The president can make it easier for reporters to gain information, and difficult for those not in favor. Simply by recognizing a reporter at a press conference, the president can increase his or her stature. The president can also help a reporter's career by selecting that person to ride on the presidential plane or by granting individual interviews.

The tendency is natural for the president to favor the reporters whose work puts him in the best light. This is not a phenomenon only of presidential press relations. Mayors and police chiefs frequently have the same opportunities and respond the same way. Foreign correspondents sometimes face the same situation. If the government of the country they are in disapproves of their dispatches the correspondent may be deported or cut off from regular news channels. Hitler and Mussolini engaged regularly in such practices. Reporters covering Germany or Italy had to decide whether and how much to temper their reports so that they could remain in the country. This is still true in many countries. Obviously a reporter's value as a correspondent is gone if he or she is deported from the assigned country.

Likewise a White House reporter's value is diminished if he or she is systematically excluded from the choicest positions on airplanes and press buses and ignored at press conferences. Factors like these perhaps account for the fact that the original stories about Watergate were uncovered, not by White House correspondents, but by local reporters working for the metropolitan desk of the *Washington Post*. Having made the original discoveries, reporters Carl Bernstein and Bob Woodward were kept on the story. Woodward maintained later in a speech that the White House correspondents are simply "sophisticated stenographers" who transmit whatever the White House wants to publicize.

This charge exaggerates the problem, but it does point up the delicate situation of the White House "regulars" who cover the president from day to day. They are dependent on the president as a news source. They prosper by placing their stories on the front pages and in the evening newscasts to the extent that the president provides them with newsworthy material.

The importance of this delicate balance is great when reporters are covering the most powerful person in the country, but it is an inherent problem for all reporters. In more general terms, it is simply the question of how much reporters can involve themselves with their sources of information and remain objective about them—even if they cover these sources for a period of years.

The Press Conference

The presidential press conference is perhaps the most dramatic institution in which the interaction of the president and the White House correspondents can be studied. It illustrates the interplay of personalities as well as issues.

During the presidency of Franklin Roosevelt a few reporters would crowd into the Oval Office for a period of banter and questions and answers on matters of public concern. The president could not be quoted verbatim, so he was free to be informal. Apparently everybody had a good time. The president had a chance to get publicity for new programs; reporters got some stories; and good relations were preserved by the president's habit of blaming the publishers, not the reporters in front of him, for any ill will he felt toward the media.

This informal meeting was too good to last. Gradually the press conference grew to be a production. More reporters wanted to be admitted, so the sessions were moved to an auditorium and became more formal. President Harry S. Truman recaptured some of the earlier spontaneity by allowing reporters to tag along on his brisk morning walks when he seemed to be at his casual best.

President Dwight D. Eisenhower allowed press conferences to be filmed for later broadcast after the film had been reviewed to protect the president against statements that might be embarrassing. The public learned something about the personality of its president and about public affairs, but the press conference became more formal still. The number of reporters increased, and some were impressed more by the opportunity to appear on national television than by the chance to develop a news story. Serious print journalists complained that the press conference was being turned into a television show, and that the reporters were being used as props for the rival medium. Television reporters pointed out that they, too, were part of the nation's press, and that home viewers were presented with an unparalleled civics lesson.

President John F. Kennedy, well aware of his charisma, opened the press conference still further by allowing it to be televised live. This heightened the drama and presumably increased the value of the show for public edification, but it tended to limit it still more as a source of hard news. The president had to be more careful than ever of what he said because there was no chance for a review of direct statements that might cause concern in foreign capitals. The Kennedy glamour proved itself again; even the reporters seemed pleased. President Kennedy displayed some of Franklin Roosevelt's skill and apparent enjoyment at bantering with the press.

Suspecting that he could not pull off a Kennedy-type press conference, President Lyndon B. Johnson experimented with other forms. Old hands in the press corps were reminded of Truman days when Johnson occasionally allowed them to accompany him as he strode around the White House grounds. Reporters complained that puffing along trying to match the presidential stride made it difficult to compose intelligent questions, but Johnson enjoyed keeping the newspeople off base. Reporters other than White House regulars complained that conferences that were frequently called without advance notice precluded the attendance of specialized writers qualified to probe into complicated subjects. President Johnson himself was so fascinated by the news that he had three television sets installed in the White House, mounted so that he could watch all three and select the sound for whichever one interested him most at the moment. He also was suspected of having a microphone hidden in his press secretary's office so that he could eavesdrop during news briefings, and occasionally the press secretary would be interrupted by a mysterious call causing him to make an addition or correction.

President Richard M. Nixon's relationships with reporters was complicated by the overt hostility that he showed for them and that they sometimes returned. NBC newscaster John Chancellor once remarked that, while most presidents have had a love-hate relationship with the media, President Nixon had a "hate-hate" relationship. Nixon's distrust of reporters was most vehemently displayed in public during a famous press conference at Beverly Hills, California, on November 7, 1962.

Through his press aide, Herbert Klein, Nixon had just conceded the election for the California governorship to Edmund G. Brown. This loss, following his close loss to Kennedy for the presidency two years earlier, was seen by most political observers as choking off Nixon's political life. Nixon had intended to let Klein handle the press conference on the morning following the election, but at the last minute he changed his mind and went into the room where reporters were assembled.

His opening statement showed his feelings: "Now that all the members of the press are so delighted that I have lost, I'd like to make a statement of my own." The same tone carried through the conference: "I think it's time that our great newspapers have at least the same objectivity, the same fullness of coverage, that television has. And I can only say thank God for

"Riddle: What's black and white . . . and makes
the White House see red, moreover?"

From the Louisville *Courier-Journal*, October 30, 1973. © 1973 The Courier-Journal. Reprinted with
permission.

television and radio for keeping the newspapers a little more honest."
And again: "You won't have Nixon to kick around any more, because,
gentlemen, this is my last press conference."[3]

Most newspaper people agreed with Gladwin Hill, who, in covering the
story for the *New York Times*, characterized Nixon's statement as "a bitter
denunciation of the press."[4] Governor Brown regarded that press conference as a "horrible mistake" and ventured the opinion that, without it,
Nixon probably would have been his party's candidate for the presidency
again in 1964.[5]

After his remarkable comeback and election to the presidency in 1968
Nixon strove for better relations with reporters, preparing diligently for
press conferences, and getting praise for the way he handled them in the
early months of his first term. This period of good relations ended with
the press revelations about Watergate. Press conferences became fewer:
one thirteen-month period went by without a single scheduled conference. The White House retaliated against the *Washington Post* for its aggressive Watergate coverage by giving stories exclusively to the *Post*'s
competitor, the *Washington Evening Star,* and by barring the *Post*'s social
reporter from covering White House functions.

The few press conferences that Nixon did hold often degenerated into
wrangling matches. Some members of the White House press corps were
accused of conspiring to "get" the president instead of trying to obtain information for the public. Some White House staffers said the correspondents were failing to do their homework and bringing flabby questions
into the conference. Dan Rather, then CBS White House correspondent,
became known for being particularly aggressive in sparring with the
president. Even the *New York Times*, no Nixon supporter, editorially
complained that reporters were not showing sufficient respect for the
office of the presidency.

It was clear that the presidential press conference was not doing much
to further public understanding of government. Even Nixon's earlier favorites, radio and television, were not pleasing the president. Comments
following Nixon speeches led to Agnew's complaints about "instant
analysis" that we considered earlier.

With the help of his press secretary, Ron Nessen, President Gerald Ford
tried to revive the press conference. The location was changed to sym-
bolize a new way of treating reporters. One of the new locations was the
White House rose garden. A more substantive change allowed reporters

[3]"Transcript of Nixon's News Conference on His Defeat by Brown in Race for Governor of
California," *New York Times*, November 8, 1962, p. 18.
[4]Gladwin Hill, "Nixon Denounces Press as Biased," *New York Times*, November 8, 1962,
p. 1.
[5]"Brown Finds Attack on Press Hurt Nixon," *New York Times*, February 1, 1964, p. 8.

to ask a follow-up question to develop an area. Reporters appear to be mildly optimistic about the new "open" White House.

A Unique Institution

The presidential press conference is a unique American political institution. Since we have the presidential instead of the parliamentary form of government, our chief executive is not forced to appear in Congress and undergo questioning by members of the opposition party. Some have suggested that the presidential press conference is the American equivalent.

In that comparison the press conference falls short. The press conference is given or withheld at the will of the president. He controls its format and its length. He decides whom he shall recognize. All these factors make it a potent weapon in the hands of a president who is skillful in its use.

Representatives of the news media are ambivalent in their views as to the value of the presidential press conference. Some say that particularly since the advent of televised conferences, the device has lost its capability of forcing the president to come to grips with the issues, and that thus it cannot produce hard news. It is all right, they say, to provide press conferences so that the public gets a chance to look at the president and see how he answers questions, but we should not delude ourselves that this is productive in helping the country understand its problems.

Reporters are disturbed by what they see as lack of cooperation by the president, and also by their own role. A president can manipulate the subject matter simply because he knows the interests of the reporters. President Kennedy said that sometimes when he was afraid the conference was getting too dull for the television audience he would deliberately turn to a reporter who he knew would ask a fairly light question that would allow him to display his quick wit in answer. This demonstrates a tendency to regard the conference as show business, with some of the reporters, wittingly or not, acting as foils for the president.

Pierre Salinger, Kennedy's press secretary, admitted that he planted questions by asking sympathetic reporters to bring up specific points. Salinger defended the practice by saying that otherwise reporters often did not broach important subjects that the president wanted to discuss in public.

Alternatives to the press conference include the granting of private interviews to single reporters. There are two reasons why presidents have seldom done this: other reporters become unfriendly, feeling that they have as good a right as anyone else to interview the president; and the president lacks the time to see many reporters individually.

Leaks and Rumors

President Theodore Roosevelt used to meet informally with reporters and provide tips and stories that could not be attributed to him. It is said that it was in this setting that he developed the successful technique of gaining major attention for his stories by providing the information to reporters on Sunday night. Monday morning was a dull news day, with editors sometimes desperate in their search for a story worth prominent display on the front page. Under those circumstances almost any story that the president cared to disclose was worth major display. President Kennedy was said to have used the same technique even more informally. He had a few fairly close friends among news writers, and he sometimes divulged information to them that he wanted circulated. This would always be used without attribution, but after a while other reporters began to recognize trends, and the practice of spotting presidential "leaks" became popular.

One of the more celebrated leaks came in connection with the Cuban missile crisis in 1962. A few weeks after the crisis was settled Charles Bartlett wrote in a magazine article that Averell Harriman, then U.S. ambassador to the United Nations, had been vacillating and ineffective in the advice he gave the president during the crisis. Since Bartlett was a personal friend of President Kennedy and since few other sources for his information were apparent, it was widely suspected that the president himself had been the source of the material critical of Harriman. While reporters must sometimes use information without disclosing the source, it is a dangerous practice because it allows the press to be used by officials, and it feeds the rumor mill.

Rumor is one of the less savory aspects of Washington reporting. As residents in a gossip capital reporters sometimes let tidbits, often inaccurate and frequently inconsequential, get into the news.

Washington journalism suffers, too, from emphasis on the main story of the day. Reporters get in each other's way as they swarm over the headline news, while many other items of national concern never come to light. Our capital city is bulging with information that needs to be reported and explained. Serious reporters should be allowed the time such work requires. Some of the talented individuals who stumble over each other in following the president around might well be employed as investigative reporters.

Another standard White House fixture is the press secretary, who is constantly in contact with the correspondents. When they are effective such individuals become decision-makers in their own right. James Haggerty, the master press secretary whom Governor Thomas E. Dewey of New York bequeathed to President Eisenhower, appeared to decide what was to be announced and when. His thinking was close enough to that of the president that great mutual trust developed. Haggerty's skill in keeping reporters reasonably happy was one of the great assets of the Eisenhower administration.

Elected nationally, the president stands out dramatically as the national leader. He wields tremendous power. Not bound by laborious legislative procedures, he can take decisive action. It is no wonder that he is the focus of national attention.

Congress and the Media

Members of Congress have less natural news appeal. Each representative or senator is one of many; each is elected from a state or district rather than nationally; the power of each is severely limited although the overall power of Congress is great; and the role of each is usually obscured by the procedures of the House of Representatives or the Senate.

While the president can have time on radio or television by asking for it, an ambitious representative or senator has to scramble to gain national attention on the media. Whereas the president may well feel that his office gets more coverage than he would desire, the average member of Congress finds it difficult to get national attention focused on his or her own activities.

These differences make for an entirely different relationship between members of Congress and the press than that which prevails between the president and the press. Normally the president can exert a great deal of control over the information that appears in the media. "News management" has been a frequent accusation against the president. Considering all the president has going for him and the natural tendencies of any man who holds such an office, it is difficult to see how the president could do otherwise than "manage the news." In a popular government any politician or statesman must act with one ear cocked toward the reaction of the voters.

Many members of Congress would probably like to manage the news, too, but they do not have the same opportunity. Within their own states or districts they can expect the media to pay attention to their actions, although even here they must be painfully aware that many of their constituents do not even know their names. Many senators and representatives seek national attention, either because they have ambitions for national office or because they are genuinely interested in promoting causes that need nationwide support.

Sometimes members of the House and Senate form groups to call attention to causes they are interested in or to rebut the president on a given issue. Steering committees of one party or the other, the Black Caucus, and party members of various committees are examples of groups that have done this. But it is difficult for individual members of the House or Senate to achieve nationwide attention. There is neither time nor space in the national media for many to project their ideas. Even if there were time and space and plenty of reporters to do the job, the public could not be expected to pay attention except to their local representatives. In contrast to the president, members of Congress must actively seek national attention or they will almost surely remain in the relative obscurity of state or local politics.

What are the characteristics of members of Congress who do manage to beat the odds and gain national attention? It would appear to be a combination of hard work, personal appeal, identification with popular issues, and good luck.

Senator Estes Kefauver of Tennessee became widely known in the 1950's when he presided over a series of hearings on crime. He moved the hearings from city to city and gained much television exposure. Partly as a result of these activities he won the vice-presidential nomination and ran on the ticket with Adlai Stevenson in 1956.

Senator Everett Dirksen of Illinois achieved national prominence through a brand of individualism that appealed to many people and was advertised through a gravelly voice that used to launch eminently quotable one-liners.

Dirksen's son-in-law, Senator Howard Baker of Tennessee, came to national prominence as minority chairman of the Senate Watergate committee, which had many hours of nationwide television exposure in 1973. All the members of that committee won some attention by virtue of their presence on the committee, but the chairman, Senator Sam Ervin of North Carolina, hit a special chord as the personification of the shrewd but simple country lawyer who successfully dealt with the city-slicker types and who was always ready with an apt quote from the Bible or the Constitution. He fitted the favorite character image of so many people that it was probably only his age that kept the politicians from promoting him as a candidate for national office.

Senator Edward Kennedy was naturally prominent as the younger brother of a president and the all-around beneficiary of the Kennedy family charisma. This combination, plus the political skill he eventually developed, made him one of the senators television reporters turn to when they seek comment.

The question of "who the reporters turn to" may become critical to the future of the persons involved and critical, too, to the future of the national leadership. The newspeople are creatures of habit as is anyone else. If they get a favorable response to an interview with a given person they are likely to try to repeat the performance. The process is self-reinforcing. As they interview a given individual they build him or her in importance in the public mind. As a result that person becomes a more important news source. One of the intriguing phenomena about the media and their sources is the manner in which the media build the public stature of individuals and then seem to be mystified that it has occurred.

What begins such a cycle of stature building? The answer is not well established, but it lies somewhere in the mystique of "news judgment." There are some obvious answers. First, an articulate legislator must be identified. If the legislator or a press secretary is capable of coining bright, quotable phrases that stick in the mind, so much the better. Presumably the legislator is sought out by the media because of some special knowledge of the issue at hand. It is helpful if he or she is a member of a committee concerned with the subject at hand. Better still if he or she is chairman or minority chairperson. If the reporter is working in television it will be a good idea to find an expert who is also good looking. An attractive appearance and a personality that comes across on the tube add to the chances for television exposure, which, in turn, may produce stories in the print media.

As we have already noted, some senators bring themselves to national attention by identifying themselves with public issues that command notice. Senator Joseph McCarthy of Wisconsin assumed prominence and importance of a kind by claiming that the State Department harbored many disloyal individuals. Lyndon Johnson was in a position of power as Senate majority leader before he received the Democratic nomination for the vice presidency on the Kennedy ticket in 1960.

Not all roads to national prominence come through diligence in the Senate itself. John Kennedy was more active as political speaker and party promoter than as a senator.

Most recent presidents and candidates for the presidency have come to prominence from the United States Senate. Exceptions were President Dwight D. Eisenhower and the man who ran against him twice, Adlai Stevenson. Eisenhower won worldwide fame as the successful leader of the Allied forces in Europe during the Second World War. Even he had to fight off a determined attempt to gain the Republican presidential nomination from a senator, Robert Taft of Ohio. Adlai Stevenson had been governor of Illinois.

Governors and generals, nonetheless, are less likely contenders for the presidency than are senators. The Senate offers a platform that skilled and ambitious individuals can sometimes turn into the presidency. Since this occurs quite frequently, the means, formal and informal, by which the news media are induced to focus attention on these individuals is of much relevance to the study of the transfer of political power.

Media Exposure Tests Policies

The press affects the politics of personalities—who gets the power. It also affects the politics of issues—what proposed policies come to public attention with sufficient force to gain acceptance.

Congress increasingly expects the president to initiate legislation, but even the president cannot get legislation through Congress unless there is some show of public support. This requires cooperation from the media.

Officials, intellectuals, leaders of special groups, and other opinion leaders use the media to encourage discussion of issues and to promote those they favor. Timing must be right and events cannot contradict information campaigns, but effective use of the media is an essential element in bringing about a change in public policy. U.S. history is full of examples.

One of the classic stories of a man who almost managed to ride an issue to power is that of William Jennings Bryan and the free silver issue. Bryan used the media of his day with consummate skill. He turned the Democratic national convention in Chicago in 1896 into a sounding board for the free silver issue, and he did it with a great speech that dramatized the issue throughout the country and has left its mark in history. His conclusion echoed across the United States: "You shall not press down upon the brow of labor this crown of thorns, you shall not crucify mankind upon a cross of gold." After this speech, Bryan, thirty-six, was nominated for the U.S. presidency. Beaten by William McKinley, Bryan was nominated again in 1900, but again lost to McKinley. In his last try for the presidency he lost to William Howard Taft in 1908.

Bryan did not lose his election attempts through any lack of skill or energy in using the media to promote the issues or himself. His media were the lecture hall and the newspapers. In his first campaign he made six hundred speeches in twenty-seven states. Before his first nomination he was editor of the *Omaha World-Herald* and he had already lectured extensively. In 1901 he founded *The Commoner*, a weekly newspaper, and used it as a forum to express his views. A lecturer and grappler with issues all his life, he died in 1925 while resting in Dayton, Tennessee, after his final battle with issues. A fundamentalist in religion, he had aided in the prosecution of John Scopes in the famous "monkey trial," which convicted Scopes, a high school teacher, of promoting the doctrine of evolution. Clarence Darrow, the famous criminal lawyer, had been defense attorney, and the trial was strenuous.

Bryan illustrates the individual who combines active public service, or aspiration for it, with the skilled use of media. Another example is Norman Thomas, who ran for president six times starting in 1928 as the candidate of the Socialist Party. He also ran for mayor of New York City as well as governor of and senator from New York State. He founded the journal *World Tomorrow* in 1918 and wrote many books and articles urging his views on the necessity of planning. The methods of Bryan and Thomas have been perfected in the 1960's and 1970's by Ralph Nader.

Nader Works the Press

Ralph Nader has demonstrated that power can be achieved without public office by a person who understands how to use the media to bring about change. From Nader's first encounter with General Motors over the safety of the Corvairs his battles have been fought in the arena provided by the media. The Corvair campaign was launched by Nader's media blockbuster, the book *Unsafe at Any Speed.* As Nader's renown has spread and his resources in people and money have increased, a voluminous report has often been the opening salute in a media campaign to achieve change. For instance, "The Company State," an eight-hundred-page report criticizing the Dupont company, was put together by a ten-member Nader's Raiders group headed by two Yale University law students supervised by Nader.

One of Nader's strengths is his credibility. One reporter describes it this way:

> Such is the credibility he enjoys that virtually every barbed utterance he makes finds its way into print. One recent morning, for example, The Washington Post ran an eight-column headline over a story detailing a series of Nader charges against the Nixon administration. Just below that, an unrelated story with a three-column headline reported on Nader's criticism of the United Mine Workers of America and its financial coziness with the coal industry.[6]

If a Nader campaign does not begin with a book or a lengthy report it may start with an article in the *New Republic* or a letter to a public of-

[6]Ward Sinclair, "The Unlikely Dragon-Slayer," *Courier-Journal & Times,* magazine (Louisville, Kentucky), April 20, 1969, 9.

ficial that Nader gives to the press. At the opening he saves part of his information to answer the expected rebuttal, the whole process adding more publicity. Other forums for Nader are the lecture platform and testimony before congressional committees. The influence of both devices is magnified by repetition through the news media.

Success in changing patterns of living in the United States and challenging established power centers requires a keen perception of issues to which media and public will respond, but it also requires the ability to carry the debate adroitly through the media, as Ralph Nader and other creators of social change demonstrate daily.

Test by Trial Balloon

The media also serve as a barometer of public opinion for leaders trying to discover whether an idea or a program will be acceptable to the public. Constant monitoring of the media provides understanding. Another method is the trial balloon. This old trick is still a standby of a cautious politician feeling the direction of the winds of opinion. An official will drop a hint to the news media that a certain policy is being considered, but will not let his or her name be used. If the idea is favorably received the official hastens to take credit, but if it is a dud he or she denies all knowledge of it. Sometimes the president will use a cabinet officer or some lower official to make the announcement. If it fails to gain acceptance the president can still deny authorship, although this will make the lower official look a bit lame.

The trial balloon technique becomes fairly obvious if one watches for it. Much less obvious to an outsider is evidence of the effect that neglect by the media can have. Theodore White says even the president needs media support to get legislation through Congress. If the press publicizes the White House program, Congress is likely to react favorably, particularly if the media have reached the constituents of the members of Congress. If the media ignore the program, Congress is likely to ignore it, too.

To some extent the media determine what we talk about and what we think about, just by deciding what information to print or air. Called the *agenda-setting function*, this may be one of the most influential aspects of the media role. Talk, thought, and interaction are necessary to make changes in our society, and in a nation of more than 200 million people, such discussion requires media participation. To the extent that the media do control the subject matter of our thoughts and discussion it is clear that they have a powerful influence on events.

Interpersonal Communication

The influence of the mass media is counterbalanced and tempered by that of interpersonal communication among the people and by that of the specialized media that influence the thinking of small groups. Elihu Katz and Paul Lazarsfeld made some early observations about the comparative influence of mass media and personal acquaintance in decision-making.

They concluded that influence does not flow directly from the mass

Figure 9.1   How the Media Influence People
This simplified version of the two-step flow theory shows the passage of influence from the media (top) to the opinion leaders (middle) and thence to other citizens (bottom). Occasionally influence flows directly from the media to the citizens. Information flow is complicated by the existence of many media, not all of which may agree on a particular question.

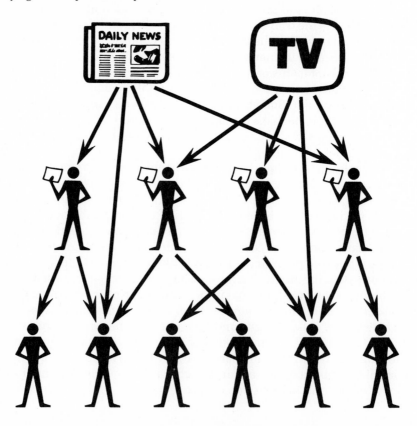

media to the whole population in an even or unbroken chain. Instead, the media influence some individuals, who may in turn influence others. (See Figure 9.1.) When people have to make decisions, according to this theory, they seek someone among their peers whose opinion they respect. They are likely to turn to different people on different subjects. If a teenager is trying to decide whether to see a certain motion picture he may read the advice of a reviewer in the newspaper or he may call a friend, probably of his own age. This friend may have seen the movie, may have read the review, or for some other reason may have information on which to base advice. If a woman is thinking about buying a new car, she is likely to consult a friend who has special knowledge about autos. The people whose advice is sought, the opinion leaders, will vary as the subject matter of the decision varies, and their opinions are respected for various reasons. One of these reasons may be that they pay attention to the mass media, but others may be that they have certain kinds of experience or that they are tied in to a special group that provides them with another source of information—some specialized medium such as a limited-circulation magazine or a newsletter.

Information, Communication, and Decisions

In voting studies researchers found that there is sometimes a group in a community whose opinions are valued in national and international affairs. These persons tend to pay attention to that kind of news in the media. Another group may be influential in local and regional affairs. This group may pay little attention to information about national affairs, but it is tied into a network that provides information on which to base views about local activities.[7]

The means by which personalities and media combine to promote the issues and to bring certain individuals into power is still poorly charted territory in the study of communications and politics.

A person seeking political power must somehow gain a forum, a position from which to speak. This is a little different concept from the media. A senator has a forum because the media report what is occurring in the

[7]Some of the studies that generated these theories are: Paul F. Lazarsfeld, Bernard Berelson, and Hazel Gaudet, *The People's Choice*, 2nd ed. (New York: Columbia University Press, 1948); Robert K. Merton, "Patterns of Influence: A Study of Interpersonal Influence and Communications Behavior in a Local Community," in *Communications Research, 1948–49* eds. Paul F. Lazarsfeld and Frank N. Stanton (New York: Harper and Brothers, 1949), pp. 180–219; Elihu Katz and Paul F. Lazarsfeld, *Personal Influence: The Part Played by People in the Flow of Mass Communications* (Glencoe, Ill.: Free Press, 1955).

Senate and because the public attaches some importance to it. An editor or editorial writer for a newspaper has a forum because some people are accustomed to look for his or her editorials and to put some faith in them. A public speaker has a forum because people come to listen to and consider what he or she has to say.

Theodore Roosevelt called the presidency "a bully pulpit." Certainly it is one of the great forums. The president can command the attention of a large segment of the American public and much of the world public whenever he wants it.

The Media Select Issues

Still another aspect of the media and politics is critical to the way we reach decisions of social consequence. If the media serve as agenda-setters for the rest of society by bringing up subjects for discussion, the next question is: How do the media determine what issues they should raise?

The answer to that question has been shrouded by much illogical debate. Whoever feels that publicity is harming a favorite cause is likely to criticize the media for bringing up the subject at all. The media are very visible targets and their defenders do not have very good answers to the question, simply because it is unanswerable. They may say: "We simply tell what happened. We didn't make it happen." When Republicans criticized the media for all the attention paid to the Watergate scandals in 1972 and 1973, media defenders answered in that vein. "After all the Republican administration brought this on itself. We simply did our job of reporting by telling about it."

This is a logical enough answer, but to some public figures the press seemed so determined to make every political story a Watergate story that other aspects of the political picture were neglected. Tired of talking about Watergate at a press conference, Nelson Rockefeller, before he became vice president, asked reporters: "What are you people going to do when this is over?"

Realistically, the media select the subjects they choose to report largely through habit and a mutual reinforcement process. The national press showers coverage on the president, providing, collectively, considerably more personnel than is needed to do the job. These things are matters of habit and custom and they tend to be self-generating. Stories from this source, no matter how routine, are almost sure to be published. Once they are published reporters and editors are so impressed by their product and that of their competitors that they decide such material really is newsworthy and then publish all similar stories from the same sources. Thus custom and habit become ingrained, and as new areas of society develop they have to fight to get their story told in public, simply because it never has become a habit to send reporters to cover their activities. A similar syndrome is observable in the bulk of historical writing. The affairs of kings, emperors, and popes are given much attention and we learn little about how everyday people lived. This habit is self-reinforcing, too, since historians look at each other's work and decide that is the way to write history. Much is lost to the world because of this habit. Records of many segments of society are never kept, or they are allowed to disappear.

Habit and mutual reinforcement are not the only factors that determine what the media pay attention to. To some extent they have information about what their readers are interested in. Many newspapers and broadcasters receive regular reports on audience habits. If a Watergate hearing is attracting a large audience it will be easy for a news director to defend preempting a soap opera. As the audience begins to taper off, the arguments about the social significance of the hearing bear less weight with the network and station management.

The existence of a television station or a newspaper depends upon its ability to attract and hold an audience, and no manager can allow personal program preferences to govern. The medium must carry material that will hold public attention.

But audience reaction is only one factor and no one can really say how strong it is in determining news content. "Gatekeeper" studies by David Manning White and others have shed some light on the matter, but these, too, indicate that selecting material for the public press is more a matter of art and imitation than of science.[8]

One understudied aspect of news judgment is the flow of subject matter from one medium to another. If the media set the agenda for public discussion and legitimize public discussion about certain subjects, do they follow certain bellwethers among themselves? After weeks of whispering after the Watergate story broke, how did the word *impeachment* finally break into the public press in 1973? After generations during which it was daring to refer to a lady's ankle in the newspaper, how did discussion of penis envy appear in family newspapers in mid-twentieth century? The thought habits of our media are as well worn as those of most of our minds. What is it that allows a new idea to be discussed?

The answers are not well documented. The vocabulary and ideas presented in our media relate to the climate of opinion and to the level of public tolerance for out-of-the-ordinary words and thoughts. One indication of the level of a civilization is the extent to which it can give a hearing

[8]David M. White, "The 'Gate Keeper': A Case Study in the Selection of News," *Journalism Quarterly* 27 (Fall 1950): 383–390. A recent application of the theory is described in James K. Buckalew, "The Radio News Gatekeeper and His Sources," *Journalism Quarterly* 51 (Winter 1974): 602–606.

to unusual ideas. It is easy to defend freedom of expression when ours is being threatened, but difficult or impossible to give a hearing to ideas that frighten us. The Puritans demonstrated this. They broke away from England because they were denied freedom of worship. Once established in New England they granted freedom of worship to everyone—so long as everyone worshiped just the same as they did.

New ideas gain currency through discussion in small groups. Some of these groups publish their own "radical" papers, which are monitored by the other media, and gradually the ideas slip over into the general media. That is the best theory available, but probably it is only a partial explanation.

Certainly the college press has had some effect. Its discussion of sexuality in the early 1960's eventually led to more shockproof readers. As the college writers graduated and started work on the general media they brought their ideas with them. By the time they had sufficient influence to inject such subject matter into the general press, enough recent college graduates had, through their college press, become adequately sophisticated that the general media were safe in slightly liberalizing their coverage.

The same bellwether role is frequently claimed for the journals of opinion such as *The Nation, New Republic, New Leader, National Review, Commonweal,* and *Commentary. The Progressive* of Wisconsin was a powerful force in disseminating the ideas of the LaFollettes.

The media differ in the freedom with which they dare approach new ideas—or ideas that formerly were not a subject of public discussion. Television has been less free than motion pictures. Motion pictures, until the middle of the twentieth century, were considerably less free than the printed media. These differences were brought about by the way audiences viewed the different media and by media response to differing controls.

But these things are changing. In the 1970's television has treated homosexuality and other delicate subjects. The practicalities of the marketplace have some effect, too. As more explicit films become available for television showing it is likely that more of the blips will give way to original soundtracks, and the more adult vocabulary will be heard on television.

Politics and the Media

Political processes determine how our wealth is distributed, who has to make the most sacrifices for the common good, the system by which we reward or punish activities. Politics, in short, determines the very nature of our existence. If our population continues to expand and our resources become scarcer it is certain that political processes will become even more vital and will affect our lives even more intimately. Will government tell us whom to marry in order to produce desirable offspring? Will it forbid some of us to bear children at all? If biologists conquer the aging process, will the government decide how long we can live?

It appears inevitable that the conditions of the future will require more social decisions in areas that are now considered private ones. Political decision is the only alternative to dictatorial decision.

The media and what they tell us are critical to the functioning of the political process. Our press and our politics are sometimes whimsical in their decisions, easily distracted from serious questions, susceptible to manipulation by clever minorities with special interests. We have relied on patchwork methods and happenstance to keep us afloat, but serious attention is beginning to be focused on the area.

Suggestions for Further Reading

Lang, Kurt, and Lang, Gladys Engel. *Politics and Television*. Chicago: Quadrangle Books, 1968.
   Reports studies of political conventions as they are shaped by television.
Porter, William E. *Assault on the Media*. Ann Arbor: University of Michigan Press, 1976.
   The Nixon administration and the media.
Reston, James. *The Artillery of the Press*. New York: Harper & Row, 1966.
   A discussion of the relationship between reporters and officials with special emphasis on the effect of the press on foreign policy.
Rivers, William L. *The Opinionmakers*. Boston: Beacon Press, 1965.
   The interplay between reporters and officials in Washington.
——. *The Adversaries: Politics and the Press.* Boston: Beacon Press, 1970.
   Theorizes that reporters and officeholders are forced into antagonistic roles.
Rivers, William L. *The Opinionmakers*. Boston: Beacon Press, 1965.
   The interplay between reporters and officials in Washington.
   Report on a workshop that considered several aspects of government and the media.
Small, William J. *Political Power and the Press*. New York: W. W. Norton, 1972.
   A discussion of press and politics with emphasis on the Nixon years, including "The Selling of the Pentagon" and the Pentagon papers case.
White, Theodore H. *The Making of the President, 1972*. New York: Atheneum, 1973.
   In discussing the campaign the author has much to say about the media.

10

News and Information Formats

Communication, even through the media, is one of the most human of occupations. Even the most impersonal billboard bears some clue about the writer. The message spoken into a camera, although relayed electronically to millions of viewers, still carries the personal stamp of the television correspondent in a way impossible for printed journalism.

Each individual communicates in his or her own unique way, although the style is developed by practice and by imitating others. Each public speaker has a personal way of inflecting the voice to modify the message. The speaker varies the tone, pitch, and speed of delivery either unconsciously or purposefully. At one time clergymen, through training and imitation, developed a style of delivery that marked each of them as a man delivering a sermon.

Radio announcers went through the same stage. Their voices dropped a few notes and assumed the timbre of a minor pontiff as they adopted the conventions of their craft. Milton Cross became the archetype. His self-assured, sonorous tones as he announced the Metropolitan Opera broadcasts each Saturday afternoon were imitated by aspiring radio personalities for a generation. Arthur Godfrey, who became one of radio's most durable entertainers, lay in a hospital bed early in his career and listened to so many Milton Cross–type voices that he decided he would maintain his natural diction. He succeeded in combining success with a natural voice. Godfrey, along with Lowell Thomas and others, helped radio to escape eventually from that particular convention.

In the more spontaneous communication of everyday conversations individuals often become stylists, too. Some people impart information by vigorous use of their whole bodies. They deliver a few shadow blows in describing a fight; they do a little jig when they tell of a dancing bear; they mime the shuffle of an old man; their voices copy the diction and accent of those they are quoting. These are the people who become known as *raconteurs*. Others are as motionless as wooden Indians when they talk, and their voices produce a monotone. The manner in which people communicate is an indicator, perhaps the best one, of personality.

So it is with the media. The manner in which they communicate is what they *are* to their audiences.

Although the media are large operations combining human and mechanical interplay, they still manage to develop personalities of their own. The *New York Times* presents a different face to the world from the *New York Daily News*. *Mad* magazine has a different personality from *Atlantic Monthly*. Formats of radio stations vary from rock and roll to classical music.

Mechanical limitations control to some extent the manner in which media present information, but media facing the same mechanical limitations will produce widely differing images. The *Christian Science Monitor* speaks in well-modulated tones, while the *Berkeley Barb* is more strident.

Organizations, like individuals, have personalities. Since the media are more visible than most organizations, their personalities are more subject to public scrutiny. These media personalities are made up of manner and format. In this chapter we will consider how manner and format interact. Aspects of manner we will consider include (1) whether communication is analogic or digital or a combination of the two, (2) the viewpoint adopted by the communicator, (3) the mixture of opinion and fact, and (4) the purpose of the communicator.

Format is also influenced by technology, or lack of it. We will examine interpersonal and media formats to see how media communication developed from face-to-face talk and how the media influence each other.

The Elements of Manner: Digital or Analogic?

Every day we communicate in many different ways. Sometimes we use a formal code such as language. At other times we act out our

News and Information Formats

meanings or use other graphic representational devices. A more formal way of making the same distinction is to say that all communication is either *digital* or *analogic.*

Digital communication uses a code. When the code is fairly elaborate we call it *language.* In the early chapters we considered the relationship of language to reality and noticed that language uses signs or symbols to represent reality. There is always an extra step in communication through language. The person talking has to translate his or her thoughts into the code, consisting of words arranged in sentences, and voice the words. The hearer has to decode the message by translating the symbols into his or her own version of reality. The language of the digital computer is binary arithmetic, which permits its data to be stored by a series of *on* or *off* indicators. The cumbersome detail of the binary system is compensated by the speed of the computer, but mechanical interpretation is needed before the information becomes useful to a human.

Analogic communication dispenses with the code and uses devices that imitate reality. A voltmeter is an analogic device. It is arranged so that an increase or decrease in voltage through the circuit being measured makes a needle move. When the needle is placed before a scale a reading can be obtained. The traditional clock face is an analogic device, since the movements of the hands correspond to the passage of time. (See Figure 10.1.) Digital clocks and watches translate the information into a number code. For harried disc jockeys a digital clock is a convenience. If they are using a regular clock they have to translate the analogic data it gives them into digital information before they can broadcast it. That is, they have to

Figure 10.1   Digital Versus Analogic Time
The digital timepiece (left) translates the hour and minutes into pure figures. On the conventional analogic face (right), the movement of the hands bears a spatial relationship to the passage of time.

encode it. If they look at a digital clock the information is already coded. All they have to do is read it off to their listeners.

Raconteurs are usually good at providing analogic information. If someone in the story they are telling shouts, they shout. If someone points, they point, too. Such communication reaches its most perfect expression in the work of a gifted pantomime artist or dancer. Such artists use no codes and so the receiver is spared one mental process in interpreting the information. He or she does not have to break down the code. Hence the popularity of Punch and Judy shows.

At some point analogic communication may become so stylized that it is symbolic and so almost digital. The studied arabesques of the ballet dancer have symbolic meanings, but their direct relation to reality is still apparent. The symbols of the alphabet developed in the same way. At first they were pictures but gradually they lost this direct connection with reality and became abstract symbols.

Different media vary in their ability to combine digital and analogic communication, but nearly all of them do it to some degree. The typing instructor who provides rules for positioning a business letter on a page and urges the virtues of neatness is showing concern for the analogic message of letters. The typography and layout of newspaper, book, and magazine pages supply nondigital information to the reader. So do pictures. Charts are somewhere between the analogic information supplied by pictures and the digital information of the text.

Radio can provide analogic cues to enrich the digital material in the spoken word. Vocal inflections, background music, and sound effects all add to the other information presented and affect the way it will be interpreted.

One of the reasons for the popularity of television is that its signal is rich in analogic as well as digital data. It furnishes information to the eye and the ear, and in both channels it can combine digital and analogic information. This breadth of channels makes television more capable than most other media of giving the audience an illusion of firsthand communication. The power of analogic communication can be heightened by the use of stereo or quadrasonic sound, and by positioning screens all around the room so that the people in the audience feel that they are participating in the event pictured.

Viewpoint

Another important variable affecting the manner of presentation is the viewpoint adopted. There are various ways to consider viewpoint, but we will discuss only one: the extent to which the communicator injects himself or herself into the information offered. This varies all the way from the continuous participation of the narrator in an interview program or talk show to the cold impersonality of the traditional news story.

Interpersonal communication involves the direct participation of the communicator. A person cannot tell a story without injecting a personal interpretation, if only by the inadvertent raising of an eyebrow. Styles of personal communications vary a great deal. We tend to regard people who impart information without involvement as "cold and impersonal," while the opposite type is classified as "warm and friendly." Once again, this emphasizes the extent to which most people relate interpersonal communication habits to personality.

Media, too, vary to the extent to which they personalize information. The mix is controlled by the traditions of the medium, by the habits of the particular people working on it, and by the technology of the medium. Television frequently injects a personal viewpoint partly because of programming habits and partly because of its technology, which projects the human voice and image. Television appears to have developed this characteristic more than films, as we shall see when we consider the audiences of the media. Film has the broad sight and sound channels of television, but lacks the regular viewing patterns given to television, and it probably suffers because it is not viewed in the familiar home surroundings wherein most people view the tube.

Radio, while it lacks the broad channels of television and film, has achieved an aura of intimacy with its listeners due to the richness of the human voice and to radio's mobility. Radio can follow its audience around and be a companion in periods of loneliness and when major attention is being given to other tasks.

The viewpoint with which information is presented has much to do with the manner in which it is received. If it is presented impersonally an air of authority may be achieved, but this is not likely to compensate for the coldness that many people appear to perceive in an impersonal presentation.

Another critical factor in the way information is received is the amount of opinion that is presented. Most interpersonal communications contain what appears to be a chance mixture of fact and opinion. Depending on how they view each other, the sender and receiver may or may not make a conscious distinction between the two modes. If the receiver is of a trusting nature or trusts the sender, he or she is likely to be little concerned with whether the sender is providing fact or opinion. If the receiver is suspicious, he or she is likely to watch for cues that indicate the injection of opinion.

The media have sometimes been accused of including opinion simply by telling one side of a story. One newspaper responded to this criticism by hiring an accounting firm to measure the space it allocated to each of the major party candidates in a presidential election. It assumed that "fairness" resulted from an equal division of space, ignoring the other subtleties of injecting opinion into the news.

There may be disagreement, too, between sender and receiver as to what actually constitutes opinion. A commentator may reach a conclusion and feel so strongly that it is correct that he or she regards it as fact and propounds it as such. The auditor may take the opposite view.

One of the great controversies that concerns the media has to do with this point. The interpretative function of the media is well recognized, but many professionals and observers alike insist that when interpretation becomes an expression of opinion the reader or listener is entitled to be told. The receiver of information has less information than the sender and so may not be able to make the distinction between fact and opinion for himself or herself.

Purposes Are Often Unstated

Like other factors controlling manner of presentation, the purpose of the communicator often is unstated, so the receiver has to infer it from the manner. The purpose may be to entertain, to inform, to persuade, or to urge to action. (See Figure 10.2.) In the background lurks a more general and more subtle purpose. For an individual it may be to appear friendly and well informed. For a communications medium it is to attract and hold an audience.

An effort to be entertaining is usually indicated by an informal, breezy style filled with anecdotes and personalities. Banter, jokes, and trivialities abound in material designed to entertain. This is the light feature story of the newspaper; the personality sketch in magazines; the talk shows, show business celebrity interviews, and game shows of radio and television.

Simple, factual style that provides no clue as to the opinions or preferences of the communicator indicates an intent to inform. The reporter seems to be saying, "This is something you might want or need to know about. Here is what happened. Here is the situation." Such an expository-explanatory style may take many forms. It often uses examples and illustrations, and it is usually impossible to tell whether the illustrative material balances all sides of an issue. Here, the reader or listener must usually rely on his or her view of the trustworthiness of the reporter or the organization for which that person works.

Persuasive material varies in subtlety from patterns in which the persuasive intent is hidden in overtly entertaining or informative material to those that follow the traditional and easily recognized argumentative structure. Calls to action are seldom indirect and they are easily recognizable.

Any given message may have several purposes. In fact, it is possible that the most persuasive messages are also the most entertaining. Certainly an entertaining message can be informative and an informative one entertaining. Although a communicator may have several purposes, normally one dominates. To understand a message completely, the receiver must know the dominant purpose of the communicator. To be persuaded without knowledge that it is occurring is to be manipulated, as the opponents of propaganda and subliminal advertising frequently argue.

The way that a receiver interprets any message is affected by many fac-

Figure 10.2   Information, Entertainment, and Persuasion
Each of the morning news and variety shows on network television has its own mixture of information, entertainment, and persuasion. "CBS Morning News" presents a lot of information ("hard news"). NBC's "Today" carries more entertainment than CBS, but more news than ABC's "Good Morning America." All sometimes present persuasive material, which can be either news or entertainment.

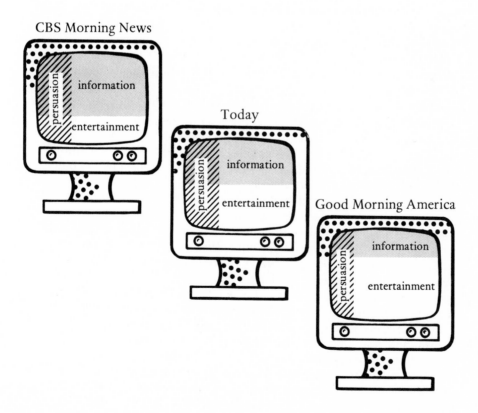

tors. Among the dominant ones is the manner of presentation, which, in turn, is controlled by the purpose of the communicator.

Purpose and manner combine to determine the format in which information is presented. We will take a look at format and how it evolved in various kinds of communication. First we will consider face-to-face communication.

Conversations

When two people converse the situation can be entirely informal and almost purposeless, or it can be highly structured to achieve a specific goal. Aimless conversations occur whenever two persons meet and find they cannot endure silence. Such conversation is a filler by which people recognize each other's presence and assure each other that their intentions are innocent.

Conversations may be informal but full of purpose, as when a son asks his father to borrow the car. Or they may be highly structured, as when an interviewer questioning a respondent meticulously follows the wording on a printed form. Interviews are purposeful conversations. When one or both of the parties to a conversation has a purpose, some structure is likely to be imposed, although it may not be overt. Interviews are used to obtain or give information, to persuade, or sometimes simply to get acquainted with another person.

Interviewing is important in many professions. The news reporter uses it constantly to get information. People use it to get jobs, and job recruiters use it to evaluate candidates and to persuade them of the benefits of working for their company. Counselors use it to advise their clients. The psychiatric interview, complete with couch, has become a part of our folklore, although not a part of everyone's life.

Interviews range from hurried questioning to summit-level exchanges that form the basis for decisions that affect the world. When a president or a secretary of state goes abroad, large staffs are called upon to help to prepare for the coming conversations with other world leaders. The "conversation" of a vacuum cleaner or encyclopedia salesperson with a potential buyer is highly structured, with counterarguments carefully planned for every sign of resistance to the sales message. The public opinion pollster plans the interview form to keep the respondent interested until the last and to ask embarrassing questions at the end. The whole form is intended to provide a simulated conversation so that the respondent responds naturally and honestly.

Professionals who use interviews in their work have studied the form intensively. For our purposes it is enough to note that interviewing is used universally with varying purposes and skill. It is a form of interpersonal communications on which many people base successful careers. Skill in conversations or formal interviews is one of the best guarantees of personal success.

Meetings

Before the days of writing people had to assemble to conduct public business, and even now most public decisions are reached in meetings. But meetings, like conversations, vary from the aimless to the earthshaking.

From bull sessions to assemblages of the Supreme Court, meetings run the gamut of purpose and structure. In purpose they may be entertaining —to exchange small talk or to hear a new comedian—or deadly serious, like a congressional committee hearing on a presidential appointment. They also range in structure from come-as-you-are informality to white tie and tails. They may allow or even require all present to participate, or they may provide for one or two to transmit information to the others assembled.

Fast transportation has increased the popularity of the convention, which brings together people from a wide geographic area for a series of meetings. Within the format there are likely to be several types of meetings. These may range from group participation, such as a cocktail party or a seminar session, to a single speaker addressing the group. The convention provides contact with different people for a short enough period that boredom is unlikely to set in. A change from the participants' everyday setting also encourages friendly, informal communication.

Direct face-to-face communication presents a wide variety of communication modes, from the entirely free form to situations so totally structured that even a wrong gesture can bring swift punishment. For example, through the contempt power a judge is allowed to punish anyone in a courtroom during a trial who commits an act that the judge construes to be detrimental to the conduct of the proceeding.

The interposition of the media in the communication process invariably imposes structure. There is less structure in interpersonal than in mass communication, but any medium makes communication a little more self-conscious and a little more planned.

Letters and Telephone Talk

In even such a simple task as writing a note to a friend we use a communications medium—a method a little less direct than the spoken word. Since talking is an activity we learn earlier and under less formal conditions, most of us are more at home in talking than writing. Perhaps when we pick up a pen we feel a little more guarded, too. Even though the communication may be intended for one person only, we can never be quite sure that another will not see it, or that it will not crop up years later and cause embarrassment.

Letters are likely to be less frank, more contrived, more structured than firsthand conversation. It is for this reason that some administrators check the references of job applicants by telephone rather than by letter.

The telephone, like other electronic media, may allow people to forget that they are not communicating firsthand, so telephone talk is likely to be less guarded than letters. It is easier to adapt one's messages to the receiver in speaking on the telephone than in writing a letter since one can monitor verbal response instantaneously.

Letters and telephone conversations leave out much of the richness of face-to-face talk, but they are effective when supplemented by it. This is why some reporters make it a point to visit their news sources in person occasionally. When a story breaks and they need information quickly they are more likely to get it on the telephone if the source knows them personally.

Telephone talk and letter-writing, even though they require mechanical devices, are interpersonal and participatory, so they are likely to be more satisfactory than mass communication. But any mechanical intervention narrows channels and provides less feedback and spontaneity than face-to-face conversation. Letters and phone calls usually take more time and money, too, so they require more planning and structure.

Because mass media try to reach large audiences, they plan their content with care and use standardized formats. Thus they are more formal than interpersonal communication.

Information Formats in the Mass Media

As do other forms of communication, the mass media provide information in formats designed to inform, persuade, and entertain. In the early writing about public affairs these goals were blended into one form. Frequently they still are, but there has been a determined effort to separate them.

The need for information and interpretation was obvious before the news media existed, and in the days of the oral tradition this need was filled by word of mouth. In the latter half of the sixteenth century Europeans began to gather in coffee houses to exchange information and opinions. Supposedly the first coffee houses were established in Constantinople in 1554. Nearly one hundred years later the first one was opened in England at Oxford. Another hundred years later, in 1754, William Bradford opened the first known "merchants' exchange" coffee house in America. Located in Philadelphia, it was called the London Coffee House.

The transition from oral to written and eventually to printed news was helped along by coffee house proprietors, who served information along with drafts from what one early writer called "the hissing urn."

At Bradford's London Coffee House, conveniently situated in the commercial district of Philadelphia, merchants met to learn the latest information and to discuss business and make deals. Bradford made available his own weekly *Pennsylvania Journal* along with latest issues of other Colonial and London newspapers. Like coffee houses in European cities, Bradford's house became the information center for the city. Letters to dignitaries visiting Philadelphia were directed to the coffee house rather than to the post office, as were messages to the Continental Congress.

Coffee houses in New York and Boston supplied the same information services for their cities. They supplemented the printed newspapers with manuscript sheets wherein their regular customers could get the latest information about ship arrivals and departures and visitors to the city. So thorough was the news service supplied by the proprietor of the New York coffee house that the weekly newspapers quoted his information with a credit line. Seven manuscript newspapers were provided by the coffee house in Boston run by Samuel Topliff, Jr. These contained records of general news, arrivals and departures of ships for foreign and American ports, and a list of visitors. Topliff maintained a boat "with two men at the ready at all times" to meet ships and collect information for the coffee house.

Topliff's zeal in collecting news is regarded as one of the reasons that no daily newspaper was successfully launched in Boston until 1813, years after New York and Baltimore had dailies.[1] With all necessary news available at a reasonable price at the coffee house, merchants were slow to subscribe to a daily or advertise in one.

Coffee houses provided meeting places as well as information. Even the governor was said to be a regular visitor to Bradford's house in Philadelphia. In their visits the businessmen provided their own interpretation of events and reinforced each other's opinions. The proprietors of the houses, by mingling with their customers, got regular feedback about the kind of information they desired. The local news supplied was usually handwritten and updated as new tidings arrived.

New England clergymen sometimes purveyed the news as well as the

[1]Alfred M. Lee, *The Daily Newspaper in America* (New York: Macmillan, 1937), p. 47.

gospel from their pulpits. And in Detroit a Roman Catholic priest stationed a crier at the church door to announce community news every Sunday. The crier also included notices of auctions and other advertising. The man who did this work, sacristan of the church, later became a publisher.

The taverns, coffee houses, and clergy formed a participant information exchange, with the consumers of the news almost as much involved as the proprietors. Little format or structure was necessary since the process was oral or handwritten. The weekly papers were gradually applying the structure of print to the news form, but the coffee houses were competitive with the dailies and their more formal approach to the news. In Boston and probably other cities, too, they delayed the advent of the daily press.

But it was the printed media that gradually brought structure to the news story.

The News Story

It is no wonder that early newspapers paid little attention to the form of a news story—the direct descendant of coffee house conversations, handwritten accounts, and town criers. In telling the story opinion was generously mixed with fact and sometimes the facts themselves were admittedly questionable.

On September 25, 1690, Benjamin Harris published in Boston the first and, as it turned out, the last edition of *Publick Occurrences, Both Foreign and Domestick*. Consisting of four 7½-by-11½-inch sheets, *Publick Occurences* had two columns on every page except the last, which was left blank. Harris planned to publish once a month or oftener "if any glut of occurences happen," but the governor and council found the sheet to contain "reflections of a high nature" and suppressed it. They also forbade any further unlicensed printing.

As the earliest attempt at a newspaper in the Colonies, *Publick Occurrences* clearly showed the effects of the oral tradition from which it sprang. Two paragraphs show how the paper moved from event to event in conversational style:

> While the barbarous Indians were lurking about Chelmsford, there were missing about the beginning of this month a couple of Children belonging to a man of that Town, one of them aged eleven, and the other aged about nine years, both of them supposed to be fallen into the hands of the Indians.
>
> A very Tragical Accident happened at Watertown, the beginning of the Month, an Old man, that was of somewhat of a Silent and Morose

Temper, but one that had long Enjoyed the reputation of a Sober and Pious Man, having newly buried his Wife, The Devil took advantage of the Melancholy which he thereupon fell into, his Wives discretion and industry had long been the support of his Family, and he seemed hurried with an impertinent fear that he should now come to want before he dyed, though he had very careful friends to look after him who kept a strict eye upon him, lest he should do himself any harm. But one evening escaping from them into the Cowhouse, they there quickly followed him found him hanging by a Rope, which they had used to tye their Calves withal, he was dead with his feet near touching the Ground.[2]

Despite the early example of Harris, Colonial publishers often ignored local news except for shipping and commercial items that they could pick up at the taverns.

Persuasive and explanatory material were the essence of the Federalist papers, the first seventy-six of which appeared originally in the *Independent Journal* of New York City in 1787 and 1788. Written by Alexander Hamilton, John Jay, and James Madison, they were reprinted widely and given much credit for the passage of the Constitution.

In the early days of the Republic the press was frequently subsidized by political parties, a fact that led to bitter partisan attacks that brought small credit to the press and contributed little to the news format. James Melvin Lee described it this way:

> Those who look over the papers of this era will find that all of the customary courtesies of life were put aside; that the papers of both parties employed the vilest, grossest epithets found in the English language; that the newspapers advanced the most atrocious charges against those holding public offices and even so forgot themselves as to attack wives and sisters in their disgraceful accounts of the personal activities of office-holders.[3]

A small news staff led to the dearth of local news and often to delayed reporting. Until the 1850's the Philadelphia newspapers had only one reporter apiece, and in the 1840's New York papers had only four or five.[4] Small staffs also provided little opportunity to experiment with the news format.

After Horace Greeley started publication of the *New York Tribune* in 1841 he became the most celebrated example of an editor who used the

---

[2]*Publick Occurrences, Both Forreign and Domestick*, Boston, September 25, 1690. Quoted in James Melvin Lee, *History of American Journalism* (Garden City, N.Y.: Garden City Publishing, 1923), p. 11.

[3]Lee, *History of American Journalism*, p. 143.

[4]Alfred M. Lee, *Daily Newspaper in America*, pp. 608, 611.

editorial columns as a forum and who thus elevated them to greater importance than the news columns. But three decades later news was predominant, and Whitelaw Reid, editor of that same *Tribune*, hailed the change in 1875. He declared that a newspaper was

> what its name expresses; a *news*paper, with the promptest and best obtainable educidation . . . of the news to attend it. I know there is another idea urged by men who are anxious to become propagandists; but whenever such men have obtained exclusive control of a daily newspaper they have ruined it. The essence, the life-blood of the daily paper of to-day, is the *news*.[5]

The dominance of the news continues to this day—in space allocated by public affairs media and in audience interest. For this reason the proper mixture of fact and interpretation is frequently debated by newspeople.

A fact is a piece of information that is either directly verifiable or generally accepted. A reporter is well within the bounds of verifiable fact if he or she writes that the governor is on a speaking tour accompanied by his wife. To say that the governor is accompanied by his lovely wife injects the reporter's opinion. Standards of loveliness vary from one person to another, so it is a judgment and not verifiable. To say that the governor and his wife are touring the state trying to build support for the women's rights amendment because the governor needs the female vote in the coming election adds background that may or may not be verifiable.

Kent Cooper, a former general manager of the Associated Press, claimed that the AP invented objective journalism because it served many newspapers of different political persuasions. In the days of the party press, newspapers quite commonly put their own party in a better light in news stories by emphasizing its virtues or even by shading the facts. With papers available representing both parties, a reader could arrive at some notion of actuality by taking both. Usually a reader took the one that espoused the cause of his or her favorite party and enjoyed the partisanship that matched his or her own.

The Associated Press could not afford the luxury of partisanship since it served papers supporting both parties, so it developed an objective approach. Such an approach is impossible to define accurately, but in general it means that a reporter sticks to the obvious verifiable facts, injects no obvious opinion of his or her own, and keeps all background and interpretative material to a minimum. The result is supposed to be an impersonal account of an event or situation that informs readers or listeners and allows them to form their own opinions.

In the name of objectivity editors sometimes imposed patterns of writ-

[5]Ibid., p. 629.

ing that resembled strait jackets. Even the common "inverted pyramid" often leads to awkward style. It requires a writer to start with either the most important or the most exciting element of a story, then proceed to relate the remainder in descending order of importance. Not only does this frequently nullify the possibility of maintaining a logical order, but it may make it impossible for the writer to create an interesting story.

It did fit the mechanical problems of the newspaper. Deadlines often required the swift writing of a headline, and usually the opening paragraph or "lead" had only to be condensed. In the days when newspapers were rapidly laid out on a printer's table stories often had to be cut. If the inverted pyramid style was followed a printer could end the story at the close of any paragraph, confident of subtracting the least important information.

But deadpan "objectivity" and the inverted pyramid style left something to be desired. Too often that something was meaning. For most people nearly every event needs some explanation. The events we meet firsthand in the course of our daily expeditions into the world are understandable because the situations are familiar to us or because we have someone to explain them. Most situations presented to us in the news media are sufficiently complicated that we need some guidance as to their meaning and their importance. The limitations of objectivity frequently kept the reporter from providing that guidance.

Curtis D. MacDougall of Northwestern University, a leading professor of journalism and an influential writer, credits deadpan reporting with leaving the American public unprepared for the U.S. entrance into the First World War and amazed at it. He holds that the interpretative reporting that developed in foreign news between the wars helped the public accept U.S. entrance into the Second World War as inevitable. Whether the effect in either case was quite that dramatic is debatable, but the trend is inescapable. The conclusion is, too: some interpretation is essential to all but the simplest of news stories.

Arguments among newspeople about objectivity continue and probably will not stop. But during the 1920's, 1930's, and 1940's the concept of objectivity enlarged so that reporters could include background material and sometimes more subtle interpretive devices. Objectivity no longer requires barebones reporting, but a new line of argument has been staked out. It centers on the question whether the reporter's opinion is now a legitimate part of a story as one of the devices of interpretation.

The dangers are that the reporter may present hasty or erroneous opinion, and that the reader or listener may confuse this with fact.

Dorothy Thompson, one of the most prominent correspondents between the First and Second World Wars, sometimes erred in her opinions, as her biographer recalls in telling of Miss Thompson's interview in 1931 with Hitler:

Building up suspense, Dorothy makes the occasion not a mere interview, but a dramatic confrontation. She also shares with the reader what turned out to be a monumental blunder. "When I finally walked into Adolph Hitler's salon in the Kaiserhof Hotel, I was convinced that I was meeting the future dictator of Germany. In something less than fifty seconds I was quite sure that I was not. It took just that time to measure the startling insignificance of this man who has set the whole world agog." Such was her self-assurance that she used these sentences as the headnote for her book's opening chapter. Hitler would soon be Chancellor of Germany and by March 1933 the Nazi dictatorship would be firmly established.

Fellow journalists were to twit for years about this historic miss.[6]

It was natural that American foreign correspondents should be the ones to open up patterns of news-writing. They were the ones on the scene and even their editors were seldom in a position to question their information or their opinions. That this freedom would produce some bad guesses was natural, too. The cause for concern is that the audience may mistake opinion for fact or, recognizing opinion, may still place too much credence on it.

Radio Uses an Informal Style

Radio news was another factor that increased the flexibility of the news story. By the early 1930's broadcast news was attracting reporters and writers from newspapers, and they found that the inverted pyramid style did not work in the new medium. For one thing, the emphasis on a catch-all lead had resulted in many reporters producing long, cumbersome opening sentences as they strove to summarize their stories. When such sentences were read over the air they were almost incomprehensible. The deadpan style of the inverted pyramid did not work over the air, either. The flat, monotonous prose was difficult to read and obnoxious to the ear.

Writers for the new medium learned to take advantage of the more personal appeal of radio. They used openings to create interest rather than to summarize the story. They varied structure for interest and packed less information into each sentence. This more personal, less formal approach softened the news writing in newspapers as writers for print imitated it.

The news magazines, particularly *Time*, had their effect, too. Along with a convoluted style, *Time* freely mixed fact and opinion in a loose

[6]Marion K. Sanders, *Dorothy Thompson: A Legend in Her Time* (Boston: Houghton Mifflin, 1973), p. 167.

structure that permitted an accent on the drama of events. *Time*'s popularity persuaded many newspaper editors to allow more freedom in matters of style.

Rules of Readability

Another influence that simplified and personalized news style was the work of Rudolf Flesch. In several books he popularized the findings of his Ph.D. dissertation at Columbia University and provided a formula by which aspiring writers could test the "readability" of their writing. In essence his advice boiled down to this: make it understandable by writing short words and short sentences, and make it interesting by using many personal references. Personal references included names of people and other nouns indicating family relationships or gender.

Flesch's influence on news style was increased because the Associated Press, worried about its image as a stodgy, though reliable news service, hired him to improve the quality of the writing of its reporters. AP copy appeared in many newspapers and was imitated by local editors and writers, and so Flesch had much trickle-down influence. His work also encouraged imitation by other readability specialists who helped keep the bandwagon moving.

Thus the local reporter began to win more stylistic freedom as a result of all these factors: radio, foreign correspondents' work, news magazines, and readability specialists. The freedom varied considerably, but still reporters were seldom allowed to express their opinions overtly in news columns. Nor were they allowed the wide latitude granted to correspondents in Europe, Washington, and sometimes in the state capital.

Radio and television lightened the news format so that it sometimes came close to being sheer entertainment. "The March of Time," a radio program sponsored by *Time* magazine, relied more heavily than its sponsor on the drama of news to gain an audience. Deep-voiced announcers and music worthy of an adventure mystery heralded dramatic re-creations of the highlights of the past week's news.

"Happy News" of the 1970's

The exploitation of news as entertainment was not a major trend, but there was another attempt at it in the 1970's. This time it occurred in television as stations battled for audiences. The "happy news" format seldom got beyond the level of local programming, but it attracted audiences and tempted stations with low audience ratings. Done with taste it presented no great threat to reliable news reporting. The broadcasters assembled in the studio for the news program were encouraged to joke with each other and to feature humorous angles in the news. But once started it was hard to control. Joking could quickly turn to buffoonery and humorous angles might bring neglect of serious news.

Frank Magid, the researcher who nudged a number of television stations to the "happy talk" formula, had a hand in planning "A.M. America," ABC's frothy morning show, which opened early in 1975. It made little dent in the audience for NBC's "Today" show and was replaced later that same year with another light offering, "Good Morning, America," presided over by actor David Hartman. CBS was doing a little better with its move in the other direction. In its morning news program it provided more hard news than either of its competitors.

The networks in general and most local stations have resisted this low road to high ratings in the same way that most newspapers have resisted the temptation to print only the light and funny stories out of the day's news.

The trend toward light presentation of the news illustrates the effect that the medium can have on the news format. Radio and television have always emphasized the show business aspects of their media, and it is not strange that this same flair for entertainment should manifest itself in the news programs they present.

Broadcast Formats

In the interview and documentary, radio and television have developed formats that have been little used by the print media. The interview can combine drama and information; it is cheap to produce; and it can be presented on a regularly scheduled basis. Every Sunday each of the three major networks invites someone prominent in the news to battle with reporters in front of television cameras, and many local stations provide similar fare on the local or state level. The necessity of providing a program each week sometimes leads to banal interviews, but occasionally a major figure in the news chooses to make an important announcement on the program or is tricked into a newsworthy admission. When that happens it becomes front-page news in Monday morning's papers. Interview programs achieve drama because they are usually broadcast live, and the public has the tingle that comes from not knowing quite what to expect. The impact of such programs comes mostly from the interplay of personalities. As such it has had some effect in persuading the print media to play up personal information about their reporters.

The television documentary is a form unique to electronic journalism, unmatched by the print media even in the prime of *Life* and *Look* magazines. Television's combination of film and sound can provide a compelling public drama. Edward R. Murrow had much to do with the beginnings of the form in the CBS "See It Now" series. But despite their advantages, television documentaries fail to attract the audience that will normally accrue to even a mediocre entertainment show, and they are expensive. In addition, advertisers tend to be leery of supporting them because they are afraid to associate their company with controversial issues.

For these reasons and perhaps others, television documentaries, in spite of some outstanding examples, decreased in the mid-1970's.

Documentaries anchored by news personalities, interview programs with almost total emphasis on personalities, and regular news programs again featuring people all illustrate the effective use made by television and radio of personalities.

Some of the researchers who help stations improve their local news ratings are confident that they can measure the effect the personality of the anchorperson has on the popularity of the news show. If the on-air news persons are perceived in a positive way, the audience rating increases. Frequently, these specialists advise the stations to change personnel, and they describe the type needed and sometimes find a specific individual for the role.

The attractiveness of news personnel has little to do with the quality of information that a station dispenses, but the public is as swayed by personality considerations in its electronic media habits as it is in politics.

In exploiting personalities the electronic media are far ahead of the print media. Researchers have found that the anonymity of reporters for newspapers puts them at a competitive disadvantage relative to television. Newspapers have fought back by emphasizing the quality of their staff in house ads and by including background sketches about reporters at the head of their articles. However, it is doubtful that such devices can compete with the powerful sense of personal involvement that a person skilled in interpersonal communication can create through the sight and sound channels of television.

Certainly the power of news personalities is one of the reasons the American public tells pollsters that it gets most of its news from television. In the intermedia competition it is easy to see where the advantage lies. In the quality of the news report it is another matter. Large-scale news-gathering requires a large organization and many technical aids. The character of the news report is determined more by the quality of the organization than by any single member, but the presence of individuals on the screen makes it easy to forget the elaborate organization that supports their efforts.

How the Media Affect Each Other

In the mid-1970's television was assuming a larger and larger role as an important—and for many people, *the* important—source of information about public affairs. Since it arrived on the scene far later than newspapers and somewhat later than radio it accepted many of the forms already created by its predecessors. The notion of what information should be regarded as newsworthy was pretty well established by the time television became available, and public affairs people in the new medium accepted the definition of news as it already existed. After all, many of the early newspeople in radio and television came directly from newspapers.

As we saw in Chapter 9, television news reporters emphasize the stories to which their medium is peculiarly adapted. A story is a better one if there is dramatic film to illustrate it. And any story that is accompanied by interesting visuals is likely to be treated at greater length than one without them.

Just the same, the fundamental concepts about news-gathering were well established by the newspapers, so they had a profound effect on the nature of radio and television news programming. It is mostly in the news-gathering process itself that the final product is shaped. Before the arrival of television, newspapers had developed the concepts of news, what people make news, and how these people should be approached. They had also reached some agreement as to what was legitimate conduct for news gatherers and what was taboo. Starting fresh, radio and television might very well have developed different conventions that would have altered the information presented to the public.

While *Time* magazine seemed revolutionary at its inception, it also inherited the conventions developed by newspapers. Its contribution was simply in the final processing of information. It started with the same notions about the nature of news and without the advantage of immediacy that radio and television had over newspapers. The result for *Time* was a clever and interesting new form of presentation, but there were no new concepts as to the fundamental nature of the information that should be presented or the proper approach to news sources.

As we have seen, newspapers responded to news needs as they were first seen by proprietors of coffee houses and mercantile exchanges. So the news concepts were transplanted from the oral to the printed tradition partly through that intermediary. In transplanting the news function to radio and television, newspeople shifted back to something that resembled the oral tradition. The resemblance to oral tradition is only partial because the electronic media do not provide for the immediate feedback that is characteristic of face-to-face talk, but it is sufficiently close that it probably has some of the same effects on the listener-viewer.

At any rate, competition with radio and television has caused newspapers to adopt some of the traditions of oral communication as transmitted through the audiovisual media. These include emphasis on personality, simplicity in style and structure, some mixture of fact and opinion, increased use of such analogic devices as photographs, and descriptive devices. None of these changes came suddenly, and all had been used before television arrived on the scene, but competition with the new medium did speed up the process.

Since the media generally regard themselves as in competition with each other, each medium strives for the attention of the audience for news and does not regard itself, openly at least, as complementary to the others.

Thus members of the audience must analyze for themselves and apply the ways in which the media are complementary. Television and radio can supply immediate information with more emotional impact than is possible through print. But the print media are unmatched in their ability to explain complicated material, to list detailed information, to allow readers to proceed at their own pace and time, and to act as a reference source.

Formats for Opinion

The media's response to the problem of mixed fact and opinion is to provide a label for opinionated material. In the printed media the labels are clear enough to the practitioners in the field. The opinion of the newspaper as an organization is printed on a separate page in the form of editorials. Editorials may be explanatory, designed to clarify an issue; or opinionated, designed to express the newspaper's opinion and to persuade others to that view. Another format that permits the expression of opinion is the signed column. Under a by-line writers are assigned space and frequently allowed to write about anything they consider pertinent and to adopt just about any form they choose. The implicit requirements are that they fill a certain amount of space and that they interest a large number of readers.

Frequently columnists choose to write on public issues, and often they express their opinion. This happens so often that some columnists have come to be recognized as conservative, as is James J. Kilpatrick; or liberal, as is Nicholas Von Hoffman. The designation is so freely admitted that

Kilpatrick's column is headed in some newspapers "The View from the Right."

Other columnists go about the job of attracting an audience by a crusading posture and the revelation of information not previously made public. The late Drew Pearson and his former assistant who became his successor, Jack Anderson, illustrate this genre of columnist.

Still other columnists are primarily humorists who use the daily news report as the basis for their satire. Art Buchwald has been highly successful with this.

The electronic media have been slow to editorialize because of uncertainty about exactly what the "fairness doctrine" (see Chapter 5) means and concern that, under it, an expression of opinion would require much time to solicit a response and a donation of time to someone with an opposing view. This situation was clarified in a 1949 FCC report and given a lukewarm endorsement in these words: "overt licensee editorialization within reasonable limits . . . is not contrary to the public interest."[7]

Even such tepid encouragement had its effect, and a number of radio and television stations began editorializing. The format made it clear that the matter was opinionated. Radio announcements to that effect were usually read before and after each editorial. Television used various methods: often an announcer or the station manager read the editorial before a camera, with announcements before and after, as on radio. Sometimes a person off camera read the editorial while a notice on the screen labeled the matter as comment. At the conclusion the anchorperson usually promised to read letters representing the opposing view.

Thus both print and electronic media go to some lengths to alert their audiences to opinionated messages. There is some question whether most persons in the audience understand the warning and respond with proper caution, but there is little more the media can do.

As news columns and broadcast reports were opened up to allow more expression of opinion and more interpretation of all kinds, it became more difficult than ever for newspeople to define in their own minds the line that separates comment from reportage.

As interpretative devices gained acceptance in the news columns of the *New York Times*, its Sunday Department, which had formerly handled most of the interpretation, became concerned. Gay Talese describes the reaction of Sunday editor Lester Markel:

> Markel was becoming uneasy about the whole new trend of thinking on the third floor [site of the daily newsroom]: the advocacy of interpretative reporting (which had long been the specialty of Markel's

[7]FCC Report in the Matter of Editorializing by Broadcast Licensees. 1 Pike & Fisher Radio Reg. 9; 201 (1949).

"Week in Review" section); the introduction of such daily "background" features as the "Man in the News" profile, the news analyses, the in-depth articles (which had been a function of the Sunday *Magazine* and the "Review").[8]

Correspondents who do stand-up pieces for radio and television also have considerable freedom to interpret. Often their material is opinionated.

New and Alternative Journalism

In the 1960's and 1970's a small band of skilled writers began combining the techniques of the journalist and the novelist. During the same period some larger cities saw the establishment of publications designed to report situations that were ignored by the regular media and to present viewpoints that had heretofore been largely left unvoiced.

The new journalism and the alternative media were largely separate developments, although they occurred at about the same time. The general effect of the two movements was the start of a re-examination of the techniques of writing for journalism, and at the same time a questioning of the standards by which information is judged to be newsworthy.

Gay Talese, Truman Capote, Tom Wolfe, Norman Mailer, and Jimmy Breslin are prominent among the new journalists. Gay Talese is a former *New York Times* reporter. Tom Wolfe, a former reporter for the *New York Herald Tribune* and the *Washington Post,* had turned to writing for *New York* magazine. Jimmy Breslin was a newspaper columnist. Mailer and Capote had established reputations as fiction writers before they turned to the new form. While some of the new writing appeared in newspapers, it was more often found in magazines and in books.

In its most dramatic form the new journalism took actual events and situations and reported them so that they had the impact of fiction. Drama was achieved by using the same techniques that novelists since Dickens had been using.

But the writers are free to use other forms, too. Freedom in format and style are the distinguishing characteristics of the new journalism. Some writers, like Talese, do not inject themselves into their writing. Others make frequent use of the first-person pronoun.

The style of the new journalism requires saturation reporting to provide

[8]Gay Talese, *The Kingdom and the Power* (New York: World Publishing, 1966), pp. 255–256.

the tremendous detail that is usually featured. Scenes are re-created in fictionlike format. Dialogue is reproduced in the same fashion. Places as well as people and their motives are described in detail. Reporters immerse themselves in the situation and then in their reports try to give the reader the same sensations. In the hands of a skilled reporter and writer the effect is compelling.

But there are dangers. New journalism sometimes describes aspects that cannot be verified. For example, describing the emotions of another person is risky business. The only honest way to do this is to ask the person described to recollect what he or she was thinking. Often a person cannot remember. Sometimes, when the emotion is unflattering, a person may not reveal it. Although analysis of characters is a well-accepted fiction technique, it is less justifiable in journalism.

Some of the new journalists are not disturbed by deviations from literal facts, from accuracy. Facts, they hold, are less important than truth, and they are not equivalent. One magazine published an account of a torture scene during the Vietnam War that, the author admitted later, was a product of his imagination. It was defended on the grounds that it might well have happened, that similar incidents did occur, and that the technique gave the reader a better understanding of what was going on in Vietnam than conventional reporting methods could have done.

The expression *new journalism* is elastic and covers many kinds of reporting. Some of them merely attempt to make conventional patterns more graphic. But an imaginative account presented as literal fact misleads a reader. It also may tempt a reporter to substitute daydreaming for investigation. To pretend that fiction is journalism cheapens both.

Harry S. Ashmore, who won a Pulitzer Prize for his work as editor of the *Arkansas Gazette,* had this comment on the new journalists:

> It is, I believe, fatal to the enterprise for the journalist to confuse his mission with that of the artist, and claim a license to shape transient and contingent facts to his own preconceived end. Nor is he in any position to fulfill the role of the scholar, who presumably has the time to pursue his examination of events until he and his peers are satisfied that he has arrived at their ultimate meaning.[9]

Alternative journalism, an independent but contemporary development, grew from a dissatisfaction with the viewpoint and subject matter of the traditional media. The alternative journals point out flaws in society that the press, through long acceptance, has tended to disregard. The virtues of "bigness" are questioned and the practices of entrenched power and wealth are fair game for the new press.

[9]Harry S. Ashmore, "The New Journalism," *The Center Magazine* 8 (July-August 1975): 55.

News and Information Formats

Changing standards of morality in sex and politics are chronicled in the alternative journals, particularly in that branch that came to be known as the underground press. Hardly *underground* in the original sense of the word, these papers are sold openly on the streets. They are distinguished primarily by their more radical approach.

Aimed at minorities, the poor, and the young, the alternative press found that it collected a readership among middle-class intellectuals. Some of the sheets, founded with scant resources, became prosperous.

Prominent in the alternative press are such journals as the *Los Angeles Free Press*, the *New York Free Press*, the *Berkeley Barb*, the *San Francisco Bay Guardian*, the *Village Voice*, the *East Village Other*, and *Cervi's Journal*. One branch of the alternative media devoted itself to press criticism. The *Chicago Journalism Review* and the *Last Post* of Montreal are examples. Often the critical journals are published by men and women who continue to hold jobs on the traditional media of their area—the very journals they publicly criticize.

The new journalism is a new combination of objectives, methods, and subject matter. It can be quite revolutionary. In its strident attacks on institutions and their practices it is a logical successor to the muckrakers of the early 1900's, who included Lincoln Steffens and Upton Sinclair.

Like the early 1900's the 1960's were times of social upheaval, and that undoubtedly was a cause of the more strident journalism. Alternative journals were made more possible by cheaper printing. A third factor in the new journalism was the competition of radio and television. The dramatic possibilities of the nonfiction novel provide one way of matching the impact of the television documentary. The latter's drama is heightened by editing, which can rapidly contrast spoken words and images collected in different places at different times. The new journalism achieves its effect by more traditional literary devices, but it can be just as compelling.

The new journalism and the documentary return the news form to its earlier state when there were fewer limitations on creative image building.

The Effects of New Formats

The result of the media responses to the oral tradition and to each other has been that the information format has become less formal in the 1970's, and inside that format the formal warning signs are often omitted. This marks a return to practices resembling face-to-face communication. After all, when someone in a conversation starts a statement with "In my opinion" we are more likely to think he or she is being pompous rather than warning us to be careful of undocumented material.

There are dangers in this trend. Reporters may rely too much on opinion instead of fact, and readers and listeners may forget to make the distinction. On the other hand, the media have never been successful in divorcing opinionated material from other kinds of interpretation. When opinions are banned they often go underground, as reporters, perhaps subconsciously, disguise them. The same thing happens in conversations, too.

Since the media magnify voices and thus the effects of words, this natural human tendency to mix fact and opinion becomes more critical for newspeople. It is a much discussed problem, but one that is not likely to be settled soon. One great advantage is that reporters are gaining the freedom to tell their stories in more human form.

This requires reporters of integrity and audiences with critical ability.

Suggestions for Further Reading

Bliss, Edward, Jr. "Remembering Edward R. Murrow." *Saturday Review*, May 31, 1975, pp. 17–20.
A firsthand account of Murrow and his influence on the format of radio news.

Dennis, Everette E., ed. *The Magic Writing Machine: Student Probes of the New Journalism.* Eugene: University of Oregon, School of Journalism, 1971.
Student writing illustrating different forms of new journalism, with a perceptive introduction by the editor.

Dennis, Everette E., and Rivers, William L. *Other Voices: The New Journalism in America.* San Francisco: Canfield Press, 1974.
Provides a systematic treatment that helps in understanding the new journalism.

Glessing, Robert J. *The Underground Press in America.* Bloomington: Indiana University Press, 1970.
History, format, and audiences of the alternative press.

Lee, Alfred M. *The Daily Newspaper in America.* New York: Macmillan, 1937.
Early chapters trace the news format in Colonial America.

MacGregor, James. "Once Over Lightly: How ABC's Av Westin Decides What to Show on the Evening News." *Wall Street Journal*, November 22, 1972, pp. 1, 22.
Tells how a news program is assembled and describes Westin's views of the limitations of any television news program.

Von Hoffman, Nicholas. "TV Commentators: Burbles from Olympus." *Columbia Journalism Review* 14 (January–February 1976): 9–13.
Argues that network television commentators, while they sound impressive, are usually bland and often confusing.

11

Fact, Fiction, Games, and Chatter

In Super Bowl VIII, 71,882 ticket holders crowded Rice Stadium in Dallas to watch the Miami Dolphins defeat the Minnesota Vikings 27–8 in some dull football action.

The lackluster activity on the field did not seem to matter. Tickets had been apportioned in advance and about 80 percent of them had landed in corporate hands. It was *the* place to be that afternoon for business executives.

Executives who did not rate a ticket presumably joined the 70 to 95 million other Americans who watched the rites on television. As a refresher for next day's armchair quarterbacks the 1,600 newspeople present filed more than 3 million words of copy.

CBS paid the National Football League $2,750,000 for television rights, charged $200,000 to $240,000 for each minute of advertising sold, and picked up more than 4 million dollars in revenue. Advertising filled 15 percent of the telecast time; live-play action time, 3 percent.[1] Figure 11.1 shows how total telecast time was distributed.

Thus the media provided a powerful magnifying glass for Super Bowl VIII, as they also do for the Kentucky Derby, the World Series, and the Olympics. Sometimes exciting, often dull, the action is always surrounded by and frequently engulfed by pomp and pageantry. Half-time shows, Rose Bowl type parades, tapes of former games or races, interviews, and nonstop talk beguile television audiences to sit through long afternoons of commercials while they await a few minutes of live action.

Three generations ago Americans would gather at a handy hayfield on an August Saturday afternoon to watch the town team take on a visiting club from the next village. Now they sit in front of television to watch games being played in faraway cities—sometimes even out of the country.

The viewer may be a native New Englander who has never ventured south of Philadelphia or west of Buffalo, but he finds a way to take sides even if it is the Vikings playing the Dolphins. Even "captive viewers," people who watch a game as a concession to a companion, pick a favorite after a few minutes of viewing. Thus the passive spectator becomes a pseudo-participant.

The liaison between sports and media is mutually profitable. It builds readers for newspapers and viewers for television. *Sports Illustrated* and other magazines live as appendages and promoters of the sports world.

Figure 11.1   Time Distribution of Super Bowl VIII Telecast

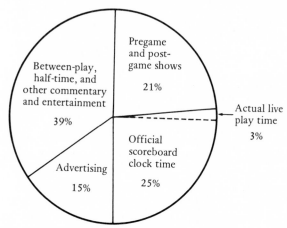

Adapted from Michael R. Real, "Super Bowl: Mythic Spectacle," *Journal of Communication* 25, no. 1 (Winter 1975): 32. Reprinted with permission.

[1] Figures on the Super Bowl games are from Michael R. Real, "Super Bowl: Mythic Spectacle," *Journal of Communication* 25 (Winter 1975): 31–43.

Sports events are entertainment. They serve as dramatic illustrations of the media's ability to focus national attention on single events. In doing so the media build an area of common interest and cultural solidarity to the nation. They also create mythical worlds for their audiences. Readers and viewers can vicariously chat with winning jockeys or owners and thus skip into another world—supposedly a more glamorous one.

Sports reports create national heroes. Their reign may be short, but the adulation is intense. Babe Ruth and Jack Dempsey received more prolonged attention than is likely to be accorded Billie Jean King, Joe Namath, or Muhammad Ali because competition for attention is greater now. Faster transportation and communication have speeded the pace of events and heightened cynicism.

Television has a great advantage in reporting staged events such as political conventions and sports events. Athletic contests occur within a prescribed area, and they are known in advance. Cameras and sound equipment can be put in place. Telecasters can anticipate the nature of the action and prepare themselves. Often the individuals staging the event are so eager for television coverage that they will arrange the action for the convenience of the broadcasters.

Sometimes the real purpose of an event is to provide a good television show. Even when promoters start with other motives, television usually just naturally takes over. The nearly seventy-two thousand persons present at Super Bowl VIII probably felt their pleasure enhanced by the knowledge that they were part of a television spectacular. The enthusiastic crowds in the stands are important background for the television show. It would not do to stage a Super Bowl in an empty stadium. A peculiar double empathy is created as watchers at home identify with those in the stands while spectators in the stands enjoy the knowledge that the event is being watched by millions through the eyes of the camera.

As television takes increasing control in order to create its spectacle for the home watchers, the original event is further distorted. If team and official times out do not provide for a sufficient number of commercials, the sponsoring network signals its needs and action is halted until the quota of commercials has been piped into millions of homes. Spectators physically present at the event can wait, and the actual tempo of the action is changed.

The event as seen at home on the screen is considerably different from that which on-the-scene spectators receive. Highlights of former games or races may be shown; personalities connected with the event can be interviewed. The Derby can be seen over again, with comments by the winning jockey, and eternally there is the genial or sarcastic voice of "your host" explaining, describing, grandstand quarterbacking, or just arguing with colleagues.

For the home viewer, the advent of the delayed replay has changed the experience. Critical plays are often shown over at once, from the vantage of a different camera. This helps viewers caught napping or those who did not trust their eyes the first time around. When slow motion and stop motion are used, many uncertainties may be cleared up. These devices put the broadcaster in a superior role.

During the tenth inning of the third game of the 1975 World Series, Cincinnati pinch-hitter Ed Armbrister bunted and then collided with Boston Red Sox catcher Carlton Fisk when Fisk tried to field the ball. Fisk's throw to second bounced off the mitt of shortstop Rick Burleson, and runners advanced to second and third. Boston manager Darrell Johnson complained of interference, but was overruled. Plate umpire Larry Barnett said it was interference only if intentional.[2]

This action paved the way for a Cincinnati win and caused bitter comment in the Red Sox dressing room. It caused comment all next day, too, by sportscasters who played and replayed the action as they voiced their opinions about it.

The printed media, too, affect events they report. Writers may look for certain kinds of material for stories and thereby focus attention on certain aspects of the sport. Often conflicts between personalities are regarded as newsworthy or certain coaches or players receive special attention, favorable or unfavorable. These things influence the sporting world and the nature of each event, but writers for print have never had the direct impact on the spectacle that television, almost casually, exerts. Sometimes the event becomes truly a television production and all persons present are players for the cameras.

Deliberate control is used to increase the interest—to heighten the impact of an event. The fact of television coverage promises drama. The presence of cameras says "something exciting is happening here." Sports coverage by television is promoted widely to build an audience. The promotion promises excitement. If little or none exists the producers, camera operators, and commentators do what they can to produce it.

One observer pointed out this straining for excitement in the television coverage of Super Bowl VIII:

> The Super Bowl VIII telecast was careful to convey a feeling of larger-than-life drama. Before the game, announcers proclaimed: "We fully believe that this game will live up to its title Super Bowl. . . . We expect this to be the greatest Super Bowl ever." The screen was filled with images of vast crowds, hulking superheroes, great plays from the past, even shots from and of the huge Goodyear blimp hovering over the field. . . . The actual game was one-sided and boring. Sports Illustrated led its coverage with "Super Bowl VIII had all the excitement

[2]Joseph Durso, "Reds Win in 10 Innings, 6–5; Take 2–1 Lead in Series," New York Times, October 15, 1975, pp. 1, 27.

and suspense of a master butcher quartering a steer." . . . But after the game the one-sidedness itself became the occasion for historic superlatives: Are the Dolphins the greatest team ever?"[3]

This has all the ring of the self-fulfilling prophecy. Psychologists say that some people succeed or fail because of their expectations. Expectation of failure makes an individual feel and act like a failure, so he or she fails. Expectation of success has the opposite effect.

Coaches try to work self-fulfilling prophecy from both directions. They may predict success and assume the prediction will help create it. Or they may point out their opponents' strengths to try to make them overconfident.

Television producers never rely on a subtle approach. If they buy television rights to a game they promote that game and their coverage of it as though it were the greatest event since the fall of the Roman Empire. Prophecies do have a way of fulfilling themselves, particularly if they are heralded through the combined voices of all the media. And if the game does not quite live up to expectations, the announcers can always pretend it did—and many will believe it.

Self-fulfilling prophecy, the planning of an event to serve a purpose, and the restructuring of reality in an ambiguous fashion are characteristics of the "pseudo-event" discussed by historian Daniel Boorstin. A pseudo-event is a false event, deliberately staged. Boorstin says the occurrence of a pseudo-event "is arranged for the convenience of the reporting or reproducing media. Its success is measured by how widely it is reported."[4]

Pseudo-events are more exciting than real ones because they are planned for the media and neatly packaged for dissemination by the media.

The media-sports symbiosis is of long standing and it is important for both. The result for the armchair sports fan is a world of semifantasy more exciting by far than the real world of sports.

In sports the media begin with a tangible world of reality. After all, there *are* athletes, and there *are* games. It is just that after the media get through, the athletes look like superheroes, and the games look like contests worthy of the gods of Greece.

Perhaps for many Americans, stuck in the mundane world of office, factory, or shop, the athletes *are* gods and the games *are* played near Mount Olympus. Sports events provide an orderly island in an otherwise

[3]Real, "Super Bowl," p. 32.

[4]Daniel J. Boorstin, *The Image: Or What Happened to the American Dream* (New York: Atheneum, 1962), p. 11.

untidy world. The final score is uncertain, but the action is governed by rules that enforce a predictable pattern for the game.

The media are only applying the rules of show business when they look for the drama and heighten its effect by comment or by immediate tape replay. Like any entertainer, they look for actions that bring crowd approval and emphasize them. This is natural and reasonable in a sports context, but we need to remember that in these circumstances the media are entertainers, not reporters.

Sports coverage, in which the media start with a real event and shape it as they report it, serves as a bridge between news and entertainment. In reporting hard news, the media strive to reflect reality; in sports reporting, the media participate more in shaping the events they report; and in entertainment, the media create the format and the content. Media people are the originators as well as the transmitters of the entertainment fare they offer.

From Vaudeville to Radio

Some show people have lived through the development of vaudeville to radio and then to television. Comedians like Bob Hope, George Burns, and the late Gracie Allen and Jack Benny lived the cycle. While folk art and popular art evolved over generations, the rapid development of the media and their devotion to entertainment have allowed a few professional entertainers to live through three distinct stages.

Before radio and motion pictures, the vaudeville houses and legitimate theaters provided a face-to-face setting for show business. The song and dance team, the clown-comedian, the musician, were staples of the vaudeville circuit. Their tours took them to legitimate stages in even the small cities of America.

The death of vaudeville, widely lamented in show business circles, was brought about by motion pictures and radio. For a while, live entertainers did their acts between showings of the feature film at movie palaces, but gradually film features and the ability of radio to keep people home brought an end to vaudeville.

Some of the performers went to other vocations or retired, but others made the move, sometimes to film, but more often to radio. With them went an adaptation of the vaudeville format that set the pattern for early comedy and variety programs.

Not all the transplanted comedians understood their new medium. The late Fred Allen described some of the resulting anachronisms in his autobiography *Treadmill to Oblivion*:

In the early 1930's when the Broadway comedians descended on radio, things went from hush to raucous. The theater buffoons had no conception of the medium and no time to study its requirements. Eddie Cantor, Jack Pearl, Ed Wynn, Joe Penner and others were radio sensations. They brought their audiences into the studios, used their theater techniques and their old vaudeville jokes, and laughter, rehearsed or spontaneous, exploding between the commercials. The cause of this merriment was not always clear. The bewildered set owner in Galesburg, Illinois, suddenly realized that he no longer had to understand radio comedy. As he sat in his Galesburg living room he knew that he had proxy audiences in New York, Chicago, and Hollywood watching the comedians, laughing and shrieking "Vas you dere, Charlie" and "Wanna buy a duck" for him.

The big comedians felt that if they entertained the studio audiences their radio success was assured. Eddie Cantor wore funny costumes, pummeled his announcer with his fist and frequently kicked his guest star to obtain results. . . . Ed Wynn made complete changes of funny hats and grotesque coats between comedy joke routines. Other popular comedians threw pies and squirted seltzer water at their stooges.[5]

Radio humor of the 1930's provided strong counterpoint to the drab hand-to-mouth existence of those depression days. George Washington Hill of Lucky Strike urged that the United States dance its way out of the depression, and President Herbert Hoover told entertainer Rudy Vallee: "If you can sing a song that would make people forget their troubles and the depression I'll give you a medal."[6]

Thus radio took the traditions of the music hall and vaudeville house to produce the nighttime entertainment of its great days, the 1930's and early 1940's. Nearly all the comedy stars came from musical comedy or vaudeville. They included Al Jolson, Bing Crosby, Al Pearce, Bob Burns, Fibber McGee and Molly, Phil Baker, Kate Smith, and Rudy Vallee. The theater influence is clear in the comedians' use of live audiences, usually in a theater setting, and the incorporation of audience reaction into the program.

Erik Barnouw commented: "Some said that radio had killed vaudeville, but it could also be said that vaudeville had taken over radio or, more accurately, that the sponsors had taken over both."[7]

In comedy and variety, radio assumed the format of the music hall and vaudeville but did little to add to it, making only minor alterations. These minor alterations sufficed for a brief period during which radio was a na-

[5]Quoted in John W. Dodds, *American Memoir* (New York: Holt Rinehart & Winston, 1959).
[6]Erik Barnouw, *The Golden Web* (New York: Oxford University Press, 1968), 2: 273.
[7]Ibid., p. 102.

tional medium. It provided relief from depression dreariness and was even cheaper than going to the movies—an important consideration in those days of thin wallets.

Radio's New Formats

Radio floundered for a time after television took over its content and its audiences, but eventually it found some successful new formats. By the early 1970's radio stations (many of them small) outnumbered television stations seven to one in the United States. More than 64 million homes in the United States were equipped with radio receivers, usually four or five per home, and radio stations attracted higher listening time than television during daylight hours.

What did radio do to make such a vigorous comeback?

First, it gave up network programming for most purposes. Arthur Godfrey lasted for a time as CBS radio's only network entertainment program, but eventually the networks were seldom used except for news and special events. The great bulk of radio is programmed locally. This allows radio to do what magazines have done for a long time—program for specific audiences. Even small cities are likely to have three or four radio stations and large metropolitan areas are often served by twenty or more. Since it would be folly to attempt to capture the entire market, station owners decide what portion they want to reach and target their programming for that segment. Or in some formats (for example, all news) they may try to reach all of the potential audience for a portion of the broadcast day.

The result is the growth of such specialized stations as country music, rock, all news, all talk, classical music, popular music, and ethnic programming. More than 150 stations in this country broadcast at least an hour a day in Spanish, and some of them program full time in that language. Some stations in the Southwest broadcast in Navajo; an Arizona station broadcasts a program in Apache; a Seattle station one in Aramaic; and an Idaho station one in Basque.

With this specialized programming and the use of disc jockeys and call-in program hosts with attractive voices, radio has personalized its appeal and so become a more intimate medium than television. (See Figure 11.2.)

The appeal has been particularly strong to teenagers, who are likely to regard radio as "their" medium. Rock music and disc jockeys whom they can hear for several hours a day are part of the reason. The disc jockeys may increase their own and their stations' appeal by presiding at teenage dances and record hops. According to Marshall McLuhan: "The teenager withdraws from the TV groups to his private radio."[8]

One researcher hypothesized that radio may be a "portable friend" to teenagers:

> Youth-oriented stations may be a significant source of socialization since they occupy the attention of many young people for significant periods of each day and personalities on these stations are highly ac-

Figure 11.2   Radio Versus Television
Radio is a more intimate medium than television.

[8]Marshall McLuhan, *Understanding Media: The Extensions of Man* (New York: New American Library, 1964), p. 268.

cessible and share the interests of the young audience. As a result, radio may have become a portable friend and an instant advisor available at the flick of a switch.[9]

The same researcher found that children with fewer friends spent more time listening to radio than did their more popular peers. Thus radio, as a private medium, may provide companionship.

Another study supported the theory that lonely adults may use radio for the same purpose. After analyzing calls to a talk show on WCAU, Philadelphia, the researcher concluded that "these findings tend to support an earlier implication that housewives who call during the morning and afternoon are victims of a temporary loneliness that accompanies their housework."[10]

Thus, by splitting the audience, appealing to special interests, and personalizing its approach radio has been able to survive as a competitive medium.

In assuming the role of latter-day vaudeville, television has gone the other way—using stars and lavish production techniques to justify its overused epithet, "spectacular." Unlike radio, it tries to be all things to all people, so its efforts to personalize its impact have all the charm of an elephant trying to curry favor with a mouse.

Lady Authors at 8 A.M.

John Chancellor, probably in a relaxed moment, once confided that one of the reasons he gave up the job of host of NBC's "Today" program was that he decided that there must be better things to do than interview lady authors at 8 A.M.

Lady authors and gentleman authors, too, have been a staple of "Today." But "Today" depends on a great many other things to keep it floating at the top of the morning news and variety shows. The show's history exemplifies the curious combination of the banal and earthshattering by which the popular media live.

News, interviews, and just plain talk have been the major ingredients of "Today." Friendly personalities and informality have also been characteristic.

In its early days, presided over by Dave Garroway with the assistance of

[9]Joseph R. Dominick, "The Portable Friend: Peer Group Membership and Radio Usage," Journal of Broadcasting 18 (Spring 1974): 162.

[10]Joseph Turow, "Talk Show Radio as Interpersonal Communication," Journal of Broadcasting 18 (Spring 1974): 176.

J. Fred Muggs, the inscrutable chimpanzee, the program could hardly have been more informal. Highlights of the previous day's sports events presented by Jack Lescoules and some light interviews and chatter filled the time between newscasts.

During the turmoil of the 1960's and the Vietnam War "Today" 's content became more serious. Senators, leading congressmen and -women, and top-level government officials began appearing for interviews in the Washington studio, and issues became as important as personalities for the program. The necessity for rehashing the news at the beginning of each half-hour segment and the general pace of the program usually left insufficient time to develop issues satisfactorily, but perhaps the same short time span for any activity kept many viewers from tuning out.

Pseudo Friendship

Perhaps the most consistent characteristic of the "Today" program was the insistent good fellowship. Everyone was on a first-name basis. Often visitors spontaneously called the hosts by their first names, although it was apparent that they had never seen them before except on the screen. The semblance of comradery and the attachment viewers developed to the program regulars were factors in "Today" 's success. The care with which new hosts were tried out indicated the importance NBC executives accorded to personality. Presumably the audience got into the habit of accepting the regulars as surrogate friends—people who could be counted on to be present five mornings a week and to be cheerful at that. In one way this is similar to the relationship between a motion picture star and the public. Movie fans meeting a star in a restaurant may feel free to approach the star and assume a first-name relationship. With the cast of a television program the relationship is perhaps even stronger because of the regularity of the performers' appearances and because they are seen in the privacy of the viewers' homes.

The feeling is an illusion, but, as an English writer pointed out, television takes pains to foster it:

> The question of friendship and what constitutes a friend is something that being a TV personality forces one to examine. I would not accept any definition of a friend that would not include the concept of a personal relationship in which affection annihilated all considerations of status and prestige. In the TV-personality-world, friendship stands for something quite different. In the first place, all the trappings of friendship—first names, expressions of affection, embraces, hospitality—are exchanged as a matter of course between two people whose relationship to each other is solely that of business acquaintances. Secondly,

efforts are deliberately made to create illusions of surrogate friendship between TV personalities and the viewing public, and it is far from unusual to meet TV personalities who say that they look on the public as their friends or to meet members of the public who behave as if friendship between themselves and the TV personality was mutual and established.[11]

Perhaps a feeling of friendship for someone seen only on a television screen provides people in the audience with some satisfaction, but it is shallow confidence that comes from reacting eternally with shadows instead of here-in-the-flesh companions.

In the media's eternal balancing of information and entertainment, information often comes off second best. Entertainment, like sugar, may make the medicine go down, but by itself it serves only to pacify the receiver. An executive of the "Tonight" program in England makes clear the central function of entertainment:

> I would say that entertainment is to *Tonight* what discipline is to the schoolmaster. No matter how fascinating the subject the instructor is trying to put across, he must have discipline in the classroom before he can hope to achieve results. With us it's much the same thing. Unless you entertain the audience sufficiently you can't begin to inform them.[12]

The comparison between discipline and entertainment is a bit tenuous, but the authors make their point. In news, talk, and interview programs, entertainment is often inserted through entertaining personalities and devices that invite the audience to fantasize that they are friends.

In some television talk and interview programs personality becomes paramount to the program. Jack Paar and Steve Allen made a parade of personalities the basis for highly successful formats. As perfected by Johnny Carson of the "Tonight" show and Mike Douglas, the form capitalizes on the desire of audiences to see performers in a first-person role. That and quick repartee become the standards for many talk formats. The talk is sometimes condescending toward the audience as one "celebrity" talks with another. But large audiences seem to bask in this atmosphere.

But the talk shows are sometimes revealing and may be a showcase for fine comic talent. Johnny Carson has maintained his position as top dog in the interview-talk format through a genuine talent for comedy, masterful use of the sly innuendo, and highly mobile features that sometimes say things that would be censored if expressed in words.

---

[11]Marghanita Laski, in *Twentieth Century*, quoted in Stuart Hall and Paddy Whannel, *The Popular Arts, A Guide to the Mass Media* (Boston: Beacon Press, 1967), p. 251.
[12]Hall and Whannel, *The Popular Arts*, p. 253.

Occasionally such shows are enlivened when people make unusual public confessions. Arthur Godfrey, for example, announced to a talk show host and the world at large that he had undergone a vasectomy.

Once in a while interviews and talk shows produce truly memorable programs that reveal the personalities of interesting people, shed light on events, or enliven an idea. It is too much to hope that such things can happen often. Television is doomed to second-rate material most of the time because of its voracious appetite—the endless hours it must fill.

A Little Ray of Sunshine

Every weekday morning in the early days of television from twenty to thirty people down on their luck used to gather outside a New York City theater. After interviews with producers a few of them would end up as contestants on "Strike It Rich," a program designed, as announcer Warren Hull used to tell the audience, "only to bring a little ray of sunshine into the lives of a few tragedy-struck people." One writer describes the show:

> A typical show would start off with a recent double amputee who needed artificial limbs but couldn't afford them. The second guest might be a black child from Harlem who had seen his mother and father die in a tenement fire. The third receiver of the show's benevolence could be a destitute farmer from North Carolina who had lost his home and barn in a hurricane. If he was a good "Strike It Rich" farmer, the hurricane had also blown away his wife, four cows, and two sons.[13]

Hull interviewed the unfortunates collected for the program, "bringing out every sordid detail of their tragedy," then he took them over to the "Heart Line Area." There, amid heart-painted scenery, they would await telephone calls from good-hearted souls offering aid. The good-hearted often did call, giving what they could—bus fare or a free operation. Others called, too, offering products and getting a good plug on national television at the same time.

"Strike It Rich" and similar shows have disappeared from national television, but some local radio shows use the same technique. They often build large followings by allowing audiences to shudder at the horror of it all and to feel a little pious at the same time.

[13]Kenneth Whelan, *How the Golden Age of Television Turned My Hair to Silver* (New York: Walker, 1973), p. 24.

These programs are closely related to the game shows that play on cupidity and frenetic acrobatics that have contestants jumping up and down, hugging each other, bestowing wet smacks on each other's cheeks, and displaying agony or joy (sometimes the expressions are the same) on their faces. Contestants are chosen for their ability to fill television screens with emotional scenes and their willingness to put up with indignities in the name of fun rather than for any ability to play whatever game is the focal point.

Prizes may be magnificent, although many winners eventually report that the benefits were mostly imaginary. One wonders what a low-income winner would do with a Rolls Royce grandiosely presented. For most the only option is to sell the prize to pay taxes on the extra income and then salvage what little is left.

Sometimes the prize may become a long-lasting entanglement. A West German station found contestants willing to appear, list their qualifications and conditions, and ask for marriage partners from the viewing audience. Although the program was dubbed the "craziest idea of the year" by a Cologne newspaper, the audience was large and each of the early contestants received from three hundred to five hundred letters from potential spouses. And since contestants were paid only travel expenses, the program was cheap to produce.

Some talk shows provide for informed interplay of ideas and information. Some game shows, such as "College Bowl," demonstrate that fun and some intellectual stimulation are not incompatible. This program, presided over by Allen Ludden, assembled teams representing colleges and universities that competed in answering questions from history, the arts, and other academic fields.

A Still, Small Voice

When college and professional sports went big time through the media the nature of the sports world, particularly its financial structure, was dramatically changed. Likewise, when religion goes big time on radio and television there is often a dramatic increase in cash flow.

In the 1950's the late evangelist A. A. Allen advertised his television programs: "See! Hear! Actual Miracles Happening Before Your Eyes. Cancer, Tumor, Goiters Disappear. Crutches, Braces, Wheelchairs, Stretchers Discarded. Crossed Eyes Straightened. Caught by the Camera as They Occurred in the Healing Line Before Thousands of Witnesses."[14]

[14]Neil Hickey, "That Old-Time Religion Goes Big-Time," *TV Guide*, February 15, 1975, p. 2.

Few media Messiahs are that blatant these days, but the great spectacles they produce bring in the audiences and the cash contributions. Stars from the entertainment industry sometimes appear on broadcast revivals, and the evangelists themselves assume the trappings of stars.

Rex Humbard mixes guitar playing with a preaching style he learned in tent revivals. A "still, small voice" told him, he says, to quit the one-night stands and "stay in Akron, build a church and televise the services. God Said, *'That's* the way to reach the human race—television.' "[15]

That was at least the way for Humbard to build his Cathedral of Tomorrow, which was designed for television and put up at a cost of 3.5 million dollars in 1958. His programs reach an estimated 15 million a week on 415 stations in the United States, Canada, the Far East, and Europe. In 1975 he was spending 3 million dollars a year just to buy air time.

The television ministry of Oral Roberts is reported to produce 15 million dollars a year, and it forms the cornerstone of Oral Roberts University in Tulsa. Other superstars of televison evangelism are Dr. Billy Graham, whose television crusades have made him famous and the friend of U.S. presidents and other notables; Dr. Robert Schuller, who broadcasts "The Hour of Power" from Los Angeles; and Dr. Jerry Falwell, who spends 5 million dollars a year on television and claims each dollar spent that way brings his message to three thousand viewers.

A number of lesser-known revivalists are at work. They begin by purchasing time on one or two stations and plow back the money from contributions into more television time. A few make it big. An estimated 100 million dollars a year is spent for television time by evangelists.

Television and radio stations provide free time to religious organizations as part of their public service obligations, but more conservative church leaders complain that this time is too limited and comes at awkward hours compared to the prime time sold to evangelists. There are other complaints, too.

Dr. Everett Parker, director of communications of the United Church of Christ, told *TV Guide* that the major Protestant religions spend about as much on food relief in India, Africa, and South America as one television evangelist spends on television time, and added, "He doesn't spend any money to help anybody."

Dr. Parker elaborated his complaint:

> Religion has no right to be exploiting people on television. Those of us who try to be responsible, but who can't afford to buy air time, get stuck in "ghetto" time by networks and stations. The fundamentalists are allowed to buy prime time because they can afford it, and because

[15]Ibid., p. 3.

the television industry is so damned irresponsible—probably the most irresponsible group you can find in dealing with the basic needs of the American people. The *real* churches are discriminated against, yet they represent the majority of the American population.[16]

The stunning success of the television evangelists indicates that they provide some sort of satisfaction for millions of people. Whether they exploit those on whose contributions they live is a question that the Federal Communications Commission and the courts have managed to avoid. If millions of television viewers believe that they are provided with a genuine religious experience, who can say they are right or wrong?

Borrowed Lives: Drama and the Media

Threads of drama run through all the media. The novel and short story are staples of books and magazines. Continued stories were once common features of newspapers. The earliest comics were funny, but between the First and Second World Wars many of them became continued tales of romance or adventure, or detective thrillers.

It was only natural that films, radio, and television should turn to drama. As they took the techniques of theater and musical comedy and combined them with literary traditions and the freedom provided by their new techniques, they altered the forms and conventions of drama. And they made drama available to millions. In the process the new media frequently cheapened drama, but occasionally they produced masterpieces possible only through the meshing of many people working together with a difficult and demanding technology.

Radio drama began early. Regular series started in 1930 with "First Nighter." This was followed in 1933 by "Grand Hotel" and toward the end of the decade by "Grand Central Station," "On Broadway," and "Curtain Time." These consisted of half-hour series without continuing characters. Scripts were bought from free-lance writers, who provided diversity and, in turn, were given considerable latitude.

At first Hollywood studios remained distant, but toward the end of the 1930's the studio chiefs began to realize the publicity potential in radio. As a result, sponsored radio drama picked up a distinct Hollywood flavor, although MGM was a long-time holdout.

[16]Ibid., p. 6.

Sick, Sick, Sick?

"Daytime Television Sick, Sick, Sick" proclaimed the headline over a description of daylight programming in the mid-1970's. The writer referred to the soap operas, or daytime dramas, and the game shows that filled many of television's hours.

Soap opera was another legacy from radio to television. The soaps in those early days began with some basic dilemma, then spun fantastic plots and subplots around it. Sometimes it took years to work out the details. One of the original stories, "Our Gal Sunday," wandered on through years of elaborate plots based on the theme expressed in every episode: "Can a girl from a little mining town in the West find happiness as the wife of a wealthy and titled Englishman?" The same basic set of characters carried through the months and years, with new ones being added to meet story demands, and with old ones disappearing as emphasis shifted.

Another early drama, "Backstage Wife," told the tale of a simple girl married to a Broadway idol. One beautiful actress after another provided drama as she sought to steal him away. "The Romance of Helen Trent" dramatized the trials of a woman trying to remake her life after her marriage ended.

> The central characters of serials fell into two categories: (1) those in trouble and (2) those who helped people in trouble. The helping-hand figures were usually older. "Big Sister" was first planned to revolve around a younger helping-hand character, but the series failed to take hold while it pursued this formula. When the heroine was plunged into a long-held and seemingly insoluble problem—she fell in love with a man married to an insane woman—the rating climbed quickly.[17]

Television's soap operas have developed enough subtlety that they cannot be classified so easily, although some critics insist that sex is invariably the major component. One writer who spent a day watching television announced that she found two couples in bed during the afternoon, and that "there was no doubt about what they were up to under those sheets." It was the same sort of thing which "causes all sorts of howls when shown at 10 P.M. instead of 2 P.M."

Extramarital affairs are common on the soaps. Women have a penchant for producing babies by someone other than their husbands; men may

---

[17]Barnouw, *Golden Web*, 2: 96.

discover grown-up sons whose very existence comes as a surprise; and all the characters are likely to have to face up to the results of some sexual misadventures in their past.

Due to limitations of time and budget, few scenes are shot outside the studio. One popular series is limited to four sets and eight characters per episode. Writers, producers, and actors work hard. They produce 255 to 260 episodes a year, while those who make the nighttime series are getting out 23.

Production demands are heavy and budgets are low, but the audience does respond. Some episodes of "All My Children" were watched by 8 to 9 million people, about 70 percent of them women. Some viewers find it difficult to wait from Friday until the programs resume on Monday.

Agnes Nixon, one of the most prolific writers for soap operas, is given credit for introducing socially significant material. Her scripts have treated venereal disease, Pap tests, child abuse, and drug-rehabilitation centers. Up to the middle of 1975 the soap operas had not considered homosexuality.

Back in the days of radio soaps a researcher found that listeners with more complex problems of their own tended to listen to more of the radio dramas. It would seem that the soap operas provide a means of escape and a road to fantasy.

With their set of characters constant over the years, soap operas also provide a familiar element in lives of their viewers. When Agnes Nixon visited a college campus to discover why students were among her viewers, one told her, "It's the only constant thing in our lives." Another said, "Every day at 1 o'clock I can go home to Pine Valley."[18] Perhaps these comments relate more to the fast pace of society than to the dramas themselves. A fantasy world can be a refuge.

As an entertainment form, the soap operas match the continued story of the magazines. Perhaps in the days when Arthur Conan Doyle was writing the Sherlock Holmes stories, readers took the same pleasure in being able to read of the adventures of the great detective and Dr. Watson, secure in the knowledge that everything would end successfully, and that the two chief characters would be back again to strike another blow against crime.

Compared with characters on most other television dramas, those on the daytime serials have a unique characteristic. They can recall the past, learn from their mistakes, and so change over the months and years. In the hands of skilled writers and performers, this ability of personalities to grow allows for three-dimensional characters—characters capable of fostering attachment and affection from the audience. It is this feature that distinguishes the soap opera from most other television drama.

[18]Rod Townley, "She Introduced a Stranger to the World of Soaps," *TV Guide*, May 3, 1975, p. 16.

Television's Other
Dramatic Forms

The situation comedy takes a number of forms, but essentially it provides a stock set of characters who involve themselves each week in a situation that provides comic confusion and a comic solution. For its effects it depends on skilled performers and the willingness of the audience to suspend its natural skepticism and go along with the gag. More often slapstick than subtle, the episodes are designed to offer a half-hour of pleasant diversion. Characters become familiar and their exaggerated reactions to chaos are anticipated with pleasure.

Lucille Ball, one of the great practitioners of the art, could never be called subtle, but her broad-stroked reactions to fabricated dilemmas amused millions. It did not seem to matter that her audience could anticipate her responses. Perhaps familiarity helped her cause.

Situation comedy characters do not develop. They are the same every week. They are a set of characters looking for a comic situation. The problem of the writers is to devise situations that will provide maximum opportunity for the comic talents of their company. The comedy differs from "high" art in that neither character nor situation nor event really develop. The heart of the method is to create humorous confusion, often by letting the audience in on a joke that will backfire on the players. Anticipating the comic action may be half the fun.

Situation comedy blends into domestic comedy, so that it is not always possible to separate them clearly. Domestic comedy depends more on an established setting and on the relationships between the people, often a family. Frequently the family head will be unmarried to allow opportunities for an occasional romantic encounter.

The people are seen as caring deeply for each other, and frequently there is a strong father figure who lives up to the title of the "Father Knows Best" series. Mother often stands in the background, keeping track of father, and setting him straight when even his judgment falters, but she invariably lets him take the bows. Perhaps the Women's Liberation movement had something to do with the change in that tendency of the domestic comedies, for we have seen produced "Phyllis," "Rhoda," "Maude," and "Fay."

Often the plot centers about a member of the supporting cast questioning one of the accepted social verities. Through the wisdom, tact, and understanding of the father figure, the backslider is returned to the fold, and the social verity is reinforced for the family and the audience.

A variation of this formula came with the "Mary Tyler Moore" show in which a woman was introduced as a somewhat diluted father figure whose good sense often solved the dilemmas of other members of the cast.

There is the suggestion in this show, too, of what was to come a little later. The happy endings sometimes require some adjustment of the characters to new situations.

Norman Lear's productions, "All in the Family," "Maude," and "The Jeffersons," turn back comedy to one of its traditional stage roles—making it the vehicle for social satire. Archie Bunker's character as the outspoken bigot and an occasional not-so-happy ending implied belief in a somewhat more mature television audience. The ratings indicate audience interest, but not necessarily maturity.

Researchers have been intrigued by the question as to whether the audience laughed at Archie Bunker, the bigot, or sided with him against his son-in-law, Mike, and thereby intensified their own bigotry. One study concluded that highly prejudiced persons are more likely than others to admire Archie. It is possible, the authors concluded, that making Archie a "lovable bigot" encourages the audience to excuse and rationalize their own prejudices.[19]

M*A*S*H provides its own seriocomic bite. The antics portrayed provide a strong counterpoint to the madness of war, which is ever present, although usually beyond camera range.

Although it often uses shock dialogue and slapstick devices, situation comedy has begun to adapt some of the techniques of Dickens, Shakespeare, and Charlie Chaplin of using comedy and drama to explore social situations.

The Western, probably the most frequently analyzed form of drama, is the basis for novels and short stories as well as radio, film, and television productions. Its central characteristic is that it is laid in the American West, usually Kansas or Texas, during a forty- or fifty-year period beginning somewhere around 1860. It is populated by cowboys on horseback, ranchers, outlaws, pretty schoolteachers, saloon girls, sometimes a tenderfoot from the effete East, and marshals. Its action takes place in plains, badlands, or mountains, or in the streets and barrooms of some raw, new town such as "Dodge City."

The Western's plots involve conflicts over women, grazing lands, gambling, the rights of a widow, or the efforts of the hero to destroy troublemakers—the habitual killer, the bank robber, or the "respected citizen" in cahoots with the outlaws.

Often, particularly in the early films, you didn't need a program to recognize the players. The good guys wore white and rode white horses; the villains wore black and rode black horses. Sometimes the plots were that simple, too. The hero was always right. There was a dangerous job to do and he did it. If a killing were required to right a wrong the hero did it, al-

---

[19]Neil Vidmar and Milton Rokeach, "Archie Bunker's Bigotry: A Study in Selective Perception and Exposure," *Journal of Communication* 24, no. 1 (Winter 1974): 36–47.

though it was clear that killing was against his nature. Neither the hero nor the audience had any doubts about the essential rightness of what he did. The hero faced great odds. Through unmatched courage and skill with a six-gun he triumphed. His reward was a ride off into the sunset to new adventures or a chance to claim the pretty schoolteacher or the head saloon girl who turned out to have a fourteen-karat heart.

One writer identified seven basic Western plots:

> (1) The Union Pacific Story centering around the construction of a railroad, telegraph or stagecoach line or around the adventure of a wagon train; (2) The Ranch Story with its focus between ranchers and sheepmen; (3) The Empire Story, which is an epic version of the Ranch Story; (4) The Revenge Story; (5) Custer's Last Stand, or the Cavalry and Indian Story; (6) The Outlaw Story; and (7) The Marshal Story.[20]

In a television broadcast actor John Wayne once remarked that in the pure Western guns do the job but that in the "adult" Western the villain is talked to death. Some Westerns have become more complicated. Many stories are still composed mainly of violent physical action surrounded by the clatter of hoofs and the clink of whiskey glasses and gambling chips. Others provide three-dimensional characters who develop a bit during the drama.

Whether pure or "adult," the Western's popularity never seems to wane for long. Thus a semblance of the Old West lives on in books, on movie and television screens, and in the minds of men and women in the United States and the many countries where Westerns are a favorite form of drama. Some sense of reality may be imparted by the use of historical characters such as Marshal Matt Dillon, Daniel Boone, or Bat Masterson and by such real places as Dodge City, Hayes, or Abilene.

Frozen in a slice of historical time, the Western has developed its own conventions. As in the situation comedies the action centers around the solving of a problem, usually by a strong central character who represents either conventional law and order or some higher law. Issues usually are clear-cut and the viewer seldom has to worry about the power of the hero to provide justice and a happy ending. Sometimes, as in *High Noon*, starring Gary Cooper, suspense builds artfully to a tremendous climax that at the end is washed away in an eruption of physical violence. In other films and programs the form may not be handled so adroitly, but always the values remain.

The Westerns also illustrate how the same form moves from one medium to another. "Gunsmoke," for example, came directly to television from radio, even bringing along its theme song.

[20]Quoted in John Cawelti, *The Six-Gun Mystique* (Bowling Green, Ohio: Bowling Green University Popular Press, 1970), p. 34–35.

Crime and detective shows, another popular form of drama, portray a world as remote for most people as that of the Westerns. As in the Westerns, television producers are simply carrying on in a well-established entertainment tradition. The "whodunit" is a traditional literary pattern that takes many forms. In film and television it varies from the bumbling antics of Don Adams in "Get Smart" to the deadly seriousness of "Hawaii Five-O"; from the stylish humor of *The Thin Man* to the flat documentary style of Jack Webb's "Dragnet."

The line between fact and fiction is blurred by such programs as "Dragnet," which bases its episodes on material from the files of the Los Angeles Police Department and constantly reminds the viewer of this fact. That this touch of realism paid off is indicated by the other police-crime shows that also use it, including "M Squad," "Naked City," and "The FBI."

Such factual allusions constantly remind viewers that, although the world they see is alien to them, it does exist. While the world of the Western is past, the world of crime drama is now. It hangs tantalizingly just beyond the vision of most citizens. Few really desire to enter such a violent and amoral world, but they like to observe it through the safety glass window of film or television, comfortable but still able to thrill at its forbidden joys and horrors.

Like situation comedies, the Westerns and detective stories sometimes provide a simulated family situation.

> From the beginning "Bonanza" was one of those special, single-parent television families. Ben Cartwright fathered his three sons by different wives, outlived all the women, and was presented to the television audience with the robust young men who constituted his total family. . . . The three sons among them constituted a single, multifaceted individual character. But the model for the rounded, complete character was always before these young men in the figure of their father.[21]

"Ironside" illustrates a family type relationship, too:

> Ironside is a former chief of police in San Francisco who has been paralyzed from the waist down by a sniper's bullet. He browbeats his commissioner into making him the leader of a special investigation team. It is the team that becomes the family. The young white police officer, the young white female police officer, and the young black assistant are more like brothers and sister than professional associates and Ironside himself is the gruff, business-like, all-caring father.[22]

[21]Horace Newcomb, *TV: The Most Popular Art* (Garden City, N.Y.: Anchor Press/Doubleday, 1974), pp. 75–76.
[22]Ibid., p. 105.

Thus Westerns and detective series provide a means of examining developing human relationships even though they are laid in settings distant from those in which viewers live and work.

Fact and Fancy

News occupies the television screen for only a small number of broadcast hours, so for most viewers television is primarily a source of fantasy and entertainment. This may make it difficult for some people to separate information from entertainment during the relatively short periods they watch the news.

Techniques blur the lines, too. "Dragnet" and other dramatic programs adopt the documentary format. New documentaries sometimes adopt the fast cutting and contrasted images used so successfully on "Laugh In." Perhaps Walter Cronkite assumes some of the father image bestowed on Robert Young in "Father Knows Best" and again in "Marcus Welby." Young and Jim Brolin, who plays his assistant in "Marcus Welby," are sometimes didactic in dispensing information about diseases that they "treat" in their television roles. Young appeals directly to the television audience in an HEW commercial. He gives the commencement address at the University of Michigan Medical School, an event reported on the evening news. Where does reality end and fantasy begin?

Some hold that soap operas are close to reality. University of Maryland psychiatrist Dr. John R. Lion told the *Baltimore Sun*: "I think the most realistic programs on TV are soap operas. They portray life with all its complexities and insolubilities." Dr. Lion said he often suggested that patients "view these programs in order to see, in admittedly caricatured form, what life is like."[23]

All of the content of the media is important to our national life, not just what frankly and directly relates to public affairs. News and documentaries are stylized rearrangements of reality. The Westerns, the mysteries, the soap operas, the talk shows, too, are all rearrangements of reality. The values they present are the values by which we live. They are worthy of study, not just to see what the media are feeding us, but as indications of what we, as a nation, are thinking about.

[23]Ibid., p. 180.

Suggestions for Further Reading

Barnouw, Erik. *The Golden Web.* New York: Oxford University Press, 1968.
  One of the author's three volumes of the history of broadcasting in America, this one covers the period from 1933 to 1953 and, among other things, describes the patterns of radio programming.

Boorstin, Daniel J. *The Image: A Guide to Pseudo-Events in America.* New York: Atheneum, 1971.
  Develops the thesis that created "events" play an important role in controlling opinion.

Halberstam, David. "CBS: The Power and the Profits." *Atlantic Monthly,* Part I, January 1976, pp. 33–71; Part II, February 1976, pp. 52–91.
  A two-part series telling how business considerations and personalities (particularly that of William S. Paley) have affected programming of the network.

Hall, Stuart, and Whannel, Paddy. *The Popular Arts: A Critical Guide to the Mass Media.* Boston: Beacon Press, 1964.
  Insights into programming formats of various media.

Newcomb, Horace. *TV: The Most Popular Art.* Garden City, N.Y.: Anchor Press/Doubleday, 1974.
  A study of the entertainment formats of television.

Post, Steve. *Playing the FM Band.* New York: Viking Press, 1974.
  An irreverent account of the author's experiences at an unconventional radio station, WBAI, New York, one of the Pacifica stations.

Real, Michael R. "Super Bowl: Mythic Spectacle." *Journal of Communication* 25 (Winter 1975): 31–43.
  An example of a media event.

Whelan, Kenneth. *How the Golden Age of Television Turned My Hair to Silver.* New York: Walker, 1973.
  A breezy and sometimes brutal account of the early days of television.

Youngblood, Gene. *Expanded Cinema.* New York: E. P. Dutton, 1970.
  Examines new formats for film and their relation to audiences and society.

A glance back at
Part Four
and ahead at
Part Five

In Part Four we considered how information relates to reality and how the formats for information and entertainment developed. Since political news is a staple of the information media, we gave it special attention.

Standards of news judgment are not well articulated, but the various media show remarkable agreement in what they select and in the emphasis they give it. This similarity is due to a common tradition, to daily imitation, and to the influence of news services, which provide most of the nonlocal content. We examined the tendency of the media to report the more dramatic and easily understood events instead of the more important, but less dramatic situations. It is important to remember that news is neither reality nor truth, but simply an aspect of the environment that media people have selected to report and thus turn into "news." Bringing news and reality closer together (they will never merge) is one of the goals of a democratic society.

We paid special attention to politics, as do the media in the United States. The president, as a prime news source, has special access to the media and therefore special power. The media have tended to magnify this power and thus, inadvertently, helped to set the stage for Watergate and other presidential excesses. The "agenda-setting" function of the media gives them influence, for the power to determine what public questions are reported determines which ones achieve prominence in the public mind and therefore are likely to proceed to some kind of solution.

We considered the formats of information and entertainment material. The manner in which information is organized affects the way it is received and the impact it has on the receiver. Information is organized differently for presentation in conversations, meetings, letters, and other information formats. The news story has evolved from oral patterns to early written and printed ones. The new journalism of the 1960's and 1970's represents a return to some of the freedom of the oral pattern.

Entertainment formats are drama, interview, comedy, and variety. Television took over radio's formats and adapted them to its own uses. A study of patterns shows much kinship between the dramatic forms of radio and television and the written novel and the stage play.

Formats used by the media have an effect on the audiences, although it often is not measurable. The audiences, their media habits, and how these habits are affected by the media are the subject for Part Five.

FIVE
The Audiences

12

Life in the Media Womb

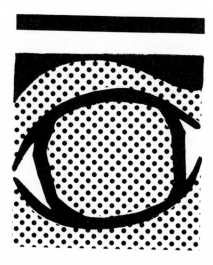

Everybody is in it; everybody can afford it; nobody can avoid it. What?

The media world, of course!

It wraps 215 million Americans in its giant womb. It mixes wild diversions and its own version of reality so that sometimes they are indistinguishable. It captures human eyes and ears so skillfully that, for most, the transition from the media world to the real world passes unnoticed. For some the media world *is* the real world.

And it has become so familiar that it does all this while allowing its users to forget that it is there.

Television is the great time gobbler for American audiences. If you knock on a door at random and do not find *both* a television set *and* a bathtub the odds are you will find a television set. And you will have to knock on a lot of doors before you find a house without a television receiver. Ninety-seven percent of U.S. homes have one or more.[1]

[1]*Broadcasting Yearbook*, 1975, p. B-154, is the source of radio and television figures in this section.

315

At least one of these sets is in operation for six hours and forty-nine minutes a day. If you leave yours dark for a full day, think of the one down the street that blinks and blares for more than thirteen hours to maintain that average figure. The average adult spends three hours and thirty minutes each day ogling the moving shadows in black and white or living color.

Only one U.S. home in every hundred lacks a radio. Most homes have more than one. Throughout the country 401.6 million radios are in working order—nearly two receivers for every person. Of every four sets, three are in homes; the other sits in a car, dangles from a neck or wrist band, or bulges from a shirt pocket.

Daily newspapers circulate nearly 62 million copies a day,[2] and the average adult spends about half an hour with the paper every day.[3]

These are the media on which the public lavishes its time most freely, but they are only the beginning. Books, films, magazines, and records take added chunks of time from media audiences. Billboards lurk at strategic spots to make their pitch. Elevator rides or grocery shopping often require involuntary exposure to music from Muzak.

Because media are everywhere it is easy to forget that they exist at all. They surround us so completely that they are like clothes. Except for fashion designers or clothes horses most people are likely to forget the existence of clothes until a streaker goes by to remind them that nearly everybody does wear them.

The media are pervasive and nearly everyone pays a great deal of attention to them. That is proved by everyday experience and volumes of research. The questions for this chapter are: How do people use media? Why? What do they think of them?

We will examine some of the main strands of "effects research." This is often guided by the requirements of the media or the needs of policymakers. Thus, for example, we have much data comparing use of one medium to another and on the effects of violence. Some scholars believe that a more basic approach would provide more enlightenment.

Foibles and Demographics

Audience foibles are of much interest to programmers, advertisers, and scholars. Do people really desert their television sets to take care of bathroom needs the moment a commercial appears? Resourceful

---

[2]*Editor & Publisher Yearbook*, 1975, p. 5.
[3]*The 1971 Attitude Survey*, the *Virginian-Pilot* and the *Ledger-Star*, Norfolk, Virginia. This study reports slightly under thirty minutes. Others have reported slightly more.

investigators have gone to municipal waterworks to find out. Some have produced records of sudden increases in water use indicating that the flush cycle sometimes does coincide with the commercial cycle.

Advertisers are more interested in demographic information. This is the classification of people into groups by age, sex, race, income, education, type of job, and section of the country. An advertiser selling high-ticket items like Cadillacs seeks an affluent audience; one selling pantyhose looks for programs appealing to women.

Thanks to the interest of advertisers and others, some information has accumulated about the characteristics of audiences.

Who reads what? Who listens to what? Who views what? These questions have been answered quite satisfactorily when the "who" is defined by demographics.

The questions are not nearly so well answered in terms of the more personal attributes of the men and women in the audience. Do lonely people watch certain kinds of programs? Do aggressive people watch more adventure shows? What are the personality characteristics of people who read editorials or personal advice columns? Some interesting studies have been done, but, by and large, media people and advertisers know little about the psychological characteristics of their audiences.

The questions go beyond the needs of program managers and advertisers to know their audiences. The answers, when they come, will help to explain why people use their leisure time in the ways they do. They will help to describe the lifestyles of America's millions.

Sampling

Researchers who supply audience information depend on the theory of sampling. This statistical principle holds that, if properly selected, a portion of a group will reflect the characteristics of the entire group. The portion (sample) of the entire group (the universe) must be selected by pure chance methods. Elaborate precautions are necessary to exclude all factors except chance, but when proper methods are used, the results are spectacular. Good sampling procedures allow the A. C. Nielsen Company to trace broad viewing patterns of the nation's nearly 70 million television households by monitoring viewing in 1,200 homes.

Determining the proper sample size for a given purpose and properly selecting the individuals or homes to be included is exacting scientific work, but it is effective. It allows researchers to conclude that Lawrence Welk appeals to the Geritol set, that Southerners like Westerns, and that prosperous people tend to like movies on television.

The U.S. Bureau of Census supplies the background information that makes the whole process work. It tells the researcher the demographic attributes of the populations as a whole. This includes such things as the age groups of people living in various parts of the country, the number of males versus the number of females, and what proportions of the populations are in what income groups and how much education they have had. Sampling methods underlie most of what we know about how people use the media.

How People Use the Media

A woman who was not used to visiting the world of the very rich had business that took her into the library of the home of one of the wealthy automobile heirs in Grosse Point, Michigan. She returned with a chuckle and a slightly smug observation. "All the classics were sitting on shelves around the room in beautiful bindings and looking as though they had never been opened. Off in a corner were the best sellers, bruised and thumb-worn. Those were the ones they read."

It is not only the rich who use the media to tell the world they have good taste. What appears on the living room coffee table is not always the main reading fare of the household. Once again, observation leads us to interesting speculation, but the studies based on sampling are our best guide to understanding how people use the media, one of the principal concerns of this chapter. To understand how people use the media we need first to consider the nature of the so-called mass audience.

The Mass Public and the Mass Audience

The word *mass* as it is used in *mass public* and *mass audience* sometimes carries a connotation that is misleading. It seems to imply the existence of one great homogeneous blob consisting of individuals with similar characteristics who respond to the media and other stimuli in about the same way. In fact, the mass audience, to the extent that one exists, consists of many smaller audiences, each with its own identity and individual characteristics.

The expression *mass audience* sometimes seems to imply a stable audience. This may be true, but is not necessarily so. While an audience for a given station or newspaper may exist over a long period, it is unsafe to assume that the same individuals are always in that audience. Individuals respond to media offerings on the basis of their needs for information and entertainment at a given moment, so that for any audience of any size, there is a constant dropping in and out of individuals.

The steady listener or the regular reader, goals of media programmers, are hard to achieve. A daily newspaper without local competition has an advantage in holding readers since it regularly supplies information needed by local citizens, but even its audience is subject to change. Some people will give up their subscriptions in disgust when an editorial blasts one of their idols. Others will quit when the carrier misses the front porch for the tenth time. Readers have alternatives in radio and television news broadcasts, and many find they can live without the paper.

Magazine circulation specialists are often preoccupied with the problem of keeping the renewal rate high. A high proportion of renewals provides a stable audience and avoids the expense of removing and adding names to subscription lists, but cut-rate offers to new subscribers combined with a hard sell sometimes make for a less stable audience. New subscribers who respond to special low rates are likely to drift away when the inducements are removed at renewal time.

As we have seen, books generally appeal to selected audiences. Publishers of academic and professional books can rely to some extent on the communication channels of those areas to publicize their new offerings, but they are not so fortunate with books intended for a general audience. The *New York Times Book Review* is available to serious readers, but it and other reviews reach a specialized rather than a mass audience. Book stores, except the largest ones, cannot supply shelf space to stock books that do not have a high volume of sales. Book audiences increased with the development of retail sales organizations such as the Book of the Month Club and the Literary Guild, which supply books by mail on a regular basis, but the audience for books remains relatively small and specialized.

In the broadcast media, audiences tend to be even more volatile. As we noticed earlier in this chapter, television comes closest to having a mass audience in the sense that it appeals to a great many individuals. But the audience is fickle and hard to predict, as network executives prove each season when they cancel out the programs that have failed to attract massive audiences and try their luck with new ones.

Volatile radio audiences have led to much experimenting with format, particularly in the FM stations. Quick accommodation to the desires of changing audiences are facts of life for harried radio programmers. Quotes from two of them illustrate the point. Bert Klienman, programming director for WPLJ, ABC's New York FM outlet:

> I don't think that most radio stations . . . have a committed listener-ship. . . . It's a fact of life in this business that we have to accept that we will not *capture* a radio listener. We will provide a service and when

the listener wants that service he will turn to us. That's why all-news stations are all news, etc. Whatever you want to call us, hit progressive or pop album, that's what we are, a service.[4]

Bob Henabery, head of programming development for ABC Radio: "There is not one who is successful who isn't running scared to some extent."[5]

Audiences are formed by individuals with mutual interests and by their interactions—their relations with each other. If a basketball game is an important event it will become important for some people that they be in the stands. Likewise, some people pay attention to certain television or radio programs so that they can talk about them the next day.

The nature of audiences is also determined in part by the nature of society. Industrial societies, in which cold contractual relationships have to some extent displaced the warm bonds of family and tribe, tend to produce lonely individuals. These people often turn to the media as substitutes for firsthand relations with family and friends. We will consider some of the research on this a little later on.

Thus, in present-day America, the mass audience is really a collection of smaller audiences, even lonely individuals, who are likely to respond in different ways to the same stimuli. This helps to explain the diversity of the media and also some of the confusion that seems perpetually to surround them.

Demographics and Media Use

Many scholarly and commercial researchers have described the audience of the various media in terms of demographics. In other words, they have tried to answer the question of what sex, age, income, education, race, and similar variables have to do with the way in which people use the media. There are dangers in this that all researchers recognize. It is dangerous to generalize from the data of a particular study because the findings may hold true for only a particular region. Another danger is that a particular factor that varies with a given reading or viewing habit may not be truly significant. For example, affluent persons tend to read newspapers more frequently than do people with less money. But the richer tend also to be better educated, so the question remains as to whether education, wealth, or something else is the causative factor. Another danger is that people change over time and no single study will

[4]"Switch Hitting on ABC's FM's," *Broadcasting*, March 13, 1972, p. 51.
[5]"It's Back to the Tried and True for Top-40 Radio," *Broadcasting*, January 29, 1973, p. 50.

show whether a given relationship is likely to continue for a long time.

Resourceful researchers are meeting these problems, but each study must be examined for its care in guarding against such threats to validity.

One of the early landmark studies of audiences is worth attention for comparative purposes. It is *Radio Listening in America*[6] by Paul F. Lazarsfeld and Patricia L. Kendall. Based on a nationwide survey conducted by the National Opinion Research Center of the University of Chicago, it provides a general picture of media habits at the time.

The study showed interesting relationships in the use of the four media studied: books, magazines, films, and radio. The media audiences are overlapping. "A radio fan is likely to be a movie fan also, while, conversely, those persons who rarely go to the movies are likely . . . to be light listeners." Similarly, those who did not read magazines regularly spent little time with radio or at the movies. Nearly all the people who read books also read magazines, but many of the magazine readers did not read books. The researchers were puzzled by the small number (5 percent) who said they read books, but not magazines. Since magazines are usually easier to read than books, no logical explanation presented itself. The researchers concluded that these people might have had unusual reading tastes or that perhaps they misinterpreted the question.

In another study of about the same period Wilbur Schramm and David White related newspaper reading to age, education, and income.[7] On the basis of their sample Schramm and White concluded the amount of news reading tends to increase with the three demographic factors they were studying. They also concluded that pictorial content is what attracted younger readers to the newspaper. Comics were the most read item in the paper for readers between ten and fifteen years old. They found no one in that age group who had read any editorials.

Among their other findings were that crime and disaster news was the content most likely to be read by teenagers and people with lower incomes. They also found that persons with college educations are more likely than others to read the serious news and less likely to use the newspaper for its entertainment value.

The findings are fairly consistent that the more affluent and the better educated are likely to be the best informed about serious content of the media. It was confirmed again in 1968 in a study in Madison, Wisconsin, which found that the persons best informed about international affairs were those in the higher socioeconomic brackets.[8]

[6]Paul F. Lazarsfeld and Patricia L. Kendall, *Radio Listening in America* (New York: Prentice-Hall, 1948).

[7]Wilbur Schramm and David White, "Age, Education, Economic Status: Factors in Newspaper Reading," *Journalism Quarterly* 26 (June 1949): 149.

[8]John T. McNelly, Ramona Bush, and Michael E. Bishop, "Cosmopolitan Media Usage in the Diffusion of International Affairs News," *Journalism Quarterly* 45 (Summer 1968): 329.

But there was a questioning of continuing validity of the demographic variables in that same year. Bradley S. Greenberg and Hideya Kumata, using a national sample of 1,528 persons interviewed by the Gallup organization, questioned whether demographic data were good predictors of media use and whether high or low use of one medium of communication could predict how a person would use another.[9]

People in the sample were asked how they used television, radio, newspapers, and magazines. The researchers found correlation only between magazines and newspapers. That is, they concluded that a person who was high in number of magazines read was also likely to be high in number of newspapers read. They found that women tended to watch television more and listened to radio more than men. They also reported that the more highly educated and those with higher incomes tended to be heavier users of newspapers. The authors commented that television, as a "low effort" medium, cut across all segments of the population. Lazarsfeld and Kendall had made a similar distinction in their study. They found overlap in use of radio and film and offered in explanation the theory that these "spectator" media required little skill from their audiences.

At any rate, Greenberg and Kumata felt they had enough evidence to question the use of standard demographic factors as predictors of media use. "Perhaps the relevance of these variables has long passed," they commented. Instead, they suggested that investigators might inquire whether more personal characteristics of individuals might offer more substantial clues as to their use of the media. Factors they offered as worthy of consideration were social interaction, self-evaluation, cognitive need for information, and innovativeness.

Such analysis is sure to provide deeper understanding of the way people use the media, but for now we must base our judgment on available information that is based primarily on demographic data.

On that basis it is safe to make some generalizations about the media.

Television

Based on the number of people who view television and the great amount of time they lavish on it, television is the most popular of the mass media in the United States. Figures quoted at the beginning of the chapter prove that.

On another basis, too, television is the most massive of the mass media. Television is as close to being a universally popular medium as any that has ever existed. Many people in the United States are functionally illiterate; that is, it is difficult for them to read and write. It is easy to see that

[9]Bradley S. Greenberg and Hideya Kumata, "National Sample Predictors of Mass Media Use," *Journalism Quarterly* 45 (Winter 1968): 641–646.

television would be popular with this group, and figures show that it is. This fits with the theories that as a "low effort," "low skills" "spectator medium," television should appeal to those with rudimentary communication skills.

However, that is only part of the story. Television also appeals to those with the most sophisticated communication skills—and all the groups in between.

Some groups use television more than others, but there is good reason to question whether the factor being analyzed is the one producing that effect. Nearly all studies show that sex is a factor in television viewing: women watch considerably more than men. Age is also a factor: the very young and persons over fifty spend more time with television than does the rest of the population. In an elaborate study based on 1970 data[10] Robert Bower made an attempt to test the extent to which these differences are actually caused by another factor—the opportunity to watch.

He reasoned that many women have more opportunity to watch the tube simply because they are home more than men. Older persons, too, have more opportunity because many of them are retired. Bower constructed what he called an "equal opportunity audience" by studying viewing patterns during the period when nearly everyone has the opportunity to watch—after 6 P.M. on weekdays and all day Saturday and Sunday. Bower concluded that two of the most highly regarded predictors of television viewing, sex and education, had no effect of viewing during his "equal opportunity" period. Other variables did not perform much better. "Region of the country, age, income, conservatism versus liberalism, and occupation all play some miniscule part of the analysis, in an ambiguous set of interrelationships, but no one of these factors by itself accounts for more than one percent of the explained variance."[11]

Bower explained his findings this way:

> The one main conclusion that may be drawn from this analysis is that the amount of time a person will spend watching television during the evening and weekend hours has little to do with who he is as a socially defined entity. Stated another way, the equal opportunity audience of television is an extraordinarily undifferentiated one in its social composition. It would appear to be very much of a "mass" audience if we mean by that term a large audience and one composed of all segments of the population in fairly equal proportions.[12]

It is possible that other factors are working that escaped Bower. For example, the reason for television's heterogenous evening and weekend

[10]Robert T. Bower, *Television and the Public* (New York: Holt, Rinehart & Winston, 1973).
[11]Ibid., pp. 32, 35.
[12]Ibid., p. 35.

audience may be in the programming rather than in available time. The networks may have become so successful at providing content with universal appeal in evening "prime time" and on weekends that all segments of the population are attracted. Until further research establishes whether this or other factors control, Bower provides the best explanation:—simply that nearly everyone watches television—men and women, rich and poor, educated and uneducated; and that the amount of watching is controlled mostly by the time one can free from regular duties and the nearness to a television set.

From studies of other media we know that availability of any medium has something to do with how frequently it is used, but obviously there is more than that to understanding media behavior. Probably the additional factors are imbedded in the personalities of potential audience members.

Television viewing time has increased gradually from the time of its introduction, indicating ever-increasing acceptance of the medium as part of everyday living. This is indicated by Table 12.1. In it Bower compares television viewing by age groups from 1960 to 1970. The 1960 figures are from a study[13] that laid much of the groundwork and supplied much comparative data for Bower's work.

Table 12–1 Median Hours of Viewing per Week / *1960 and 1970*

Age	1960	1970	Base: 100 percent = 1960	Base: 100 percent = 1970
18–19	26.25	25.33	84	182
20–27 }	22.31	29.05 } 28.70	473	261 } 331
28–29 }		27.33 }		70 }
30–39	23.66	28.08	544	356
40–49	22.60	26.83	463	378
50–59	25.39	28.93	400	311
60+	25.25	28.21	440	419
Total	23.82	28.20	2404	1977

Source: From *Television and the Public* by Robert T. Bower. Copyright © 1973 by Holt, Rinehart and Winston, Inc. Reprinted by permission of Holt, Rinehart and Winston.

[13]Gary A. Steiner, *The People Look at Television: A Study of Audience Attitudes* (New York: A. A. Knopf, 1963). Interviews were conducted in 1960, but the study was not published until 1963.

The Total row shows that weekly viewing time in 1970 was 28.20 hours, an increase of 4.38 hours, or 18 percent, over 1960. The 1970 figure cited here is lower than the one for 1974 cited earlier in this chapter. Figures from different studies will vary somewhat, but the trend toward increased viewing is unmistakable. The comparison in the table assumes that the 1970 and 1960 samples were representative of the population as a whole. Scanning down the 1960 and 1970 columns it is also apparent that viewing for each age group increased except for the eighteen-to-nineteen-year-old viewers. For this group the viewing time declined from 26.25 hours per week to 25.33. This is almost an hour less viewing, a decrease of 3.5 percent. Also, we see that while the teenagers were the heaviest viewers in 1960, they were the lightest viewers in 1970. While not catastrophic for the television industry, it is a cause for worry if it indicates the start of a declining trend in viewing. For students of the media it raises interesting questions.

These questions have to do with viewing habits of individual age groups as the people in them grow older. The comparisons straight across the table that we made earlier are of different age groups at a given time. If we follow the diagonal lines we can look at representatives of the same age group ten years later. These, of course, are not the same people interviewed ten years earlier, but they are samples from the same age group. Since everyone is ten years older, those in the teenage group in 1960 are in the twenty to twenty-seven or twenty-eight to twenty-nine groups a decade later. Thus we see that members of each group appear to have increased their viewing as they grew older. Earlier data on the 1970 teenagers are not available for the previous decade, so all we know about them is that they viewed in 1970 for fewer hours than the teenagers of 1960.

Newspapers

While television viewing appears to be scattered through the population without much regard for age and education, newspaper reading is a bit heavier among the older and the better educated.

A study by the American Newspaper Publishers Association in 1973[14] followed an often-used procedure in assessing readership. Persons were asked if they had read a newspaper "yesterday." This produces more accurate results than asking people if they read a paper "regularly," for a person is asked to describe a specific act of the previous day.

On the basis of this procedure, the ANPA study concluded that on an average weekday 77.4 percent of the adult population of the United States reads a daily newspaper. This is slightly lower than the comparable 1961 figure of 79 percent, but this may be because the 1973 sample included a

---

[14]ANPA, *News and Editorial Content and Readership of the Daily Newspaper*, ANPA News Research Bulletin No. 5, April 26, 1973.

larger proportion of younger adults, fewer of whom are regular newspaper readers. The 1961 sample included no one below twenty-one, while the 1973 study lowered the cut-off age to eighteen.

Better educated and more affluent persons are more likely to be newspaper readers. The same ANPA survey showed that 88 percent of the college graduates but only 70 percent of those with an eighth grade or lower education had read a newspaper "yesterday."

Newspaper reading generally increases in higher income households. The ANPA study disclosed this trend, but it also showed that people in the $15,000 plus annual bracket are somewhat less likely to read a paper than those with $7,500 to $14,999 annual income. Table 12.2 gives details.

The newspaper-reading habit increases with age, but drops off a bit around retirement age. Table 12.3 gives the figures for the ANPA survey. It shows, too, the usual tendency for women's readership to be lower than that for men.

These trends have long been recognized and appear to be fairly consistent. For example, in 1949 Wilbur Schramm and David M. White concluded that "the amount of news reading tends to increase with age, with education, and with status. News reading increases very rapidly through the teens, reaches a peak somewhere between the ages of 30 and 50, and thereafter drops off slightly."[15]

Table 12.2   Newspaper Reading by Household Income and Sex

Percentage of Respondents having read a newspaper "yesterday"

	All respondents	Male	Female
Under $5,000	67%	66%	68%
$5,000–$7,499	69	72	67
$7,500–$9,999	81	83	79
$10,000–$14,999	88	92	83
$15,000 or more	79	75	84

Source: Adapted from ANPA News Research Center, *News and Editorial Content and Readership of the Daily Newspaper,* News Research Bulletin No. 5, April 26, 1973, p. 20. Reprinted with permission.

[15]Schramm and White, "Age, Education, Economic Status," p. 150.

Radio

The technology that produces miniature radios helped the industry to survive the onslaught of television. That technology also helped change the habits of listeners. Radio became a more personal medium, one that could be used wherever one happened to be, and often was a companion in solitude.

Radio also tended to be the medium of young people, not only for rock and other forms of popular music, but for more serious content as well. In Portland, Oregon, for example, it was found that radio was used for local news by 38 percent of those under thirty-five, but by only 17 percent of those fifty years of age and over. For national and world news the pattern was the same: 26 percent of those under thirty-five, but only 13 percent of those fifty and over used radio for that purpose.[16]

Figures in various surveys show different amounts of exposure to radio as well as the other media. Time of year, construction of questions, and availability of other media in a given locality, all are likely to create such differences. A rough average might be that about 80 percent of the population listens to some radio each day.

Magazines

In one national survey 5 percent of the persons interviewed said they read no magazines; 87 percent said they read between one and

Table 12.3   Newspaper Reading by Age and Sex

Percentage of respondents having read a newspaper "yesterday"

	All respondents	Male	Female
18–24 yrs.	66%	69%	62%
25–34 yrs.	68	72	64
35–49 yrs.	82	82	82
50–64 yrs.	85	86	84
65 or older	84	86	83

Source: Adapted from ANPA News Research Center, *News and Editorial Content and Readership of the Daily Newspaper*, News Research Bulletin No. 5, April 26, 1973, p. 20. Reprinted with permission.

[16]Chilton R. Bush, *How Portland (Ore.) Adults Use TV and Radio for News*, ANPA News Research Bulletin No. 4, March 2, 1972.

three; and about 1 percent said they regularly read seven or more.[17] As with newspapers, people with more money and more education are more likely to read more magazines. Whites are slightly more likely to read more magazines than blacks, and age appears to have little relation to the number of magazines read.

Books

Book-reading habits show the same tendency as magazine-reading habits, but educational level is even more discriminating. In the Lazarsfeld and Kendall sample, 50 percent of college graduates, 27 percent of high school graduates, and 11 percent of grade school graduates said they read at least one book in the previous month.

The figures for book and magazine reading and, to a lesser extent, those for newspaper reading tend to support the theory that the electronic media require less effort. Many individuals can read well enough to do routine tasks, but sustained reading is sufficiently difficult to be tiring and irksome. Another factor probably is the availability of the electronic media compared with the printed. Once one has acquired a television set and some portable radios, the programs from these media become available with only slight additional effort. Newspapers and magazines are available through subscription, but even that effort requires some volition, and books generally have to be sought out.

Having considered *who* pays attention to the media, it is time to ask: *how* do people use the media?

The Constant Companion

For some people the media are constant companions.

One hot summer Sunday a *New York Times* reporter found a Long Island man using media in a frenzied fashion. Warding off the boredom of a long weekend, this hapless individual was sitting in his patio sipping a drink, surrounded by the remnants of the Sunday newspapers, reading a magazine, glancing up occasionally to keep track of the baseball action on a portable television in front of him, and reaching down frequently to adjust the volume of a portable radio carrying a description of still another baseball game. The man's wife and children had gone off to the beach leaving him to fight boredom with all the media at his command.

It is stories like this that remind us that all the carefully collected statistics may be measuring somewhat different things. One person may dip into the newspaper quickly to catch the result of the third race at Aque-

[17]Greenberg and Kumata, "National Sample Predictors," p. 644.

duct. Another may read the closing price of half a dozen stocks he holds. Still another may scan favorite comics. Such users of the paper are "readers" as well as are those who systematically look through the paper, starting at the front or back and seeking items of interest on each page. Studies show us that most readers do look at every page, but even for these people "reading the paper" is likely to mean different things.

Colin Cherry has suggested that reading the newspaper counts for less than "having" the paper.[18] The paper's regular arrival on our doorstep and the reassurance it brings of the existence of the outside world may be its most important role.

Certainly for a medium such as the newspaper, which strives to appeal to the entire cross-section of the population in its area, the various people who "read" it will do so for different reasons, and they will find different things of interest.

The same question is valid for the electronic media. What does a man or woman really mean by reporting that he or she views television for, say, five hours a day? Some people sit in front of the screen and watch, period. Some turn the set on and go about their business. It relieves the monotony of their housework, piecework, or handicraft.

In his study of media habits in Portland, Oregon, Chilton Bush found that many other activities may accompany television "watching." An inspection of Table 12.4 brings us back to the bored Long Islander.

Since the activities vary in the amount of concentration they require we can only guess at how much attention was really devoted to the television program. Eating, drinking coffee, or smoking take little attention away from television. But talking with one's spouse or other friends, reading a newspaper, gardening, or cleaning could mean that very little attention was given to the turned-on television set. For most people really reading the paper and really watching television at the same moment is nearly impossible. One activity or the other must be tuned out.

Some of the media are admittedly designed and used for "background." When the Muzak organization hires a well-known band to record, it insists on toning down the distinctive style of the band so that few people will recognize it. The organization seeks to provide music that will be soothing but will not register on the conscious minds of its hearers. Some radio programs are designed for background purposes. Dave Garroway, first host of NBC's "Today" television program, said that he perceived his role as providing low-profile material that would not interfere with the morning duties to which his audience had to attend. He visualized his image as "somebody else around the house"—a protection against loneliness, but demanding little attention.

[18]Colin Cherry, *World Communication: Threat or Promise? A Sociotechnical Approach* (London: John Wiley, 1971).

Most media try to do the opposite—to "grab" the attention of the audience. Advertisers almost impose that effort on the media. A medium that the audience can ignore would not be a good salesperson.

Nevertheless, many people do other things when they are using the media, and some people apparently regularly "pay attention" to several media at the same time.

The media habits of the president are always of interest to the journalists who report them, and they serve to illustrate the point. What, for example, caught the restless mind of Lyndon Johnson as he used to sit in the White House simultaneously watching three news programs? Was Dwight Eisenhower ill informed because he professed to read no news-

Table 12.4 Viewers' Activities While Watching the Dinner-Hour Television Program

	Total	Men	Women
Eating; having a snack	47%	53%	41%
Preparing dinner	25	14	37
Household chores; busy with children; gardening; cleaning house	14	6	22
Visiting with friends; talking to spouse; phone conversation	9	8	10
Drinking coffee or other beverage	7	12	2
Reading newspaper	7	12	2
Handcrafts; sewing; painting; knitting; cleaning paint brushes	7	2	12
Reading other printed matter	4	6	2
Miscellaneous; smoked a cigarette; played with children	5	10	—
Total	125%	123%	128%
Number of respondents	100	51	49

Source: Chilton R. Bush, *How Portland (Ore.) Adults Use TV and Radio for News*, ANPA News Research Bulletin No. 4, March 2, 1972, p. 21. Reprinted with permission.

Life in the Media Womb

papers regularly? Was part of Richard Nixon's "isolation" brought about because he read summaries of the news prepared by his staff instead of reading newspapers and listening to radio and television for himself? What is Gerald Ford's definition of "reading the paper" if he reads all those mentioned in this clipping and runs the country, too?

> **Washington (UPI)**–President Ford reads 10 newspapers a day, three news magazines a week and regularly watches network news programs, says press secretary Ron Nessen.
>
> Nessen was asked Monday about Ford's daily reading habits and replied that Ford regularly reads seven morning papers: The Washington Post, New York News, New York Times, Wall Street Journal, Christian Science Monitor, Chicago Tribune and Baltimore Sun.
>
> He said the President also reads three afternoon newspapers: The Washington Star, St. Louis Post-Dispatch, and his hometown Michigan newspaper, The Grand Rapids Press.[19]

Why Do People Use the Media?

Habit is the best explanation of why people use the media. If one gets used to waking up with a clock radio every morning he is likely to continue this. If one gets used to looking at the dinner-hour newscast on television she is likely to continue to do so. The newspaper becomes a regular visitor and that, too, becomes part of the ritual of living. We may read the paper just because we always read the paper.

But habits can change. They can be reinforced. They can be broken. New habits are always being developed.

Wilbur Schramm suggested that people seek news for immediate reward or for delayed reward. He put it this way:

> I think it is self-evident that a person seeks news in expectation of a reward.
>
> This reward may be either of two kinds. One is related to what Freud . . . calls the Pleasure Principle, the other to what he calls the Reality Principle. For want of better names, we shall call these two classes *immediate reward* and *delayed reward*.
>
> In general, the kinds of news which may be expected to furnish immediate reward are news of crime and corruption, accidents and disaster, sport and recreation, social events, and human interest.

[19]"President's Reading Habits Told," United Press International, Lexington, Kentucky, *Leader*, July 9, 1975, p. 12.

Delayed reward may be expected from news of public affairs, economic matters, social problems, science, education and health.[20]

Immediate reward news provides gratification: a smile at a story of a child's prank, a shudder at a bloody killing, a twinge of envy at the latest escapade of a movie star. Delayed reward news has to do with news of public affairs, tax rates, the state of the stock market, information that readers or viewers need to adjust their lives to the pressures of the world.

Schramm suggests that immediate reward news provides a dream world, while the delayed reward links the receiver to reality.

Schramm's theory suggests that some news is a form of entertainment. If this is true, then it is reasonable to think that news watching and news reading may be, in part, at least, a fun thing. We can sit idly in front of our television and enjoy watching the world go by, complete with moving images in living color. We can commiserate with other people in their disasters and count our own blessings.

The idea that news reading represents play, serious play, but still play, is supported by another scholar, William Stephenson:

> What has to be explained about newsreading, fundamentally, is the *enjoyment* it engenders. Even bad news is enjoyed in the sense at least that *afterwards,* upon reflection, we can say that it was absorbing, interesting, and enjoyed. So, also, *play* is enjoyed, though during the game we may be so intent upon winning that we are unaware of any feelings of pleasure. We are to propose that newsreading, in developed forms, is subjective play, and that communication-pleasure . . . explains the enjoyment: newsreading is therefore attended, normally, by a certain inflation of the self. Newsreading, so regarded, is a complex subjective skill, the importance of which is little understood.[21]

Stephenson also says:

> In its most primitive form one would have the "feebly socialized" newsreader, passing from one enticing bit of scandal to another entertaining murder; in a developed form one has the skillful reader of the New York *Times,* pursuing his orderly way through a complex subjective minuet, in which there is order, elements of ritual and much else of a highly playful nature. The outcome is a feeling of enjoyment . . . *after* one has been so absorbed in the reading.[22]

[20]Wilbur Schramm, "The Nature of News," *Journalism Quarterly* 26 (September 1949): 260.

[21]William Stephenson, "The Ludenic Theory of Newsreading," *Journalism Quarterly* 41 (Summer 1964): 368.

[22]Ibid., p. 369.

Stephenson points out that news reading is voluntary and says that it is separate from the reader's real life—"rather, it is an interlude, an act of 'pretending,' a temporary event, satisfying itself and ending there."

The theories of Schramm and Stephenson suggest that the media, even in their most serious content, the news, provide enjoyable pastimes for their readers and listeners. The pastime may be intellectual, as it is for Stephenson's *New York Times* reader, or it may simply gratify the sensations for the moment, as it does for Schramm's reader of immediate reward news. Schramm sees the reader or listener pulled into a fantasy world by immediate reward news or into the real world by delayed reward news. Stephenson sees the possibility that the play approach to news may help readers to understand their cultures more fully. He cites the theory that play explains cultures and therefore the play approach to news provides

> freedom for the person, at times, to see through the cultural conditioning of news. It is not that he becomes more penetrating in thought, but merely that he can at times *exist*, as a child does when he freely plays, and thus, every now and then, be free to push to one side the trappings of what everyone else swears is the truth.[23]

Why do people pay attention to the news? To be amused certainly, to be forewarned of possible dangers and opportunities ahead, and perhaps intuitively to seek the insights that the mosaic pattern of news may provide.

The habits of paying attention to the media provide rewards or else they would vanish. Since the media in their content embrace much of the world and much variety, the reward will differ for each member of the audience.

Part of the question is whether people are responding to the media themselves or to the content of the media. As we saw in earlier chapters, McLuhan and Innis say that the nature of a communications medium is more important than its content. This suggests that people relate to the medium, regardless of the content. But the question is still open. Do people have a feeling about television or just about the programs that television brings them? Do they welcome the newspaper at the door or do they react simply to the content of the pages?

The common-sense answer is that people respond to both, and the studies seem to bear that out. This can work to the advantage or disadvantage of the media. Television newsman William Small wrote a book whose title, *To Kill a Messenger*, reflected his view that television is blamed by its audiences for the bad news it brings them. On the other hand, television benefits, too, from the general picture many people hold of it as a

[23]Ibid., p. 374.

light, friendly, cheerful medium primarily devoted to entertainment.

People pay attention to the media partly because they are lonely or depressed. The electronic media are available as mood changers. Turn on the radio and we can hear the cheerful voice of the disc jockey commiserating with us about having to get up on a cold morning. Good cheer is the stock-in-trade of the disc jockeys, especially those who broadcast in the morning hours when many in the audience feel the need of an elixir to get them ready to face the day. But, while the news may be dismal, all the media attend to their function of putting a bright face on the world.

In nearly all its many hours of programming, television seeks to entertain, and usually with light fare. When the news is of wars, floods, famine, rape, and murder, it is a threatening element in a media world that is otherwise filled with perpetual fun and games. Perhaps even the commercials are welcome in the reports of the grim news of the day. Things may be going to pot all over the world, but we can take some small comfort in the blandishments of advertisers who assure us that though we may have lost our teeth we can still buy a magic potion that will keep our dentures tight so that we can bite as well as the handsome men and women on the screen.

Even newspapers, whose main fare is news, take pains to provide a cheerful context when they can. Sports news, whether the home team won or lost, is essentially news of good cheer. The comics provide a chuckle, and so do the feature items used on the front page as "brighteners."

For some people all of the time and for all of the people some of the time, the media serve as a quick pick-me-up, an escape from the routine, a mood changer. Ancient Rome's *circus maximus* was designed to serve as an escape hatch for the weary plebeians of the Empire. The programming sometimes consisted of throwing Christians to the lions to bring a vicarious thrill to the hearts of the multitudes and keep their minds off any possible thoughts of revolution.

Television is ideally suited to provide escape and enchantment in a make-believe world and, as we shall see, back in 1960 it was already filling that role.

"TV Is Wonderful"

Listen to the rapture with which people described television to interviewers for the Steiner study[24] done in 1960: "TV is wonderful—just wonderful. Why TV has brought me the whole world. I just love it. . . . I just love every minute. It's the most thrilling thing of my life."

[24]Steiner, *The People Look at Television.*

And in answer to the question about what happened when the set was out of order:

> I feel like someone is dead.

> We went crazy. My husband said, "What did I do before TV?" . . . We couldn't do anything. Didn't even try to read a paper. Just walked around brooding.

> I nearly lost my mind. The days were so long, and I just couldn't stand to miss my continued stories.

> I went from house to house to watch TV, or to the filling station, or went to bed early because I was lost for something to do.

Not all viewers were so completely sold on the medium. Here is a minority evaluation from the Steiner study: "TV engineers are going to roast in hell till eternity as a result of what they have done."

Steiner found general satisfaction with television, but satisfaction tempered with reality. For example, his interviewers asked which among certain amenities of modern-day life people would keep if they should have to do without all but one for two or three months. Only 5 percent of both men and women said they would keep television. Voted as more worthy of keeping were the family's automobile, refrigerator, newspaper, and telephone.

Some persons interviewed admitted to a considerable guilt feeling about the amount of time they spend viewing television. Quotations from men and women interviewed seem to typify an ill-defined malaise:

> Too often I feel that I have wasted my time. I have a country home in which I haven't installed TV because I do not want to be tempted to waste my time. I watch too much.

> I spend too much time. Can't control myself. A TV addict.

> My wife stole a tube and pretended something was wrong with the set. We went back to reading, the kids got better grades, and Mom was easier to live with. I think it was a sneaky way to do it though.

Steiner's own comment is apt: "In short, television . . . is considered more good than good *for* you."[25]

Responses favorable to television outnumbered unfavorable ones in a ratio of two and a half to one. The factors most likely to influence a per-

[25]Ibid., p. 77.

son's attitude toward television were education and religion. In general, the more education a person had, the more likely he or she was to be critical of television, but this tendency did not show up very strongly except in persons who had continued their education beyond high school. Jews tended to be more critical than Catholics or Protestants.

On the average, men and women with more education earn more money so there was a tendency for higher income groups to be more critical of television, although this was less pronounced than for education alone. Age groups showed no significant variation in direction of opinion, although older men and women tended to be more extreme in their views, whether favorable or unfavorable. No differences were found between men and women.

When Steiner analyzed viewing patterns as revealed in diaries kept by families in the metropolitan New York area, he found that watching matched the offerings of the networks, with light entertainment gaining most attention, but considerable attention was given to news programs. "Heavy entertainment" (serious music and drama) and information and public affairs programs received very little attention from viewers.

Education accounted for fewer viewing differences than many might expect. The college-educated watched fewer programs, but they emphasized light entertainment only slightly less than those with considerably less education.

Not So Wonderful Ten Years Later

Ten years later Steiner's study was replicated by Robert T. Bower.[26] Many of Steiner's earlier findings were found to still hold true. People were less ecstatic about television, but they still heartily approved of it, and tended to increase their rating of it in comparison to other media.

Again in 1970 those interviewed said that if forced to give up some items they would discard television before parting with their automobiles, refrigerators, or telephones. It was an even choice between television and newspapers. Details for 1960 and 1970 appear in Table 12.5.

This comparison may be a little unfair to the media since some of the other items may be necessities. Nevertheless, it demonstrates that, enamored as it is of television, the American public retains its perspective.

Again in 1970 the more highly educated wobbled in attitude and action. They spent slightly less time with television than others, but when

[26]Bower, *Television and the Public.* As in the Steiner study, the report was made three years after the interviewing. Interviews were conducted in 1970.

they watched they looked at the same things as the rest of the public. Seldom did they give up amusing programs for the more serious fare they asked for.

A comparison of the 1960 and 1970 data produced the illogical findings that, despite their decreased enthusiasm for television, people spent more time viewing it. Bower theorized that this contradiction might be due to the increase of leisure time—people had more free hours, so they watched more television. This supports the theory that one of the great determiners of media use is availability.

Another contradictory aspect was that, despite their slightly lower rating of television as a medium in 1970, most people rated the programs slightly more enjoyable than had those in 1960. This indicates that sometimes at least, people do make a separation in their minds between television as a medium and the content it offers.

What emerges from these two landmark studies is a picture of an audience less charmed by the medium itself, but more interested in specific content, and one whose viewing time is controlled more by the spare time available than by any more serious motive. In 1960 television was still something of a novelty. By 1970 it was more an accepted part of everyday life.

Table 12.5   Media Rated Against Other Items

Responses in 1960 and 1970 to question "Here are some things that many people take for granted today. But, imagine, if you can, that for two or three months you could have only one of these and you'd have to do without the rest. If you could only have one of those things, which one would you choose? What would be the second, third item you'd want?"

Percent who say	First choice 1960	First choice 1970	Second choice 1960	Second choice 1970	Third choice 1960	Third choice 1970
Refrigerator	38%	38%	24%	31%	15%	16%
Automobile	31	41	28	28	17	13
Newspaper	11	5	12	8	16	13
Telephone	10	11	21	22	27	34
Television	5	5	14	11	24	24
Don't know / NA	5	1	1	0	1	1

Source: From *Television and the Public* by Robert T. Bower. Copyright © 1973 by Holt, Rinehart and Winston, Inc. Reprinted by permission of Holt, Rinehart and Winston.

Where Do You Get Your News? Whom Do You Believe?

Finding the answers to these two questions has taken much time and money and occupied the talents of researchers for more than two decades. The media and their defenders are much concerned. It is the road to prestige and profit to be able to claim that one's medium is the prime source of the most believable information.

One of the most indefatigable of the researchers into these twin questions has been the Roper Organization, which has asked the questions of a national cross-section of the population since 1959. Results for the "most news" question are shown in Table 12.6.

Television has shown a fairly dramatic increase in use as a source of news. Newspapers have suffered a slight decline. Radio's loss has been quite severe, and magazines, never a major contender, appear to be holding their own. Other people as a news source remain low, but quite constant. Given what we know already these findings should not be surprising. Television has established itself as the major all-purpose medium. People spend a great deal of time with it, and expect it to fill more and more of their media needs.

Table 12.6 Major Sources of News

	Dec. 1959	Nov. 1961	Nov. 1963	Nov. 1964	Jan. 1967	Nov. 1968	Jan. 1971	Nov. 1972	Nov. 1974
Television	51%	52%	55%	58%	64%	59%	60%	64%	65%
Newspapers	57	57	53	56	55	49	48	50	47
Radio	34	34	29	26	28	25	23	21	21
Magazines	8	9	6	8	7	7	5	6	4
People	4	5	4	5	4	5	4	4	4
Total	154%	157%	147%	153%	158%	145%	140%	145%	142%
Don't know / no answer	1	3	3	3	2	3	1	1	*

Source: Adapted from *Trends in Public Attitudes Toward Television and Other Mass Media, 1959–1974,* p. 3. A report by the Roper Organization, Inc. for the Television Information Office, 1975. Reprinted with permission of the Television Information Office.

*Less than 1%

Television's increase in believability at the expense of the other media is even sharper, as the survey summarized in Table 12.7 reveals. The wording of the question posed by the surveyors has become traditional: "If you got conflicting or different reports of the same news story from radio, television, the magazines and the newspapers, which of the four versions would you be most inclined to believe—the one on radio, or television, or magazines or newspapers?"

The other media, particularly newspapers, have become concerned. The American Newspaper Publishers Association commissioned several studies to probe the question more deeply. One of the most interesting is the one already mentioned by Chilton Bush. It endeavored to discover how people use the various media to obtain news. Among its findings were the following:

Radio is an important news source for younger people in the sample. "Eighty-four per cent of adults under 25 years of age listened to radio news 'yesterday.' Only sixty-eight per cent of the people in that age group received a newspaper 'yesterday' and only 49 per cent viewed television news."[27]

"Thirty-four per cent of the people who watched a television news program watched only part of it."

As we noted earlier, many people were doing other things as they watched television news.

Many people watched television news just because the set was on. Respondents gave such answers as these: the children had the set on; they

Table 12.7 Credibility of Media

Most believable	Dec. 1959	Nov. 1961	Nov. 1963	Nov. 1964	Jan. 1967	Nov. 1968	Jan. 1971	Nov. 1972	Nov. 1974
Television	29%	39%	36%	41%	41%	44%	49%	48%	51%
Newspapers	32	24	24	23	24	21	20	21	20
Radio	12	12	12	8	7	8	10	8	8
Magazines	10	10	10	10	8	11	9	10	8
Don't know / no answer	17	17	18	18	20	16	12	13	13

Source: Adapted from *Trends in Public Attitudes Toward Television and Other Mass Media, 1959–1974*, p. 4. A report by the Roper Organization, Inc., for the Television Information Office, 1975. Reprinted with permission of the Television Information Office.

[27]Bush, *How Portland (Ore.) Adults Use TV and Radio*, p. 15.

always turn the set on when they get home from work; the news followed some favorite entertainment program; it was too hot to sleep so they turned on the late news.

On the other hand, many people gave evidence of consciously seeking news programs. For example, 56 percent said they are aware of the time a news program comes on, that they arrive home from work at news time, and that they watch the clock. At least one person mentioned using the oven timer as a reminder.

Bush's study also confirmed the findings of others: that television tends to be favored as the source of national and world news, but newspapers are preferred as the source of local news.

Bush also commented that some of the people who get most of their national and world news from television tend to define news narrowly as "happenings." "On reflection, however, as when they are asked why they read a newspaper, they broaden their definition to include ads, society news and general news presented with more details and perspective than television supplies."[28]

Greenberg and Roloff in their literature review[29] ask the question whether the public looks at television and newspapers from the same frame of reference. If they do not, then the credibility research may not be valid. They suggest that "one goes to the newspaper to find out something," but that the public has a more general view of television more related to "the anticipated entertainment that will be received." The people answering the questions of Roper and others may not make the switch from television in general to television news, they reason.

Greenberg and Roloff also hold that the traditional role of the newspaper may make people perceive it as less credible than television. Newspapers often take a stand on community issues and seek to be leaders. People who disagree with it may find it less credible than the relatively bland offerings of television.

They also say that television has two more distinct advantages over newspapers in being credible. Television's pictures provide a feeling of reality that newspapers have not matched. The audience is likely to feel that it has "seen" an event, and so find it impossible not to believe it. Another innate advantage of television is that the audience can associate with the warmth of the personalities delivering the news and thus be persuaded of the credibility of the medium.

Since their stock-in-trade is basically serious news, newspapers are more vulnerable than television and radio to the dilemma posed by the public's general preference for light, entertaining material.

[28]Ibid., p. 39.
[29]Bradley S. Greenberg and Michael E. Roloff, *Mass Media Credibility: Research Results and Critical Issues*, ANPA News Research Bulletin No. 6, November 4, 1974.

Ed Zelman, president of Carl J. Nelson Research, Inc., of Chicago, has this comment about the serious news:

> The so-called hard news simply isn't read by many people. Our surveys consistently show this—dating all the way back to World War II. I think people are fed up with it. Unless there's a substantial victory or defeat in war or a major development in the middle of an important political campaign, not many people will pay attention to it.[30]

What Does It All Add Up To?

In this chapter we have cited figures, studied trends, analyzed research findings. What does all this tell about the audiences of the media? What is it like to live in the giant media womb?

We can make some generalizations:

1. The audiences for all the media are large in terms of numbers. Everyone but a few hermits is in the audience for at least one of the media—and probably for several.

2. Television is used by more people than any of the other media and its viewers include all social groups and classes. It is the most nearly universal medium.

3. People with more education tend to rely more on the printed media than do people with less education, but they spend nearly as much time with television (and generally watch the same programs).

4. Individuals use the media to escape from their immediate surroundings into a dream world, but they find information of practical use.

5. Habit is a strong factor in media use.

6. Paying attention to the media is different things to different individuals. Some give it all their attention, some use it for background for other activities. The media that require reading skill demand the more concentrated attention.

7. Audiences prefer light, amusing material and often ignore the more serious content of newspapers and television.

8. The amount of time spent on the media is linked to the amount of leisure. The more leisure time, the more time will be spent on the media.

[30]Darrell Sifford, "Is Anybody Out There Reading the Hard News?" *APME News*, January 1974, p. 3.

9. Availability is a factor in media use. Many people apparently watch television programs just because the set is on. Some people listen to the radio whenever they are riding in their automobiles. More books are read in urban centers where bookstores and libraries are easily available.

10. The audience seeks (and presumably receives) rewards for using the media, but most individuals are passive in accepting whatever the medium is offering them at the moment.

11. The media are so pervasive that they become an ordinary part of everyday life, and it is possible that many people do not make regular distinctions between the worlds brought to them by the media and their immediate physical environment.

Suggestions for Further Reading

Bower, Robert T. *Television and the Public.* New York: Holt, Rinehart & Winston, 1973.
Reports on an elaborate survey of television viewing habits.

Bush, Chilton R. *How Portland (Ore.) Adults Use TV and Radio for News.* Reston, Va.: American Newspaper Publishers Association, 1972.
Analyzes patterns of media use.

Cherry, Colin. *World Communication: Threat or Promise? A Sociotechnical Approach.* London: John Wiley, 1971.
Provides a philosophical approach to the study of media use.

Greenberg, Bradley, and Michael E. Roloff. *Mass Media Credibility: Research Results and Critical Issues.* Reston, Va.: American Newspaper Publishers Association, 1974.
The authors review some of the literature studying media use and raise basic questions about research directions.

News and Editorial Content and Readership of the Daily Newspaper. Reston, Va.: American Newspaper Publishers Association, 1973.
A useful source of information about newspaper reading habits.

Schramm, Wilbur. "The Nature of News." *Journalism Quarterly* 26 (September 1949): 259–269.
An examination of the nature of news.

Steiner, Gary A. *The People Look at Television: A Study of Audience Attitudes.* New York: A. A. Knopf, 1963.
The prototype study for the Bower work cited above.

Stephenson, William. "The Ludenic Theory of Newsreading." *Journalism Quarterly* 41 (Summer 1964): 367–374.
Develops the "play theory" in a consideration of news appeal.

———. *The Play Theory of Mass Communication.* Chicago: University of Chicago Press, 1967.
A fuller development of the "play theory."

13
Communication and Conduct

"You are what you eat," one writer on nutrition used to proclaim. That may be true for the body, but for the mind and for society it should be "you are what you communicate."

Communication is social interaction. This communication-interaction occurs at many levels and in many ways. At the interpersonal level it is usually spontaneous and seldom analyzed. In mass communication it is often calculated and scrutinized.

But the payoff is in results.

What is the effect of communications on society? More specifically, what is television doing to political institutions, to public taste, to individual patterns of behavior? More specifically still, what is the effect of a single program, article, or speech on a group or individual?

The question of effect lurks behind all others. Are we interested in who controls the media? Why should we care unless the owners affect society through the media they control? Do we care how many murders occur on

"Police Woman"? What difference does it make unless violence makes the audience more violence-prone?

The flood of information from the media somehow changes people and society. What are the effects and what, if anything, should we do about them?

Some Basic Propositions

Many competent researchers have spent a great deal of effort in furthering our understanding of communication and how it changes the world. The work has been done for different purposes, from different perspectives, and with differing methods. But underlying it all are some basic propositions. They concern the nature of (1) the source, (2) the medium, (3) the channel, (4) the message, (5) the receiver, and (6) the surrounding situation.

The Source

Message source is an elusive concept. Researchers may identify sources differently, depending on the frame of reference in which they are working. Receivers, too, may disagree on the source of a message. For example, reporters interviewing a person who has just left the office of the president of the United States are likely to try to find out whether what the person says is a reflection of the president's view. In other words, is the president the real source of the information? If the president is the source, the information is assigned special importance.

One of the common distinctions used to separate propaganda from other kinds of information is whether the true source of information is disclosed. It is one thing to read of the virtues of a new automobile in an advertisement signed by the company that makes it, and quite another to get the same information in a story about new cars in a newspaper or magazine. One can allow for the auto maker's bias in an ad, but one has a right to expect an objective evaluation in an article. If the manufacturer has somehow controlled the information in the article it has become propaganda.

The receiver's perception of source is a critical element in the communication process. The president speaking to the nation over television has a different effect than would a prominent gangster reading the same words. A person may be perceived differently at different times. President Nixon's debacle was caused partly because he was viewed with increasing distrust by the American public in the final months of his presidency.

The source affects a message in interpersonal communication, too.

When a father speaks to a son, the effect is different from what it would if the mother, or a brother, or a stranger said the same thing.

The Medium

As we saw in Chapter 1, a communications medium is the means by which a message is carried through a channel. The mass media, television, radio, newspapers, and the rest, are highly visible institutions, and the public's opinion of them affects the manner in which messages are received. A common question has to do with the credibility of the media. Are newspapers more trustworthy than television as sources of news? Later in this chapter we will see that there is evidence that individuals do receive information differently from the two different media.

Newspapers or television in general may be regarded as reliable or unreliable, and individual units may build up their own reputations. The old *New York Sun* built up and cherished a reputation for accuracy. It was best expressed in a little girl's letter to the editor inquiring if there really was a Santa Claus. The little girl, Virginia Hanlon, said that her father had suggested she write the *Sun* and told her that if something appeared in the *Sun* it was true. The much-quoted editorial, "Yes, Virginia, There Is a Santa Claus," was the paper's response. The editorial reflects an innocent age, but also it indicates the payoff of a newspaper that tried to build itself up as a reliable source of information.

Good will is a dollars and cents asset for any business, often figured in when it is sold. For the media it is especially important.

The Channel

The channel used (sound waves or light waves, for example) controls the manner in which a message enters the human nervous system. As we saw in Chapter 2, Marshall McLuhan believes that the human sense appealed to is a critical factor in the determining of the effect of a message.

Spoken communication has more direct access to the central nervous system than does written or printed communication. As children we learn to decode speech at an earlier age than we learn to decode print. This advantage seems to persist for most people throughout their lives. It is probably reinforced by the fact that speech is a more personal form of communication. And it takes less effort. It is easier to listen than to read; easier to talk than to write.

This distinction appears to be true for nearly everyone, but it is magnified for major segments of the population. Many individuals never learn to read without some effort and never do feel very comfortable with printed information. For the television and film are especially welcome.

The questions for social scientists are fascinating. Will the pervasiveness of television change the nature of our society? Will the struggle to produce a literate population end as most people decide that reading and writing competence is no longer necessary? Will such a change alter the social and political structure of the nation? Marshall McLuhan predicted vast changes. Tom Wolfe summed up the questions by titling his chapter on McLuhan "What If He's Right?"

The Message

Both the content of a message and the way it is delivered affect how it is received.

At one time newspapers made a sharp distinction between news and feature styles of writing. News presentation was supposed to be factual, unadorned with adjectives or expressions of opinion, simple to the point of dullness, with frequent mention of the source of information. In feature articles, writers were given more freedom to use literary devices to lure the reader. They could include description, colorful quotes, maybe even a little opinion to liven their tales.

We have seen how, under the pressure of competition from magazines and then radio and television, newspapers have enlivened their presentation and so recognized that manner affects reception.

Interpersonal styles have much to do with personal effectiveness. Some people are persuasive by nature. Others learn it. Many never take the trouble to learn how to be persuasive. Ray Birdwhistell, who has studied the effect of gestures on interpersonal communication, says that by their gestures and posture many people actually contradict what they are saying with their voices. Birdwhistell has described these people as "masculoids."

The electronic media, particularly television and film, have an advantage over the others because they can make their messages more personal. They can, if they choose, ignore the fact that they are addressing a vast group and speak directly to each listener. Actress Helen Hayes in a radio talk once said that she was not addressing "the vast radio audience," but was just sitting here talking with "you." It is significant that, of all the content of television, it is the advertisers and newscasters who most consistently face into the camera and address the audience directly.

The content of the message also affects how it is received. Some messages are inherently unbelievable. Every once in a while reporters stand on a street corner and try to give away dollar bills. Invariably they get a story from the fact that many passersby simply refuse to believe what they see. Nobody stands on the corner and gives away dollar bills, so even if our eyes tell us it is happening, we had better stay away—there must be a catch.

One researcher found evidence that, at the early stages of the Watergate investigation, many people did not believe what they were being told by the media simply because they found the story unbelievable.[1] It was not a matter of trusting or not trusting the media, the researcher concluded, but simply that the story was too fantastic. We will examine his reasons later in this chapter.

The Receiver

As different filters over a lens can make the sky more blue, the clouds more richly hued, the roses more crimson, so each person has a set of filters that color the information he or she receives. Some people will believe almost anything, others remain skeptical of everything. Some people are moved by appeals to motherhood and homeland; others respond to step-by-step analysis of data; still others respond to neither emotion nor logic.

Discovering a favorite subject matter is sometimes an entree to someone else's mind. When strangers find themselves together at a party there is a period when they feel around for a conversational subject of common interest. Usually it starts out with very general themes: the weather, food, and high prices.

Sometimes an object in their presence provides a touchstone. There are dangers. It is not safe to comment on the shiny bald head of the man across the room unless you are sure that man is not a relative or close friend of the person you are talking to. Sometimes objects are displayed so that people can use them to bridge conversational gaps. Such a "conversation piece" is defined by one dictionary as "an article of furniture, bric-a-brac, etc. that arouses comment or special interest in a room."

Eventually two people can usually find some subject in which both have some interest. It may be needlepoint, raising children, or the Ming Dynasty. If some such common subject matter does not appear, one or the other of our two trapped nonconversationalists is sure to sidle off with a vague wave toward the refreshment table or the bald-headed man across the room.

Occasionally the real communication process is not revealed by the words being used. A man and a woman may find each other so interesting that a question like "Do you think it will rain?" is charged with emotional overtones. The real message is being carried not by the words, but by intonation, posture, gesture, or eyelash movement.

Each of us examines incoming messages through our particular set of filters. We accept, reject, and modify according to our preconceptions. The nature of the receiver is clearly a critical factor in assessing the effects of any message.

[1] Alex S. Edelstein, *Media Credibility and the Believability of Watergate*, ANPA News Research Bulletin No. 1, January 10, 1974.

The Surrounding Situation

In interpersonal communication we respond differently, depending upon whether we are talking to one person, to a small group, or to many people.

The media vary in their ability to control the situation in which their messages are received. Motion picture producers, before the days of television, could be quite sure that their product would be viewed by a group in a darkened theater. Since there is nothing else to look at under those circumstances, producers could expect undivided attention and some interaction in each audience that viewed their film. The situation changes drastically when the same film is shown on television. It may be viewed in small groups or by isolated individuals. It will be interrupted by commercials. Viewers are sitting in their homes with all the attendant distractions. Surely the different viewing situation has some effect on the response of the viewers, and surely film producers would like to take that into account when they produce the film.

The audience receiving situation for radio has changed considerably since television's arrival. When radio had the broadcast field to itself it was often the center for group listening in the evening; now it has become more personal and portable, as we noticed in Chapter 12. It is more likely now that one person by himself or herself is listening, whether it is the commuter on the way to work in an automobile or the teenager alone in his or her room. There is a physical manifestation of this change in the way radio receivers are packaged. In the late twenties and early thirties radio sets were often built into impressive cabinets that occupied prominent places in many living rooms. Now radios are more likely to be hidden behind car dashboards, or combined with clocks in small portable enclosures, or even fitted into dolls or balls as novelties.

Television cabinetry is undergoing something of the same change. While expensive cabinets are still the center of many living rooms, others are becoming less obtrusive. Many sets are smaller, more portable, and less ornate. In this utilitarian mien they turn up in kitchens, dens, and bedrooms. As more and more families acquire two and three sets, television, too, may become a more personal medium. We shall examine some of the effects of this change in connection with children's viewing a little later, but the effect on the manner in which television's multitude of messages are received is still largely a matter of conjecture.

Researchers in the employ of newspapers have found that many readers put aside regular times when they read the paper. Such a period may be before or after dinner or late at night when they can be alone. Such reading environments differ considerably from that of the urban breadwinner who reads his or her daily paper while hanging on the strap of a subway car or in the crowded confines of a Penn Central, Illinois Central, or BART commuter train.

Again, we must admit that we know little about the manner in which the different situations affect the manner in which the message is received. We do know that a tabloid is easier to handle in the rush-hour crowd of a subway train, and many people may read the tabloids because of that convenience.

To summarize, the effect of a message is controlled by the nature of the communicator, of the medium, of the channels used, of the message, of the receiver, and of the situation. Since all these variable factors involve many subvariables, it is easy to understand why the effects of communication are difficult to analyze.

We will need to keep these variables in mind as we examine some of the social effects of the media.

Social Effects of the Media

Five main theories help to explain some of the less obvious social effects of the media. They have to do with (1) social regularity, (2) status conferral, (3) agenda-setting, (4) narcotization (actually dysfunction), and (5) surveillance of the environment.

Social Regularity

Regularity means doing the expected, normal thing. Generally when we walk as well as when we drive we use the right side of the right of way, and give way in that direction when we meet another. Most persons dress in a way that is acceptable to their peers. Most refrain from stealing and otherwise respect the property of others. All of these actions are examples of social regularity—doing things as the people around us expect us to do them.

Why do we do things in accepted ways? Generally because we are rewarded for such conduct. By their friendly attitude, by accepting us in their groups, others express their approval of our conduct. If the conduct involves some sacrifice on our part, such as giving up a golf game to coach a Little League team, others may express their approval in words, or even vote us a badge of merit or life membership in the PTA at the end of our period of service.

The media, too, provide reinforcement for socially accepted conduct. They tell us about boys and girls and impecunious old ladies, who, upon finding large sums of money, turn them over to the police for return to their rightful owners. By their accounts of arrests for selling drugs they constantly remind us of the fate of transgressors. They help us to stay sober by recounting the punishment of those arrested for drunk driving or public intoxication. They remind us of the rewards of a lifetime of devoted labor by chronicling the eulogies and gold watches awarded to the faithful at the end of fifty years of service. All in all, they promote social regularity by reminding us, day in and day out, of the rewards of regularity and the penalties for its lack.

This theory holds up well for the news and public affairs content of the media. Some of the counterculture media do not promote the regularity of the general culture, but they do tend to enforce the regularity of their own subcultures. The entertainment content of the media does not always provide such reinforcement of regularity. A common criticism is that television and films overemphasize violence and do not sufficiently point out that an unfortunate end comes to those who resort to it. We will reserve a discussion of that particular maggots' nest for the last pages of this chapter.

Status Conferral

Another commonly accepted function of the media is that of raising certain individuals into prominence and thus putting them into an advantageous position for leadership and personal profit. We discussed this status-conferral function in Chapter 9. It is particularly important in the context in which it was discussed there—political activity—but it functions in many other areas too. Society pages, a disappearing feature of American newspapers, were once the happy preserve of the rich and the well connected. Many newspapers preached democracy in their editorial columns, but devoted fawning coverage to the doings of a supposed elite on their society pages. Thus bolstered by constant public deference, the privileged few were encouraged in their belief in their own superiority. Worse, the general public was bamboozled into a half-hearted admission of the divine right of the dowagers and dandies.

Such blind acceptance of whatever exists is another way in which the media sometimes promote institutions that have long outlived their utility.

Agenda-setting

As we observed earlier in connection with politics, the media help to decide what people talk about and thus what they think about. This general idea has been discussed under a number of names. Its latest sobriquet is agenda-setting. In certain areas of discussion the media and the general public are talking about the same things. This is hardly a revolutionary concept, but it is worth examining a bit. The theory holds that, while the media often do not make up peoples' minds on public issues, they do set the stage for discussion and decision by deciding what people will talk about. Thus they may effectively block a decision on an issue simply by ignoring it. The general public remains ignorant of it. Leaders are probably aware of it, but such is the inertia of government that they can do nothing about it without some public pressure.

Thus the media are in a powerful position, according to this theory, because they control what people will talk about, think about, and thus what issues will receive public attention and progress to some kind of resolution.

This theory rids the media of the onus of making decisions in the name of the public, but it still ascribes much significance to their role. Since the media cannot pay attention to every facet of life something like this must occur. Walter Lippmann pictured it graphically years ago when he suggested that the news media are like searchlights that send their beams out over the countryside and illuminate first one, then another aspect of the landscape, holding each in their light for a moment or two, then moving on.

What determines the particular situation or events that the media illuminate? Are the media the energizing agent when an issue comes to the fore, or are they responding to an interest they see in their audiences?

The relationship between media, issue, and audience is a circular one. It is seldom that the media can or will combine their efforts so effectively that a single issue is forced into prominence. It is more common for one element of the media to bring an issue to the fore more tentatively. If public discussion ensues other media pick it up, and the issue stays in the public mind. Since the media live on public interest they cannot afford to stay with a single issue or group of issues too long if the public shows little interest.

It is not just the agenda-setting function of the media that puts issues on the front burner. It is a process that occurs somewhere in the chemistry of the interaction between the media and their audiences.

The Narcotizing Dysfunction

Still another effect of the media results not from a function at all, but just the opposite. That explains its exotic name—the narcotizing dysfunction.

The media do their job so well, according to this theory, that they become an end in themselves instead of a means to an end. They charm their audiences so that people think they have done their duty by simply paying attention to the media. Citizens become "well informed" and spend so much time doing so that they do not have time to act upon the information they have absorbed.

At their worst the media act like a drug. Semanticist S. I. Hayakawa, former president of San Francisco State College, put the extreme view into words: "The kinship of the LSD and other drug experiences with television is glaringly obvious: both depend upon turning on and passively waiting for something beautiful to happen."[2]

[2]Gerald S. Lesser, *Children and Television* (New York: Random House, 1974), p. 29. Quoted from a 1969 article in the *Boston Globe*.

Communication and Conduct

Sociologists Paul F. Lazarsfeld and Robert K. Merton take a more conservative view than Hayakawa, but still regard the problem of passivity as serious:

> The individual reads accounts of issues and problems and may even discuss alternative lines of action. But this rather intellectualized, rather remote connection with organized social action is not activated. The interested and informed citizen can congratulate himself on his lofty state of interest and information and neglect to see that he has abstained from decision and action. . . . He comes to mistake *knowing* about problems of the day for doing something about them.[3]

In *Future Shock*[4] Alvin Toffler relates onrushing events and the speed with which the media force details onto their audience to something akin to the narcotizing dysfunction. He suggests that too many messages arriving too rapidly will produce information overload and throw people into a state of shock wherein they are incapable of any intelligent action. The Lazarsfeld and Merton theory, although less dramatic, is more plausible. Before they are sent into shock by an information overload most individuals are likely to ignore some of the information and spend so much time intellectualizing about the remainder that they separate themselves from the reality of events.

Surveillance

Another common theory of the function of the media concerns their role in surveillance of the environment. This theory sees the media as a kind of early-warning radar system for their audiences. They give advance warning about events that may affect the lives of readers and listeners. Since they serve many people the media often cannot give their audiences all the information they need about developments, but they provide an alert so that people with special information needs can go to other sources for details.

The five theories we have considered about the effects of the media are promoting social regularity, raising individuals to positions of leadership, setting the agenda for public discussion, narcotizing the audience, and surveying the environment. Taken together only the narcotizing dysfunction seems to be in contradiction with the others. This is not a bad average considering the tremendously varied factors that must enter into any analysis of the effects of the media.

[3]Paul F. Lazarsfeld and Robert K. Merton, "Mass Communication, Popular Taste and Organized Social Action," in *Mass Communications*, 2nd ed., ed. Wilbur Schramm (Urbana: University of Illinois Press, 1960), p. 502.
[4]Alvin Toffler, *Future Shock* (New York: Random House, 1970).

It is plain enough that different individuals use the media for different purposes. Some may use it as a means of escaping reality while others may be using it to get close to the world of events. In other words, some may be using the media to drop out while others may be using them as steppingstones to power.

The media do different jobs for different people. But usually they provide a service for society. Any society has to be based on an area of commonality, and, when societies get as large as the United States, the media are the only hope for providing it.

These theories concern the effects the media have. We will now consider theories about how the media achieve their effects.

Puppets or People?

At one time many persons held the alarming theory that the mass media controlled their audiences like puppets on a string. A direct line of influence stretched from each newspaper office or radio station (or more likely from some "propagandist") to every reader or listener, giving the media a stranglehold on the public mind. This notion of direct action was dubbed the "hypodermic theory."

Some supporting evidence was offered. Orson Welles had unwittingly thrown the nation into a panic when he broadcast a radio adaptation of H. G. Wells's novel *War of the Worlds* on Halloween night, October 31, 1938. Using a simulated news format Welles had actors sounding like news announcers at remote points detailing the arrival of the dreaded little men in their space ships. Despite announcements that it was all in fun, people began tidying up their lives for the final accounting, setting up expeditions to meet the intruders, or just plain fleeing for their lives.

One New Jersey housewife later told an interviewer: "We decided to get out. We took blankets and my granddaughter wanted to take the cat and the canary. We were outside the garage when the neighbor's boy came back and told us it was a play."[5]

Hadley Cantril, a social psychologist at Princeton, conducted a study of the event that has become a classic. He concluded that, of the estimated 6 million people who heard the broadcast, at least 1 million "became frightened or disturbed." Cantril added: "Long before the broadcast ended people all over the United States were praying, crying, fleeing frantically to escape death from the Martians." He remarks in another place: "Probably never before have so many people in all walks of life and in all parts of

[5]Hadley Cantril, *The Invasion from Mars* (Princeton: Princeton University Press, 1940), pp. 47–48.

the country become so suddenly and so intensely disturbed as they did on this night."[6]

Hitler's hypnotic tirades on radio and the great military spectacles he provided for the German public were also cited as evidence of the potentially devastating power of the mass media.

But the Martian invasion was an exception, although a frightening one, and Hitler had help from other quarters than the mass media alone.

A landmark study[7] of voting in the 1940 election turned up additional evidence. Instead of influence proceeding in a straight line from the media to each individual voter, various factors intervened. These factors, called *intervening variables*, were usually conversations with other people. Such personal contacts were often the deciding factor in how people voted.

Such studies support the theory that the more personal media are usually the more persuasive ones. Nothing can be more personal than a family member or close friend or neighbor, but the media appear to differ in the extent to which their impact is personal. Television, as we have noticed, tends to benefit from its ability to simulate personal communication. The 1940 study found that specialized magazines, despite their smaller circulations, were mentioned as frequently as those of general circulation as reasons for switching from one candidate to another.

In short, other people and the more personal media are often more influential than the mass media. This emphasizes once again the need to consider many factors in order to assess the effects of communication.

Believability of the Media

Many experiments indicate that the extent to which a person believes a given bit of information depends in part on his or her perception of the source. As the voting studies indicated, a story from a trustworthy friend may gain more credence than would the same information from a newspaper or broadcast. On the other hand, one of the media may be such a credible source that its account of an event is considered more trustworthy than an acquaintance's firsthand recital.

Carl I. Hovland and others in a series of experiments at Yale found that information was more likely to influence opinions if it was said to come from an authoritative source. Not all studies came out that way and the effect was not permanent, but the pattern was clearly established.

[6]Ibid., pp. 47 and vii.
[7]Paul F. Lazarsfeld, Bernard Berelson, and Helen Gaudet, *The People's Choice* (New York: Duell, Sloan and Pearce, 1944).

After studying the same problem in a different setting, Alex Edelstein, a University of Washington researcher, concluded that the image of the source is not the most important factor to a person who intends to use information as the basis for decision. Edelstein asked people in Longview, Washington, what source was most important in providing information about Watergate. Then he asked why. After interpreting the "whys" he came to this conclusion:

> The evidence seems to be that most people can shake off the "image" of any particular institutional source of communication as irrelevant, whether it is in learning something useful from an individual, a newspaper or a television network. In short, we don't know how relevant source images, in the abstract, are to the individual who is confronting a problem with which he is trying to cope. . . . source credibility is not the most critical variable at the point of decision-making, but . . . elements of content availability and channel dimensionalities are of equal or greater significance.[8]

Edelstein suggests that audiences use five criteria in assessing the utility of the media: completeness, integration, and comprehension of content; availability; "channel dimensionalities" (for example, the advantages of watching an event on television as opposed to reading about it in the newspaper); trustworthiness; and reliability.

After studying reactions to Watergate news Edelstein concluded that the issue was credulity of the audience rather than credibility of the media. He put it this way:

> Rather than media credibility being the central problem in relation to Watergate—and by inference, in relation to other social and political events—the more significant problem was the capacity of people to believe or disbelieve Watergate actors and events. Thus the issue was credulity rather than credibility or lack of credibility of the media.[9]

Another strategy used to discover how people evaluate their media has been to ask individuals to rate their "ideal" station or publication. They are asked to check the position of this ideal on a series of scales composed of opposite adjectives, such as fair-unfair. Statistical analysis determines what groups of adjective pairs fit together to form evaluative factors.

One national study produced five factors that explained 75 percent of the variance in judgment by the public of the ideal magazine, newspaper, radio station, and television station.

Here are the five factors and their components:

[8]Alex S. Edelstein, quoted in Bradley S. Greenberg and Michael E. Roloff, *Mass Media Credibility: Research Results and Critical Issues*, ANPA Research Bulletin No. 6, November 4, 1974, p. 6.
[9]Edelstein, *Media Credibility*, p. 29.

General evaluation: pleasant-unpleasant, valuable-worthless, important-unimportant, interesting-boring
Ethical evaluation: fair-unfair, truthful-untruthful, accurate-inaccurate, unbiased-biased, responsible-unresponsible
Stylistic: exciting-dull, fresh-stale, easy-difficult, neat-messy, colorful-colorless
Potency: bold-timid, powerful-weak, loud-soft
Activity: tense-relaxed, active-passive, modern-old fashioned[10]

In general terms this means that the concepts listed here are largely the ones that people keep in mind, consciously or unconsciously, when they form an opinion of one of the media. Other studies using the same general method have turned up fairly comparable figures.

Edelstein's studies clearly point up the idea that a person receiving information judges it by its plausibility, its completeness, the manner in which it is organized, and related factors. They demonstrated that the individual characteristics of each member of the audience are critical in media effects. The studies that analyze factors people consider in evaluating their media show that, despite individual differences, people do tend to agree on which are most important.

Reassured by this conclusion we can go on to consider what people say when asked which media they find most trustworthy.

Funds for some of the research into these questions have been supplied by newspapers and broadcasters. Each industry, quite naturally, would like to prove itself the most "credible." It is a matter of prestige and of profit. The payoff comes in the fierce competition for advertising dollars. Space or time salespersons make more sales if they can assure their customers that the medium they represent is the most credible. It is natural to think that an ad will be more effective if it appears in the most trustworthy medium.

Ad salespersons must content themselves with trumpeting whatever advantages they can find for their medium. Students interested in communications must concern themselves with the subtleties. One such subtle distinction was found by the study just cited that produced the five factors in media evaluation. Percy Tannenbaum and Jack McLeod, the authors of the study, found that the public applies these factors differently to each medium. They sorted out the amount of emphasis put on each of the five factors for print and broadcast media.

Table 13.1 shows their findings. They indicate that people judge the print media more on the basis of ethical standards while they place more importance on potency and activity in evaluating the broadcast media.

---

[10]Percy H. Tannenbaum and Jack M. McLeod, "Public Images of Mass Media Institutions," *Paul J. Deutschmann Memorial Papers in Mass Communications Research*, December 1963, pp. 51–60. Quoted in Greenberg and Roloff, *Mass Media Credibility*, p. 5.

The findings indicate that each medium may play quite a different role in the lives of most people. The blanket classification "communications media" for newspapers and television, for example, is convenient, but it may help us to forget that they provide quite different experiences, that they are used differently by the public, and that the public's view of them is not based entirely on the same considerations.

An additional problem in interpreting research results is that it is difficult to know exactly what a question means to a person trying to answer it. Social scientists have demonstrated that a slightly different wording can produce quite different answers.

People respond differently, too, if they are asked to differentiate between local and nonlocal news. A series of studies has shown that people tend to use newspapers more than television for local news and to trust them more. The closer to home an event is, the better newspapers fare in such studies.

Another not so strange finding is that people generally tend to have more confidence in the particular medium they use most. One study, for instance, reported that 81 percent of those who said they used television most also put more faith in that medium. Only 14 percent of the heavy television users put more faith in newspapers. On the other hand, 48 percent of the heavy newspaper users also put most faith in it, while 37 percent of that group found television more credible.[11]

Table 13.1 Factors in Evaluation of Print and Broadcast Media

	Print	Broadcast
General Evaluative	37.6%	41.0%
Ethical Evaluative	20.6	8.0
Stylistic Evaluative	17.0	13.6
Potency	13.7	21.3
Activity	11.1	16.1

Source: Percy H. Tannenbaum and Jack M. McLeod, "Public Images of Mass Media Institutions," *Paul J. Deutschmann Memorial Papers in Mass Communications Research*, December 1963, pp. 51–60. Quoted in Bradley S. Greenberg and Michael E. Roloff, *Mass Media Credibility: Research Results and Critical Issues*, ANPA Research Bulletin No. 6, November 4, 1974, p. 6. Reprinted with permission.

[11]Richard F. Carter and Bradley S. Greenberg, "Newspapers or Television: 'Which Do You Believe?'" *Journalism Quarterly* 42 (Winter 1965): 28–34.

After an extensive review of the literature Bradley Greenberg and Michael Roloff found that certain demographic characteristics related to belief in newspapers or television:

1. Young people find newspapers less credible, older ones find the newspaper more useful.
2. Women are more oriented to TV, and men to the newspaper, in both credibility and usage.
3. The more educated, the higher in SES [socioeconomic status], and the socially upward-mobile are more reliant on the print media. They may trust them more also.[12]

Despite a considerable amount of research, many questions still need answers. One of the most critical questions is whether print and electronic media are sufficiently similar that attempts to compare them on a credibility scale have any real meaning. Television, for example, is heavily weighted toward entertainment. Can many people separate the entertainment and news function of television sufficiently to compare it with news in other media?

Is it possible to compare a medium that offers firsthand views of events in the making with one that relies on printed accounts? Is it possible, for example, for an individual to compare the "believability" of a televised press conference in which he or she has seen and heard the president speaking with a printed account of that same event? Does the many-channeled television automatically provide for a viewer a sensation of authenticity that cannot be matched except by film or firsthand experience in the event itself?

Greenberg and Roloff suggest that future studies might be more effective if the comparisons they seek to make are more specific. For example, instead of comparing a general idea like the believability of television versus newspaper news, they suggest that the local news on a specific local channel might be compared with the local news in the newspaper a person usually reads. Greenberg and Roloff also suggest explorations of the effect of immediate news of television compared with the later but more detailed information that appears in newspapers.

What is the image of television? Of newspapers? Of radio and magazines? The answers have not been found, but researchers are finding better ways to ask the questions.

Meantime, we will take a look at the bogeyman of all the media, but that currently bothers television more than the others—the portrayal of violence.

[12]Greenberg and Roloff, *Mass Media Credibility*, p. 27.

From the Washington *Star*, January 16, 1976. Reprinted by permission of the Washington Star Syndicate, Inc.

Children, Violence, and the Media

Two tales, one a bit suspect, will get us to the problem.

The first is of a farmer who lived by himself and, beset by loneliness, bought a parrot. To achieve some companionship from the bird the farmer resolved to teach it to talk, starting with the word *uncle.* He sat up during the long winter nights ordering, begging the bird to say "uncle." Never a word from the parrot. Finally the farmer decided on sterner measures. He got a stick, told the bird to "say uncle," and whacked the bird beside the head at every refusal. Still no results.

Finally the farmer gave up and threw the parrot into the chicken coop. Hearing a commotion he went back and opened the door to find the parrot with a stick in his claw, shouting "say uncle" and whacking the bewildered chickens across the beak.

More prosaic, but more "credible" is the report of laboratory cats that were placed so they could watch as other cats, already trained, pressed a lever as a light came on and were rewarded with food. The cats that had an opportunity to observe firsthand learned the routine faster than those that had not had the chance to watch.[13]

Both stories illustrate the "monkey see, monkey do" syndrome. People, as well as parrots and cats, tend to imitate.

Especially children.

This explains the worry and the fury that center around children, violence, and television. Are we, by allowing children to watch excessive violence on television, bringing up new generations each more violence-prone than the last?

[13]Quoted in Gerald S. Lesser, *Children and Television* (New York: Random House, 1974). The parrot story is from Albert Bandura; the cat experiment was by E. R. John, P. Chessler, F. Barlett, and I. Victor.

Communication and Conduct

Supporters of the theory can build up a frightening case. They do it by citing examples. For instance:

- A seven-year-old boy sprinkled ground glass in the stew. He wondered if it would work as well at home as on television. His plan was discovered before he got his answer.
- A nine-year-old in Massachusetts bringing home a bad report card suggested to his father that they send his teacher a box of poisoned candy. "It's easy, Dad," he said, pointing out that the plot had worked beautifully on television.
- An eleven-year-old, aided by a seven-year-old friend, burglarized Long Island homes, taking $1,000 in cash and other items. Television had taught him the techniques, he said.

The modeling effect works. Some children are going to imitate the bad things they see on television. Some grownups do, too.

Do children and adults imitate the good things they see on television? Presumably they do, for there is no reason to believe that the modeling effect works only for antisocial behavior.

But the argument goes, there is much more bad than good on television, so television is destructive.

"Bad" content usually means graphic portrayal of crime and violence and material that is thought to be too sexually explicit. Again, the evidence is not hard to find.

The National Association for Better Radio and Television stated that a child between the ages of five and fifteen sees 13,400 persons destroyed by violence on television.

George Gerbner of the University of Pennsylvania, after an elaborate study of television violence, found that eight in ten television dramas portrayed scenes of violence, with violent episodes averaging about five per play and eight per hour. And violence increased in children's programs:

> The average cartoon hour in 1967 contained more than three times as many violent episodes as the adult dramatic hour. The trend toward shorter plays sandwiched between frequent commercials on fast-moving cartoon programs further increased the saturation. By 1969, with a violent episode at least every two minutes in all Saturday morning cartoon programming (including the least violent and including commercial time), and with adult drama becoming less saturated with violence, the average cartoon hour had nearly six times the violence rate of the average adult television drama hour, and nearly 12 times the violence rate of the average movie hour.[14]

[14]George Gerbner, "The Structure and Process of Television Program Content Regulation in the United States" in *Television and Social Behavior. Vol. I; Media Content and Control,* eds. G. A. Comstock and E. A. Rubinstein (Washington, D.C.: U.S. Government Printing Office, 1972). Quoted in Robert M. Liebert, John M. Neale, and Emily S. Davidson, *The Early Window* (New York: Pergamon Press, 1973), p. 24.

The cycle of violence dipped a bit in the mid-1970's. Gerbner, working with Larry Gross, also of the University of Pennsylvania, found violence in 73 percent of the television programs studied in a 1973–1974 period. Prime-time violence was down to 54 percent of the television dramas. But studies indicated that some heavy television watchers were more fearful and that others were less sensitive to violence in their own lives.

Because the cause-effect relationship is difficult to establish researchers often cannot make broad generalizations even after exhaustive studies. Often it is relatively easy to point out that two things go together. For example, a child may commit a violent act after seeing a similar act on television. Was the program the cause? It may have been. On the other hand, the child might have done something similar without exposure to television.

Certain individuals are more likely than others to explode into violence. Such action may be triggered by television or by other experiences. Obviously not all of society's violence can be blamed on television.

The other media are criticized in the same way. It is not uncommon for investigators to find newspaper accounts of garish crimes in the possession of criminals.

News accounts of dramatic crimes sometimes appear to generate a spate of similar acts. Clarence Kelley, director of the FBI, cites the case of a "D. B. Cooper" who hijacked an airplane bound for Seattle on November 24, 1971, then makes this comment:

> When Cooper parachuted from that airplane and vanished, he fired the imagination of news reporters and a lot of impressionable people. Vast quantities of publicity made his exploit seem bigger than life.
>
> Of course, there had been other aircraft hijackings, but this was the first extortion hijacking with a parachute embellishment. Cooper became a folk hero. A song was written about him, and T-shirts bearing his name were peddled.
>
> However, the really significant aspect of all this was, soon after Cooper's highly publicized episode, there were 15 attempted skyjackings, in which skyjackers demanded parachutes as well as money. The detailed television and newspaper accounts had been instructive as well as stimulating.[15]

News as well as entertainment content of the media creates the modeling effect. Individuals who are on the brink of some antisocial act may be pushed into it by information from the media. Comic books, films, plays, and novels have been accused of the same effects. Plato posed the same question in *The Republic*:

[15]Clarence Kelley, "Television Is Armed and Dangerous," *TV Guide*, March 8, 1975, p. 6.

And shall we just carelessly allow children to hear any casual tales which may be devised by casual persons, and to receive in their minds for the most part the very opposite of those which we would wish them to have when they are grown up?

The problem has been studied on a grand scale, both in Great Britain and the United States. Britain's early large-scale study was done in the mid-1950's. At that time not all of Britain was served by television, so it was possible to compare viewers and nonviewers and, by follow-up interviewing, to compare children's habits before and after television became available to them.

With the restraint that was to become typical of later studies in the same area, the authors concluded:

> All in all, the values of television can make an impact if they are consistently presented in dramatic form, and if they touch on ideas or values for which the child is emotionally ready. Extrapolating from these findings, one would expect that in the crime and detective series the constant display of aggression by both the criminal and the upholder of the law would also make an impact on those children sensitized to such cues.[16]

It was found that children tended to become more frightened when viewing in the dark and when no adult was in the room. Television was found to be very similar to movies and radio "in the amount of fear it engendered and in the types of programmes which children found frightening."

The British researchers found little evidence that children who watched television were more aggressive or maladjusted than those who did not. But they found no support for the catharsis theory, that viewing violence drains away latent tendencies toward violence by providing vicarious experience.

Stylized presentations such as Westerns were found to be less disturbing than other types of violence. Detective programs, which sometimes develop the character of the criminal and arouse sympathy, were often more disturbing to children than programs featuring black and white one-dimensional characters, such as Westerns. Children were less bothered by violence in unfamiliar settings, apparently because they were less likely to think such things could occur in their neighborhood. A series with familiar patterns and expected endings as well as a regular hero also made violence less disturbing to children.

This study, conducted in the early days of television in Britain when programs were less violent than those in the United States today, an-

---

[16]Hilde T. Himmelweit, A. N. Oppenheim, and Pamela Vince, *Television and the Child* (London: Oxford University Press, 1958), p. 18.

swered questions people were asking about the general effects of television on children.

The more recent studies in the United States have focused more sharply on one aspect of television effect: does it, through violence, tend to increase the amount of violence in society?

Certainly the incidence of violence in the United States is on the increase, although this increase began long before the days of television, and other factors are partly responsible for it. The number of violent crimes in the United States increased more than 200 percent from 1960 to 1973, and the crime rate is increasing at several times the rate of the population increase. Under these circumstances it is no wonder that efforts have been made to assess the effects of television violence.

America's most massive study of television and violence was set in motion in 1969 by a letter from Senator John O. Pastore, chairman of the Senate Subcommittee on Communications of the Senate Commerce Committee, to then Secretary of Health, Education, and Welfare Robert Finch. Senator Pastore said, "I am exceedingly troubled by the lack of any definitive information which would help resolve the question of whether there is a causal connection between televised crime and violence and antisocial behavior of individuals, especially children."[17]

Senator Pastore went on to request Secretary Finch to direct the surgeon general to appoint a committee of distinguished men and women to "devise techniques and to conduct a study . . . which will establish scientifically insofar as possible what harmful effects, if any, these programs have on children."

The resulting study took three years and 1 million dollars. Its meaning is still being debated.

Twenty-three studies were funded. The researchers who conducted them were free to report and interpret their findings in whatever way seemed suitable to them. The committee submitted them along with its report. The entire report was finally published by the U.S. Government Printing Office in seven volumes. Some difference in interpretation of such a mass of information was inevitable. Given the powerful conflicting interests involved it was perhaps inevitable, too, that the differences would lead to bitter accusations. The final report was a result of many compromises between members of the commission, who felt a special loyalty to the broadcast industry, and the representatives of the general public.

The hedging resulted in misunderstanding of the meaning of the report, and several of the researchers who had contributed studies later indicated in response to a questionnaire that they felt their work had been misinterpreted.[18]

[17]Quoted in Liebert, Neale, and Davidson, *Early Window*, p. 149.
[18]Matilda B. Paisley, *Social Policy Research and the Realities of the System: Violence Done to TV Research*, Stanford University, Institute of Communication Research, 1972.

Surgeon General Steinfeld made his interpretation clear enough in testimony before Senator Pastore's committee:

> Certainly my interpretation is that there is a causative relationship between televised violence and subsequent antisocial behavior, and that the evidence is strong enough that it requires some action on the part of responsible authorities, the TV industry, the Government, the citizens.[19]

In 1975 *TV Guide*[20] magazine, in a special issue devoted to television violence, quoted industry executives and others. Here are some excerpts. Frederick S. Pierce, president ABC Television:

> Violence on television continues to be a subject of major concern to all broadcasters. . . . Are there too many police or detective "action" series on television? The answer is probably yes and I look for more comedy, dramatic and variety series in the season ahead.

Robert T. Howard, president, NBC-TV Network:

> Although findings have not been conclusive, the possibility that televised violence may influence behavior, particularly in the young, cannot be ignored. . . . While television violence may be an inflated issue, it is still something that every broadcaster who believes in social responsibility must take seriously.

Robert D. Wood, president, CBS-TV Network:

> We at CBS have long been involved in a continuing examination of violence in television entertainment . . . our goal is to be responsive to potential problems without . . . destroying the creative freedom.

Richard E. Wiley, chairman, Federal Communications Commission:

> I am not in a position to resolve the scientific dispute [about the effects of televised violence], but I do share Dr. Steinfeld's conclusion that the evidence is clear enough to justify changes in broadcast-industry practices. I am convinced, however, that these changes should be brought about by reforms within the industry itself and not by the adoption of rigid governmental standards.

Torbert H. Macdonald, chairman, House Subcommittee on Communications:

[19]Quoted in Liebert, Neale, and Davidson, *Early Window*, p. 155.
[20]*TV Guide*, June 14, 1975.

Violence on television is a serious problem which is getting worse instead of better, despite repeated promises by the networks to the contrary.

John O. Pastore, chairman, Senate Subcommittee on Communications:

Violence on television and the effect that it has upon young minds is not a figment of my imagination. All you have to do is watch the tube and you can understand it. . . . In 1972—when the Surgeon General appeared before our committee—he substantiated these fears and declared in no uncertain terms that there is a causal relationship between violence on television and the behavior of children. Subsequent research has further confirmed the validity of this conclusion.

After a study done in England during the mid-1970's Bradley Greenberg concluded:

There is a relationship between watching programs high in violent themes and aggressive attitudes . . . this relationship is a moderate one at best, and one certainly cannot attribute a child's aggression solely, or largely, to watching TV violence.[21]

This quotation is instructive for its restraint. The author uses the word *relationship*, not the word *cause*. He is careful to point out that the relationship is "moderate."

There is good reason for restraint in judgment on this matter, and the reason is that our information is scanty. Educational psychologist Gerald S. Lesser comments "Researchers have not taken much interest in television's effects upon children; consequently our knowledge is pitifully thin." In a footnote he mentions that a bibliography prepared for the National Institute of Mental Health lists 496 studies, then comments: "They provide little illumination."[22]

The Needle Goes Up

Why violence? Simple. "Every time you have violence the needle goes up."

Roy Huggins gave that direct explanation to King Features Syndicate columnist Nicholas Von Hoffman. The needle Huggins was talking about is the meter that registers response from experimental audiences watch-

[21]Bradley S. Greenberg, "British Children and Televised Violence," *Public Opinion Quarterly* 38 (Winter 1975): p. 545.
[22]Lesser, *Children and Television*, p. 235.

ing test films. If they like what they see they twist their dial to "good," which pushes up the needle.

Enthusiastic audience reaction plus competition make it hard for television producers to provide anything but violence. Huggins said it this way: "The man who finds the way to get around the standards will beat you in the ratings."

Not too complicated, is it? Producers know audiences like violence. If one producer does not provide it another one will, and whoever does it will get the audiences.

Robert Blake, star of "Baretta," complained to Von Hoffman that politicians simply keep raising the violence issue to get votes. "There's no statistic I've ever seen or read that indicates any kind of correlation between what people see and their eventual behavior," Blake said. "We've been slaughtering Indians for a long time. We did it before radio and television."

The government of Ontario is not reassured by the cowboy and Indian tradition. In April 1975 Premier William Davis appointed a Royal Commission to determine whether there was a link between violent movies and television programs and a rising crime rate. "We believe," he said, "there is a danger . . . that the increasing exposure to young or impressionable minds of extreme violence may have a relationship to violence in the community."[23]

A More Cheerful View

Gerald Lesser, chairman of the board of directors of Children's Television Workshop, sees some hope in the success of the workshop's premier production, "Sesame Street." He points out that "Sesame Street" attracted large numbers of children even though it did not disguise its educational purpose. Thus it proved that education can be entertaining, and that good entertainment can be educational. Not a startling discovery, but one that had heretofore been demonstrated on only a small scale and in isolated instances. The reality of the education-entertainment relationship is that education has to be at least a little entertaining, and that entertainment is almost sure to provide at least a little education.

Another lesson of "Sesame Street" is that children can learn from television. This is hardly a new thought to anyone who has heard tots chanting the latest detergent commercial, but it takes on a new meaning when the material learned is something that schools have been trying to put over with sometimes limited success.

[23]United Press International dispatch in the *Lexington* (Kentucky) *Leader*, April 15, 1975.

Perhaps the grimmest lesson from "Sesame Street" is that dollars call the tune in educational as in commercial television. Joan Ganz Cooney, president of the Children's Television Workshop, and Lloyd N. Morrisett, chairman of the workshop's board of trustees and president of the Markle Foundation, raised 8 million dollars to provide planning time and production for the first programs. This put educational television on a par, for once, with commercial television.

Another hopeful sign from "Sesame Street" is an indication of the possibility that children and grownups, too, if given the chance might not insist on violence and the bizarre in their programs.

Lesser calls it the "power of the ordinary." He describes a little girl exploring the fuzz on a puppet; a small boy recovering his confidence after he momentarily forgot a number; a little girl taking pleasure in being able to supply names in both English and Spanish. Lesser comments:

> For children, television can do more than supply drama. It can show them that there are other people out there in the world, going about their lives, sharing this exact moment in history with them, all having no meaning in terms of drama whatever. It is when the ordinary escapes from the dramatic that television seems to come alive.[24]

When television reaches this level it comes closer than at any other time to true interpersonal communication—the sharing of experience.

Attempts at Resolution

Although even network officials acknowledge that increasing violence on television, coupled with increasing crime rates is a cause for concern, relatively little has been done.

One approach would be to somehow modify the system that rewards whatever producer and whatever network can raise the level of violence another notch. With highly rated programs placed in the same time periods the viewing audience frequently has little choice. Thus three national networks and several local channels compete in providing the same fare—with the objective of each to attract the largest audience and so the largest income per commercial minute.

It is conceivable that some form of cable television will break the mass audience into more specialized segments and thus provide variety for the audience as well as escape for the producer who is truly interested in

---

[24]Lesser, *Children and Television*, p. 250.

quality. A varied and discriminating audience might be provided by some combination of pay television, cable, and satellite technology. This possibility is discussed in Chapter 14. At this stage attempts at prediction turn rapidly into speculation.

Barring some improvement of programming through advances brought by technology, the road to change in content takes the form of either constant pressure, probably through advertisers, or direct government intervention.

Pressure on program sponsors has proved to be a fairly successful device for Action for Children's Television (ACT). Through this method ACT has been instrumental in eliminating advertising of vitamins to children and cutting down commercial time on children's programs. Joan Ganz Cooney said in a radio talk that as few as six letters to a sponsor can have an effect.

Governmental action through Congress or the FCC is fraught with grave philosophic and legal considerations. While the rights of free speech and a free press have sometimes been used as a blind by the media, their basic principles are critical to an open society. Would these rights be violated if categories of material already forbidden were increased to include specific types of violence? To a civil libertarian any abridgment of freedom of information is abhorrent. But as society becomes more lawless some civil libertarians are beginning to wonder whether they are defending the right of free speech or the right to make a dollar by irresponsible programming.

Chairman Wiley of the FCC feels that his role is not to enforce compliance with any set of government standards, but to urge the industry to develop and enforce its own. When such "persuasion" is done by the licensing agency, it is only one step removed from direct governmental control, but it is more palatable. The motion picture industry developed and enforced its own code, and it is quite likely that television will be inclined to do the same thing as pressures mount.

Chairman Wiley's "jawboning" had one effect. In April 1975 the board of directors of the National Association of Broadcasters adopted a plan to provide family viewing hours from 7 to 9 P.M. on the East and West Coasts and an hour earlier in the Central Time Zone. During this period programs "inappropriate for family viewing" would be kept off the air.

The plan was to go into effect in the fall of 1975. Even before that some objections were raised. The most obvious one was that many children are not in bed by 9 P.M. (or by 8 P.M. in the Midwest). Some critics fretted that "adult" programming after 9 P.M. or 8 P.M. would become even more violent. But broadcast executives and Chairman Wiley hailed the plan as an achievement.

At the least it was recognition of a problem.

Communication and Conduct

Instinctively we know that communication affects how each of us acts, thinks, and interacts with others. The effects of home training, schooling, and all other aspects of our culture reach us through communication channels. The impact of society is changed to some extent by the communication process through which society sends its messages to each individual. Before the days of large-scale media, elders in family and tribe conveyed the messages that developed attitudes and controlled conduct. As the media have become more pervasive and more vivid they have taken over some of this control-through-communication. As the most vivid and pervasive of the media of the 1970's, television has been widely criticized for its real and imagined influence on society. Research to separate the real from the imagined effects is immensely difficult and so far not very conclusive, although it is quite safe to say that children are likely to become more violent if they are exposed to a steady diet of violence on the tube. One factor that may force media directors to concern themselves is the increasing tendency for the public to interact with the media. We will consider the manner in which this is happening in Chapter 14.

Suggestions for Further Reading

Blumler, Jay G., and Katz, Elihu, eds. *The Uses of Mass Communications: Current Perspectives on Gratifications Research.* Beverly Hills, Calif.: Sage Publications, 1974.
A fairly difficult volume with selections of uneven quality, but it presents some of the questions inherent in this kind of research.

De Fleur, Melvin L., and Ball-Rokeach, Sandra. *Theories of Mass Communication.* 3rd ed. New York: David McKay, 1975.
Treats communication effects in a sociological framework.

Edelstein, Alex S. *Media Credibility and the Believability of Watergate.* Reston, Va.: American Newspaper Publishers Association, 1974.
Distinguishes between the inherent believability of a piece of information and the credibility of a communications medium.

Goldsen, Rose K. "NBC's Make-Believe Research on TV Violence." *Transaction* 8 (October 1971): 28–35.
A critique of NBC's panel study of television violence and suggestions for other methods of study.

Lesser, Gerald S. *Children and Television.* New York: Random House, 1974.
An educator who participated in the planning of "Sesame Street" tells its story and, in the process, discusses the possibilities of television in enlarging individual experience.

Liebert, Robert M., Neale, John M., and Davidson, Emily S. *The Early Window: Effects of Television on Children and Youth.* New York: Pergamon Press, 1973.
A review of television's effects, generally critical of the medium.

Toffler, Alvin. *Future Shock.* New York: Random House, 1970.
Widely discussed, this book considers the possible consequences of "information overload."

Vidmar, Neil, and Rokeach, Milton. "Archie Bunker's Bigotry: A Study in Selective Perception and Exposure." *Journal of Communication* 24 (Winter 1974): 36–47.
Questions whether the Bunker show actually decreases bigotry.

A glance back at
Part Five
and ahead at
Part Six

One thing is clear enough—the media have increased their dominance over the lives of most people in the middle decades of the twentieth century. Writers sometimes stretch the point when they say that the media environment is the real environment, but certainly the media are supplying more and more of the information consumed by the public, and up to the mid-1970's the media kept taking increasing bites of the American citizen's time. Studies show that different people have different ways of using the media, but that the media loom large in the lives of most people. Studies are based on demographics (population breakdowns such as age, sex, socioeconomic status, and so on) and on psychological attributes. It is likely that the latter, as they come into more general use, will be more productive of insights into how people relate to the media.

There has been much theorizing as to how the media affect individual and group conduct. Controversy has swirled about all the media in turn, and in the 1970's it was television's turn. The problem is that the programming that attracts the largest audiences (sex and violence) is suspected of producing the most antisocial conduct. Since large audiences are vital to television, its managers are reluctant to give up sure-fire audience gimmicks, but it is becoming increasingly difficult to justify some of the programs. The problem is particularly acute with children. Studies are not too conclusive, but increasingly they show some relationship between television violence and violent acts committed by children who have seen the programs. Family viewing time, initiated in the 1975–1976 season, limits sex and violence in early evening shows, but it seems to be a weak effort. Certainly better solutions are needed.

Technology does not appear to offer a solution for that particular problem, but it shows promise on some others. We will examine these opportunities in Part Six.

SIX

New Technology and New Opportunities

14

Back Talk, Cross-Talk, and the Media

When a family goes to a ball game parents and children share an experience. They watch the action and discuss it with each other and with the people sitting around them. They smell the odor of hot dogs and beer and probably of sweat and garlic. The total experience is spontaneous, immediate, and full of the flavor of "going to the ball game."

Crowds at a sports event are engaging in one of the rites of the oral tradition we discussed in Chapter 2. Such firsthand, oral communication has a great advantage over media communication in that it is *interactive*. Interactive communication allows for immediate response and counter-response. It permits continuous adjustment to new ideas. It extends to everyone with lung, larynx, and vocal chords the privilege of using the principal communications channel—sound waves.

Point-to-point communications media, the postal and telephone systems, for example, allow for interactive communication, but the mass media provide basically one-way channels. Making the mass media more interactive is a ponderous process, but not impossible. Former FCC Commissioner Nicholas Johnson tells ways to make television more interactive in his book *How to Talk Back to Your Television Set.*[1]

While the mass media are good at putting great chunks of information in front of a great many receivers, they are not very good at getting response from the people they serve. Turning millions into receivers of information should not be an end in itself. Spending hours in front of the tube and reading a newspaper every day are pointless activities except as diversions unless they lead to meaningful action. Full participation in the communications process means the ability to talk back to the communicator and to talk with other participants. Such full participation requires that citizens have some control over media content, and that they have a chance to express their own views in the media.

Those who control the media acknowledge that they have a public service to perform, but most insist that only they can be the judge of what they print or broadcast. To the suggestion that under some circumstances a judge might order them to print certain things verbatim, publishers reply that they cannot give to a judge the right to edit their newspapers.

Broadcasters are in a somewhat more precarious position than the print media because they are licensed by the government, and statutes require certain responsibilities in return for the use of the radio spectrum. But broadcast executives, too, stoutly argue the injustice of demands that they open their facilities to anyone with a reasonable complaint.

Publishers and broadcasters also argue that an attempt to open their space and time to all comers would create only confusion. If they had to print or broadcast everything that anyone wanted to bring in, they say, it would be impossible to create any orderly publication or broadcast format.

Some of the ways that have been suggested for making the media more responsive to the public are:

- Making the media common carriers of information
- Guaranteeing the public a right of access to the media
- Setting up press councils to monitor media performance

Some of the ways the media themselves have tried to become more "participatory" are:

- Regularly criticizing themselves and other media
- Providing formats to regularly report audience opinion
- Giving time or space for audience response
- Establishing ombudsmen to hear complaints

[1] Nicholas Johnson, *How to Talk Back to Your Television Set* (Boston: Little, Brown, 1967).

The Media as Common Carriers

The suggestion that the media should be open to all comers is not new. It was expressed graphically and forcefully in 1947[2] by the distinguished members of the Commission on Freedom of the Press under the chairmanship of Robert Hutchins, then president of the University of Chicago. Members, some of them distinguished legal scholars, borrowed a concept from the world of transportation when they suggested that newspapers should become "common carriers" of information. They had a specific model in mind.

Railroads provide a good example of common carriers. Under their charters they are required to treat all customers alike. If one manufacturer is allowed to ship a certain number of pounds of material of a certain size from point A to point B for a certain fee, another manufacturer must be given the same rate for a similar shipment. This principle is essential in a competitive economy. If railroads were allowed to vary their rates at will they could make or break many of the businesses that depend on them to bring in raw materials or parts and to distribute products to their customers. Obviously people desiring to start a furniture manufacturing plant in a North Carolina town could not compete with an established manufacturer in the same place if they knew it would cost them twice as much as their competitor to bring in their wood and other materials and to ship out their finished furniture.

In the 1870's John D. Rockefeller gained control of 90 percent of the oil business, partly because the railroads were not required at that time to treat all shippers equally. Already the dominant oil shipper in the Northeast, Rockefeller used this leverage to negotiate a deal with several railroads that provided a rebate on Rockefeller's shipments. Competitors would pay the regular rate, but the difference between that and Rockefeller's rate would be paid to Rockefeller's company.

It is easy to see how such manipulation created the demand that railroads become common carriers, which meant that they must treat all customers alike, that they should carry all kinds of materials so long as they are not illegal, dangerous, or excludable for some other justifiable reason.

The common carrier concept has helped shape public thinking about the proper conduct of transportation systems. The legal minds of the 1946 Commission on the Freedom of the Press recommended that the same principle should be adapted to monitor the performance of the communications media. From one point of view, the business of the media is to

[2]Commission on Freedom of the Press, *A Free and Responsible Press* (Chicago: University of Chicago Press, 1947).

move information (facts and opinions) around the country. Everyone should be treated fairly in the movement of this information. That is, everyone is entitled under the Constitution to say what he or she wants to say and to hear what he or she wants to hear. The only way to reach many others is through the media, so the right to speak freely must include the right to use the media freely. The transportation barons were forbidden to discriminate in the movement of people and goods. Why should the media barons be permitted to discriminate in the movement of information?

Some media systems operate the way the railroads, buslines, and airlines do. The telephone and telegraph networks offer point-to-point message transmission. Everyone who makes a call from Boston to San Diego is charged the same rate, and the telephone company exerts no control over the content of the message so long as it is not illegal. The Postal Service offers point-to-point message service in its first-class mail. The content of letters is entirely private, and there are serious penalties for illegally opening first-class mail except in certain unusual situations, best known to the CIA.

The mass media differ in critical ways from point-to-point message systems. Economics and technology so far have not made it possible for the mass media to tailor their messages for specific individuals. As consumers of the mass media each of us receives a grab bag of information addressed "to whom it may concern." The average newspaper article is read by about 20 percent of the people who see a newspaper. This would indicate that most people who read a newspaper find only a small portion of the information it contains of much interest. It is inefficient to supply the public with such a vast amount of information that it disregards, but we do not have a better way of doing it. Thus mass media managers are not engaged in point-to-point transportation of information, but are trying to put together a package that will be of sufficient interest to enough people to persuade them to read their newspaper or watch their television station.

For this reason it is difficult to see how the common carrier concept can be practically applied. The governing principle has to be that an item of information should have sufficient interest to enough people to justify inclusion. The fact that any single individual has a consuming interest in an item does not justify distributing it to all points. For example, it is quite conceivable that someone would have a vital interest in sending or receiving the multiplication tables, but this is hardly justification for printing them in a newspaper or reciting them over the radio.

The common carrier concept may eventually be applicable to the information media, but that must await the development of sophisticated technology that will enable each reader or listener to order material to suit his or her individual mood and need. Until then, the media must be allowed to select content on the basis that it interests many people. Proponents of the right of access seem to be suggesting, not that the media be common carriers, but that, once they open a subject for discussion, they be required to report it in sufficient detail that all aspects are covered and the individuals involved are treated fairly. Most media managers say they intend to do this, but they want the crucial decisions to be theirs and not something forced upon them by others. The question as to when a person has received fair treatment, for example, is one in which there is room for the exercise of judgment and in which one's judgment is likely to be affected by his or her involvement.

Right of Access

Jerome A. Barron gave the most coherent expression of the arguments for the right of access to the media in an article in the *Harvard Law Review* in 1967. Calling the "marketplace of ideas" a romantic, outmoded concept, he asked for a legal guarantee of the right to insert novel and perhaps unpopular ideas into the media.

Perhaps in the eighteenth century the concept of the marketplace of ideas made sense, Barron argues, but now the mass nature of the media, their declining number, and their commercial propensities have made it difficult or impossible for new ideas to find expression in them. He explains the blandness of the media this way:

> The aversion of the media for the novel and heretical has escaped attention for an odd reason. The controllers of the media have no ideology. Since in the main they espouse no particular ideas, their antipathy to all ideas has passed unnoticed. What has happened is not that controllers of opinion, Machiavellian fashion, are subtly feeding us information to the end that we shall acquiesce in their political view of the universe. On the contrary, the communications industry is operated on the whole with an intellectual neutrality consistent with V. O. Key's theory that the commercial nature of mass communications makes it "bad business" to espouse the heterodox or the controversial.[3]

Barron charged that the media are using the free speech and press guarantees

> to avoid opinions instead of acting as a sounding board for their expression. What happens . . . is that the opinion vacuum is filled with

---

[3]Jerome A. Barron, "Access to the Press—A New First Amendment Right," *Harvard Law Review* 80 (1967): 1641. Quoted in Donald M. Gillmor and Jerome A. Barron, *Mass Communication Law: Cases and Comment* (St. Paul, Minn.: West Publishing, 1969), p. 121.

the least controversial and bland idea. Whatever is stale and accepted in the status quo is readily discussed and thereby reinforced and revitalized.

The First Amendment, he argues, is "somewhat thin" if people can express themselves only at the pleasure of the media managers. One result of media aversion to new ideas, he holds, is that those holding them are forced to resort to violence to get a hearing. This reverses the traditional process by which the media sometimes serve as a sort of safety valve—with the expression of radical ideas serving as a substitute for civil disturbance. Once an idea has been projected into the media by violence or other means, it usually gains the protection of the First Amendment and the media proceed to discuss it. But the alien idea, until it breaks into the press, gains little protection because of the First Amendment.

Barron is at odds with many media managers and legal scholars in his demand for a "contextual approach." He says that the First Amendment should be interpreted to compensate for the innate differences in the impact of the various media. He rejects the idea that persons who are denied access to newspapers and broadcast media receive equal treatment because they can avail themselves of media with lesser impact such as sound trucks and pamphlets.

> Competitive media only constitute alternative means of access in a crude manner. If ideas are criticized in one forum the most adequate response is in the same forum since it is most likely to reach the same audience. Further, the various media serve different functions and create different reactions and expectations—criticism of an individual or a governmental policy over television may reach more people but criticism in print is more durable.
>
> The test of a community's opportunities for free expression rests not so much in an abundance of alternative media but rather in an abundance of opportunities to secure expression in media with the largest impact.[4]

Barron's most interesting suggestion is that the requirement for the publication of a new idea should be judged, not on the number of its proponents in the community, but on the degree to which it is already expressed in the media.

Provocative as Barron's ideas are, he has few suggestions for implementing them beyond speculating whether it should be done by the courts, Congress, or the administration. In a later writing[5] he argued that

[4]Barron, "Access to the Press," quoted in Gillmore and Barron, Mass Communication Law, p. 125
[5]Jerome A. Barron, Freedom of the Press for Whom? (Bloomington: Indiana University Press, 1973), p. 6.

at the very least aggrieved parties should be allowed to buy space to express their views and that public figures who are attacked should be granted the right of reply.

A precedent has been established for the broadcast media by the Federal Communications Commission regulations and in the federal laws.[6] A broadcaster who attacks a person or group or opposes or supports a political candidate must, within twenty-four hours, notify the party or candidate attacked (or the opposition to a candidate endorsed), furnish a copy of the script, and offer equal time for a reply. This doctrine was held to be constitutional by the Supreme Court in the *Red Lion* case.[7]

Broadcasters have argued that the requirements are burdensome and expensive and that they will tend to make for bland political programming because broadcasters will deem it not worth the trouble to involve themselves in controversies. Nonetheless, neither Congress nor the FCC has shown much interest in eliminating the requirement.

The U.S. Supreme Court declined to extend the right of reply to newspapers in 1974 in *The Miami Herald Publishing Company* v. *Pat L. Tornillo, Jr.*[8] The decision invalidated a 1913 Florida statute that would have required a newspaper to print a response from a candidate for public office whom it had criticized. In forthright editorials the *Miami Herald* had urged voters to reject Pat Tornillo's candidacy for the legislature. One editorial said, "it would be inexcusable of the voters if they sent Pat Tornillo of Tallahassee to occupy the seat for District 103 of the House of Representatives." Tornillo demanded that the *Herald* print his reply verbatim. When the paper declined he brought suit.

The 1913 law had been invoked only once before when the court refused to enforce it, and few thought it would be taken seriously now. The Dade County (Miami) Court ruled the law unconstitutional, but, on appeal, the Florida Supreme Court reversed the decision, 6–1. The court said its action would "encourage rather than impede the wide-open and robust dissemination of ideas and counterthought which is essential to intelligent self government."

Although unexpected, the decision of the Florida Supreme Court drew some interesting reaction in the United States Senate. Senator John McClellan suggested to the Senate that there might be a need for a national law similar to the Florida statute. The suggestion was not taken lightly since Senator McClellan was in an influential position as chairman of the Senate Appropriations Committee and of the Judiciary Subcommittee on Criminal Laws and Procedures. The senator held that since the Supreme Court had made it extremely difficult for a public official to win in a libel suit the right of reply was even more important.

[6] *47 U.S.C. 315.*
[7] *Red Lion Broadcasting Co.* v. *FCC*, 395 U.S. 367 (1969).
[8] 418 U.S. 241 (1974).

Senator Alan Cranston of California, a former correspondent for International News Service, responded that "the Senate must resist the temptation to set up Big Brother as the arbiter of fairness in the press."[9]

When the case came to the Supreme Court, Barron, representing Tornillo, used the same general arguments that appeared in his *Harvard Law Review* article. Unimpressed, the Court unanimously held that the Florida statute was unconstitutional.

Chief Justice Warren Burger, writing the opinion, based his central argument on the First Amendment:

> The Florida statute fails to clear the barriers of the First Amendment because of its intrusion into the function of editors. A newspaper is more than a passive receptacle or conduit for news, comment, and advertising. The choice of material to go into a newspaper, and the decisions made as to limitations on the size and content of the paper, and treatment of public issues and public officials—whether fair or unfair—constitute the exercise of editorial control and judgment. It has yet to be demonstrated how governmental regulation of this crucial process can be exercised consistent with First Amendment guarantees of a free press as they have evolved to this time.[10]

Justice Byron R. White, author of the *Red Lion* decision affirming the fairness doctrine for the broadcast media, held that the First Amendment prohibits government tampering with the content of the print media. He specifically denied that the public utility concept is applicable to newspapers.

Access to the media is not necessarily increased for those who are willing to buy time or space. As we saw in Chapter 7, the courts have generally held that the privately owned media are free to reject advertising on controversial issues. The courts have also held that in advertising as well as other content broadcasters are governed by the traditional interpretation of the fairness doctrine, which requires them to report all aspects of controversial issues of public importance, but in so doing they are allowed "significant journalistic discretion."

The decisions regarding commercial time and the *Miami Herald* decision seem to make legal access to the media a closed issue for the moment. Nevertheless, there is no indication that proponents of legal rights of access have changed their views. Clearly the media must function in the public interest if they are to maintain their independence, and the public must be persuaded that they are functioning in the public interest. The fact that the issue could come to the U.S. Supreme Court at all reflects some lack of public confidence in the media. Whether such lack is jus-

[9]"Senator Cranston Opposes 'Right-to-Reply' Law," *Editor and Publisher*, February 16, 1974, p. 12.
[10]418 U.S. 241 at 258.

tified is important, but justified or not, its very existence is a matter of concern to the media and to everyone interested in the free circulation of information and ideas.

Most members of the press want to present all sides of public issues. Editors of the *Miami Herald* pointed out that they had printed a number of letters to the editor from Mr. Tornillo and that they felt they had been fair to him. What they resisted was the *demand* that his reply be published, on the theory that giving in would constitute a violation of freedom of the press.

Press Councils

Press councils are another way that has been tried to relate the media to their audiences and the public to the media. However, in testing this idea, the United States has been years behind Europe. A Press Fair Practices Commission was begun in Sweden in 1916, and a number of other European countries, including England, have adopted versions of it. Generally the councils are designed to provide a forum for criticism of the media and an avenue of communication between the media and their audiences. In the United States the Commission on Freedom of the Press recommended in its 1947 report the formation of an independent agency to assess the performance of the press. The commission suggested that such an agency should report annually on the status of the press and urged that it compare "the accomplishments of the press with the aspirations which the people have for it. . . . Such an agency would also educate the people as to the aspirations which they ought to have for the press.[11]

Like much of the report of the Commission on Freedom of the Press, this suggestion did not stir much favorable reaction among media people. Their principal fear appeared to be that a press council would limit their freedom to edit. Despite these worries the *Littleton* (Colorado) *Independent* set up an advisory board in 1946. Eight editors met with individuals representing the fields of sociology, journalism teaching, economics, psychology, political science, public opinion polling, race relations, and international relations.[12]

In 1966 the Mellett Fund for a Free and Responsible Press announced modest funding to try local press councils on an experimental basis. Two conditions were established. First, the councils would not be empowered to change the content of the media; and second, they would not be organized by the media. The funds were distributed to universities, which

[11]Commission on Freedom of the Press, *A Free and Responsible Press,* p. 100.
[12]Donald L. Brignolo, "How Community Press Councils Work," Freedom of Information Center Report No. 217, March 1969.

took a leading role in the formation of the first councils sponsored by the Mellett Fund. Stanford University organized councils in Bend, Oregon, and Redwood City, California, under the direction of William Rivers. Southern Illinois University was made responsible for councils at Cairo and Sparta, Illinois. A specialized version of the council idea was tried in Seattle, where media representatives and individuals from the black community formed the Seattle Communications Council of Media Leaders and Black Citizens.

Much variety is possible in the way a press council is organized and operated. One basic consideration is how the persons from the community should be chosen and by whom. Should they be recognized community leaders? Should they represent various community groups? Should an effort be made to have them constitute a cross section of the community? Obviously the composition of the public representatives will have much to do with how a council functions. A related question is who should represent the media and how such persons should be selected.

Should the council monitor just one of the media in its community or all of them?

Another concern is whether a council should hold open or closed sessions. The latter alternative is difficult to defend in days when there is much agitation to open every government meeting to public scrutiny, but some feel that closed sessions make for frank discussions.

Different councils have assumed different functions. The Seattle council, for example, seems to have become primarily a channel for the voicing of the discontent of the black community. The organizer of the Seattle council described its meetings this way:

> The monthly council meetings brought together individuals dissimilar by race and environment, occupation and age, training and experience. At meetings one heard quiet statements and shouted denunciations, carefully-phrased thoughts and nearly-stuttered obscenities. Through it all the ear hears—if it would—black men tell of the pain of being black, of being an invisible, powerless minority in a white society which for generations had ignored or abused them.[13]

This description would lead one to believe that the main attempt at the meetings was to present the black view to media people present and to obtain a better reporting of black problems in the Seattle media. Apparently that occurred.

> The outstanding *Post-Intelligencer* story during this period was written by a council member, Lou Guzzo, managing editor of the *P.I.* Guz-

[13]Lawrence Schneider, "A Media-Black Council: Seattle's 19-Month Experiment," *Journalism Quarterly* 47 (Autumn 1970): 445–446.

zo's column, "Blacks Must Have Justice," angered a number of whites but came like a breath of fresh air into the black community where a black separatist newspaper reprinted it.

The *Times* and *P-I* [sic] opened their pages to the reporting of black affairs. Photos and stories of black fashions and foods appeared in the women's pages and the Sunday magazines also carried material on black history, experiences and attitudes.[14]

The council organizer reported that the council had failed in its goal of creating a sense of community, but cited

> a growing recognition on the part of the media individuals regarding the specifics of the black perceptions of white society, a gradual willingness to use their media to bridge the gap between the two societies, and early gropings to do just that.[15]

The effects of the general councils, like the Seattle experiment, are hazy. In Sparta and Cairo, Illinois, publishers said they became more aware of public expectations and made changes, chiefly in increasing the amount of local news and displaying it more prominently. Redwood City publisher Ray Spangler said that the existence of the council made him "reflect more carefully" on the performance of his paper. Publisher Robert W. Chandler of the *Bend Bulletin* saw fewer results from the council. He commented: "I cannot point to anything we have done to improve our practices, and I think we were doing pretty well prior to the start of the council."[16]

The value of local press councils is still a matter of debate. At the very least they provide an avenue for conversation between media people and the public whom they try to represent. At their best they would help to promote the spirit of community that seems to have eluded the Seattle council. Two men who worked closely with local press councils have sharply differing views. Rivers has said they are not a necessity in every community but would have greatest value in large cities, where much of the population is at odds with the power structure. Ben H. Bagdikian has said that press councils are a necessity in all communities and that the alternative is some kind of forced intervention in media affairs.

The only statewide press council, which is in Minnesota, has for sanctions only "jawboning and bad publicity" according to Austin C. Wehrwein, editorial writer for the *Minneapolis Star*. Wehrwein reviewed the five cases handled by the Minnesota Press Council in its first twenty-three months of existence and concluded that it had been accepted by both the press and the public. The council has, he said,

[14]Ibid., p. 447.
[15]Ibid.
[16]Brignolo, "How Community Press Councils Work," p. 73.

become a substitute for, or an alternative to, libel suits. While on the one hand the council declined to fashion a new "access" doctrine, on the other hand, it narrowed an editor's discretion to define proper redress. It plunged into headline accuracy review, a touchy problem. And while it refrained from judging the validity of editorial opinion, it reserved the privilege to judge the "factual accuracy and honesty" of editorials, certainly another tender topic in journalism.[17]

The council, now independent of the Minnesota Newspaper Association, is made up of twenty members, half from the media and half from the public. Its chairman is Associate Justice C. Donald Peterson of the Minnesota State Supreme Court, who was co-chairman of the Twentieth Century Fund group that planned the National News Council. Wehrwein thinks that media opposition to the news councils comes from either the belief that they will be ineffective or the belief that if they do work they will limit press freedom and encourage government interference. In his opinion, neither fear is justified by the early experience in Minnesota.

In the summer of 1973 the National News Council came into existence, inspiring mixed reactions among media people and public. A private organization, it has no powers of enforcement. It investigates complaints about the media, serves as an intermediary between the media and the public, and publicizes its findings.

William B. Arthur, the last editor of Look magazine and now executive director of the National News Council, sees the council as an agency that will protect freedom of the press. He likes to point out that the council's purposes as stated in its incorporation papers is "to serve the public interest in preserving freedom of communication and advancing accurate and fair reporting of the news." The council originally reviewed complaints only against the national news media,[18] but at its December 1974 meeting it voted to "accept legitimate complaints about press and broadcast performance from any citizen anywhere in the United States."[19]

Although the council proceeded cautiously, nonetheless, news executives worried.

Arthur Ochs Sulzberger, publisher of the New York Times, refused the cooperation of his newspaper and explained the action to his staff in these words:

[17]Austin C. Wehrwein, "A Council Judges the Press, How Minnesota's Experiment Has Fared So Far," Louisville Courier-Journal and Times, September 2, 1973, p. E3. Wehrwein writes a regular column in the Minneapolis Star called "Watching the Media."

[18]For the council's purposes the national news media were defined as the national wire services and syndicates, the national radio and television networks, Newsweek, Time, U.S. News and World Report, the Christian Science Monitor, the New York Times, the Wall Street Journal, and the Washington Post.

[19]Jane Levere, "News Council Votes to Act on All Press Complaints," Editor and Publisher, December 14, 1974, p. 10.

As we view it we are being asked to accept what we regard as a form of voluntary regulation in the name of enhancing press freedom. We respect the good intention of the fund, but we believe the operation of such a council would not only fail to achieve its purposes but could actually harm the cause of press freedom in the United States.[20]

While many executives were cautious about the council, many others accepted it willingly as a way of expressing their view that the news profession really is a public trust and as a means of giving the public some participation in decisions that vitally affect it.

Vigorous Mutual Self-Criticism

Another suggestion of the Hutchins commission was that the media engage in "vigorous mutual self-criticism." Newspaper editors of the day responded rather grumpily if at all. One paper found a diatribe that one personal journalist hurled at his competition a hundred years ago and blandly asked if that was the sort of thing the commission had in mind. More likely what the commission had in mind is better represented in Figure 14.1.

The idea has merit. Some newspapers have been accused of criticizing everything, but feeling outraged when anyone ventured a comment on their own performance. Newspapers had art, film, and theater critics. They criticized government officials freely in their editorial columns, and some sportswriters felt called upon to offer their views as to the efficacy of the local coaches. But there was little regular public criticism of the press. The columns of the late A. J. Liebling in *The New Yorker* provided one of the few sources of informed evaluation of press performance.

Some newspapers, more sensitive to the problem in recent years, have gone to what appears to be the ultimate step—subsidizing their critics. They have hired competent people and given them space to critique the paper in public. Such critics need strong constitutions and ironclad contracts. If they do their job well their friends in the newsroom will be few and the publisher will be cool.

The best-known example of such an in-house critic was Ben Bagdikian, resident termagant of the *Washington Post*. Bagdikian's column made it impossible to doubt either his critical ability or his feeling of independence, although he admitted that his relationship with other *Post* employees was not the best. When Bagdikian left for other work the *Post* filled

[20]"N.Y. Times Won't Work with Press Council," *Editor & Publisher*, January 20, 1973, p. 36.

the position by hiring Charles B. Seib, former managing editor of the *Washington Star*.

A different version of the in-house critic is found in Charleston, West Virginia, where the *Gazette* assigned its city editor to write a weekly column evaluating the newspaper. In it he supports and criticizes the paper's policies, sometimes even taking his publisher to task. The possibility that no one working on the paper and directly on its payroll can be objective has publisher W. E. Chilton III considering contracting with someone completely outside of the organization to do the column.

Encouraging Audience Response

The same *Charleston Gazette* offered its own right of reply shortly after the Supreme Court announced its decision in *Tornillo v. The*

Figure 14.1 "Vigorous Mutual Self-Criticism"

Butterfield-CIA flap shows TV journalism in unflattering light

By CHARLES B. SEIB
© The Washington Post Co.

WASHINGTON — The Alexander Butterfield-CIA story, which flared and then fizzled out in one brief week, provided a good — but not reassuring — case history of enterprise journalism as it is practiced on television today.

There was a shoot-from-the-hip quality to it as well as a disturbing disregard for a man's reputation and for the public's need to make sense out of the strange doings in Washington.

The story had its beginning in an effort by two congressmen to defend their turf — namely the House investigation of the CIA. Reacting to a move to kill or restrict the investigation, they committed a little leak. They told reporters that they had learned of a CIA practice of "infiltrating" federal agencies, even to the extent of placing an agent in a high-level position in the Nixon White House.

The next day, July 11, shortly after 7 a.m., the two top network morning shows — the CBS Morning News and the NBC Today Show — came up with a name — the same name. They produced former Air Force Col. Fletcher Prouty — live on CBS and taped on NBC. Prouty said the high Nixon official with CIA ties was none other than Alexander Butterfield, who in 1973 started Richard Nixon's slide toward disgrace by disclosing the White House taping system.

Butterfield was a CIA "contact officer" in the White House, Prouty said. His source: E. Howard Hunt, a long-time CIA man who later was sent to prison for his connection with the Watergate burglary.

Just what is Butterfield supposed to have done for the CIA? That didn't come clear. On the CBS show, Prouty said Butterfield's function was "to open doors for CIA operations." On the NBC show he

[Commentary box:]

Commentary

Charles B. Seib, a former managing editor of the Washington Star, is ombudsman and an associate editor of the Star's rival, The Washington Post. As such, he monitors the Post and other media for fairness, accuracy and professional competence. His reports appear weekly in the Post.

assented to a description of Butterfield as a "man with CIA connections."

Imprecise descriptions to be sure, and far from identifying Butterfield as a CIA spy. But in the context, the implication was clear. Butterfield was the CIA's man right on the edge of the Oval Office.

Neither network provided a response from Butterfield or verification from any other source. NBC did couple a flat denial from Mrs. Butterfield with the Prouty charge. CBS put Prouty on the air without any denial, direct or indirect, but a half hour later reported that Mrs. Butterfield said the charge was "ridiculous." Both networks said they tried hard to locate Butterfield before the broadcasts, but without success.

The story hung there for two and one-half days. Prouty elaborated on his charge. It was widely carried in the print press, usually coupled with CIA denials and with emphasis on Prouty's statement that he was not calling Butterfield a "spy."

Then Butterfield, who had not been reached by reporters, astutely accepted an invitation to appear on the CBS show, "60 Minutes," that Sunday evening. There, before a prime-time audience of about 20 million viewers, he indignantly denied Prouty's story.

"Not a shred of truth," he said under questioning by Mike Wallace. At another point in the interview: "I have never been their designated contact man. That is absolutely false." Later: "I had no contact whatsoever with the CIA."

Since then, Hunt has denied that he told Prouty Butterfield was a CIA contact. And Sen. Frank Church, who heads the Senate CIA investigation, has said no shred of evidence has been found to support the charge. Nevertheless, the Butterfields feel that his job search (he was eased out of his post as head of the Federal Aviation Agency last March) has been seriously hampered. And it is a fact of life that undoubtedly there will be some who will say, years from now, when his name comes up: "Oh, yes. He's the guy who scuttled Nixon for the CIA."

In retrospect, it is clear that all concerned — Prouty and CBS and NBC — were careless in their handling of a man's reputation and of an important and complex story. Not only does it appear that unjustifiable harm was done to Butterfield, but a great disservice was done to the public in that the Butterfield story drew attention away from a very serious question: Just what has been the nature and extent of the CIA's involvement in

the operations of other government agencies?

CBS reporter Daniel Schorr and NBC reporter Ford Rowan were asked for their afterthoughts on the Prouty broadcasts. Schorr defended the use of Prouty without supporting evidence on the ground that in an earlier situation Prouty's information stood up. Rowan defended his broadcast on the ground that he had received some support for Prouty's story from several other sources.

Conceding these points, one must still ask why they didn't take the time to check on Prouty's story more fully or at least wait for Butterfield's response.

Schorr said that although CBS learned the evening before the broadcast that NBC also had Prouty, competitive pressure was not a factor in the decision to go ahead. He noted, however, that Thursday was a dull news day and that the Morning News people were happy to get a good lead story for Friday morning.

Rowan conceded that competition was a factor in his pressing to get the story on the air. He said he didn't know that CBS had Prouty, but that he thought ABC might have him. "In a situation like this," he said, "my thought is to get it on the air and see how it flies."

This one appears to have crashed.

From the Louisville *Courier-Journal*, July 31, 1975. © The Washington Post. Reprinted with permission.

Miami Herald. As of July 6, 1974, the *Gazette* incorporated this guarantee in its editorial masthead. A person whose judgment or conduct is criticized by the paper's editorials is guaranteed the right to respond in the paper. The paper promises to display the replies as prominently as the original editorials.

The *Gazette* had previously offered its readers the right to reply, but decided to spell it out after the Supreme Court decision. In an editorial, publisher Chilton explained: "While applauding the U.S. Supreme Court decision that voided the Florida law, the Charleston Gazette remains sensitive to its responsibility for providing access and clarification of issues."[21]

Four years before spelling out the right of reply, the *Gazette* established a Bureau of Accuracy and Fair Play that is pledged to investigate complaints by citizens who feel they have been misrepresented or treated unfairly. For practical purposes, Chilton told *Editor & Publisher*, most people simply call the city editor, editor, or publisher when they have a complaint.

Action Line Columns

Another way that newspapers try to give readers a feeling that they are direct participants in the media is through the use of action line columns. These encourage readers to write or telephone in when they have problems, and the action line editor tries to provide a solution. *Chicago Today*, the *Chicago Tribune*, and the *Chicago Daily News* each reported in 1973 that they were getting about four hundred queries a day. Each editor has a staff of four or five to deal with the complaints and answer questions for readers. Readers complain about products that do not work, ask help in locating missing relatives, or request aid in getting government agencies to act. One reader wanted to know how to make a chain out of gum wrappers. A syndicated column prepared in Washington uses brand names in reporting complaints.

Often the problems are trivial to all except the complainant and perhaps a few others, but when a newspaper solves a problem the reader feels closer to the paper and is comforted by the thought that he or she has a place to turn.

The *Miami Herald* printed this question and answer, a fairly common kind of action line interchange, in its column:

---

[21]"Reply Format Instituted by W. Va. Newspaper," *Editor & Publisher*, July 20, 1974, p. 11.

My section of SW 104th Court has at least 500 potholes. For the past seven years the county has been faithfully patching each and every one of them but the potholes must eat the patching compound. I dare anyone to drive over this road and tell me it doesn't need to be resurfaced. —Mrs. D.J.

[Answer] The county took your dare, and agreed with you. The road was in need of repair. The Metro Public Works Department finished resurfacing SW 104th Court between 24th and 28th streets today.

Letters to the Editor

The old reliable audience response feature of the newspapers is a letters to the editor column. Nearly all newspaper editors welcome letters and print all that they can make room for. Usually the only limits of freedom of expression are those of libel and good taste. Readers frequently write to sound off about their gripes against the newspaper, the city government, or to complain about the weather.

It is said that Benjamin Franklin wrote an anonymous letter to the editor of his own paper—to himself—which he duly published and used as the basis for some commentary. If so, he was probably not the first and certainly not the last editor to write for his own letters column. When things got dull, the letter was sometimes used to inject a little life into the editorial page.

Editors of today's newspapers condemn that practice and usually insist that letters bear the names and addresses of the writers. This is insurance against crank letters and a guard against pressure groups that sometimes try to flood the column with letters supporting their pet positions.

A lively and well-edited letters to the editor column is regarded as a valuable asset to any newspaper. Readership studies show that many people pay attention to the opinions of their neighbors as they appear in the paper.

Radio Talk: Much Interaction

Radio talk shows provide the highest level of interactive communication of any of the mass media.

Radio has the great advantage of immediacy. Talking on the telephone to a disc jockey or talk show host is not so very different from any other kind of conversation. It does not require any special skill, such as the ability to write a letter, and there is the immediate reward of knowing that one is talking to an audience—an opportunity available to few people.

As we saw in Chapter 11, radio stations are so competitive that their managers frequently have to scramble to devise a format that will attract listeners. Also, radio stations can operate profitably without appealing to everyone in their areas, as television and newspapers try to do. This ability to program for segments of the mass audience instead of every last member of it allows some freedom and promotes creativity.

This freedom and creativity are apparent in a remark by Frank Stewart, general manager of KTRH (AM) in Houston. Asked where he got the nerve to go to an all-talk format, Stewart said, "We did a survey and 74% of the people voted for music. So I said to myself: 'Frank, I know where you can get a 26 share.' "

The all-talk format includes more than audience-participation shows, but these are usually important aspects of it. Audience participation shows include answering teenagers' requests for the rock-and-roll favorites; back-fence gossip sessions; swap sessions in which housewives can trade recipes, cleaning formulas, and shopping advice; and public affairs programs featuring government officials, doctors, or specialists in psychology or sex.

WCAU (AM) in Philadelphia, owned by CBS, features news in morning and evening "drive time," heavy play-by-play sports broadcasting during evenings and weekends, and audience-participation talk shows the rest of the time. The host interviews an outside specialist and lets the audience participate. WCAU's telephone system allows twelve persons on one conference call, so sometimes the host, an outside guest, and several members of the audience can talk together.

Sometimes advertisers resist uninhibited talk shows. Station WERE (AM) of Cleveland made a sudden switch from a traditional format to "very aggressive talk" in February 1972. Paul Neuhoff, vice president and general manager, told *Broadcasting* magazine, "In three days we lost a million dollars in billings."[22]

Neuhoff added:

> At 7 o'clock that morning you could picture people tuning in for that prestigious news the station always had. And there was Gary Dee shouting at some lady: 'Why don't you go gargle with razor blades?' They all went off. We had had every bank, every utility on the air. They all left."

WERE used the slogan "people power" to express its concern for its listeners. Program manager Robert V. Whitney explained: "We wanted to

---

[22]"Talk Radio: In the Middle of America's Conversational Mainstream," *Broadcasting*, May 28, 1973, pp. 35ff.

say that everybody has power, including the ordinary guy who feels kind of powerless; we wanted to provide a soapbox."

The unrestrained language, too, was deliberate. "People like to hear tantrums, and people yelling at one another," Whitney told *Broadcasting*. He described some of his talk shows hosts as "zippy personalities. . . . These personalities were willing to mirror—in the extreme sometimes— the way people really feel. People really get angry. So these personalities were willing to be angry."

Not every one in Cleveland expressed pleasure with the format. Enough people complained in enough places that the FBI investigated the station six times. but no charges were filed. Meanwhile the station management says it has more than regained its lost advertising revenues, and presumably some people in its audience are strengthened by "people power."

The Ombudsman: "Dear Omnipotent"

In 1713 Sweden created the office of *Hogsta Ombudsman* (Supreme Commissioner) to protect citizens against government wrongs. Thus was formally begun a system for guarding civil rights that flourishes today in many countries of the world; and thus was that difficult Swedish word, *ombudsman*, launched to become practically synonymous with a citizen's advocate.

Over two hundred and fifty years later the idea was proposed for newspapers in an article in the *New York Times Magazine*.[23] Barry Bingham, Sr., chairman of the board of the *Courier-Journal* and the *Louisville Times*, and Norman E. Isaacs, then executive editor of those papers, put the plan into effect that same year. John Herchenroeder, a long-time news executive at the papers, was named to the position. Herchenroeder has found that some people have difficulty with the title, and he has been addressed as "omnibusman" and "Dear Omnipotent." But he is generally regarded as the most effective ombudsman in any newspaper in the country.[24]

Other newspapers have adopted simpler titles, including "Mr. Go Between," "Reader Contact Editor," and "Public Access Editor." Whatever the title, the general purpose remains the same—to receive and investigate reader complaints, to correct those that deserve it, and to explain the rest.

Herchenroeder received about four hundred calls the first year, five hundred the next and, by 1973, was receiving nearly three thousand calls

[23]A. H. Raskin, "What's Wrong With American Newspapers," *New York Times Magazine*, June 11, 1967.

[24]Keith P. Sanders, *What Are Daily Newspapers Doing to Be Responsive to Readers' Criticisms?* ANPA News Research Bulletin No. 9, November 30, 1973.

a year. Readers are encouraged by stories and advertisements to call at any time, day or night. Off-hour calls are recorded. Isaacs called it an early warning system, saying: "For the first time we have a continuing flow of information about reader reaction. We thus have the opportunity to make quick assessments of whether what we have done is of a serious nature or not."[25]

At the *Washington Post* the ombudsman is designated as the paper's internal as well as external critic. In addition to a weekly column on the news business, he writes critical memoranda to editors and criticizes orally. At the *Minneapolis Star* and some other papers, the ombudsman (called "Reader's Referee" at the *Star*) mails out clippings of stories, asking persons mentioned to indicate any errors.

The executive editor of the *Omaha World-Herald* supervises the accuracy checks and keeps a running record of flubs by individual staff members.

Smaller papers are less likely to have a formally designated ombudsman, with complaints being received by editors or the publisher. One of the smallest papers to formalize such a system is the *New Castle News* in Pennsylvania. Complaints are discussed with the newsroom people involved and reported back to the person who complained.

The *Milwaukee Journal* provides an ombudsman and also holds monthly dinners at which representatives of local organizations are encouraged to discuss the paper's performance.

In a study of reader-response systems Keith Sanders found that 52 percent of the papers in his sample used some kind of accountability system and that they were "generally pleased with the results." Radio stations, too, notably WEEI in Boston, have used the ombudsman concept successfully.

Not all newspeople are persuaded of their desirability, however. Bill Maddox of the *Port Arthur* (Texas) *News* expressed the doubt of a number of editors:

> Hasn't it become perfectly clear that this nation's press—while so busy examining itself—almost forgot to examine the people, places, and things called for by its traditional role? Because of Watergate, we can now come out from under the rocks and be bold again—that is until those in high places begin to attack us again and lead us to believe, by golly, that we'd better set up press councils, "bureaus of accuracy," etc., which serve as self-imposed intimidations. We don't need 'em."[26]

Accepting criticism is not fun, even for those who regularly dish it out. But the media need to hear from their audiences. They need back talk—the good and the bad.

[25]Ibid., p. 66.
[26]Ibid., p. 80.

With Chip on Shoulder

The media need to promote cross-talk, too.

Letters to the editor and radio talk programs can be sounding boards and rallying points for community opinion. This, too, is a job of the media: to generate discussion on issues of common concern. Sometimes a touch of emotion helps.

Vituperative as they often were, the personal journalists of the nineteenth century were at least provocative. Provocative media exist today, but they are relatively few and they do not receive much attention. They may be less profitable because advertisers tend to steer clear of them. Good, noncontroversial middle-of-the-road programming is the safest bet.

Unfortunately, middle-of-the-road programming is often go-to-sleep programming. A few weekly newspapers still dare to be provocative, and, as we saw, some of the new radio talk shows are provocative almost to the point of verbal violence. A shrill, strident press sometimes gets results where dignity fails. Until the happy day arrives when nobody ever needs to shout at anybody else we will need some tough-guy media: to get some blood boiling about worthwhile issues; to create the turmoil that precedes the consensus on which democracy thrives.

Media, Interaction, and Technology

Freedom of speech, freedom of the press, and freedom of assembly were provided by the Bill of Rights in the hope that they would help to provide interactive communication on public issues. There was no intent to protect the special rights of a few who would own a great communication system. But as media have become large commercial enterprises, there has been a tendency for a few individuals to control their content. The problems in giving an opportunity to many individuals to interact with each other through the media are complicated by a system of information delivery that makes many receivers dependent on a few senders of information. It takes much social ingenuity to expand the power of individuals to communicate through the media. We have examined some of these attempts in this chapter. In the final chapter we will consider the possibility that new technology may help the communication system to become more interactive.

Suggestions for Further Reading

Barron, Jerome A. "Access to the Press—A New First Amendment Right." *Harvard Law Review* 80:1641, 1967.
The article that fanned discussion of access to the media, it questions whether Supreme Court interpretation of the First Amendment enhances freedom of information.

——. *Freedom of the Press for Whom?* Bloomington: Indiana University Press, 1973.
Argues for access to the media by the public.

Brignolo, Donald L. *How Community Press Councils Work.* Columbia: University of Missouri, School of Journalism, Freedom of Information Center, 1969.
A report on early press councils in the United States.

Carnegie Commission on Educational Television. *Public Television: A Program for Action.* New York: Bantam, 1967.
An attempt to reconcile the educational possibilities of television with the reality of financing them.

Jacklin, Phil. "A New Fairness Doctrine, Access to the Media." *The Center Magazine* (May-June 1975): 46–50.
Suggests that any outlet over a certain size should be required to make 10 percent of its time available for citizen access.

Rivers, William L. et al. *Back Talk: Press Councils in America.* San Francisco: Canfield Press, 1972.
Firsthand and readable accounts of some local press councils.

Sanders, Keith. *What Are Daily Newspapers Doing to Be Responsive to Readers' Criticisms?* Reston, Va.: American Newspaper Publishers Association, 1973.
A survey of newspaper use of ombudsmen and other reader-response devices.

15

Interaction and the New Technology

Communication has brought about many of civilization's triumphs. It is the process by which knowledge is passed along, consensus is achieved, and people and materials are organized for great undertakings.

Small wonder that thoughtful citizens expect great things from each new development in the means of sharing information.

Sometimes they expect too much too soon.

Printing changed the world. So did radio and television. Will new combinations of information technology change us again?

Are we, as we are told at least once a day, "on the threshold of a communications revolution?"

"Communications irresolution" is a more accurate description of our state.

We possess a magnificent technology and amazing devices. We have the equipment and the skill to link them all together into a national, multidirectional communication system.

If we went to that trouble we could do all those things we are constantly being told about. We could watch first-run movies in our game rooms in near perfect color—probably on three-by-six-foot screens. We could vote on presidents and policies almost instantaneously by touching some device near our "home communications center." We could order groceries and dry goods from home, and command some distant computer to take the money out of our checking accounts. On cold winter mornings we could show our sore throats to the doctors on television, then take our three aspirin tablets and go to bed without ever leaving home.

Some of us could work in our own special communications cocoon, never going to an office, but shuffling "hard copy" printouts and responding to lifelike shadows on screens and to well-modulated voices coming from high fidelity speakers.

We could . . . but why go on? We all know the fairy tale.

But it isn't a fairy tale. It all could happen.

If we want it to.

But do we?

Scholars, businesspeople, and thoughtful citizens are peering ahead, trying to figure out what can happen, what will happen, and what should happen. For some there is background fear. The days ahead look a little too much like the cold, electronic, ruthless world of George Orwell's 1984. For some there is resignation. Can we strengthen human values as we radically increase our dependence on machines?

For all there is excitement and confusion. Just the existence of a new way of doing things alters our outlook. There will be changes. What new technologies are on hand? What forces are at work to shape the way they will be used? What dangers exist? What opportunities are in the offing?

The Cable Is the Link

The catalyst that could open the communications cornucopia is cable. Combined with satellite transmission and microwave relay, it offers broad information highways complete with two-way traffic. It could free society from that damning limitation of mass communication—it is always from the few to the many. It could be truly responsive to the information needs of each individual.

The telephone system already makes the United States a "wired nation." Adding cable would be like substituting a sixteen-lane superhighway for the rutted creek bed that serves as a road up an eastern Kentucky "branch." That is why cable is called broad-band communication. It can carry a heavy load of varied information.

The coaxial cable itself has been in use for several years. As adapted to cable television it is from one-half to one inch in diameter. The covering is a flexible aluminum tube. Inside is a copper conductor surrounded by insulating material. A single cable can carry up to forty-six channels. Some systems envision installing two such cables to double the number of channels. Transistorized amplifiers are needed to boost the signal about every quarter of a mile.

Potential substitutes for coaxial cable are fiber optics, which have been developed in the Bell Telephone Laboratories, and "waveguides." Fiber optics may be used to guide laser beams. The waveguides are hollow pipes that can be used to channel waves in the band shorter than microwaves, but a bit longer than light waves. Waveguides are necessary since such waves are affected by weather conditions.

Since the signal on coaxial cable deteriorates after a few miles other means will have to be used to interconnect local cable systems. The most logical candidates for this job are microwave or satellite relay systems.

Microwaves, just longer than light waves, can be focused in much the same way, so they can be transmitted as coherent beams. The antenna is placed at the focal point of a parabolic, or "dish," reflector with a two- to twelve-foot diameter. A similar device at the receiving end takes the signal from the air. Sender and receiver can be up to seventy miles apart, depending on their height and the intervening terrain. Sending and receiving units, back-to-back, can provide long-distance channels.

Satellite relay is an alternate method of interconnecting cable systems. Ground stations would receive the signal from the satellite for transmission to cable systems in their area. Eventually hardware may become cheap enough that home receivers can take a signal directly from a satellite.

Along with improved transmission will come improved terminal equipment that will result in much better picture quality. The small screens of the 1970's with their obvious line patterns will probably appear crude in later generations. The long-predicted flat screen, as large as three by six feet, will provide theater-quality images in the home.

In Columbus, Ohio, a cable system has a feedback capability that shows which sets are in use and to what channels they are tuned. Additional response systems are sure to be built into home receivers. Eventually sophisticated devices may make it possible for a person at home to use a dial similar to that on the telephone to request a wide variety of special-interest programs or information.

The production of hard copies on paper of material sent over cable indicates that there is even the possibility of merging electronic transmissions and printing, although facsimile by itself has never caught on as a method for delivering newspapers.

The Foot-Draggers

Whether these and other predicted communication wonders will come about, how rapidly they come, and their results are all problematical. The technology is here or on the horizon, but economic and political considerations could block the way.

As with any innovation, the "cable revolution" is opposed by interests whose power would be displaced or diluted. Cable's economic opponents include over-the-air broadcasters, who fear that their mass audiences will be fragmented; segments of the motion picture industry, who fear that the "home box office" will replace regular movies theaters; and the telephone companies, which fear the loss of their near monopoly of point-to-point transmission of information.

Also slowing down the blossoming of the wired nation is the vastness of the undertaking and the large amount of capital that will be required.

Meanwhile, regulators sit at every level of government. They are subject to many pressures. Fortunes will be made and lost in the coming realignment of the communications industry, and the smell of money and power always focuses pressures on regulators.

Cable's Competitors

The communications of abundance promised by cable is a direct threat to the business interests of the television networks and stations. The fewer channels available the more valuable each one is since profits increase in direct ratio to the size of the audience. Presumably the ideal situation from an owner's point of view would be to control the only channel in town.

Since it is not good politics to say that they are fighting cable to preserve their own fat purses, television owners argue that they serve the public interest because they provide "free" what the public would have to pay for on cable television.

The argument makes sense *if* one is willing to disregard the costs of owning and operating receiving equipment and *if* one forgets the indirect costs to the consumer of advertising.

The ifs stick in the craw of proponents of cable. They argue this way:

> The average color television set today costs $350 and has a life expectancy of seven years. An average receiving antenna installation costs approximately $90 and has a similar life expectancy. The cost of the

basic system is therefore about $63 a year. To this must be added the average cost of repairs at $35, and $12 for electric power for a total cost to the homeowner of close to $100 per year. For that the average viewer has a selection of five stations which are received with various degrees of quality. . . . In contrast, the average cable system today delivers twelve stations, with excellent quality, for an approximate cost of $60 per year. In other words, for a further investment of a little over half as much again, the viewer has a choice of over twice as many program sources, and with better overall quality.[1]

The free TV argument is further complicated by those who argue that consumers ultimately pay the cost of the programs through increased prices of the advertised products they buy. Those arguments, which apply to all media that accept advertising, were examined in Chapter 7. They are inconclusive. Some products are less costly because advertising allows manufacturers to mass-produce them and cut costs. For other products, advertising may be used simply to call attention to superficial differences between competing products.

Burned once, the motion picture industry is fighting pay television as it once fought over-the-air broadcasters. Perhaps if pay television entrepreneurs can get their hands on first-run films, they can close the motion picture theaters and put the exhibitors out of business. But the industry revitalized itself after television's first onslaught, and it is likely to do so again.

Pay television ("feevee" in industry slang) is not likely to darken movie theaters unless and until the picture is bigger and the sound more realistic on the magic box in the game room.

The role of the telephone companies is uncertain. They range in size from the giant American Telephone and Telegraph Company and its Bell system, through the smaller General Telephone, a subsidiary of Sylvania Electric Company, to two thousand–odd rural exchanges. AT&T, which provides most of the long-lines service, is particularly vulnerable to competition from satellite transmissions and microwave relays. Standard telephone lines are incapable of carrying television pictures or other broad-band services, but the AT&T lines are already carrying much of the digital information that links computers and terminals—a growing business.

In the 1960's the telephone companies made an attempt to get into the cable business by announcing that they would construct cable systems on their poles and lease them to operators. They proceeded slowly, however, and in 1970 the FCC expressed its desire to provide competition in the

---

[1]George R. Townsend and J. Orrin Marlowe, *Cable: A New Spectrum of Communications* (Spectrum Communications, 1974), p. 70.

field by ordering the telephone companies out of the cable business. They were required to sell the few systems that they already owned.

In June 1968 the FCC had already provided evidence that the telephone companies could not expect to be shielded entirely from competition. By that time the Carter Electronics Corporation, a small Texas firm, had made and sold about thirty-five hundred devices that enabled owners of mobile-phone systems to tie them into the telephone network. In 1965 the phone companies began threatening to cut off the service of people using the devices. Thomas F. Carter, president of the company, filed an antitrust suit in a federal court, which referred the case to the FCC. Until that time the telephone companies insisted that no "foreign" equipment could be attached to the telephone system. The FCC ruled unanimously that the companies must allow such installations. As a result, telephone subscribers have hooked up antique telephones, answering devices, and computer terminals and saved the phone company's rental fees.

A more serious threat to AT&T's monopoly position came in 1969 when the FCC authorized a small company called Microwave Communications, Inc., to construct a broad-band microwave system paralleling telephone lines from Chicago to St. Louis. MCI President John D. Goeken spent $400,000 to win the battle. He promised services not provided by AT&T, a guaranteed error rate in data transmissions, and lower rates. His victory produced 750 additional applications to provide similar service.

AT&T's stranglehold on point-to-point electronic communication appears to be ending, but it and General Telephone are in little danger of losing their near monopoly in providing voice telephone service. Competing phone service would be expensive and inconvenient. Since it would siphon off resources it might also lead to a deterioration of service. But the telephone companies, like the television and motion picture industries, will offer strong competition to cable in the years ahead.

In the race to dominate the communications industry, competition will be a factor. So will government regulation.

Regulation: Three Layers Deep

In cable's early days regulatory agencies paid little attention to it. Now that it is showing signs of becoming an important medium, cable has to answer to regulators at all three levels of government: local, state, and federal.

Originally cable provided television service where it was otherwise unavailable or where it was needed to improve reception from distant stations. The local television repairworker or appliance store proprietor might erect a high antenna, string cable on telephone poles, and bring the signal into the homes of families that would pay five dollars a month for the service. Usually that individual would go down to the village council to get permission to string the cable since it was using the public streets.

Council members were often interested in getting the service, so they granted a franchise without much debate. Often no conditions were attached, not even a completion date. As systems grew larger they were seen as profitable enterprises, and later councils demanded payment of a percentage of income to the village or city in exchange for the franchise.

As cable has become more sophisticated, issues have become more complex, and few village or city governments have the expertise to evaluate companies seeking franchises or to write appropriate conditions. Franchise periods normally run for ten years, so a community suffers when its council makes a wrong decision.

In medium-sized cities with their own television stations the broadcasters began to fear cable's ability to bring in distant signals and so take away their audiences. Thus broadcasters began to make their influence felt at the local level, and they invariably delayed the growth of cable.

Connecticut became the first state to assume control over cable in 1963 when the General Assembly assigned its Public Utilities Commission the duty of awarding all cable franchises. But state governments have been slow to take jurisdiction. By 1975 only four states had established cable commissions and only nine others had authorized any direct state control. Table 15.1 shows the number of cable systems, their subscribers, and state regulation as of 1975.

The Federal Communications Commission did not exert control over cable in the early days of the industry. When it did, the control was largely negative. Former Chairman Rosel H. Hyde and former Commissioner Kenneth A. Cox influenced the commission to favor the interests of over-the-air broadcasters at the expense of cable.

The FCC defended its protection of over-the-air broadcasters on the grounds that cable operators could not serve rural areas; that cable might put small stations out of business; and that only the urban areas would get any television service.

In trying to provide television stations for small communities as well as large, the FCC assigned a large segment of the radio spectrum to television. The federal government uses about one-third of the available spectrum in the United States, and the FCC had to allocate the rest among many users. In addition to radio and television stations, it had to consider the needs of amateurs, aviation, marine, land-mobile, astronomical, and other users.

In making the assignments in 1949, the FCC reserved twelve spaces (channels 2 to 13) of the choice VHF range for television. It also saved the upper range of the broadcast spectrum from 470 to 890 megahertz for

UHF television (channels 14 to 83), although this has since been slightly reduced.

This was a large assignment of space to television, but in practice it did not result in the large number of small stations the FCC had hoped for. The choice channels in the VHF band were assigned first, usually to well-financed operators in larger cities. The UHF band was saved for later assignment or for educational uses.

But UHF stations are at a disadvantage in competing with VHF. More power is needed and equipment costs more. Moreover, until 1964, when a federal law required that all new receivers should be all channel, few sets could get UHF channels. In addition, the VHF stations, since they were on the scene first, usually got the network affiliations, which almost guarantee financial success.

Sometimes the big-city stations used repeaters, which carried their signals into smaller communities and so discouraged the formation of new and smaller stations in the UHF range.

The result of all this is that more than 70 percent of 1,191 channels assigned in the UHF spectrum have not been activated, and there is little prospect that many of them will be.

The FCC was cautious in extending its jurisdiction over cable, and at first it used its power to protect broadcasters. In 1965 it issued an order requiring cable systems to carry the signal of every television station in its area and protected local stations from having their programs duplicated on cable for fifteen days before and after broadcast.

The next year the commission forbade cable systems in the hundred largest television markets to import signals from distant stations without specific approval from the commission. This slowed the growth of cable in the areas where it might have made great strides and certainly its richest profits were to be found. The FCC was attempting to encourage the growth of UHF stations in the big cities.

The FCC's 1972 rules, which still form its basic policy toward cable, softened its protective position toward over-the-air broadcasters in favor of cable. The complicated regulations still require cable systems to carry the programs of all local stations, but allow cable penetration into the larger markets. The number of distant signals that can be imported is related to market size. To protect smaller stations, cable systems in their territories are more limited in the number of channels they can bring in.

The 1972 rules also require systems to allocate channels for free use by the public, for education, and for the local government.

Until 1968 pay television was authorized only for experimental use, and even now limitations on programming are designed to protect television from siphoning certain viewing attractions. Thus pay cable may not show films released for general distribution between two and ten years old, or sports events that have been broadcast in the past two years.

Table 15.1 Cable Regulation in the United States

Only four states had established cable commissions by 1975, but several had assigned cable regulation to their public utilities or public service commissions. States were showing a lively interest in cable, as the "action pending" column indicates.

	Systems[a]	Subscribers[a]	PUC/ PSC[b]	Cable commission	Official study groups	Action pending	Local enabling legislation
Alabama	75	175,791				X	
Alaska	7	4,723	X				
Arizona	27	60,641					X
Arkansas	63	94,847					
California	285	1,278,351				X	
Colorado	37	70,951					
Connecticut	3	25,781	X				
Delaware	8	57,281	X				
Florida	108	416,572					
Georgia	69	207,918					
Hawaii	8	22,754	X				
Idaho	42	60,218					
Illinois	70	228,303				X[c]	
Indiana	58	388,892					
Iowa	38	56,976					
Kansas	77	135,748					
Kentucky	103	125,905					
Louisiana	33	78,139					
Maine	29	43,902			X		X
Maryland	27	83,479				X	
Massachusetts	41	136,225		X			
Michigan	64	212,187				X	
Minnesota	71	118,920		X			
Mississippi	57	133,513					
Missouri	59	118,643					
Montana	33	85,244					
Nebraska	43	51,600					
Nevada	6	29,008	X				
New Hampshire	33	68,903					X

Table 15.1 Cable Regulation in the United States (cont.)

	Systems[a]	Subscribers[a]	PUC/ PSC[b]	Cable commission	Official study groups	Action pending	Local enabling legislation
New Jersey	32	179,419	X[d]				
New Mexico	28	78,427					
New York	156	634,114		X			
North Carolina	36	122,946					
North Dakota	10	19,190					
Ohio	137	439,152					
Oklahoma	75	130,179					
Oregon	91	163,345				X	
Pennsylvania	300	952,781				X	
Rhode Island	1	3,125	X				
South Carolina	33	59,782			X		
South Dakota	17	29,660					
Tennessee	57	109,055					
Texas	219	592,470				X	
Utah	7	5,694					
Vermont	36	49,713	X[d]				
Virginia	54	122,419	X[e]				
Washington	101	236,334					
West Virginia	134	231,737					
Wisconsin	64	113,077			X	X	
Wyoming	25	53,602					

[a] *Television Factbook*, No. 44 (1974–75 ed.).
[b] PUC is the public utilities commission; PSC is the public service commission.
[c] Pending court decision; all other pending action is legislative.
[d] Regulated by an office or division within the PUC or PSC.
[e] The Virginia Public Telecommunications Council has assumed some control over cable television by establishing minimum technical standards to ensure effective use by state educational broadcasters.

Source: *Broadcasting and Cable Television: Policies for Diversity and Change*, Committee for Economic Development, New York, 1975, pp. 118–119. Reprinted with permission.

Despite such limitations, Time, Inc., has invested 7.5 million dollars to set up a network to feed programs to a cable system by satellite.

Regulation of the broadcast industry is further complicated by the establishment of the Office of Telecommunications Policy in the executive office of the president. This got off to a strong start, but the general slow-down of federal executive activities brought about the Watergate scandal has kept it from making any major immediate impact.

Governmental confusion about communications goals as well as means of achieving them are reflected consistently in its attempts to regulate the broadcast industry. Radio and television in turn were hailed as the agencies that would eradicate ignorance and provide the public information stream needed in a democratic society. Regulation was not successful in bringing that about.

The FCC does not license cable systems, leaving that to the state or local governments, but it does set standards and requirements. The three layers of control sometimes bring incredibly complicated regulations. For instance, Anne W. Branscomb, a communications lawyer and former counsel for TelePrompTer, the largest cable system, has this comment:

> The Massachusetts regulations defy the most diligent MSO [multiple systems operator] to comply. In order to qualify its Massachusetts operations, TelePrompTer had five people working several weeks attempting—not entirely successfully—to provide the information required to file for certification of its Worcester system (which serves less than 1 percent of TelePrompTer's total subscribers). This could not be considered cost-effective by any accounting method which allocated time proportionately to operations involved. . . . A prudent MSO would be well advised to pull out of Massachusetts unless it had a very substantial investment and a highly profitable operation.[2]

The confusion as to who should regulate cable and how much control should be exerted reflects uncertainty in the public and often unreal expectations as to what the new technology can do to solve human and social problems.

A Larger Battle

The turmoil over cable involves more than the fortunes of a few entrepreneurs. It is today's version of the continuous battle over technology. As such it represents the frustrations, dangers, and dreams that ac-

---

[2]Anne W. Branscomb, "The Cable Fable: Will It Come True?" *Journal of Communication* 25 (Winter 1975): 51–52.

company any major technological change. New centers of power and wealth are created in one of society's highest stakes games, and they will form the social values of the future.

The bright and beautiful promises of technology always mask the threat of hidden dangers. For all the warmth and energy it gives, fire still occasionally rages out of control. Nuclear power can build a finer environment, but the bomb itself or its fallout could destroy that environment. There is always the danger that humankind will invent itself out of existence.

Communication technology threads the same familiar path between blessing and bane. Like every other new technology it changes the world by its very existence, but the nature of the changes can be controlled by the manner in which it is used. But pace and scale increase so that more people over larger areas are affected in less time. If new machines lead us into box canyons or over cliffs we will get there a little faster than before. Before the effects of innovations can be predicted the changes are already facts.

Information controls change, so communication, as the process by which we exchange information, is critical in all efforts to control the evolution of society. Changes in the way we communicate change our lives.

It is not hard to find examples, even on a global scale. The flow of international communication is predominately from the richer to the poorer nations. As the rich nations export pictures of their relatively comfortable, affluent lives, citizens of the poor nations naturally want to emulate them. Since the world lacks the resources to provide everyone with the amenities enjoyed by the average middle-class American, the stage is set for conflict. The activities of Third World nations in the United Nations show that this struggle is beginning. Whatever the outcome, the world will be different. Thus media and the way they are used alter the world.

Ghetto rioting is partly a communication event. For generations business leaders riding from elegant Westchester homes to lavish Manhattan offices closed their eyes to the human misery as they passed through the squalor of Harlem. A riot was one way for ghetto residents to say, "We really are here. We have troubles. We need help."

A better communication system might have made the riots unnecessary. A blood bath is an expensive and dangerous way to get a message across.

Cable by itself does not promise the technology that might allow society to forestall riots by heightening understanding. But cable represents an opportunity to merge several communication systems to make each more effective. However, there are many unsettled questions. They involve the availability of money and where it should come from; the kind of regulation that will produce a desirable amount of competition; where the control points should be; and what kind of goals should be established.

Paying the Bill

Estimates vary as to the costs of a wired nation. Anne Branscomb gives some idea of the range of estimates and the options available:

> The costs of wiring the nation are staggering: $1.2 trillion for a completely switched dial-access system like the telephone or $123 billion for a traditional tree-branched system. Recent estimates, based upon 86 million families to be served in 1985 utilizing microwave interconnection, arrive at a more realistic figure of $82.5 billion, comparable to the current investment of $67 billion in telephone plant and annual construction commitments of $12.5 billion in the telephone system.[3]

Restrictions that keep the telephone companies and the television networks out of the cable business choke off one logical source of cash. The present cable industry, which serves about 10 million homes, will not be able to generate the large sums of money needed for a long time.

Where will the money come from? The stock market was a likely source when cable was a glamor stock. The FCC's rules relaxing restrictions to allow cable to expand into the big cities did not prove to be the boon that was expected. TelePrompTer and Manhattan Cable ran into tremendous expense trying to cable New York City. The recession of the early 1970's was a factor, but the cable stocks were especially hard hit. At the same time the cost of borrowing money became too high for cable operators.

It is not at all unlikely that new capital will come into the industry from regular business channels to eventually provide the needed funding. Other suggestions have been that television networks and stations be allowed to participate and that public funds be used to provide, in whole or part, the money necessary to construct a cable utility. Both suggestions raise questions: one about the control of monopoly; the other about the separation of government and sources of information.

Competition Versus Monopoly

In large-scale society such as that of the United States, where some enterprises have to be on a gigantic scale to be successful, there is always the question of the proper balance between competition and regulation as a means of ensuring that they will be responsive to public needs.

[3]Ibid., p. 48.

Space exploration is so expensive that the U.S. cannot afford competing firms; so it is a government monopoly. Other industries may be natural monopolies because of the logic of their operation. The telephone company and urban transportation systems are examples. Where competition does not exist, for one reason or another, the usual procedure is for the government to take over the operation or regulate it closely.

Cable systems are natural local monopolies. Competing cable companies serving the same neighborhoods would be prohibitively expensive as well as inconvenient. To achieve their full potential, local cable systems must be interconnected, probably into one national system.

The power inherent in controlling this much of the national communications pie is enough to make one wonder if the prize is worth the gamble.

Problems of regulation would become complex if an interconnected cable system were combined with powerful AT&T's Bell system or one of the television networks. Far smaller industrial complexes have been able to control the state regulatory commissions, and even had enough influence over the federal regulatory agency to decrease its effectiveness.

Although government ownership of communications facilities is common in Europe, the United States has a long tradition of separation except for the mail service.

The most helpful idea that has been advanced in this dilemma is simple, but dramatic. It is to separate technical control and ownership from control of content.

Perhaps if we are to construct such a superhighway to the human mind we should control it as if it were a highway: let all on it who come along, let them carry anything they desire, so long as they abide by rules designed to ensure the safest possible passage for all.

The Federal Communications Commission has made a start in insisting that systems provide a public access channel. Facilities are available so that anyone can tape a program or message, and it will be sent out on the access channel on a first-come, first-served basis.

Anyone could rent a channel and program it, financing it in any of several different ways. Some might sell advertising to produce formats much like present-day television programming. Others might charge the persons receiving the information. Others might get foundation or government grants to produce programming considered in the public interest. Professional or public-interest groups might meet expenses out of dues.

The costs of public access and educational and governmental channels would, then as now, be borne by the community, since rates would have to be set high enough so that the cable operator could maintain such channels out of regular revenues.

Separation of ownership and programming would simplify some aspects of regulation and make other kinds unnecessary. Rates for use of a channel could be made equal for all comers or varied according to the kind of traffic. Either way it would be possible to set objective standards and monitor compliance. Rates could be set to provide a reasonable return to the cable owner. Technical standards, too, can be established and uniformly enforced.

If a few unused channels were always available and if public access channels were kept open competition would be the best regulator of content. No technology will ever give everyone equal "access" to the public, for access depends upon industry and skill in presentation as well as the availability of channels. In a group discussion some of the participants have more "access" than others because they speak better and are more aggressive in presenting their ideas. But open, available channels would remedy the problem as well as technology ever will.

The traditional problems of control of indecency and blasphemy will always be with us. They are social problems that will require constant adjustment, but the availability of channels should make it possible for society to keep restrictions to a minimum.

If channels were available to all comers it would be immaterial whether system operators programmed one, several, or none of the channels themselves. If they chose to provide programming on one or more channels they would, in effect, be renting the channels from themselves and would be in competition with the other channels, just like any other programmer. Presumably present television stations and networks would rent one or more channels and become, in effect, programming services.

Perhaps newspaper publishers would eventually deliver their papers on a rented channel by facsimile. Such a move would allow publishers to get out of the manufacturing business—they could sell their great presses and concentrate on their essential job: processing information. They would also be relieved of one headache—getting the paper into the hands of the reader quickly and regularly. Studies have indicated that some subscribers cancel because they are dissatisfied with the service provided by the newspaper carrier. With electronic delivery of the paper the subscriber would at least be relieved of the worry about whether the newspaper carrier was going to land the evening edition on the porch roof or toss it through the living room window.

The Uncertain Halo

Would all this make any difference? Nobody will be any better informed by reading a newspaper delivered by cable than by someone delivering it to the front door. Barbara Walters or Eric Sevareid will not be any more persuasive if they come to us on cable instead of through the radio spectrum. "Sesame Street" will not teach the alphabet any faster just because it arrives by cable, except as the quality of the image is improved.

Cable television, barely out of its cradle, has been fitted with a king-size halo. The fitting was premature, although there is hope that the infant may grow with the job. The problems of maintaining and improving a society that distributes freedom and opportunity without prejudice can never be solved by technology. But an interactive communication system with access for all could provide the means of solving many social problems.

The United States is still a long distance from reaching its goal of providing adequate educational opportunities for all. Education by television has proved to be very good and very bad, just like education in the classroom. But plentiful educational channels would at least make it possible to distribute the best. And it would do it so cheaply that a rich nation like the United States could not afford to do without ETV.

It is possible that a large number of channels will decrease the pressures on the few channels that tend to make it a medium by which people exploit each other. Some channels could be devoted not to "selling the market," but to filling the needs of the people at the receiving end.

A larger number of channels at least opens the possibility of choice being available to a viewer. Too often the alternatives are practically zero as a viewer tunes the receiver. Does the viewer want to watch this crime show or another one copied from the same format? Does this situation comedy fit his or her mood better than another that offers the same pat, unreal solutions to contrived complications? As the sports seasons grow longer, it sometimes becomes necessary to choose whether one prefers to watch the game climaxing the baseball season or the one opening the football season.

There is nothing inherently wrong with viewing a sports spectacular if one can take the arrogance of a Howard Cosell or the florid rhetoric of a Heywood Hale Broun. Mary Tyler Moore may provide a beneficial half-hour away from reality. Even the Westerns and crime shows may have their place. At least they provide the assurance of expectations understood and fulfilled, a satisfaction often withheld by the real world.

But there ought to be alternatives—real ones.

Perhaps cable can provide some. Maybe it can make it possible for one to learn a language at some time more convenient than 5 A.M. Perhaps a home do-it-yourselfer can get a few tips on how to move a wall without bringing the house down around his or her head. Perhaps parents would like to get some tips on how to cure diaper rash, or nature lovers would like to sharpen their perception of bird calls. Perhaps some with even more bizarre tastes would desert the hilarity and money-lust of a game show to attend to an analysis of Marcel Proust's *Remembrance of Things Past*.

People are seekers: seekers of experience through information. Some will seek no matter how difficult the road, but many will not venture beyond the click-stops of their television tuner. If the alternatives on the four or five channels available are not alternatives at all, but simply warmed-over mixtures of the same potion, the hunt is lost for the hesitant seekers before it is begun.

With many channels available a hesitant or inadvertent click on a channel control knob may open a new interest—perhaps some viewer can, for a time, see the world through a new set of filters. If response equipment helps the viewer make firsthand contact with new people and new organizations, then no small thing has happened.

But there is no assurance that such things will occur. Even the optimist has to remember that television was making the same promises thirty years ago. Now, while it has its peaks, it spends most of its time deep in the valley of the lowest common denominator of audience appeal.

Making the Halo Fit

Even though an integrated communication system will not solve all our social problems, the possibilities are real. We need to make the most of them.

First, we need to look at the good in the communication system we have and preserve it. The news-gathering system in the United States has developed strong traditions of independence and responsibility and is a vital force in maintaining an open society. The men and women who supply the news may use different media and techniques to reach their audiences, and the economics of the media may make them less dependent on advertising revenue, but the great traditions of American journalism must be preserved and strengthened. As the media change, conscious attention will be needed to see that the basic values of a free society remain unaltered.

Another area that needs attention in times of rapid change is preserving a workable balance between collaboration and competition of the media. In the early days of radio, as we have seen, newspaper proprietors tried to keep the new medium from competing with them in providing news to the public. Since radio has certain natural advantages in providing a rapid bulletin service, the public is ill served by insisting that news distribution be limited to the printed media. Through Ed Murrow, Lowell Thomas, and other gifted radio newspeople, the new medium demonstrated that it could fill a need, and gradually it found a role in distributing news. Newspapers adjusted and they survived.

Newspapers gave up trying to provide a bulletin service and gave up the practice of publishing extras when radio proved it was more efficient at providing that service. Hard copy home printers, if they become common, are likely to give newspapers new problems. It is difficult to see how good quality printing will ever be entirely replaced, but newspapers may adopt an electronic delivery system or they may supplement their printed service by some kind of an electronic bulletin service.

It is becoming less and less valid to associate any particular service with the nature of the medium that provides it. News is no longer the sole province of newspapers. The public will benefit most if the media adopt the policy of using whatever delivery system is most appropriate for the type of information being offered.

Sometimes this will require collaboration. The value of such collaboration is apparent to anyone who has watched late-night rock concerts on television while listening to the sound over high fidelity stereo synchronized with the telecast by a local FM station.

If the purveyors of news could learn to recognize their audiences as seekers of information such collaboration might become more common. Radio and television talk shows, by reviewing books and interviewing their authors, encourage listeners to read books. Competition appears to keep radio and television newscasters from performing a similar service for their listeners. If they are reporting a situation that is well backgrounded in a current magazine, it would be logical to tell their readers about the article. Apparently for most this sort of action seems too much like helping a competitor.

Competition adds spice to the journalist's work day and provides many benefits to the public. But competition need not get in the way of efforts to respond to the needs of an audience viewed as seekers of information.

One of the great promises of an interactive communication system is that more people can be involved in communication as senders as well as receivers and so take a more active role in public decisions. This is the principle under which public access channels are required in cable systems. Access channels are just the first step in enlarging participatory communication.

Most cable systems have not yet opened public access channels and those that do exist have been started so recently that not much is known about their effects. New York City's cable systems were among the first, opening their public access channels on July 1, 1971. Alan Wurtzel, a Queens College faculty member, analyzed the content of the two public access channels of TelePrompTer Manhattan for two years, from July 1, 1971, through June 30, 1973.[4] Content categories used and a summary of findings are shown in Table 15.2.

[4]Alan Wurtzel, "Public-Access Cable TV: Programming," *Journal of Communication* 25 (Summer 1975): 15–21.

The small amount of political information is explained by TelePromp-Ter's opening of a separate channel for candidates in primary and general elections. Informational programs dominated the channels, accounting for more than 71 percent of the total time. Entertainment, with 14 percent, and instructional material, with 4 percent, were next.

Because informational programs were so dominant, Wurtzel further analyzed that category. He found that two types of information, "general" and "community," accounted for nearly 75 percent of the material. Table 15.3 shows his complete breakdown.

The "general" category, accounting for 45 percent of the information programming, indicates that the access channels provided a wide variety of material to anybody who cared to watch.

The interests of minority audiences were represented by programs produced by such organizations as the Gay Activist Alliance and Homosexuals Intransigent. Some programs were in Chinese, some in Spanish, and one series was presented in the sign language of the deaf. Some pro-

Table 15.2   Public Access Programming, Content of TelePrompTer Manhattan's Two Channels / *July 1971–June 1973*

	Number of programs	Amount of time (in hours)	Percentage of total time
Entertainment	1,044	863.06	14.06%
News	17	70.53	1.14
Public affairs	241	174.60	2.84
Informational	6,965	4,378.98	71.37
Religious	221	164.60	2.68
Instructional	333	260.61	4.24
Sports	34	29.73	0.48
Political	7	19.40	0.31
Children's	179	101.00	1.64
Miscellaneous	37	22.86	0.37
Experimental art	60	49.91	0.81
Total	9,138	6,135.28	99.94%

Source: Adapted from Alan Wurtzel, "Public-Access Cable TV: Programming, "*Journal of Communication* 25 (Summer 1975): 17. Reprinted with permission.

grams tried to teach such skills as sewing, flying, or yoga. During the two years studied, the researcher found that both the number of programs and the amount of time increased from the first to the second year.

This small study of public access cable indicates it is possible to allow many different groups to present a wide variety of material. However, information on audience response is sparse.

Hypothesizing from what is known about audience habits, one researcher estimated, in a community of 100,000 adults with a 14,000-subscriber cable system, the average audience for a public access channel would be between 50 and 180 viewers.[5]

A video program produced by amateurs can hardly hope to compete for an audience with the slick productions of motion picture and television artists backed by large budgets. Programs produced by amateurs on public access cable do not need the mass audiences of the networks, but they need some audience.

Some professional aid is needed to help television amateurs overcome their timidity of the new medium and to help them assess what is interesting enough to hold even a tiny audience. One researcher who spent a month watching the access channels in Manhattan came to this conclusion:

Table 15.3   Information Programming on Public Access Channels

	Number of programs cablecast	Percentage of programs cablecast
Ethnic	146	2.09%
Community	2,079	29.84
Health	590	8.47
Public relations	469	6.73
Consumer	174	2.49
Political	381	5.47
General	3,126	44.88
Total	6,965	99.97%

Source: Alan Wurtzel, "Public-Access Cable TV: Programming," *Journal of Communication* 25 (Summer 1975): 18. Reprinted with permission.

[5]Rudy Bretz, "Public-Access Cable TV: Audiences," *Journal of Communication* 25 (Summer 1975): 22–32.

Interviewers and guests manifest a peculiar knack for spending large amounts of time on matters which are least likely to be meaningful or interesting to viewers . . . Organizational statistics and administrative details tend to fascinate organization presidents—being their life work—but bore viewers.[6]

Along with new methods of communications must come new kinds of literacy. Despite valiant struggles over generations, 26 million Americans cannot read or write well enough to pass a driver's test or apply for a job in writing. Job failures and life failures result from lack of ability to read and write. These 26 million people cannot enter the group of participating citizens who have a voice in the public decision making process.

The day may come when people who cannot effectively produce a cable television program will be cast out of the mainstream of U.S. society in the same way that illiterates are today. Skill in the audio and visual techniques that produce the television experience are important requisites now for achieving a position of influence.

In a time when our democratic process requires that we enlist the participation of the maximum number of people, schools and colleges cannot afford to neglect teaching the "literacy" of the media.

For professional and amateur producers alike care is needed in combining interest and information. The gap between entertainment and information is worse than the generation gap and it has been around much longer. Educators sometimes assume that something that is important will be interesting. Entertainers sometimes work on the opposite theory—that they must be banal to be interesting.

Neither is correct. The so-called entertaining content of the media may very well be as important in influencing the nature of society as all the public affairs and news programs put together. People learn by imitation and without conscious effort. Sometimes the lessons learned when one is being "entertained" are all the more compelling because no one expects us to learn anything. "Sesame Street" attracted many children who enjoyed watching just for its entertainment value. Perhaps it was because these children were under no conscious pressure to learn that the program put over its objectives so well.

Every society must have some common base of experience. Participating in the great events of one's time is the best way to develop a common experience. The next best is through communication about these events. In the days of wandering herdsmen and hunters the tribal myths were reinforced by storytellers and minstrels around the campfires at night. Today continentwide society in America needs a complicated media system to do the same job.

[6]Pamela Doty, "Public-Access Cable TV: Who Cares?" *Journal of Communication* 25 (Summer 1975): 36.

The Enemy Is Anomie

Many people in America feel lonely, without influence, and generally disconnected from their fellows and from society. Social scientists call the condition *anomie*. These are the people who agree with such statements as "The rich get rich and the poor get poorer" and "What you think doesn't count much any more."

These are the people who have given up on society and on themselves. If enough Americans begin to feel this way we will lose our chance to make a democratic system work.

No communications system, by itself, will remedy such a feeling of disengagement with society for large numbers of people, but an interactive system would help more citizens to participate. At least communication can demonstrate that others share the same problems and are seeking answers. Maybe an interactive communication system could persuade people that what they think does matter.

Many Factors Affect the Media

It is fitting that this book should close with a chapter on the technological changes in the media. Such advances have extended humans' ability to communicate over time and space and in so doing have provided new opportunities for people to better understand themselves and their fellows. But technology is only one of the forces that control the communication process. Others are social, economic, and human.

Social, economic, and political systems and principles determine how the media are controlled. As we have seen, open societies favor minimal controls and maximum opportunity for many to participate. Closed societies restrict the information system and allow only the favored few to originate messages.

The economic system affects media ownership patterns and determines how the media gain the financial resources they need to survive. We have considered the arguments over the desirability of advertising and advertisers' control over media contents; and we have seen the worries aroused by the tendency toward consolidation of ownership of the media in the United States. Certainly the media are influenced, for good or bad, by their owners and by the advertising system. So economic forces as well as governmental and social policies have much to do with the content and control of the communication media.

Most important of all is the way that humans interact with their communications systems. We have seen that there is much theory on this subject and some substantial research. Individuals respond differently, depending on the nature of a message and the manner in which it is presented. Also critical to the communications system is the way the people communicate face to face, and the way face-to-face communication relates to media communication.

We have also seen that the media mold their society even as society molds them. The process is circular and it is not always possible to separate cause from effect.

For any society the communication system and the way it is used are critical, for communication and control are closely interlinked. Freedom to act is impossible without freedom of expression.

An open society needs a communication system in which any person with an idea can get a hearing, in which information is available to all, and where audience needs and desires determine media content.

Technology and economics conspire together to provide the opposite. As media units become fewer and larger the tendency has been for fewer people to control the attention of larger audiences. The mass information system is largely a one-way street, with information going from the few to the many.

Technology that is here already or on the horizon can be used to build a communication system that will allow for more active participation by more people or it can increase the tendency for fewer individuals to control the media. The tendency for increasing central control is strong. The only antidote is understanding and action by many.

Suggestions for Further Reading

Adler, Richard R., and Baer, Walter S. *Aspen Notebook: Cable and Continuing Education*. New York: Praeger, 1973.
Report of Aspen Institute research on uses of cable.

Aranguren, José Luis. "Freedom, Symbols and Communication." *The Annals* 412 (March 1974): 11–20.
Considers social effects of symbols and media communication.

Branscomb, Anne W. "The Cable Fable: Will It Come True?" *Journal of Communication* 25 (Winter 1975): 44–56.
An assessment of cable's problems with financing and regulation.

Etzioni, Amitai, Lander, Kenneth, and Lipson, Sara. "Participatory Technology: The MINERVA Communications Tree." *Journal of Communication* 25 (Spring 1975): 64–74.
An imaginative experiment using existing technology to increase citizen participation in public communication.

Free, John. "Tuning in Your TV to Electronic Newspapers." *Popular Science*, January 1976, pp. 62–63.
A brief, illustrated account of one form of "electronic newspaper."

Gattegno, Caleb. *Towards a Visual Culture*. New York: Outerbridge and Dienstfrey, 1969.
An approach to teaching through television, this book provides insights into possible future uses of the medium.

Henderson, Hazel. "Information and the New Movements for Citizen Participation." *The Annals* 412 (March 1974): 34–43.
Citizen groups and their role in the information system.

Servan-Schreiber, Jean-Louis. *The Power to Inform*. New York: McGraw-Hill, 1974.
A wide-ranging series of essays on the press, mainly in America, by a French writer, this book provides perceptions valuable in predicting the future of the media.

Sparks, Vernone. "Local Regulatory Agencies for Cable Television." *Journal of Broadcasting* 19 (Spring 1975): 221–233.
Rationale for local regulation with an extensive bibliography.

Wiener, Norbert. *The Human Use of Human Beings: Cybernetics and Society*. Garden City, N.Y.: Doubleday, 1954.
Contains seminal ideas on communication technology and society.

Wilhelmsen, Frederick D., and Bret, Jane. *Telepolitics: The Politics of Neuronic Man*. Plattsburgh, N.Y.: Tundra Books, 1972.
McLuhanesque predictions of the effects of television on society.

Wurtzel, Alan. "Public-Access Cable TV: Programming," *Journal of Communication* 25 (Summer 1975): 15–21.
This study is instructive for the light it sheds upon possible future use of public access channels.

A glance back at Part Six and ahead at Tomorrow

Part Six considers the social and technological changes that may make it possible to remove from mass media their main curse—their inability to provide an interactive situation for their audiences. As we need an interactive democracy, we need an interactive media system—a system that resembles the all-encompassing interaction around a tribal council.

Chapter 14 described some of the devices that the media use to give their audiences chances to talk back to the media and to talk with each other. These efforts are a beginning, but scarcely more than that. One of them, letters to the editors, are almost as old as newspapers themselves and have, over the generations, provided a useful safety valve and a rough indicator of public sentiment.

Chapter 15 considers new combinations of technology that may increase the interactive possibilities of the media. It is at the intersection of various technologies that most of the possibilities exist. Cable combined with satellite transmission may eventually create new networks. If they can be provided cheaply enough, they can serve small audiences with special-interest material. Cable also offers the opportunity for audience response, the instantaneous feedback that the communication process surrendered when mass media took over.

The computer, too, is likely to become a crossroads where audience and media can interact. A marvelous information machine, it may open new worlds for audience services when it is combined imaginatively with other media.

It is not likely that new media will crowd out entirely those now serving the United States. Surely present media will have to adapt as newspapers have adapted to television. More specialized media will produce smaller and more specialized audiences, which will in turn produce a different kind of society. Of one thing we can be sure, the media and society will evolve together.

The constants in the equation are the human elements: the need for integrity of a high order on the part of the men and women who control the media, and the need for understanding of the media by the audiences they serve. The media change the lives of their audiences, and it is only through understanding of the media that audiences can control that change.

Index

characteristics, 318; volatile nature of radio listening, 319
Master of Revels, 114
Mather, Increase, 118
Matrix, 53
Mauldin, Bill, on symbols, 9 (Figure 1.1)
Maxwell, James Clerk, 66
Media
antitrust regulation, 162–167; believability, 355–359; and Congress, 174, 246–249; content selection problems, 85–87; cross-ownership, 159; determinism, 31; factors in evaluation of, 358 (table); interaction, 238; manipulation, 223; rated against other conveniences, 337 (table); regulation, congressional view, 174; responsibility, 87, 88, 97–101; responsiveness, 376; revenue sources, 179 (table); selection of issues, 254–256; self-regulation, 136–139; social effects, 350–353
Media Communication
compared to interpersonal, 18–21; distortion through selection, 19–20; technology and content, 20
Medium as factor in credibility, 346
"The Medium Is the Massage," 30
Meetings, 267
Mein Kampf, 19
Mellett Fund for a Free and Responsible Press, 383
Merton, Robert K., 353
Message
affected by manner, 347; affected by receiving situation, 349; source as perceived by receiver, 345
Metcalf, Lee, 92, 161
MGM, and radio drama, 301
Miami Herald, 383, 389
Miami Herald v. Tornillo, 133, 381
Microwave Communications, Inc., 401
Microwave relay, 397
Middle Ages, 52
Miller v. California, 129–131
Mills, Wilbur, 91
Milwaukee Journal, 393
Minneapolis Star, 202, 385, 393

Modern Photography, 63
Montgomery (Alabama) Advertiser and Journal, 222
Morris, Lewis, 119
Morrisett, Lloyd N., 368
Motion Picture Producers and Distributors of America, 136
Motion picture revenues, 65 (table)
Murrow, Edward R., 69, 277
Music, and oral tradition, 32
Muskie, Edmund S., 161
Muzak, 329

Nader, Ralph, 197, 250
"Naked City," 307
Namath, Joe, 288
Nation, The, 256
National Advisory Commission on Civil Disorders, 99
National Association for Better Radio and Television, 361
National Association of Broadcasters, 137
on family viewing hours, 369; on licensing, 167–168
National Cable Television Association, 171
National Citizens Committee for Broadcasting, 171
National Gazette, 111
National Institute of Mental Health, 366
National News Council, 386
National Opinion Research Center, 321
National Review, 63, 256
NBC, early newsgathering efforts, 67
Nessen, Ron, 243
Networks
and news services, 160–161; ownership, 161
Neuharth, Allen H., 188
Neuhoff, Paul, 391
New and alternative journalism, 281–283
New Castle News, 393
New formats, effects of, 283–284
Newhouse, S. I., 155
"New journalism," 100–101
New Leader, 256
New Orleans, battle of, 6
New Republic, 256
News
creation, 224, 226; editing, 213 (figure); leaks, 88; media, and structuring of reality, 212; mix, 225; packaging, 227;

patterns, repetition of, 214; -reality gap, 229
Newspaper(s)
development, 56–61; main function, 56; weekly, 61
Newspaper circulation trends, 58–61
compared to population, 58 (table); per household, 59 (table)
Newspaper Preservation Act, 166
Newspaper reading patterns
by age and sex, 327 (table); by income and sex, 326 (table)
News reading, theories about, 331
Schramm on immediate and delayed reward, 331; Stephenson's play theory, 332
News sources
major, 338 (table); disclosure of, 135–136
News values
drama, 216; human interest, 219; importance, 219; interest, 215; public record, 220; timing, 218; famous people, 217
Newsweek, 138
New Yorker, 387
New York Journal, 119
New York Free Press, 283
New York Society of Newspaper Editors, 221
New York Sun, 57, 346
New York Times, 67, 84, 386
control of advertising, 196–197; on invasion of Cuba, 96; on issue advertising, 195; and Nixon's 1962 press conference, 243; on Pentagon papers, 120
New York Times Book Review, 319
New York Times Magazine, 392
New York Times Service, 73
New York Tribune, 271
New York Weekly Journal, 200, 231
Nicholas, Czar of Russia, 106
1984 (Orwell), 397
Nipkow, Paul Gottlieb, 70
Nixon, Agnes, 303
Nixon, Raymond B., 154, 156
Nixon, Richard M., 23–24, 88, 90–91, 93, 331
and "created" news events, 236; increased presidential

DATE DUE

-12.15. '81	
10.22. '81	
11.08.'84	
M6.06.'85	
18.01.'85	
11. 29.'86	
FEB 2 8 22 90	
Aut 3/8 FEB 27 91 rej 4/3	
MAY J5 '91	
MAY 0 4 2000	

BRODART, INC.   Cat. No. 23-221